LOVE AND TRUTH

JEAN BORELLA

Love *and* Truth

THE CHRISTIAN PATH OF CHARITY

Translated by G. John Champoux

Angelico Press

Book and cover design
by Michael Schrauzer

*The "commandment" of love is only possible
because it is more than a requirement.
Love can be "commanded"
because it has first been given.*

Benedict XVI, *Deus Caritas Est*, 14

*Be not conformed to the present world,
but be transformed in the renewing of your intellect.*

Paul, Romans 12:2

*If I should distribute all my goods to feed the poor . . .
and have not charity, it profiteth me nothing.*

Paul, I Corinthians 13:3

CONTENTS

Contents

PRELIMINARY NOTE

AFTER ITS INITIAL PUBLICATION BY ÉDITIONS
de Cèdre in January 1979, *La Charité profanée* (*The Desecration of
Charity*) was reprinted in 1988 by Éditions Dominique Martin Morin,
which republished it in 1991. After this, for several years the book went
out of print and the chance to present a truly new edition presented
itself. This might have involved the republishing of an identical version. When we began to draft it in 1966, the Church had entered, with
the ending of the Second Vatican Council, a very turbulent period:
in the words of the great theologian Henri de Lubac, everything was
foundering, and Pope Paul VI did not hesitate to speak of the 'smoke
of Satan'; all the truths of the faith were called into question by the
apostles of a revolutionary neo-Christianity. Forty years later this
Communist messianism has lost most of its appeal. The revelation
of the crimes of Stalinism and Maoism in all their monstrous scope,
as well as the collapse of the Soviet dictatorship and the Berlin Wall,
have destroyed the hopes that Christian progressives had placed in the
strength of Marxism. Parallel to this, under the powerful impetus of
an extraordinary pope, a restoration of the Church was being carried
out: thanks to John Paul II, thanks to Benedict XVI and his exceptional theological authority, "Rome is in Rome anew," as the Abbé
Luc J. Lefèvre, the first editor of *La Charité profanée*, confided to us
on the morrow of the Polish pope's election.

However, although the state of the Church was henceforth reestablished, although the possible collusion of Christian factions with
Communism is now hardly anything but a memory, potent fault-lines
persist in the ecclesial fabric, the legacy of a recent and tumultuous
past, exacerbated by a steadying of the Church in the truth of its
tradition. The reasons that impelled us to take up the pen have not
ceased to be of merit. Moreover, they are inherent to the very nature
of the religion of God-Love which seems wondrously in accord with
the religion of the love-god, the ideal of the modern world: If God
is Love, is not every love God?

Our book has never had any other ambition than to critically examine the relationship spontaneously established by the sensibility of

our contemporaries between these two propositions. This examination supposes first of all that we proceed with a philosophical study of what is understood naturally by the word *love*, chiefly under its 'charity' form. But next this requires that we take into consideration what Christ reveals to us about the truth of supernatural and divine love and that we pinpoint its metaphysical implications as to man, the world, and God.

This is why, setting aside polemical matters, we thought we could retain what was essential to our analyses. However, in some respects, this is a new book. First, we have endowed it with a considerably more extensive account of cosmology, as well as a fresh study of Plato's and Aristotle's doctrines on the soul. Next, we have updated references wherever we thought it necessary, and striven to rid our text of its incorrect expressions: obscure turns of phrase, referencing errors, inaccurate data, etc. And lastly, we have adjusted our formulations when they no longer corresponded to the deepening of our reflection. For all these reasons the need for a new title was imperative, a title to express more directly and calmly the essential object of our quest.

This book, begun in April 1966, went through several 'completions' in 1970, 1972, and 1974 until its first publication in January 1979. And from those years until the present time so much has been incorporated into this book, with the help of so many friends. Without the tireless dedication (in particular) of Annie Cidéron and Bruno Bérard, who have devoted countless hours of work to it, as well as Pierre-Marie Sigaud, who has accepted it into his *Théôria* series and, as an exacting proofreader, has given it the benefit of his editorial skill, this book would not have seen the light of day. I offer them here the expression of my deepest gratitude.

PART I

The Confusion of the Psychic and the Spiritual

CHARITY IS A THEOLOGICAL VIRTUE; THAT IS, it has God as its object. But, being also a virtue, it has man for its subject. Initially, then, it would be fitting to describe the relationship between man and charity. This involves a kind of phenomenology of charity wherein this virtue is grasped in its spontaneous exercise. This phenomenology (or description) makes plain the theoretical possibility of its corruption. Next, we must show how this possibility is actually realized today, that is, how the modern awareness of charity is seriously blind as to its true nature. Here we have a kind of psychoanalysis of charitable awareness. We are, in this case, ready to deal with the confusion between the psychic and the spiritual (or between the natural and supernatural) to its full extent, a confusion actualized by the illusion of love. For this is something that not only affects individual awareness, but also Christian society as a whole: it is Christianity's soul which is perverting the theological into the sentimental while mutilating itself in a parody of sacrifice. Having lost the transcendent sense of the sacred, it recovers the sentiment of its sacrificial love only by denying its very self. We have here a kind of psychodynamics whose laws can be formulated in a quite rigorous manner.

Hence the three following chapters:

1. Man and charity
2. The illusion of charity
3. The basic law of psychodynamics

I

Man and Charity

THE RELIGIOUS AND HUMAN LIFE OF THE
Christian is determined by the practice of the three virtues of faith,
hope, and charity. This truth is known to all. We have of course the
daily experience of our theological inadequacy, and dare not claim
to practice these virtues to perfection. But we have no doubt about
their nature. We are convinced that we know all about them; we only
lack courage and perseverance. But perhaps we also lack intelligence.
Is what we spontaneously consider an act of charity, for ourselves or
others, always truly one? In his relationship to the virtues in general,
and to charity in particular, can anyone be satisfied with what a philosopher would call a naive awareness? Should we not equally live our
charity with a critical awareness? Is the charity which we practice, or
desire to practice, always and automatically a theological virtue? At a
time when universal love has become something primarily self-evident
and demanded by humanity, it seems indispensable to ask: is it not
possible that, perhaps unknown to us or through some secret conniv-
ance, our charity might be corrupted? We will deal first with whether
this charity, about which we are so naively certain, is only an illusion.

I. CHARITY CAN BE CORRUPTED

If each theological virtue can be subjected to corruption, it is essentially because 'theology' is divine and 'virtue' human. The nature of
theological virtues is, in fact, to teach our human substance how to
be conformed to its divine finality. In practice, no virtue is of itself
sanctifying. It only prepares human substance for the reception of
grace, even though it corresponds to a divine quality in its essential
reality, and it is in this way a grace, insofar as God mercifully consents to let creatures share, according to their capacity, in the infinity of His treasures. What we are saying is that theological virtues
exhibit a dual aspect, existential in their human reality and essential
in their divine reality. If the grace of the sacraments descends from

5

heaven to earth, the grace of the virtues allows us to ascend from earth to heaven.

Basically, virtue is nothing but the grace of this aspiration towards the Most High, and in this respect one might say, since the virtues have a common essence, that each of them is to be found again in the other two. Faith, the adherence to an anticipated knowledge, is the hope of attaining God's Truth and the love of this Truth. Hope rests upon faith, as upon its initial motive, and is justified in the love which cannot deceive us. Lastly, charity combines faith and hope because it realizes, as much as nature here-below will allow, what faith promises and what hope awaits. This is why, on the ladder of the virtues that ascends from earth to heaven, charity is the one nearest heaven, even touching it in its highest expression.

We might try to grasp this mutual immanence of the virtues more precisely. But everything transpires as if there were only a single virtue characterized by three fundamental aspects, each theological virtue representing one of its aspects more specifically. This is what an analysis of Faith will show.

Insofar as Faith is the first of all the virtues, which is to say the foundational virtue, it includes a maximal 'essential' polarity and a minimal 'existential' polarity. It constitutes the minimum required on man's part in response to divine initiative, which is first Word and then announced Truth. Inasmuch as it is announced, we should listen to it; inasmuch as it is Truth, we should believe it. What listens is the intellect; what allows adherence to the contents of what the intellect receives is the will. If man were pure intellect, his intellection would also be his being, and the reception of the Word would be instantaneously deifying. But man is not made of pure intellect, and virtue—supernatural in its essence—requires an effort from human nature. Thus Faith, the prototype of theological virtue, brings to light these three aspects of every virtue: a human existence, a divine essence, an effort or tension of existence toward the essence. Nevertheless, at the interior of this prototypical virtue, we rediscover the triad of virtues: faith corresponds more directly to the Divine Essence because it is as if completely determined and absorbed by its objective content, the Word of God; hope more directly corresponds to the tension and effort of existence toward the essence; charity corresponds more directly to human existence inasmuch as it gives itself, which is to say inasmuch as it accepts being determined by its relationship with God.

As a consequence, the corruption of each virtue will be manifested, according to its intrinsic bipolarity, as error, inversion, and illusion: as error in what concerns the pole of essence, and this more especially has to do with faith; as inversion in what concerns the tension uniting and separating the two poles, and this is tied to hope, the meaning of which can be inverted and degraded into human hope; as illusion in what concerns the pole of existence, and this has to do with charity, for charity is first of all existence, which is to say reality, and the corruption of reality is not error but illusion.

As stated, in faith the pole of essence predominates, which means that our adherence is in some manner absorbed by those contents to which it adheres. For want of this absorption the content of the Truth to which one adheres is crushed beneath the weight of a volitive adherence and faith becomes blind, which is to say a purely formal affirmation, devoid of this Truth's content, which alone would be able to determine and complete it. To adhere to the Divine Word is, then, to efface oneself, to become quiet, to be silent in and from oneself. Faith requires our transparency.

Now this transparency rightly belongs to the intellect, since the intellect is the sole human modality whose nature is suited to the light of Truth. Consequently, we understand that the corruption of faith can result only from an obscuring of the intellect and not from a weakness of the will. Certainly, for lack of will, faith can be lost. But its loss is not its corruption. At the extreme, the truths of faith should be able to be known without the will adhering to them. An atheist could be a theologian. But in reality this is only an extreme, for will and intellect are not so separable just because the latter may understand perfectly what the former in no way adheres to. It is one same being who loves and understands, a being whose intellect and will are only modalities, and just as one cannot want what is absolutely unknown, neither can one know that which one in no way adheres to. Thanks to this transparency of the intellect, it is not the human subject who absorbs the Divine Object, but rather it is the Divine Object, seen then as Truth, that pervades and absorbs the human subject.

It can be said that the movement of charity is exactly the reverse of faith's. Here it is the pole of existence that absorbs (so as to realize it) the pole of essence, or at least 'recovers' it. Charity is the gift of self. It is the only possible way to be oneself, since it is love of one's own death. At final count, earth must prove itself not totally unworthy of heaven. At final count, man must prove himself not totally unworthy of God. At final count the human substance must absorb the divine substance, even though it be in this way consigned to its own annihilation, for the finite cannot contain the Infinite without breaking apart and being dissolved into Peace. Finally, man must accomplish what God Himself cannot do in His place. The corruption of charity, consequently, cannot be that of the intelligence. Certainly it is not absolutely independent, but an orthodox faith may cohabit — precariously — with a deviated charity. The corruption of charity is then that of the human will and, yet more profoundly, that of the ego's self-affirmation. Every act of love implies that the ego sets itself up and affirms itself. But this affirmation, allowable in the measure that the ego affirms itself in order to give itself, can be closed upon itself and take itself for its own end. Such is the corruption of charity which we will now attempt to describe.

2. THE SOLITUDE AND JUSTIFICATION
OF THE WILL IN CHARITY

What does it mean for man, or the pole of existence, to have to 'absorb' the essence? We have said: it is the desire for his own death. Charity is, in effect, realization, or it is even an obligation for realization, whereas faith is in some way a definitive and terminal anticipation. Through faith we already possess what we shall possess for all eternity. True, this possession is virtual and not actual. It is possession by anticipation. Everything is given to us in faith, and nothing more will be given to us. But we also know that everything within it escapes us, and this is why we cannot be, with respect to it, the plaything of an illusion: the being of faith is totally given and totally inaccessible to us. We can only commit an error of understanding bearing on the content, never an illusion of being bearing upon the very act of faith. We cannot mistake faith for its contrary. If we believe, we cannot believe and doubt at the same time. We can only ask God to increase our adherence, not to convert it into another faith. And this is, paradoxically, the reason why, as St. Paul says, faith "will pass away." For what completes faith, what makes it pass from virtue to sheer Reality, is faith no longer, but beatific knowledge. Faith is thus devoured by its transcendent content. Faith is this trifle that separates me from and unites me to Supreme Goodness. Faith is all or nothing: all for man who is nothing without it, nothing in God where it is nothing but the All itself. Perfect Faith is this diamond, the crystallization of the divine truth, which is dissolved, transpierced with Light as by a lightning-flash, in the instantaneity of the Absolute. But charity is realization, a passing from the virtual to the actual, the power of passage, not realization accomplished but the becoming of sanctification. Every spiritual way, inasmuch as it is a way, a guiding path, is a way of charity, is a way of the will to love. And because it is passage, it will not pass away, for the passage to Eternity is eternal.[1] Thus there is given to the human substance as such, inasmuch as it is only human and not a mirror of the Divine Light as in faith, there is accorded to this substance the power to prove that it is indeed the image of God, that it is indeed a creature, which is to say a work of God.

Here is a creature — we know with absolute certainty that God has made it, which means that this substance has been fashioned, modeled by God himself, by nothing less than the all-powerful Creator. To touch a creature is to touch God. God has placed his hand upon the body I touch, the figure of this body is the very deed of God become flesh, it is the divine act as form and matter. And so likewise for stone, tree, or wind. In truth we touch God everywhere.

There is in man as such then something of God, some datum to be conveyed. God has not denied us His immanence. The human substance is, by itself, capable of almost divine behavior. It can love, that is to say want to give itself, and, we repeat, no one can want to give himself in my stead, not even God. But this autonomous movement of which the creature is capable is that of its death and annihilation. Besides, how could it be otherwise? If it is truly human existence

---

1 In metaphysical terms, this means that the relative, or relationship, is a 'necessary' dimension of the Absolute. The mystery of the Holy Trinity expresses this truth translated into theology by the notion of 'subsistent relations'. Cf. Part 4, ch. 12.

9

which wills, if willing is to love, if this existence is the will to love, what can it will if not itself?

Now this existence is nothingness. It is separation from Being, or rather its very being is separation. If the will of man is the expression of his existence, in that mysterious moment wherein God abandons man to himself because no one can will in his stead, then, condemned to be himself, he exhausts the possibility of his own ontological separativity in the oblation of his nothingness. Such is the act of charity. And Jesus, suspended upon the cross of the world, utters the cry of the human substance crucified upon its love: "My God, my God, why have you forsaken me?"

In this movement of oblation that is charity, and because it can do nothing else, because it fulfills exactly everything that it is capable of by itself, the human substance discovers a kind of justification. And this justification is so much the more irresistible if it eludes, by nature, all ratiocination. It is not with words and reasonings that the charitable individual is justified, but through the fundamental act of his existence. In love there is clearly something that seems to relativize every intellectual certainty. A simple declaration of those revealed truths that form the content of faith is enough to make us see the full measure of our imperfection, an imperfection that as such fades away before the perfection of the Divine Object. But in love there is a capacity for reality that as such redeems or blinds us to our unreality. The strength of this reality, in the intrinsic nature of its will, necessarily ignores all that is not itself. And even more, it is the strength of this ignorance, it *is* ignorance, and this is why Christ Jesus says: "Why have you abandoned me?," an utterance that is a question wrought from love, a cry of ignorance that opens the door to Supreme Knowledge. To know, for faith, is also to understand what is unknown except, as St. Paul says, by reflection in a mirror. But the desire for reality, which inhabits faith and compels St. Thomas to touch the Resurrected One, constrains human substance to pass from shadow to reality. This is that charity by which the soul throws itself completely into the oblative affirmation of its own existence. At least the human subject has this possibility.

Thus, little by little, we are approaching that truth that we would like to establish: of all the virtues, and by its very excellence, charity is the most corruptible. If faith and hope will pass away, as St. Paul says, this is because the human dimension of these virtues will pass away, the promises of faith will be realized and the expectations of hope will be fulfilled. But if charity will not pass away, this is because in it the human dimension as such is endowed with an almost divine power. In the very bosom of God the creature does not 'cease' giving itself to its Creator, since it realizes in this way the truth of its created existence. From the point of view of spiritual psychology, in which we have situated ourselves, and excluding the metaphysical point of view, which will be envisaged later, it may be said that the act of charity constitutes the upper limit which can be reached by human nature. But at the same time that it opens the door to the highest possibilities, charity is exposed to the utmost perversion. Without doubt the act of charity consists, on the side of human nature, in 'absorbing' the Divine Essence even so far as to die of it, and this is enough to prevent the possibilities of corruption. But we have also shown that in this movement of betrothal there is a moment of pure solitude, of pure autonomy, that of the will willing itself in the indivisibility of its desire, necessarily abandoned to itself, suspended like Christ between earth and heaven upon the cross, a will which has renounced the reflected light of faith and which has not yet attained to the Essential Light of the Divine Word. It is at this moment that the charitable power can invert itself, for nothing has been accomplished yet, the *consummatum est* has not yet been uttered, the consuming of essence and existence has not yet been realized. In reality the cross is not only erected between heaven and earth, it is also placed horizontally between Good and Evil, between the good and bad thief, between the good thief of existence and the bad thief of existence, for the existence of every creature, in its ontological separateness, is a theft of pure and absolute Existence, to which it must be sacrificially restored. Thus the horizontal dimension is integrated into the vertical and salvific dimension through the sacrifice of its extension and its reabsorption into the point of its origin. This reabsorption is symbolized by the good thief who is turned toward Christ, that is to say who returns toward the crucial point from which he emanates from all eternity. And Christ expresses this 'punctualization' by declaring: "I say to you, this very day you shall be with Me in

Paradise" (Luke 23:43).[2] But the will can desire to lower the vertical direction down to the horizontal one, so as to gather salvific power from it for its own profit. This is what the bad thief cries out: "Save us from the Cross" and not: "Save us by the Cross." What is a power for spiritual oblation can become a power for bodily possession. This very strength is astray from its destiny as offering, from that which alone can complete its sacrifice, and, by the same movement, is in agreement with itself in the adoration of its own nothingness.

3. THE CRITERION OF CHARITY

The great love of Christ is a Love-Passion, the Passion of human substance devoured by the Divine Essence. Passion, that is to say the realization of the truth of human nature which is ontological passivity.

Consequently, if it is indeed true that the human substance is at first a desire to give itself, it can only *be* by giving itself to that which alone can receive it in the total nakedness of its gift, i.e., to that which is other than itself, to that which is of another order or another dimension, and it is precisely this which the vertical branch of the Cross symbolizes. It is by means of this that the horizontal branch (human substance) is crucified; therefore it is by means of this that it is determined in its very horizontality. Now what is of another order than human substance can only be of the spiritual order, which is to say directly answerable to the Holy Spirit. If charity is love, it will be said that the object of this love determines it. But even more can be said. If love is total gift, it is only real, and at first realized, if this gift is possible. And the total gift is only possible if the One to whom the gift is addressed can totally welcome it. In this way do we lay out a formal and intrinsic criterion for the gift itself. It is charity itself that, unless being an illusion, rigorously requires in the totality of its gift, in order to be real, the totality of welcome. Whoever gives himself totally is not to be denied, for the very possibility of the existence of a total gift implies that it be welcomed totally. This is why, when the charitable power is turned

---

2 The formula 'with Me' means integration with the Divine Self; the formula 'even today' means the permanent actuality of this integration, the *hic et nunc* of deifying grace.

toward what, by nature, cannot complete it, it becomes the illusion of love, blinded by the certainty of its own desire.

This might also be expressed in the following way: there is a truth to existence as such, or even an obviousness to existence as such. Charity is of the order of existence so that the truth of charity is that of its existence first. This truth, in its form, instinctively relativizes the formal truths of faith which, in contact with its obviousness, seems to reveal the unreality of these formal truths. However, faith is in its depths a demand and desire for determination, it is the movement of that which gives itself toward That which fixes it. If it can be turned away from spiritual realities, which alone admit of a true determination, in order to turn toward secondary realities, which admit of a relative determination and hence are relatively illusory, *it can at the same time also bring to these secondary determinations the sentiment of absolute reality which characterizes it,* and it is quite precisely in this that the corruption of charity resides. We repeat: there is in the charitable power the existential sentiment of an invincible reality, which appears to consign the certainties of faith to the rank of mental approximations. If it is strictly true that such an existential intuition is justified only inasmuch as the charitable power is an annihilating oblation to the All-Reality of the Spirit, it is no less true that we may address this oblation to determinations incapable of welcoming it, but whose incapacity and limits are veiled and covered over by the formal limitlessness of the charitable power. In the reality of its essence, that is, in its nature, charity implies sinlessness, just as in its principial determination, namely the Spirit, which alone can give it specificity. But this would not be the case if we were to consider it within the subject where it resides. This sinlessness of the charitable movement in itself, only perfect in its determination by the Absolute, gives way in the human subject, when this determination is no longer perceived distinctly and sought after, to an indefinite corruptibility, since charity is a movement, a power, a dynamism, a will, and since every movement not ascending toward the Infinite for its fulfillment descends toward the indefinite for its perdition. Charity is naturally supernatural. Therefore it can only fulfill its nature in supernaturality. But, being supernatural by nature, blinded by its own nobility, it can also dream of realizing itself in the naturality of exterior things. Today the time has come for this corruptibility, implied in the very possibility of charity, to be realized.

2

The Illusion of Charity

WE ARE LONG ACCUSTOMED TO VIEWING Christian charity as an upsetting power. This is, we think, the very essence of Christ's teaching. To the folly of the cross, about which St. Paul speaks, we spontaneously adjoin the folly of love. Fear of Pharisaism—and not the sense of God—orients our conception of charity. But is every folly an authentic sign of true charity? Is it enough to go to extremes to fulfill the divine commandment? When Christians dream of shedding someone's blood in the name of love for someone else, one is at least right to ask oneself: is this still the charity of Christ? We are not arguing here that care be taken about the cogency of some political attitude, but only about its relationship with the theological virtue. True, the modern world is rife with injustice; true, in many places on earth the strong crush the weak and mortally oppress them; true, at the spectacle of these sorrows a well-born soul is naturally indignant and seeks to reestablish justice. But, when we introduce into the natural awareness of rights the supernatural and 'radicalizing' ferment of Christian charity, are we not carrying out a subversion of both orders? Does not the excess of our temporal commitments, by a kind of inverted Pharisaism, become the easy conscience and alibi of a Christianity emptied of its content?

I. CHARITY IS REVOLUTION

Christian charity has gone mad. Proofs of it abound: we will quote only these few lines taken *at random* from a Christian review,[1] lines in which a priest replies to a reader of the opinion that a disciple of Christ does not have, as such, the right to take part in the armed struggle of, for example, a Che Guevara: "Above all we should not forget that the second commandment is like the first, and that anyone

1 The review *Signes du Temps*, Feb. 1968. This review has long ceased publication, but has been reborn under other forms.

who says he loves his brother and loves him in word only is a liar. We are not all called to take up the machine-gun, for we do not all have the right [*sic*]. At least let us not condemn those whose two good hands are ready to be either chained or to take up arms. What are we doing with our own hands?"

In the same issue, after a panegyric for the Maoists "who have just undertaken a tenacious campaign against egoism," we find this information concerning the Congress of Havana of January 12, 1968: "...a group of priests participated in the congress and expressed their solidarity with the revolutionary struggle. This movement must grow rapidly. It is clear, in fact, that revolution has become the only remedy for the present bloodshed."

These few quotations have only an indicative value. They testify to a general state of mind that has invaded Christianity to various degrees and has become 'part of the woodwork'. Undoubtedly they will be judged excessive. "What we have here," some will say, "is the overflow of an excess of charity, but it is still charity."

If truth is not allowed to be truth, however, it is then necessary, in spite of everything, to attempt to get to the very heart of this illusion. We have shown why charity, the virtue of virtues, was by its very nobility the privileged place of the greatest possible corruption, in conformity with the adage: *corruptio optimi pessima*. Now we will try to see how, in the illusion of charity, this corruption is realized through the confusion of the psychic and the spiritual. Undoubtedly it could be shown, by recalling some doctrinal principles, how the attitude we have singled out contradicts the truth. We are unsure if this contradiction will be perceived. Awareness of it risks being quickly obscured again by current widely held assumptions. Will we be understood?

2. A CHARITY THAT WANTS TO ENJOY ITSELF

Pure charity is a charity unaware of itself. It never experiences itself as such and, if necessary, denies any notion of itself. In its lived reality it is an existential instinct which makes the human soul run distraught toward the Love of the Beloved. It is the bride of the Song of Songs who goes everywhere seeking the supreme Lover, and will cease weeping and groaning only when she has found Him, when she finally rests upon His heart. What determines this charity then is the truth of the Spirit. But, when charity is no longer an oblation to the determination of the Spirit, there is no longer anything to reveal this truth to it. It must then know itself as charity, must experience itself, must feel itself, must perceive its own sacrificial movement so as to be in possession of an objective certainty of itself. It becomes, for itself, its own object. Therefore its certainty is no longer of a spiritual order, but of an exclusively psychic and sentimental one, which is to say of the order of the felt. *It is the very sensation of the gift which becomes the criterion and measure of this gift.* They are the psychic effects of the psyche's movement which become a certainty of movement. Let us take the image of a hand motionless in the water. With immobility we feel neither water nor our hand. But if we stir the hand, the motion reveals its own existence and that of the water. 'Objectively' the water is itself only the 'subjective' sensation of our hand. The same goes for the soul. Its sacrificial movement as such, independent of every spiritual orientation, becomes an end in itself, for, with every impulse, it reiterates the lived certainty of sacrifice.

3. THE PSYCHOANALYSIS OF REVOLUTIONARY CHARITY

Our thesis is as follows. In order for there to be an illusion of love two things are necessary: on the one hand a movement of the soul which requires a certain psychic energy, an energy which we call (charitable) *power*, and on the other a qualifying of this movement which determines it — illusorily — as *charitable* (power), as a movement of love. In the case of spiritual charity the power to love is given to man by God, and it qualifies as love when man gives himself to God. In the case of the illusion of *love*, what then is the origin of the power and from whence then does (illusory) charity come? We say that the feeling of power is engendered by a 'liberating' transgression, and that the illusion of love results from the 'sacrificial' desecration of Christianity.

Now the Christian revolutionary, as a matter of fact, is incited to transgression and desecration, as we have just seen, since, having renounced the only objective criterion, that of the Spirit, he is condemned to a parodied objectivity, that of a counter-subjectivity actualized by the transgressing and desecrating of his Christian soul. We will describe this process briefly.

Let us consider a Christian soul in harmony with a Christian world. The commandments of God and the Church, which define an order in the double sense of the term, constitute the structure of this world and determine its psycho-spiritual 'climate'. When the equilibrium of exchanges between the soul and its environment is established, this environment keeps watch over the charitable soul while enclosing it in an objective doctrinal setting. The components of this setting, which 'think' for it, become a natural fact for the soul itself, a fact that it spontaneously discovers within itself. The stability of this setting does not exclude adversity, but it constrains the soul to seek out its own surpassing and the world's at the interior of itself and the world, at the 'center' where the Spirit dwells, so that this surpassing is an obliteration. For anyone who loves with a true love, the narrowest horizon encloses the infinite fullness of Love; the garden of his heart is a limitless forest.

But when the center is no longer sought after, and therefore when the spiritual tension slackens, the soul, in a kind of altogether ephemeral state of undifferentiated equilibrium, loses the feeling of its own existence. It then turns towards the periphery in order to rediscover that tension by which the feeling of its existence is conveyed. The Christian soul and the soul of Christianity are basically the same thing; it is the 'animic climate' of a spiritual life in the first case and that of a Revelation in the second, an environment outside of which there can be neither spiritual realization nor manifestation of Revelation. For spirituality in the pure state is concentration upon the Absolute; Revelation in the pure state is the elusive lightning-bolt of the Divine Light. One would be an instantaneous reabsorption, the other a timeless irradiation. Neither one nor the other would therefore be possible for man, as such, without a milieu for manifestation to soften the insupportable dazzle of the Spirit. We could also say this: the pure essence of Revelation is of such a subtlety that it is practically ungraspable, or, if one prefers, invisible for man. In the same way, the focal-point where all spiritual efforts converge is so tenuous that the soul seeking it has the impression of perpetually missing it: "the door is narrow." But spiritual one-pointedness and revelatory transcendence are mercifully projected into the animic substance (individual or collective) under the form of rays which trace the structural axes of this climate on the one hand, at the same time that, on the other hand, this irradiation permeates their qualitative contents in a manner impossible to describe. It is in this way that a traditional world is engendered, like an ocean illuminated by the Spirit, one molecule of which is the human soul. This is what is called Christianity.

For traditional man this animic climate, this Christianity, is his very soul and the bride prepared by the Spirit. Out of this he draws those instinctive truths, those natural virtues that determine his mental horizon and the coloration of his psychism.[2] It bears him along like the ocean bears its waves. It is the Spirit 'animized' and, in a certain manner, subjectivized.

But when the soul, turning away from the Spirit, turns towards its own contents, the psychic *reflections* of the Spirit (a thousand suns shine, as it were, upon the crest of each wave), these contents or reflections become foreign objects to the very extent that they are no longer experienced as reflections, which is to say when the link with the ray issued from the spiritual Sun, the outcome of which they were, is broken. They are then transformed into temptations to liberation, because what was the axis of structure and qualitative determination has become limitation and constraint, and, at the same stroke, a source of revolt. However, the soul is not able to forget, at a single stroke, that these are its own structures. It wants to rise up against itself, it is itself that it must destroy. No longer does it want to recognize itself. It denies and blasphemes the visage of its own childhood; it wants to degrade the memory of its purity, beauty, and glory. Only this working of the Counter-Spirit can engender this feeling of liberating power and sacrificial renunciation haunting the hearts of the reformers. This power is that of transgression, or, if one prefers, the Fall. And everyone knows that the impact of a fall is proportional to its height. It is from the highest point of itself that a soul must fall. One may only desecrate one's own treasures, and,

---

2 The extremely important notion of natural virtue will be studied in the second part of ch. 4.

if what is denied were worthless, there would be no reason to reject it. Nothing is comparable to the joy over destruction, and the most intoxicating destructions are those of the most sublime edifices. There is and there can be no other source of power for the 'secularized' soul than that of its own ruin. For true spiritual power engenders no sentiment of power in the soul, but only and continually a sentiment of impotence and weakness. "When I am weak, then am I strong," says St. Paul.[3] At the outset spiritual tension puts the relative soul in the presence of the absolute Soul. And this tension is an immobile movement. Each one of our impulses is absorbed and volatilized in an absolute and boundless Space. On the other hand, once the Absolute is renounced, the psychic tension through which the greedy soul experiences itself can only go from the relative to the relative and from fall to ruin. Nevertheless the sensation of power, gained by exhilaration from destruction, is reinforced with the feeling of justification gained by an exhilaration from sacrifices. In this indefinite desecration to which a certain kind of Christianity is committed, the human soul plays for itself the comedy of charity. The charitable power seems to rediscover its most incontestable objective criteria. Does it not sacrifice what for two millennia has been its flesh and blood, that blood of our soul which no one until that moment had dared to shed? The closer I cut to the heart, thinks the reformer, the more violently the blood spurts and gleams, and, in its very gushing, the more life becomes visible, sparkling and incontestable, and the more blinding, certain, and irrefutable becomes my charity.

Such is the nature of the charitable illusion; such is also its end. It is dependent upon a veritable sado-masochism and is nourished by its own debasement. But when the destruction of Christianity will have been accomplished, when there will no longer be anything to kill, when from the tiara of St. Peter in its 'unbearable triumphalism' right down to the last hymn of the last peasant in some remote countryside in its 'laughable childishness' everything will have been definitively tossed onto the Constantinian rubbish heap, then, before the *tabula rasa* of the Christian desert, before the stretched-out sheet of a charity at fall's end, it will be necessary to invent new decadence,

---

3   2 Corinthians 12:10.

to create new ruptures of level, in order to rediscover the delicious falling sensation, where the sound of a dizzying caress glides along the skin of the soul.

In summary, what constitutes the very substance of the charitable illusion is the confusion of the psychic and the spiritual. In its truth, charitable power, under its two aspects of power on the one hand and charity on the other, is entirely governed by the Spirit; in its corruption, the illusion of love is supplied by the sacrificial desecration of Christianity, and the illusion of power by transgression and a 'liberating' fall.

3

The Basic Law of Psychodynamics

INTRODUCTION: THE NOTION OF ENTROPY

We would now like to show that the production of psychic energy is linked to the fundamental laws of what could be called psycho-dynamics, and that the illusion of charity, denounced by us continually, is only a particular case of it, one in which a religious factor is added to the general factors of the psychism's energetics. To speak in a more precise and brief manner, we will transpose into the psychic realm the second thermodynamic principle, called the Carnot-Clausius principle.

This principle, discovered by Sadi Carnot in 1824, then corrected and made precise by the German physicist Clausius, who gave it the name of entropy (*entrope* in Greek signifies in-volution, return), is considered to be the most general law of physical phenomena. Leaving aside its mathematical formulation, which uses integral calculus, we will content ourselves with providing a rather intuitive idea of it.

This law is concerned with energy production, measured under the form of heat (hence the name thermodynamic = 'heat-energy'), in a mechanically *isolated* system; that is, it receives no energy from without. For there to be a production of energy (and therefore work), a system (a steam-engine for example) must have two sources of heat at different temperatures, so that a passage from the warm source to the cold source is made possible — it being understood that heat is a form of energy. Without a cold source, the warm source would retain its quantity of heat; no passage could occur. Now it is this passage that is equivalent to energy production and that is transformed into work. But only a *portion* of the energy is transformed into work. As for the remaining heat, it "will go to the cooler source."[1] The warm

---

1 J. L. Andrade e Silva and G. Lochak, *Quanta*, trans. P. Moore (London: Weidenfeld & Nicholson, 1969), 51.

source is chilled, the cold source is warmed, and at the end of the process both sources are thermally equal: exchange between them is no longer possible. Thus the remaining portion of heat not transformed into work is lost through its absorption by the cold source. There is a degradation of energy. We start with a differentiated state, with a disequilibrium, and each time there is a production of energy in an isolated system we arrive at a state of equilibrium in which, temperature being equal throughout, no energy production is possible. Someone has called this "death by tepidity."

Carnot writes: "to heat any substance whatever requires a body warmer than the one to be heated; to cool it requires a cooler body." The cold source is no less indispensable than the warm source. He concludes: "wherever there exists a difference of temperature, motive-power can be produced."[2] As for Clausius, rectifying certain mistakes of Carnot who had encouraged physicists to reject his principle, he reaffirmed and reinforced it by showing that "heat cannot of itself... pass from a colder to a hotter body."[3] It follows that "an *isolated* system never passes twice through the same state."[4] This energy-producing passage, from a thermally differentiated state to a state of undifferentiated equilibrium, is expressed mathematically under the form of a function which measures the *entropy* (etymologically: return to equilibrium) of a system: the more a system draws closer to energy equilibrium, the more entropy is said to increase; in this case we are speaking of positive entropy. The increasing entropy of a mechanical system very precisely defines what is called the degradation of energy: all work consumes energy, and for an isolated system this consumption is irreversible.

Philosophers—especially André Lalande, who has contested Spencer's 'progressive' evolutionism—have been most interested in the entropic principle. They have related it to the theme of time and have seen in it a concrete verification of time's irreversibility: there is

---

2 Cf. *Reflections on the Motive Power of Heat*, 2nd rev. ed. (New York: John Wiley & Sons; London: Chapman & Hall, 1897), 49 ff.

3 *The Mechanical Theory of Heat*, trans. W. R. Browne (London: Macmillan & Co., 1879), 330–1.

4 J. Perrin, "Le second principe de la thermodynamique," in *Revue Metaphysique* (1903), 183.

a natural direction in the energy production of physical phenomena.

If we consider now the physical universe in its entirety as an 'isolated' mechanical system, since, from the viewpoint of secular science, there is nothing outside it, it must be concluded that the universe tends towards a maximum entropic state where no energy production will occur any longer: all differentiations having been reabsorbed, a quantiative homogeneity would reign everywhere in a deathly equilibrium.[5]

We will say no more about a subject that could lead us too far afield. Essentially, we would like to draw attention to this incontestable principle taught by physics: there is energy production only when there is difference and disequilibrium, inequality and heterogeneity. This principle is transposable into the psychic realm, that is, into the human world, so that it is possible, in tandem with thermodynamics, to speak of psychodynamics. And since dynamics only starts with a difference, the question that faces us — a most serious question for a humanity on the entropic path of disenchantment through atheistic isolation — is this: from whence will come a life-giving differentiation?

I. THE SPIRIT IS THE SOURCE OF PSYCHIC ENERGY

Production of psychic energy only begins with a differentiation or a disequilibrium. What 'animates' and 'sustains' the movements of the individual as well as the collective soul, what gives a soul the certainty of its own life and strength, is the existence of a qualitative differentiation. But in conformity with the entropism of all natural movements, the production of this energy is accompanied by a degradation and tends towards equilibrium at its outer limit. The power of differentiation is exhausted in its very manifestation, so that movement may only continue with the appearance of a new differentiation, of a rupture of the previous entropic equilibrium, but a differentiation necessarily situated at a qualitatively lower level. In the same way a waterfall is at its maximum force at its lowest point, but, since it no longer follows

---

5 Some thinkers, Raymond Ruyer for one, have spoken of negative entropy or *neg-entropy*, in connection with living things. A property of living things, in fact, is to pass from an initial poorly differentiated state — an egg for example — to a final very differentiated one: feathers, skin, nerves, bone, blood vessels, etc.

a vertical descending direction and since it flows away according to the horizontal direction, this force progressively diminishes.

Now the relation of the soul to the Spirit engenders, by its very existence, a qualitatively near-absolute differentiation. We say near-absolute for it is clear that an absolutely absolute differentiation is equivalent to the negation of all differentiation. But a purely relative differentiation is likewise equivalent to its negation. Only the notion of the relatively absolute can reflect the existence of differentiation.

The presence of the Spirit of God at the soul's center gives rise to a fundamental and almost ontological rupture of equilibrium in the latter. We could just as well speak of the presence of the supernatural within the natural. And because this rupture of equilibrium is in some way absolute and cannot be abolished, it necessarily escapes entropic degradation. It represents what some philosophers, thinking about the creative power of life — there are more differentiations, more 'information' or differentiated organization of living matter, in the chicken than in the egg — have called a negative entropy or negentropy. But, if entropy is negative, this means that in reality the direction of movement is reversed. The spiritual movement of the soul draws its power from its weakness, it climbs back towards the source of its being; in giving Itself, the Spirit does not diminish Itself; in making the snow and ice of the soul melt with the fire of Its Love, It absorbs it and gives it life. For the surging of the Spirit within the soul is the revelation, *uno intuitu*, that by itself the soul is dead substance and that by Itself the Spirit is substantial life.

2. THE THREE PRESENCES OF THE SPIRIT

The Spirit is present in the soul in three ways: with an ontological or subjective presence, with an illuminative or revelatory presence, and finally with an objective or qualitative presence. Through Its ontological presence It founds the subject's existence: in It we have Being. Through Its revelatory presence It effects the illumination of faith, by which we become more precisely aware that the Spirit is the source of our life; It actualizes our spiritual awareness: in It we have life. Thus the second presence draws the human being toward the first presence (being or existence) while revealing it to consciousness.

Finally, through its objective presence, the Spirit, as previously shown, determines the Christian soul's qualitative contents ('natural' virtues, sentiments, images, and ideas): in It we have movement. Thus the third presence corresponds to the *ad extra* radiation of the second presence, that is to say the radiation of Revelation. Conversely, the second presence draws spiritual awareness into an *ad intra* movement of return to the center. Spiritual or religious awareness, in fact, effects the 'return of the prodigal child'; it connects the periphery of the soul to its center; it learns from Revelation that the Spirit, which is 'within us', is the Being without whom we would not be, and, through this confronting of caused being with Causal Being, it realizes the nature of every human awareness, which is to be aware of a difference, since it reveals at the heart of a human being a near-absolute differentiation. As a result only religious awareness (which is to say faith) can check the natural entropy of a human soul. With the disappearance of this awareness the second presence is no longer perceived. Only the ontological and qualitative presences remain to combat this entropy. The ontological presence is neg-entropic of itself: it is perceived by each of us, even outside of faith, as not non-existent: I am not a nothingness of being, I am 'miraculously' differentiated from nothingness. But by itself, the qualitative presence is evidently inoperative, it only acts in the presence of religious awareness; the latter having disappeared, the Christian soul's qualitative determinations in their objective content, far from being a help, are perceived as obstacles, as objections. Now it is from these 'objective' determinations, perceived as 'objections', that a rupture of equilibrium, productive of enough energy for a new animation of the psyche, can appear. This is the energy of transgression. But it is then that the soul is drawn into an indefinite entropic degradation. And this is why.

Every differentiation, which is a source of energy (or of negentropy), is effected from a given, and its energetic power is a direct function of the irreducibility of this given. The superior form of the given (of the gift) is grace. Spiritual awareness realizes the perfection of the given in opening itself to the donating grace. But, quite to the contrary, transgression, because it transforms the given into a construct, exhausts the force of differentiation at a single stroke. What in fact is transgression? It consists not only in a revolt against an order considered to be sacred (the objective presence of the Spirit); once transgressed this order, formerly possessing the obviousness of a natural or supernatural law, ceases to appear as a given and becomes a construct. The qualitative determinations of the Spirit, at once ordination of the soul and order for the soul, are then regarded as 'products of history', as petrified deposits which have exuded "countless treasons of Christ's message." Accounts offered in explanation of these products, showing how they were constructed, and those genetic explanations essentially based on Marxism and psychoanalysis, will transform the determinative graces of the Spirit into "alienating structures and neuroses."

What is not taken into account is that, in abolishing the given, one abolishes the differentiation, thereby reestablishing entropic equilibrium, the equilibrium of death. If in fact the structure and contents of the Christian ambiance are just products of a human history, just human works, they immediately lose their character of irreducible objectivity, which made them almost immutable norms relative to the variations of individual souls. They cease being of a nature differing from that of changing and fallible men. They then cease being 'supports' for action, poles of attraction, and rules of life as well. Everything which would regulate the behavior of religious men — customs, laws, manners, practices, moral instincts, taboos, festivals, sacred time, costumes, songs and dances, legends — in short, everything which a religion gives birth to in the world of its deployment, and which the human soul should literally *wear*, because the soul is of another nature and willed by God — all of this being no longer anything but a contingent work, then the soul, in order to escape the entropic equilibrium, that is in order to feel itself 'alive', must turn towards the destruction of other givens.

Basically, for lack of faith and in order to live, the soul is condemned to indefinite transgression. But the curse of transgression resides in this, that it exhausts, in its very manifestation, the momentarily engendered energy. To denounce the objective forms of the Spirit's presence in the Christian soul surely produces in this soul an energy-generating rupture of equilibrium. But, doing this, do we not see how the human soul is thereby placed above all these forms, since they are only its own work, and therefore that it is the one supplying the energy, an energy it illusorily believes is drawn from their destruction?

28

3. STAGES OF THE CHRISTIAN
SOUL'S DEGRADATION

Seeing that the human soul is condemned, once the radical differentiation realized by religious awareness is abolished, to supply itself with energy believed drawn from this very abolition, it is clear that in conformity with the law of entropy it is situated on a level energetically lower than its starting point. In other words — and such is the perfectly rigorous law identified by our analysis — there is only 'life' for the (individual or collective) soul if the soul is inserted within a religious structure, which is defined by a fundamental relationship of differentiation: created/Uncreated. Outside of this insertion the soul, in order to satisfy the desire for the life which is its light ("that life was the light of men"), is obliged to appropriate the vital energy from itself, out of its own stock, and thus dooms itself to exhaustion.

The stages of this psychic degradation are easy to determine: they are correlative to the three presences of the Spirit. One first proceeds with the destruction of the supernatural religious order, corresponding to the second presence; next, to that of the natural religious order, corresponding to the third presence; and finally, an almost perfect homogeneity being realized among all components of the 'human world', so that any energetic exchange is impossible, the modern counter-spirit then attempts to fabricate differentiation artificially. But this last attempt consumes energy which can only be appropriated from that original energetic stock out of which existence is formed in its 'miraculous' differentiation from nothingness.

Neither the supernatural nor the natural order is an entropic equilibrium; they are both hierarchical equilibriums. They do not eliminate tensions and oppositions; to the contrary, they permanently 'maintain' them because they are the effect of the Spirit's presence, and in this way they escape the degradation of every physical system. These orders are not characterized by uniformity but by difference, not by homogeneity of elements but by their qualitative heterogeneity. Nevertheless they constitute an order because they are subject to the principle of unity, that is to say because this principle is transcendent to the totality of elements which it embraces and governs. But the elements retain their properties and continue to be distinguished from each other by their qualitative diversity, which is to say basically by their nature. In other words, in order to be an order, such an order has no need of embracing identical elements; its unity does not result from the nature of its elements (it is not a result), but it is a principle of hierarchically organizing all elements with respect to each other. This order is truly an order, which is to say a coherent system of relationships predominating over the elements bound together by it.

Entropic order is exactly the reverse of true order; it merits the name of disorder rather well. In order to form a 'whole', its elements have to be as identical as possible and differ among themselves in number only. This case is only realized through the mathematical notion of a set, which shows that this is then the lowest degree of unity. In such a set the relationships articulated by its components with each other are nonexistent, their mutual coherence is almost nil. This is actually a caricature of unity, or even its inversion. Each component is found at the same energetic level as the others; it can exchange nothing with them. It is moreover nearly impossible to distinguish between them. None of them can supply proper characteristics capable of being the object of discrete 'information'.[6]

Such is clearly the direction of the post-conciliar reforms. In the supernatural religious order we find a universe characterized by multiple qualitative differences, the first of which, as we have said, is the spiritual awareness of the created/Uncreated distinction, a distinction

---

6 This is the information theory which today unifies thermodynamic and probaabilist theories. After Boltzmann, who has brought entropy back to a statistical equilibrium in showing that entropy, S, should measure the most probable state, P, of a system: $S=K \log P$, Wiener, Shannon, and Brillouin have shown that all of these theories could be translated in a general way into terms of information, since information can be appropriated from a system only on the condition that it has not attained its state of equilibrium. An image will enable this matter to be understood. If we deposit white powder and black powder into a receptacle from two separate cups, the two powders will be mixed together at the end of an indeterminate time. There is no *probability* that the contrary will occur. Statistically, the black grains and the white grains will *end up* uniformly distributed, and the mass will be grey. The receptacle's system thus will have attained its entropic undifferentiated state, which is also therefore its most probable state. So much for Boltzmann. Now for N. Wiener. If I look at the receptacle at the beginning, I can distinguish the black powder from the white: I receive two pieces of information. At the end of a certain time I see nothing but grey: I receive (or deduce) one piece of information. Information varies in a direction that is inverse to entropy.

reflected in the religious universe as that of the sacred from the profane: sacred space (the temple as opposed to ordinary buildings),
sacred time (Sunday as opposed to weekdays), sacred language (Latin
as opposed to the vernacular), sacred dress (cassock and monastic
habit as opposed to lay clothing), sacred functions (the priesthood as
opposed to the trades), sacred institutions (Church and civil society),
etc. Each of these distinctions maintains an equilibrium of tension,
not an equivalence of death, a tension not without conflict. But are
not the elements of a vault held together in this way, while opposing each other? If we consider now the natural religious order, the
same remark applies: it is an order defined by structures of qualitative
oppositions: the opposition, according to essence, of man and woman,
parents and children, master and disciple, prince and subjects, past
and present, honest people and the dissolute, normal and pathological,
etc. Now, as much in the supernatural order as in the natural, there
is not a single one of these aforesaid tensions and oppositions which
the post-conciliar reformers have not attempted to destroy.

For the supernatural religious order, this work of the destruction of spiritual awareness began with the end of the Middle Ages.
It continues even today, but with less strength, since the aimed-for
result is already very nearly attained. Just think then of the feeling
of power experienced by souls in the Renaissance (which is for us, in
many respects, a burial of human beauty and dignity), and you will
see those principles which we have expressed verified. At the other
extreme of the cycle the example of Nietzsche, with the extraordinary,
almost prophetic inspiration animating his work, verifies again what
energy is set free at the destruction of spiritual awareness. But, in
reality, this energy is appropriated from the soul itself, thus exhausting
its own vitality, which is proven by the madness into which Nietzsche
sank. Nevertheless this work, after having borne its fruits of physical
death in the satanic saga of Nazism, begins only today to bear its
fruits of spiritual death.

Post-conciliar Christianity, then, has sought to abolish not so much
religious awareness as its works, namely all forms assumed by the distinction between sacred and profane. Let us not forget that what is
rather comical is that these destructions were effected in the name of
a community spirit, even though, as we have seen, this can only end in

31

the disappearance of mutual relationships, in the destruction of every cohesion among the elements of order. Individuals are condemned in this way to the solitude of numerical identity.

With the destruction of religious forms, we are already reaching the second stage, the stage of the destruction of the natural religious order. These stages are moreover in continuity and often even contemporaneous with each other; they can only be distinguished by abstraction. Today we are at the apex of this phase.

Post-conciliar Christians are far from being the only ones at work here. But the surprising thing is that for some time now they have lent a hand so obligingly. The advancement of women,[7] the cult of youth, the rejection of all control, more-or-less anarchic democratism, faith in progress, the promotion of leisure-time activities, the negating of the pathological category — all of this has very nearly achieved a state of dogma for a neo-Christianity in revolt against the dogmas of faith. At the same time — and with this we are entering the third stage — a parallel undertaking unfolds, one which seeks to build from negentropy artificially. Attempts are made to set up differentiations and oppositions everywhere, even where, up until now, they were never perceived. Marxism and Freudianism are marvelous instruments for such a task. Extrapolating to every domain of human life the fruit of theories proper to a segment of society and relative to a given era, Marxism raises 'class struggle' to a principle, even and above all where it is impossible to speak of classes. Everyone participates in this struggle: the condition of women reflects the alienation of the working class, teaching has a 'class content': these and a thousand other idiocies, although in fact only verbiage at its worst, as just so many 'scandals' and 'injustices' confer an illusory interest upon ephemeral conflicts. During this time the human soul rediscovers a feeling of life. Likewise psychology and psychoanalysis discover internal conflicts and indefinite difficulties, both pretty nearly imaginary, but capable of making an insipid daily life interesting again: teaching, the education of children, sexuality, fashion, hair-style and nutrition are the favored domains of these pseudo-problems. All of this is far

---

7 Cf. my book on the question of women and the priesthood, *La femme et le sacerdoce* (Paris: L'Harmattan, 2013).

from being inoffensive, however. Beyond the time spent in vainly trying to resolve insoluble (because nonexistent) problems, the formidable psychic bustle deployed in this case (just think of the efforts of innumerable organizations of psycho-sociology which put considerable means into play: managerial publications, reviews, congresses, symposia, seminars, exams, inquests, etc.) consumes an energy which, at this time, can only be appropriated from the soul's very existence. This is how the soul tends, inexorably, toward its own annihilation.

With these considerations our examination of the different aspects of the confusion between the psychic and the spiritual is complete. We have seen this confusion manifested in the individual order as well as the collective. We have seen the corruption of charity affect the soul of each Christian as well as the soul of Christianity.

Now it is time to approach true charity, the truth of charity.

PART II

The Natural Determinations of Charity

THE CHIEF ATTRIBUTE OF THE THEOLOGICAL
virtues, as we have seen, is to conform human existence to the Divine
Essence, according to their respective natures. Every virtue first puts
down roots in human existence. Thus we are led to ask what this
human existence must be in order for it to provide a natural terrain
adequate for true charity. Charity does not, in fact, possess its practical determinations within itself. It is a power to do something; but
what must be done, what gives a content to its power for action, is
necessarily received from the cultural setting within which it unfolds.
It is this cultural setting that provides the defining facts, or what
might be called the natural facts, of this Charity.

We can see why the question now broached is of such importance.
The frightening crisis which shakes the Church, and which, if not
resolved, will entail the destruction of the entire Western world, is a
crisis of natural facts, or again a crisis of the Christian soul. By Christian soul we do not mean only the soul of a man taken singly, insofar
as he is Christian. We are also speaking of the soul of Christianity,
of the animic atmosphere proper to the Christian collectivity. Surely
this soul does not exist outside of individual supports which are the
Christians themselves. But it does nonetheless define a non-subjective
reality, insofar as it is the soul of the Christian people. It makes up the
environment in which Revelation takes shape. Revelation in itself is
actually pure and non-formal light. It transcends all creation, even the
angelic: "Heaven [the world of the angels] and earth will pass away,
but my words will not pass away." Divine Truth is immutable and
eternal. To manifest Itself It requires an environment, an ambiance
to receive and actualize It. This rapport between Divine Revelation
and the human world, which It wishes to enlighten and save, may be

understood as being modeled on the creation of the world, for the appearance of a religion is truly the creation of a world. And just as in the beginning the Spirit of God brooded over the primordial Waters of universal Existence, so in Christian Revelation the Divine Spirit broods over the animic waters of human existence to manifest Itself there by illuminating them; otherwise the Eternal Word remains unmanifested and there is no Revelation in the proper sense of this term. One could even recall here the cosmological model of Aristotelian hylomorphism, namely that every created thing is composed of a form and a 'matter', Eternal Truth constituting the form of Revelation and human substance the matter. Finally, the mystery of Revelation finds its perfect prototype in the mystery of the Incarnation, the Word of Truth made flesh. This is why it can be said that the mystery of Revelation is realized in the very mystery of the Revealer. Now the mystery of the Incarnation requires at once the operation of the Holy Spirit and the virginal substance of Mary: the Holy Spirit had prepared a human Bride, the prototype of the Christian soul welcoming Revelation.

However, the commandment to love is equally addressed to man viewed in his own nature, and not only in his cultural soul. To speak of the natural determinations of charity is to speak therefore of a dual natural putting-down of roots: both in a certain social nature and in a certain human one. We shall characterize these first determinations as cultural and the second as anthropological.

In closing, we will clarify the meaning of these two terms:

1. By *culture* is to be understood the ordered complex of mental and symbolic representations received through tradition, by means of which a society is not only capable of intelligently assimilating all information from man, the world, or God, all the while retaining its identity, but is even able to enter actively into a relationship with them. These representations and symbols (language, rites, myths, dance, gestures, customs, calendar, clothes, etc.) are not to be viewed in an abstract way by themselves, but are to be lived directly in the manner of instinctive behavior, thus forming real cultural instincts. This is why we call them natural virtues. Our question is therefore the following: what are the natural virtues thanks to which a society can at the same time intelligently assimilate and put into practice — without corrupting it — the theological virtue of charity?

2. By *anthropology* is to be understood an integral and coherent conception of the human being. Such a conception must be seen from two different and correlative points of view: man may be considered either in his essence or in his constitution. Thus, to say of man that he is the image of God is to define him otherwise than by declaring him composed of a body and soul. In the first case his basic, synthetic quality is stated, as therefore is his spiritual destiny. In the second one his analytical structure according to the elements out of which he is formed is stated. In the latter, man is a natural being participating in the inherent multiplicity of the created. In the former, to the contrary, he is situated with respect to God as participating in His essential unity. The first anthropology could be called essential or metaphysical anthropology; the second structural or natural anthropology. Now, if it is clear that metaphysical anthropology expresses and defines the profound truth of natural anthropology, it is no less certain that the latter defines the former's conditions for realization and must therefore be in conformity with it. This is why our question will be the following: what must a human being's natural structure be so that, upon the base of such a constitution, it may enter into the way of love and thus realize the spiritual destiny assigned to it by its essence?

First we will examine in Chapter 4 the relationship of man to religion, which is to say the conception which he naturally has of the religion that he practices. This conception is itself correlative to a certain type of culture and civilization. This in turn will be the object of Chapter 5. Finally, in Chapter 6, we will analyze, by way of counterpoint, the central themes of modern civilization that are destructive of all nature.

After examining cultural determinations, we will next examine anthropological ones. A first approach to them according to the philosophical method will be attempted, so as to identify the fundamental elements of man's constitution (Chapter 7). Next we will search for the presence of these elements in the New Testament (Chapter 8). Finally we will rediscover them in Greek, Jewish, and Christian anthropological traditions (Chapter 9).

4

Religion and Man

THE QUESTION UPON WHICH WE WOULD LIKE
to focus is rather unusual. It could be formulated in this way: when one
is neither a saint nor a theologian, what does 'to be a Christian' mean?
This is not a question of knowing how the ordinary man reads the
Gospels or participates in liturgical worship, but of how he is situated
with respect to religion as a whole, how he 'sees himself' as a Christian.

The answer to this question and the central theme of this chapter
is that, as sublime as it may be, a religion, in order to be practicable,
must be comprehensible for a collectivity, in default of which men
turn away from it and forget it. But this comprehension is only possible at the price of a diminishment of the most transcendent aspects
of Revelation. This is what we will see now.

I. RELIGION MUST BE COMPREHENSIBLE
FOR A COLLECTIVITY

We have said that Revelation requires an animic climate that receives
and realizes It: God speaks, man receives the Word and realizes It
according to what he has understood. Therefore it is the mode of
comprehension that determines the mode of realization. Let us focus
our attention on this comprehension.

What is the comprehension in question? And, first, what must be
comprehended? Not a Word of knowledge but a commandment, or
rather — for Christ, the Word of God, is Way and Truth — a Word
that is at once knowledge and action indissolubly. Now supposing
that the doctrinal aspect of this Word can be understood without
any error of interpretation,[1] it would not be the same for Its aspect
of realization, for no 'user instructions' can indicate how and in
what spirit a commandment should be applied. And this is related
to the intellect/will duality: intellect without will is impotent and

---

1 But not in full, for it is infinite.

will without intellect is blind. Whatever may be the degree of their union, for non-deified man there is always (apart from the grace which comes specifically to supernaturally harmonize the will and intellect) something unintelligible in his will and some radical impotence in his intellect. But religion is not only the business of exegetes, theologians and specialists in parensis.[2] It governs the life of a whole humanity. Consequently, it cannot only be the object of a theological reflection that strives to acquire the purest comprehension of it. In some way it must be directly, spontaneously, and immediately comprehended by the humanity receiving it. It is this collective comprehension that is involved here. It does not exclude theological and spiritual research for some individuals, yet for itself it ignores it. This collective comprehension of religion may open onto what is today, in actual fact perhaps, called 'sociological Christianity'. But without sociological Christianity there is no longer any religion.

How is this collective comprehension that makes religion 'possible' manifested? We answer that it is manifested under the form of what we have called natural facts and virtues, the facts thus corresponding to the reception of the Word, to its understanding, the virtues corresponding to its realization or application. By natural facts we understand first of all what is naturally obvious. Soon we have to go further and see that a natural fact [évidence] is also a proof [évidence] from nature. For the moment let us stay with the first sense. Christ's message must at least include, for the Christian soul, a significance which appears as naturally evident; otherwise religion is no longer possible. If someone who is neither a theologian nor a saint, that is to say the vast majority of people, has to perpetually question what he understands of the Christian Truth, this will certainly lead, not only to doubt, but even to weariness and indifference. This majority willingly acknowledges that there are dimensions of Revelation that elude it. However, when they think 'Christian religion', 'Gospel', they think of something specific even though unformulated. And it is vitally necessary for them to think of something spontaneously, to have a certain 'idea' of Christianity directly translated into apparently automatic behavior, into a veritable instinct for religious conduct. Lacking this instinct the faithful are like a flock without a shepherd.

2 Parensis designates everything involved with the moral life.

2. MY KINGDOM IS NOT OF THIS WORLD[3]

The Revealed Word, we have said, is made to be understood and realized. It is hearing and actualization, and so addresses intellect and will at the same time. Revelation, at the same time that it comes to restore man, requires the agreement of these two principal powers set at variance by original sin: *"Estote factores Verbi sed non auditores tantum,"* says St. James. "Be doers of the Word, and not hearers only." Virtue is in a certain manner the power for this agreement, and is, in its highest expression, identified with it. It always consists, in fact, in the capacity to subject the will to the intellect, to want what the intellect has understood.

When the intellect is perfectly submissive to the word of Truth, and when the will is so generous and so *good* that it never refuses to give itself freely to the Truth which the intellect shows it — such is prototypically the case for the Virgin Mary — then the determinations of human nature are as if erased, absorbed, and annihilated. Such a human substance is truly *ever virgin.* And the saints are called upon to participate in this privilege, which Mary possessed *a priori* and by essence, through the grace and merits of Jesus Christ.

But the response of a collectivity could not be the same as that of a single man. There cannot be an erasing of its natural determinations to the degree encountered in Marian virginity; otherwise the collectivity would no longer exist as such. And yet it is indeed necessary, in spite of everything, that the agreement of will and intellect be assured at this level. Such is, one could say, the problem posed to the Christian soul more than to any other religious collectivity, for Christ's Revelation is not founded upon a social order; the Kingdom is not of this world.

Mosaic law established a holy people and organized the earthly city according to the express will of God, teaching in this way what human nature should be. But the Word of Christ often seems to negate or destroy every human society. "Hate father and mother," "give all your goods to the poor," "tear out an eye guilty of impurity" — these precepts cannot receive a meaning for a merely human and natural

---

3 John 18:36.

order. We understand clearly that Christ has not come to abolish the Law but to fulfill it. Nevertheless theology has come to see in these requirements counsels for perfection that are not imposed equally on all, and although in fact nature may be spiritually integrated and not abolished, this does not mean that (before its assumption) it does not enter into conflict with the Word of the Absolute, revealing by this its very imperfection.

With this remark we already touch upon the heart of the problem of present-day Christianity. The whole modernist crisis could be reduced to this pattern: the wish to realize here below the Kingdom which is not of this world because they actually no longer believe in the hereafter. This desire can only lead to the destruction of the world and religion. This is what we are witnessing. The destiny of our religion is enclosed in this word: "many are called, but few are chosen." The first part of this sentence establishes Christianity as a religion, the second part establishes it as a spiritual way of perfection. The fundamental and deadly contradiction of Modernism is to confuse these two orders and then to ignore them. It claims to confer an exclusively social and collective bearing on precepts having an essentially spiritual and, strictly speaking, 'esoteric' — that is to say interior — bearing. This is why modernists are opposed to a social-reality 'religion'. By this opposition they crush the human relative under the weight of the Divine Absolute and destroy the natural order.

3. THE NATURAL VIRTUES PROTECT US FROM THE WORLD

Our entire analysis tends to show that religion is 'possible' only if it finds an echo in human nature such as it is. This is the minimal indispensable condition. It is indeed necessary that the virtues of human nature, in their spontaneous and almost instinctive functioning, feel themselves in harmony with the requirements of religion, at least relatively, even if nature in its ultimate finality, in order to fulfill itself in perfection, must accept self-renunciation. But such a renunciation should not be required of an entire collectivity.

Thus a mother who teaches the Catholic religion to her child begins by making an appeal to his natural virtues, to his natural taste for the beautiful, the strong, the good, and life itself, in order to define the fundamental axes of his religious 'understanding', an understanding lived and not thought, and upon which abstractions and necessary corrections could be built later. But religion must first "say" something if it is to have an obvious sense, if it is to correspond to known and familiar experiences.

However, in order to rely on the virtues (which is to say the strengths or capacities) of human nature, one has to admit that such a nature exists. This is precisely what modern philosophy claims to deny, either in the name of freedom (Sartre), under the pretext that the idea of such a nature would be contrary to this freedom, or else in the name of the human sciences (Structuralism, Foucault) which would show man as fabricated by society and culture, and changing with them in such a manner that there is no permanence of a supposed nature.

We shall not discuss such theses at present. And besides, how do you refute the imaginary? We will only say this: to speak of a nature is to posit a defined and limited order on the one hand, and, on the other, to bestow necessity and obviousness upon this order.

For want of such a limitation, man is directly confronted with the indefiniteness of the world's possibilities. Being able to be anything, he is no longer anything. And in the same way, for want of such a necessity and obviousness, man is subjected to pure contingency and permanent variability. It would then be for him as it would for any living organism destitute of functional laws, which must at each instant invent new ways of digesting, breathing, reproducing — such an organism would die instantly. So for the human soul, whose natural milieu is precisely culture.

Man must be provided, therefore, with natural facts: all of those ideas formed about himself, about his limits, about life, death, and love, trace an enclosure, a veritable earthly paradise of the human soul, where the soul is isolated from the cosmic indefiniteness and uncertainty that Christ has called the outer darkness, and where the soul receives the right to be itself. This knowledge of human nature, a lived and concrete knowledge, elevates these facts into nearly absolute norms, at the same time that it effects an initial 'election' among the multitude of earthly possibilities, which eventually prepares the human being for his unitive election in glory.

43

4. THE NATURAL VIRTUES 'PROTECT'
THE HUMAN FROM THE DIVINE ABSOLUTE

Condemnable in its literal sense, this surprising statement of our heading draws attention, however, to that error, typically modernist and Lutheran in its root, that consists in denying the order of nature in the name of the Absolute, and finally in destroying (pagan) religion in the name of pure faith. In effect, just as the modernists want to open the Christian soul to the totality of worldly multiplicity, in defiance of human nature, so in their pride they want to crush this soul beneath the weight of divine transcendence; they take, they say, the Gospel literally — as a matter of fact they take literally what appears to agree with their ideological sensibility, which essentially consists in giving themselves a good conscience by condemning the 'rich' or the 'bourgeois'. Thus no one has ever yet seen a progressive tear out an eye because his sight was impure, or else preach the Gospel to trees and cats, even though these are creatures and we should preach the Gospel to every creature. There is in this attitude, we think, a consequence as it were of the Kantian moral view that claims to directly confront human action with the Absolute, and rejects as impure all natural motivations. Clearly, in gauging our actions by the standard of the Universal, we risk not finding a single good one, and Christ Himself has said: "Why do you call me good? God alone is good." "*Nemo bonus nisi unus Deus*" (Mark 10:18). Doing this one is then assured of not being deceived. But what is true in the perspective of a *via negationis*, of an apophatic theology and spirituality, is *a deadly lie at the level of the common way* because it pretends to something to which it truly has no right. Beneath the rule of Marian virtue it is right that the human soul be directly submissive to the determination of the Absolute, and that this situation alone is in conformity with the letter of the Gospel. But to take the Gospel literally, should it only be from the point of view of theoretical understanding, supposes an exceptional spiritual intelligence and an extremely rare purity of heart.

Thus the natural virtues apparently have for a function to assure the equilibrium of the human substance between the pressure of the world and that of the Absolute. Religion addressing itself *a priori* to a human collectivity, it is also necessary that this collectivity be able to exist and that, in a certain manner, it ignore the radical character of divine injunctions. "My kingdom is not of this world." This does not just mean that it will be realized in the New Heavens and the New Earth; this also means that it cannot be realized here below. The order of the human world, such as it is, could not contain the Kingdom of Christ without perishing instantaneously. This is why, if in its manifestation the Absolute mercifully veils its insupportable splendor — Moses can approach the Burning Bush, Christ is transfigured for only an instant — the relative must be no less mercifully blinded by the natural effect of its own opaqueness, which is specifically tied to its relativity. To believe that nature as such can realize the perfection of supernature as such is to destroy both nature and supernature. The commandment to love, in its absoluteness, seems to ignore all relativity. Divine logic is in some way a logic of all or nothing. But neither does God wish the death of a sinner, and between God and man there is a 'game' whose transcendent subtlety defies all analysis, a game which is that of mercy itself.

The key to this mystery resides in fact in the very nature of the created. For, as good as creation may be, according to the text of Genesis, it nevertheless remains imperfect with respect to God's supreme Goodness — besides, the work of the second day is not declared good... It is then incapable, as such, of realizing absolute Goodness. The earthly Paradise is not the heavenly Paradise. But, on the other hand, as much as creation may be wounded by sin, its natural goodness is not however entirely destroyed. It is this residue of natural goodness which constitutes the 'good earth' within which the Word of Christ will take root and bear fruit, and which will thus be, little by little, supernaturalized. It is also this which, from the Garden of Eden down to ourselves, constitutes the healthy and generous soil of paganism, and which expresses itself through the customs, legends, folklore, and mythology of the forests and mountains, that knowledge of beings and things which Father Bonnet once called the third Testament. We are born pagans, Tertullian said; we become Christians. What is true for each particular being is also true for the soul of the entire Christian community; its native essence is this pagan soil, permanent and necessary, the authentic vestige of paradisal Nature, apt for serving as a humble and vigorous 'material' for the Divine

Gardener. But if sexuality, the joy of the body, family life, the taste for effort and work, the bitterness of suffering, the power of death, if all of the natural dimensions of human existence are destroyed in their secular and spontaneous movement and rendered problematical, then this earth is withdrawn from the Word of God, the earth in which it could germinate, and is replaced with the abstractions of psychoanalysis or sociology. And lacking a nature to transmute, supernatural grace can no longer act. It is true that these virtues of nature, being pre-Christian, do not know, in their most living and most intimate strength, the death-dealing transcendence of Christ's Way. But man needs must be allowed to grow in stature and courage. Human childhood, though, should not be crucified.

5. TWO EXAMPLES OF THE NATURAL VIRTUES: MEDIEVAL ART AND THE AGONY OF CHRIST

Progressively we have been led to pass from the function of natural virtue to its nature. And, as announced above, natural virtue corresponds not only to what is naturally obvious, but, more profoundly, to the evidence of nature itself and consequently to its strength (the Latin *virtus*). Surely the existence of natural virtues does not go without a certain overestimation of the created. However, by this these virtues manifest an aspect of the innocence of creation, which makes it apt for expressing spiritual realities directly. Out of this comes that sentiment of inimitable familiarity with the divine which medieval sculpture and painting elicit: God is so close to man that the sacred artist can represent Him under the most natural human attitudes. And these human attitudes and gestures, a carpenter planing a board, a peasant woman spinning her distaff, are so beautiful and so good, so true, that they have no need of any 'distancing' in order to be sacred. They are so in themselves, in their immemorial truth: immemorial because conforming to the nature of things and man, and therefore to the Divine Will which has willed this nature. Here there is no worldly frivolity, nor dramatic tension, nor aggressive simplicity, nor pridefully expressive complication, but a sweet gravity, a meditative and fresh interiority, man such as he is, neither more nor less, working exactly as he ought, yet his attentive heart inhabited by a mysterious infinity.

Finally, we think we find the scriptural foundation of the natural virtues and the whole strength of human nature in Christ Jesus suffering His agony in the Garden of Olives and praying that this chalice be taken away from Him. How can we see, in this first sorrowful mystery which the Rosary offers for meditation, an episode of human weakness? There can be no weakness in the Word Incarnate. This mystery is that of a combat between the strength of human nature which experiences its goodness and beauty and Divine Power which requires their sacrifice. In Christ Jesus it is the whole of human nature that suffers from having to be annihilated. And how should it not suffer, why would it not be sad unto death? Was there ever, since the creation of the world, a man comparable to Jesus? Was there ever a body of more noble stature, richer blood, a strength more royal and tranquil? This man has existed. Among the myriads and myriads of beings which God has cast into existence, no masterpiece has surpassed this one. And His human soul — no other is comparable to it for fullness and acuity of intellect, for courage and purity, for nobility and generosity. It is the soul of a king's son, last scion of David's lineage, in whom is summed up the flower of all human greatness, one of the most noble races of the world. Yes, He has existed. Two thousand years ago we would have been able to meet this prince in Palestine, walking the burning roads with his grand sovereign step, and the entire earth would have been justified in our eyes because this man existed. Let us understand that human substance is capable of this beauty, and that yet it was necessary for it to perish. In this case it suffers before its destruction, as Jesus had wept before Jerusalem because He loved His religion as much as His own soul. This is neither a revolt or a denial, it is the utterance of Adamic nature, it is living splendor sorrowful at entering into the darkness of death, the cry wrung from being as it is torn asunder in the night beneath the silent olive trees.

5

Man and Civilization

FOR THERE TO BE EVIDENCE OF NATURAL VIR-
tues there must be a nature. This nature is that of man himself, but
for him it exists only in a virtual state. It demands to be actualized,
but first revealed. This revelation and actualization are in principle
the work of civilization, particularly under its cultural aspect. The
essential function of a culture is to give form to the human soul in
conformity with its natural virtualities. Therefore several questions
have to be answered: What are human nature and its virtualities? How
might these virtualities be actualized by our surroundings? On the
other hand, how can the cultural milieu actualize these virtualities; or,
more specifically, what kind of culture is required to actualize human
nature's virtualities? In summary: What is human nature? What is its
actualization? What actualizes it? We will try to answer these three
questions briefly.

I. QUALITATIVE ANTHROPOLOGY

Beginning with the Aristotelian definition, we will first say that man
is a rational animal. Mankind, among all other living beings, is characterized by the presence of mental activity which thus defines its *generic
essence*. This generic essence is not to be confused with the intellect, for
there is an animal, a vegetable, and even a mineral intelligence. But only
man 'thinks' or abstracts, which is to say that his intellectual activity
ordinarily works upon objective reality by means of concepts, and not
directly upon objects themselves. However, man is also masculine or
feminine, and this designates his *sexual essence*, which must never be
reduced to a simple anatomo-physiological disposition, but characterizes a whole behavior. Lastly, man is a particular individual, has a
particular character, a particular temperament; and this defines what
we shall call his *singular essence*. These three essences should be neither
juxtaposed nor superimposed: each constitutes particular determinations of the individual essence, or even virtualities. A trans-individual

49

or trans-personal essence can be envisaged then in relation to this individual essence characterizing our natural being, the individual essence
being only the projection of what characterizes our supernatural being,
that is to say our *in divinis* reality, upon the 'earthly' plane.

We have spoken of the virtualities of the individual essence which
are the generic, the sexual, and the singular essences. Let us consider
the first two. Obviously, it must be observed, they do not exhaust
human nature. Man is not only *homo rationalis* and *homo sexualis*,
he is also *homo politicus* and *homo religiosus*, in the sense that society
and religion form part of human nature. But, not seeking to establish an exhaustive classification, we will leave aside the question of a
general and systematic theory of qualitative anthropology. After all,
both the generic and the sexual essence imply *homo politicus* and *homo
religiosus*, as the course of our analysis will show.

Virtualities are not indeterminate possibilities. The rational and
sexual essences are not just anything whatsoever, and this is why we
have called them essences. They must be considered as virtualities of
determination, or virtual determinations. On the other hand — and
this is important — although belonging to the individual domain
these determinations are not for all that subjective, which is to say
characteristics of the subject as such. To the contrary, they constitute objective dimensions of the subject's *interior*. My reason and my
sexuality are (respectively) first reason *itself* and sexuality *itself*, and
this is indeed how they are experienced by the subject: reason is a
constant effort in the order of knowledge to obey the principles which
the subject experiences within himself as constraints, just as sexuality
arises in the subject as a stranger who relates to him as a body-object
within the body-subject, and which desires recognition by others as
object. Through sexuality the body seems to acquire an autonomous
reality, from whence it comes about that all sexuality is troubling.

2. CULTURE ACTUALIZES HUMAN NATURE

Why do these determinations exist in the state of virtualities? Or why
do they manifest themselves as internal constraining demands that
call for a form-giving actualization capable of defining their contents?
Basically the question amounts to this: why does man not have any

instincts, that is, have at his disposal any innate 'know-how', like other animals? The answer lies in the human being's mental nature. Animal instinct *is* in some way equally virtual, has to be actualized under the action of the psycho-biological environment, and in this respect there is no difference between man and animal. But man's natural environment is not of the biological but of the cultural order, which implies that culture has to be present as a nature and not as an artificial construction. Man is immersed in culture like a fish in water. This does not mean that culture is a universe within the universe; it means that, for man, the psycho-physical universe is wholly cultural, or that man apprehends it through a cultural modality, that is to say as a world of representations, meanings, values, and symbols. Man knows only what he has learned, even if he only learns what he already knows, while the animal does not learn how to make a nest or migrate. Therefore instinct is not virtual in the manner of internal determinations of human nature.

To say that the determinations of human nature are virtual is therefore to say that they should be given (determined) form, and this necessity, as we have said, stems from the mental nature of the human being, for otherwise this mental nature would have no *raison-d'être*. Only that which enters into man by means of the generic form of humanity, the mental, can take form in him. Now, as previously defined, mental activity consists in conceiving or abstracting, working with symbolic thinking about things and not directly with things themselves, or rather working with things themselves by means of their concepts. Mental activity is characterized then by a distance with respect to things (this is true for exterior things as much as for interior 'things'), and it is in this distancing that man's freedom is manifested. Apprehending his own determinations thanks to his mentality, the human being is only able to achieve them if he is in possession of mental forms capable of actualizing these determinations. Or, since man only works with things with the help of concepts, concepts about himself are necessary for him to work upon himself. If man is never taught what he is, he will never be and never become it.[1] This is why

---

1 Three-quarters of present-day philosophical and socio-psychological output revolves around the question: nature-culture-man. Thousands of works are dedicated to it. We think, however, that the thesis profiled here provides an adequate solution to the question.

no one is without culture. Culture, the sum total of intellectual representations, is truly a mental objectivity; one could say that intellect is an objective act of a civilization in which human mentality draws upon intelligible forms, and thanks to which the virtual determinations of its nature are given form.

What remains to be considered is how the singular essence is actualized. In itself the singular essence seems imperceptible. Actually, as soon as one tries to analyze it, to define what makes up the proper nature of an individual in his singularity, one discovers non-singular elements that refer back to the bio-cultural milieu that has informed them. It is here that sociologists of every persuasion, cultural anthropologists, biologists, and physicists, who reconstruct the individual out of the prejudices of their perspective, triumph. And in doing this they belie common experience, for each of us, although unable to define his own nature with precision, nevertheless experiences its existence in a very real and altogether indubitable manner, such as in expressing one's subjectivity. Thus, the philosophy-fiction of Sartrism can indeed affirm that man chooses himself, but builds out of this a series of rigorous yet perfectly delirious syllogisms. Nonetheless what remains is that, according to Paul Ricoeur's expression, "we have a way of choosing not to choose." And we add that we have a way of acting and reacting by which we are not acting.

Both Sartre and Ricoeur deceive themselves, the former by only considering the contents of the singular essence, the latter by only envisaging the pure subject, which is imperceptible upon the plane where he (like Sartre) has placed it. What must be said is that the individual essence, although inaccessible in a direct way, is indirectly manifested by the unique way in which it lives its own determinations and, consequently, by the way in which it adapts itself to external determinations of its life-setting, or by the way in which it reacts to this. In itself the individual essence should be considered as the outcome of an encounter between the archetypal or personal essence (our nature *in divinis,* such as it exists within the eternal Word) and the environment within which this supra-individual essence is manifested. Within itself the archetype, the internal principle of being, our divine name, is not subject to those just-mentioned objective determinations, to sexual determination for example; for, as St. Paul says, "in

Christ there is neither male nor female." But these determinations are included in our nature by virtue of possibilities related to its creative development. Now the personal essence cannot be manifested as such upon the created plane.[2] On the other hand, by virtue of the principle of inverse analogy governing the relationships between heaven and earth, what was a center and pure interiority above is revealed below, in an external and somewhat peripheral manner, through the contours and profiles which it impresses upon external determinations in adapting to them, determinations under whose action its own virtualities are crystallized according to an original mode manifesting this personal essence in individual mode. If the existential projection is represented by a vertical line and the environment by a horizontal one, their meeting-place will be the individual essence. In this way one has traced the symbol of the Cross, and it is to be understood that the realization of an individual's archetype can only be effected by ascending along the vertical through a crucifixion of the individual essence. "If the grain of wheat does not die, it will bear no fruit." Its fruit is also its causal root, namely its archetypal reality. This is why Christ also said: "The one who wishes to become my disciple [that is: the one who wishes to become what he is in Me] let him take up his cross." He does not say *the* Cross but *his* cross, the cross specific to each one of us, which traces our individual essence when it is defined as the meeting of the internal principle and the environment. To take up one's cross is to realize this crucifixion of the personal archetype dynamically, the personal archetype that is the individual essence statically, by crucifying it, to lead what was dispersed in the horizontal periphery back toward the crucial point.

Clearly the potential nature of the singular essence, actualized by adapting itself to the regulative data of the existing environment, effects a kind of selection out of this data and can only adapt to what is in accord with its internal determinations. It is the same for the sexual, religious, and political essences in such a way that, from all points of view, human nature is only able to be actualized, or man is only possible, if the bio-cultural environment is capable of actualizing it, which is to say that it provides this nature with easily

2 This also means that only in God are we able to become ourselves.

assimilated themes. In other words, man is only possible if external determinations of the environment are in agreement with the internal determinations of our soul. Water is the natural environment of fish, but there are toxic waters.

3. ONLY TRADITIONAL AND SYMBOLIC CULTURE CAN ACTUALIZE HUMAN NATURE

This remark brings us back to the third question formulated at the beginning: what type of culture is required for such an actualization? It is the sought-for end which must provide the answer. Natural virtues need to be formed in man, he needs to be given instincts. Only a culture of the essentialist, traditional, and mythological type is apt for doing this.

However, a first objection should be raised: how can instincts be learned? Does not every apprenticeship pass through a mental — that is to say discursive and deliberative — knowledge, whereas an instinct is direct and unconscious? On the other hand, are not the representational elements of culture that are charged with guaranteeing this apprenticeship, as such, opposed to the blind character of instinct?

Our reply to the first of these questions will be brief. The expression 'mental knowledge' must not lead us astray. In reality it is the intellect that knows, mentality being only the refracting medium through which cognitive activity is effected. Mentality is a mirror, but it is the intellect that sees. Now, by definition, the intellect is direct and intuitive in its own essence. And this is true for all information received through the medium of the mentality, whether it be a sensation, a concept, or a cultural symbol. Each time it is the intellect that is awakened, and what it grasps, at least in principle, is not an abstraction but the thing itself, or the concept or the symbol in its essence. No one can see a rose without becoming conscious, in a certain manner, of being before the rose in itself, of being in the presence of the rose's essence.

Now what about cultural representations? Our reply here will be of somewhat greater length.

Certainly, if these cultural representations are themselves the product of ideological, individual, or social constructions, they can yield no natural evidence in such a case. They speak of nothing but human restlessness. This is the situation of what is falsely called 'modern culture', a chaotic mixture of aesthetic flights of fancy and psycho-sociology. But it happens otherwise in traditional and symbolic cultures, the representations of which appear as well-nigh sensible objects, as age-old and natural data. These cultural essences are indeed learned and clothed with a mental form. But they do not for all that become abstractions. They impose themselves almost instinctively upon the individual and transform themselves into veritable interior norms. This is why we must more precisely define now the nature of these cultural representations, but first define what should be understood by the expression 'traditional civilization'.

A traditional civilization must be essentially understood as one based on Tradition, that is to say on the transmission of elements of divine origin. What has a beginning in time is in fact necessarily new with respect to the preceding time and therefore, far from qualifying as traditional, should be regarded on the contrary as revolutionary. And even if this element determines an entire temporal sequence, in such a way that the title of tradition will be falsely applied to it (as when one speaks of a Republican tradition), in the very measure that it is taken for a model it can only engender other revolutions, since it teaches first of all the negation of the past. It is clear then that a true tradition can be only of non-temporal origin. Such is the nature of traditional civilization, normal civilization. Cultural forms appear there as natural revelations issuing from the depths of the ages. They convey a permanent and non-temporal teaching. This was the case with medieval civilization. We could say that in such a civilization culture constitutes a veritable *cosmos noetos*, an intelligible world whose cultural forms are essences or Platonic 'ideas'. These cultural essences illuminate the human environment, instructing each one according to what he is capable of understanding, offering to the human mentality natural self-evident facts that actualize the virtues of its nature.

This evidence provided by traditional civilization is natural to an eminent degree. For these cultural essences, although born of the civilization, are not fabricated by it. They are the product of no geographical, historical, economic, or socio-psychological determinism, although the soil, the race, the technology and lifestyles impress upon them the style proper to such a civilization. In reality these cultural essences must be considered as reflecting, upon the plane of a determinate human grouping, eternal archetypes, and this is what their divine origin means. They are permanent possibilities, principial determinations of primordial Nature. They 'express', they 'speak to' the nature of things and hence of the Divine Will which has willed this nature. A close parallelism is to be seen here between the soul of a man and the soul of a civilization. Just as the individual essence is actualized through the personal archetype meeting the environment, so cultural essences are produced through the celestial archetypes meeting a particular human world. Thus there are, for example, the archetypes of man and woman which are reflected in the culture and in the individual essence at the same time. However, while they are only revealed in culture and presented according to their symbolic prototype, they are realized in the individual essence. And this is, we think, what Goethe had in mind when he said that a man in the presence of a woman is the eternal masculine in the presence of the eternal feminine.

In a practical way, then, the cultural environment gives its instruction under multiple forms whose inventory would be impossible to take. Everything in a traditional civilization being symbolic, everything communicates the vision of essences; everything teaches man what he is and what he ought to be; everything furnishes him with an eternal theme by which he can give form to his life, which he assimilates and adapts according to the style proper to his singular essence. The architecture and sculpture of the cathedrals; the legends and customs expressing such or such an aspect of man or of his activity; the craft cultures with their symbolism, still alive today in the Compagnonnage, and where the cosmos as a whole is related to the craft's basic components, the so-called 'folklore' traditions with their songs and popular customs which play, in an almost ritualistic manner, the game of a man and a woman in love, of marriage, birth, death and work, which, in the order of their temporal succession, connect mankind to the great cosmic rhythms while integrating his most intimate life with the life of the collectivity. All of this communicates a wisdom coming from the depths of the ages, venerable and majestic, and yet miraculously fresh, inexhaustibly young, brimming over with the great smile of creation. Thus the Middle Ages was the only era of Western history in which a true popular culture existed.[3]

The cultural models furnished to man by civilization give him the means to live. "Ah! rites. Give us rites!" said Rilke.[4] To live is to choose, for such is fallen man that there is always a distance between what he should do and what he can do. To choose is to refer oneself to or to act according to a model. This is why man cannot live without essences. All of the reproaches made against the global Platonism of past ages come from an abstract conception of essences, and from a deadly ignorance of the conditions of our life. If man has no idea about what his sexual being means, he can no longer live this sexuality but only submit to it like an animal. And who will give him this idea? He himself is quite incapable of producing it. A superhuman genius would be needed, the very genius of the species. The social sciences? But far from teaching us how to live, they themselves would have, if they were capable of it, everything to learn from life. It can only be then an objective essence, an archetypal nature provided by civilization, an essence from which man draws infallible determinations for his behavior. This essence that participates in the nature of things can be represented and presented only within a myth or a symbol. To live one's sexuality is to live a myth, is to let the genius of the species speak in oneself. It is not "I and thou," but through "I and thou" it is the realization of a nature which surpasses us and to which we are *responsible* as to a higher function, that is to say whose nobility obliges us. In such an instance, the essence is lived as that

3   Historians as little traditional as Jacques Le Goff—and not displeasing to our modernist and ignorant clergy—readily agree with this. To such clergy, enemies of the Middle Ages and the Counter-Reformation, we dedicate this excerpt from Le Goff: "The humanists abandoned one of the primary tasks of the intellectual, which was to have contact with the masses, to connect their knowledge with teaching.... [The Renaissance] was first of all a recoiling.... Those who knew how to read were a small favored elite, and were happy that way. Others were no longer fed on crumbs from the scholasticism which had been provided them by the preachers and 'artists' of the Middle Ages, all of whom were trained by the universities. It was perhaps necessary to await the Counter-Reformation for an art to appear which—in a perhaps questionable form, but one full of didactic intentions and an enthusiasm for propagating new ideas—would seek to have the people participate in cultural affairs" (*Intellectuals in the Middle Ages*, trans. T. Lavend [Oxford, UK, and Cambridge, MA: Blackwell, 1993], 165–66).

4   "Ah! rites. Give us rites! Everything happens and loses itself in discourse." R. M. Rilke, *Requiem 1* (1900).

cosmic function with which man is clothed and which he ought to assume. How do we love, say that we love? How do we hate, suffer, and rejoice, be a man or woman, a carpenter or school teacher? What should man do with the share of human nature he has received? The only possible answer to such a question is traditional civilization, integrating human nature into cosmic nature by means of the symbol. In this way it presented a man truly formed, it provided a true human substance, in all its strength and virtue, to which were applied the determinations of the Absolute.

6

Counter-civilization and Evil

I. CONSTRUCTIVIST DESTRUCTION

To ask what natural proofs inspire charity today is to pose an unanswerable question, for there are no longer any natural proofs, only constructed ones. By definition, only what offers itself as a proof of the nature of things is naturally obvious. The existence of natural proofs implies then a cultural field of the essentialist type, requiring belief in the reality of an archetypal world. But the whole movement of modern civilization in all domains since the seventeenth century consists of an immense and permanent denaturing or de-essentialization. This movement — rationalism — is carried out through the reduction of all understanding to reason. Now, for reason, to understand is to build out of the data within its grasp, which implies in the first place that it deny the data's very quality as a given. What is incomprehensible to reason is that there may be an objective datum. Cartesianism, to the extent that it is presented as a rational construct of the world, and Kantism, which deems pure data to be completely unknowable, and which substitutes for the "objectivity" of the *a priori* structures of human knowledge, a mathematical axiomatism that rejects primary, self-evident mathematical findings — principles — , replacing them with decidedly manufactured conventions, leave no doubt in this respect.

But, inevitably, the same situation also occurs in the so-called social sciences, the results of which can never be anything but a destructive construction[1] of all human data and, at the extreme, of man himself, as is apparent in the conclusions of the philosopher Michel Foucault. In such a case the idea of man, the notion of human nature, is conceived

---

1 Freudian psychoanalysis is likewise rationalist. Freud has always rightly affirmed this. He constructs the hypothesis of an unconscious, inaccessible as such but inferred from its effects. Certain philosophers have not failed to relate this Freudian unconscious to Kant's regulative idea. In our own time Lacan wanted to show that the unconscious is structured like a language. He was thus able to 'purify' the Freudian Id of what still remained of the all too natural.

to be the product of a certain era, corresponding to a certain state, a certain structure of culture. It is thought that things should be seen in this way, and in so doing Foucault esteems himself to be in agreement with the most certain requirements of modern epistemology. Structuralism, he asserts, is only the present-day scientific process applied to consciousness, which seems directly opposed to the point of view we have developed.[2] But in reality Structuralism, the negator and destroyer of every nature, purely and simply ignores this point of view. It has never been conscious of it and has never understood it. Its ignorance is not therefore deliberate, not the result of a careful and concerted reflection; it only testifies to a narrowness of ideas and, in truth, to a kind of congenital lack of understanding. Nature, such as Foucault conceives it and such as he denies it—nature which, according to him, should play the role of an explanatory *deus ex machina*—is itself a creation of Structuralism. It is denied inasmuch as it would be an absolute principle, but this principle is only conceived of in a 'philosophical' style, in the manner of the abstract entities of the metaphysical age in Comte's theory. Clearly, this conception is due to a decadent philosophism where concepts are only the cadavers of essence, but it in no way corresponds to that lived Platonism which constitutes the doctrine of all the Earth's civilizations. The experience of life is spontaneously Platonic, and also necessarily so. Man can only live his sexuality under the mode of an essence; otherwise it becomes a problem.

This movement of denaturation, which has been going on for centuries—how could we hope that it has not radically changed our cultural atmosphere? Nature has been chased from every refuge which could have stabilized human behavior. The corporeal itself, where it seems today that only instinct should act, has been subjected to the same treatment. Modern man is content to live this corporeal data as a construct, thanks to a 'responsible and adult sexuality' in particular and other such stupidities of the same ilk.

This movement is not however purely speculative. One could even say that, if it were only a question of philosophy, it would not have played such a decisive role. In fact it has been taken over by

---

2 Cf. Jean Borella, *The Crisis of Religious Symbolism* (Kettering, OH: Angelico Press, 2016), 251–93.

the industrial counter-civilization, the unique theme of which resides in the substitution of a technical process for a natural one, through which man has the illusion of rendering himself 'master and possessor of all things'. Thus the 'real' universe, within which man lives, is an entirely constructed or fabricated one.[3] Everything speaks to him of his power, everything is an objectification of this power. Not only have the cities and houses, the food and clothing, the games and knowledge been industrialized, but also human instincts, over which technology claims to give mastery, or rather which it enables to be used in an industrial manner. Here again sexuality is a particularly convincing example, and we have surely not seen everything yet.

The natural virtues no longer figure in the exercise of human nature, the mode of employment supplied by science does; in this world of concrete and pills, it is the industrial product that does. In all things man discovers material attestations of his pure power. Certainly not of his domination over the universe, for no part of the universe is brought into subjection as such, but, rather, of a universe of domination. In a modern city nothing speaks to the soul in its native tongue, but everything proclaims a technical power which has never had any other goal but itself. Nevertheless a tree remains a tree, a mountain a mountain, and man, whatever may be said and whatever the appearances, has not fundamentally had a change of nature; but today everything aspires to persuade us of the opposite.

2. THE NATURAL VIRTUES RELATIVIZE EVIL

When a civilization makes impossible the perception of natural facts, and hence the natural virtues flowing from them, the individual is yielded up to the indeterminacy of his own will. In other words, without essential determination there is no longer any practical

---

3 Traditional civilizations likewise allow for technology, but not as a substitute for nature. The difference between a tool and a machine is that man is the mover or regulator of the tool, while, by definition, the machine possesses its own movement, or else there is no machine. The primary character of mechanization is its 'a-humanness'. This is why there can be no solution to the human (and social) problems posed by mechanization. Industrial technology may appear, to modern sensibility, much less inhuman than traditional technology as such. But we have in mind here no moral evaluation. We are dealing with a perfectly objective criterion.

determination. As Existentialism has seen so clearly, the intervention of a theoretically pure will strikes all acts produced by it with radical contingency. They could always be different from what they are. Now the substitution of a construct for data implies the intervention of the will, even where qualitative determinations have their field of activity, so that all of the social sciences find themselves likewise subjected to the same *contingency principle*, if we might venture such an expression. A new original sin is accomplished, itself only a remote consequence of the Adamic fall.

Although these claim to be irreconcilable adversaries, we can now understand how Existentialism and Structuralism converge. Existentialism presents itself in fact as a voluntaristic subjectivism, whereas Structuralism poses as a rationalistic objectivism. But both join together in their denial of nature. The human essence is no less constructed for Sartre than for Foucault. And above all, as an unnoticed and never-denounced outcome, a Promethean voluntarism is no less present — a subjacent presence — in Structuralism than in Existentialism. This will is the will to possess. And this is why it is also an indefinitely repeated renewal of the original fall, which is essentially a fall from being into having: "They wanted to possess what they were," one old master has said. Modern philosophy wanted to possess what man's nature was, and what better proof of possession than to offer the possibility of constructing our very being? But only what is artificial, and hence what illusorily poses as a nature, can be constructed. Every construction is first a destruction, that is to say a denaturing.

This idea is likewise found again in the Marxist notion of work as the construction of man (man building himself) through appropriation and transformation of the world. Expressions such as "make history," "take one's destiny in hand," "build the world," etc., share in the same ideology.

In conclusion, to the very extent that natural data is a vestige of the earthly Paradise, modern civilization, by destroying such data outside and inside of man, intends to exhaust the ultimate possibilities of the original fall. Now — and this has been known for a long time — the result of the loss of Paradise is man's confrontation with the totality of the mortal contradictions of the created, which the divine will ceases to mercifully veil. Leaving Paradise, Adam discovers with terror the indefiniteness of Evil before him, as far as the eye can see. And this is precisely what we will now observe with respect to industrial civilization.

As already mentioned, the natural virtues form a protective shielding for that paradise which is the traditional human soul. Being virtues of nature itself and mediating the determinations of the Absolute, they relativize at the same time the relative, letting the relative as such exist within It, in the order of its finitude, in a way that makes it impossible to confuse with the Absolute. They allow the apprehension of Evil within the world as an inevitable dimension of the created cosmos. In such an attitude modern man, inasmuch as it is necessary for him to denigrate the past, sees egoism and fatalism. Yet nothing could be more false. History teaches that few periods have been as fruitful as the Middle Ages in Europe in the realms of urban infrastructure and technology. Wherever the historian turns—the foundation of a city,[4] forest-clearing, road construction, the setting-up of an oil press, landscape arrangement[5]—he encounters the work of the Christian Church.

> Contrary to a still-too-widespread opinion, the ardent faith of the Middle Ages was not, as a corollary, indifferent with respect to practical realities. A Catholicism enamored of *qualitative* perfection is sometimes opposed to a Protestantism more inclined toward productivity and science, both *quantitative*. But this thesis clashes with the capital fact that perhaps the most important technical revolution before that of the steam engine occurred in the Middle Ages precisely at the time of the demographic growth from the tenth to twelfth centuries.[6]

4 Recall that, according to the American sociologist Lewis Mumford (*The City in History* [San Diego: Harcourt, 1961]), the way in which the medieval city is conceived corresponds to a perfection compatible with urban civilization. The tracing of roads, the allocation of dwelling-places, the disposition and form of the ramparts compose an ideal 'living-space' for the happiness of man.

5 Many French landscapes were composed, in fact, by monks in the Middle Ages. Some of our modern landscape architects, moreover, have begun to study these remote ancestors, whom they willingly recognize as their masters.

6 René Taton, *Histoire générale des sciences*, vol. 1, *La science antique et medievale*, 2nd rev. ed. (Paris: P. U. F., 1966), 626. We dedicate this text in particular to Father Schillebeeckx and to all Modernists in general who love to repeat, as an unproven

In reality traditional man's attitude to Evil corresponds to an almost instinctive and spontaneous valuation of the possible and the impossible: suffering and death are, at final count, inescapable and therefore accepted *a priori*. They constitute the limit and horizon of every human activity, the boundaries within which it is enclosed and of which it is always aware. But within this *a priori* and thanks to it, there is a place for a human activity by which man cultivates his garden. Again it is necessary that there be a garden, which is to say an enclosed space, the enclosure of which is that ontological limitation inherent in the created which is called evil. It is not that suffering provokes neither revolt or despair for traditional man. Mothers would not cry less sorrowfully over the death of a child, or a wife over a husband's. But glimpsed through this personal sorrow was the echo of a cosmic sorrow by which, as St. Paul has said, even the stones groan. Each one's sorrow was tied to the sorrow of the Universe bewailing the absence of God, and the terrible reality of the impossible defined the order of our powers and satisfactions.

3. MODERN CONSTRUCTIVISM ABSOLUTIZES EVIL

Seeing that man has lost these natural virtues of valuation, evil becomes total, invading all of the created. And we would volunteer the following: either evil is considered as a necessary dimension of the created, or man believes himself capable of its radical elimination. The first attitude implies a relativizing of evil because, first of all, evil is only a dimension of the created, that of God's absence, thus supposing the other dimension, that of His presence, and next because once evil is recognized "it is still necessary to live," and because the order of life cannot but ignore in a certain manner the order of death. This is only possible inasmuch as this order of death is a reality as sure as the world itself. To the contrary, the second attitude implies

---

truth, that in the Middle Ages the earth had been forgotten to the profit of Heaven (thesis of Feuerbach and Marx). As Father Schillebeeckx is a scholar, so that he could not but have known the facts attested to by this text drawn from a quite official history, it must be concluded that he is lying when he declares: "for centuries the Church was essentially preoccupied with formulating truths while it did little to better the world." *Les Catholiques hollandais* (Paris: Desclée De Brouwer, 1969), 10.

a radicalizing of evil, for its avoidance is a continual temptation, as is a sense of obligation to eliminate it wherever man encounters it. Here then is the crux of the matter. Man, having lost consciousness of the reality of the impossible, is condemned to the impossible, that is to defeat. And its evil is redoubled with his defeat in a deadly and indefinite reciprocity. Also, the disappearance of the natural virtues is just as grave for the will as for the intellect.

On the one hand, the constructivist perspective urges the intellect to ignore the inescapable character of evil, to live in the illusion of an omnipotence for which there are only structural errors; on the other hand the will, placed everywhere in the presence of freedom, finds within itself no essential determination proper for orienting its activity and thus for limiting it. For this perspective everything is always possible. The will of traditional man is predetermined by a whole sum of evidence, which stands out as indisputably as the mountains or the course of a river. It would be inexact to say that this evidence is so obvious that no one has any awareness of it. But an awareness of it is precisely like that of a mountain or the sky: we are aware of it because it is there and it is there because we are aware of it.[7] While so many things are not possible or are truly dreams, some are truly possible and become realities. Earth is not heaven — such is the fundamental axiom of traditional man — and heaven is more important than earth. Consequently, it is not of *absolute* importance if men die of hunger, support injustice and oppression, suffer atrocious sickness — the essential is elsewhere. Today this is a hard saying and should never be a topic for discussion, but, whatever the propriety called for here, it has to be said. For it is necessary to know what is finally the most important, and for this there is no other method than the confronting of values with absolute value. If it is true that man does not live by bread alone, then it is strictly inevitable that there are men who die of bodily hunger for the sake of another nourishment. This should not mean and has never meant that famine, war, plague, and injustice are indifferent things, or that it is not necessary to do everything possible to feed, heal, pacify, and free men, but only that it is not possible to

7 Hegel, traveling in the Alps, contemplated the mountains. His friends asked him, he who was accustomed to speaking at length about everything, what he was thinking about. He replied simply: *"Das ist so,"* "It is so."

do it all, by right as well as in fact; were this not so man would be living by bread alone. This is how the natural virtues, which could, at the extreme, be expressed by a kind of vital egoism, would relativize the human will while predetermining it.

But when the natural virtues have disappeared, nothing is able to relativize the will any longer and it is abandoned to itself, that is to say to the totality of its will which is the will for Everything. A supreme and permanent wisdom would be needed for it to limit its desire. No society is capable of such a wisdom. But furthermore such a will by definition cannot be realized upon the plane of the relative. Those without virtue are condemned to envision only totalist and hence *a priori* unrealizable solutions, because they are immediately confronted with the totality of the relative. One cannot want everything and the opposite of everything, nor should a civilization have the right to pledge man to this contradiction. Traditional man is protected by the natural virtues against the totality of the relative. Theoretically, he knows that evil and suffering are everywhere, but existentially ignores this. He sees evil wherever he lives and, allowance made for that about which nothing can be done, for him there is a possibility for action because his field is limited and because it is natural to help his neighbor. *For modern man the field of activity is, quite the contrary, the entire world, and what must be fought is evil in its totality.* Since such an activity is practically impossible, this can only lead to a theory. The will then cedes to reason the constructing of an economic and social system for the elimination of all structural errors. Every charitable activity henceforth passes through the mediation of an abstract construction where charity is definitively alienated. This alienation stems from the analytical nature of reason, which not only renders us unable to gain any clear idea of the charitable impulse, but may even make it impossible.

An analogy with the famous arguments of Zeno is called for here. The basic aim of these arguments is actually to show that reason is powerless to understand motion, whatever its nature, and not the blunt denial of motion, as is all too frequently stated. Far from being denied, movement is first of all a given here. Next we ask ourselves under what conditions it is possible. And lastly we conclude that the adding-up of these conditions is not equivalent to the given with

66

which we have started. Reason does not join up again with reality. In order to go from A to B, we have to pass through the middle, C, of AB. To go from A to C, we have to pass through the middle, D, of AC. To go from A to D, we have to pass through the middle, E, of AD, etc. Since there is an indefinite number of points between A and B, an indefinite amount of time would be necessary to travel across them and the body in motion would never arrive at B. When Zeno of Elea expresses this reasoning in the famous fable of Achilles and the tortoise, we might think, for example, that Achilles represents reason and the tortoise movement. It is therefore permissible to attribute a symbolic value to these arguments. They describe, at the dawn of Western philosophy, the destiny of human reason when it seeks to get a clear idea of a given through a regressive analysis of these possible conditions. It cannot achieve this unless by admitting, through intuitive knowledge, to the intervention of a vertical and transcendent causality at all points of the horizontal series, a causality of another order than the series of prior conditions.[8]

Zeno's reasoning, which might be called conditional regression, is precisely the one indulged in by modern man with respect to the problem of evil. *Denying the intuition of natural evidence, he is intent on analyzing the conditions under which a complete elimination of evil is possible. From condition to condition, the entire world must be reconstructed in all its facets.* This reconstruction being indefinite, the charitable impulse is definitively alienated. How many times have we heard it said that it was a sin against charity to be content with giving food to a man who was hungry, for, according to good Marxist analysis, this would only reinforce the system of exploitation; the problem must be seen in its totality? Thank God it is the partial solutions that have prevailed, on the plane of practical realities, up until now: all good sense has not yet vanished, and it is necessity that writes the laws. But that it will always be so is uncertain. Everything indicates that the deadly mirage of totalist solutions is gaining a more and more profound control over minds, that there is nothing to stand in its way. Obsession with evil and its radical elimination becomes more and

8 It is not possible to develop here the consequences flowing from this principle. We will only point out that it touches upon the question of the angels as secondary causes, and that it pertains to the basic distinction between determinism and causality.

more all-consuming. Everywhere Satan offers himself as an indefinite bait that devours the energies of men.

At the beginning we asked what evidence inspires the charitable power. We can now reply: *it is the evidence of a universal human misery and the need for a radical human happiness.* In the name of this totalist need, we are witness to the destruction of partial equilibriums, to the disdainful refusal of limited remedies. Let small partial joys perish provided that the purity of the system reigns. In a practical way, then, the charitable power is determined by theories issuing from modern rationalism, with the most totalist theory the most appreciated. And if Marxism finds itself contested by a more radical and totalist system, the charity professionals that today's clergy have become will no doubt reject the old and adopt the new with so much the more eagerness and love.

4. THEORIST ALIENATION AND UNIVERSAL MISERY

And so a radical change in the Christian mentality is produced: the evidence providing a driving force for charity today, as well as the spontaneously envisioned solutions, often derive from socialist, progressive, or at the very least democratic theory. Surely it will be objected that the words of Christ make it our duty to do away with suffering everywhere, for whatever is done to His least brethren is done to Him, and that, consequently, if sociology, economics, and psychology provide the best instruments for charitable activity, they need to be adopted. Our answer to such an objection is that this question pertains to natural law and not to the supernatural commandment of charity. We have, in this presentation, intentionally left aside all that concerns the natural law, because here it is not a matter of economics and politics. But such a law does exist. Not that its decrees are positively defined, but, once its decrees are taken into consideration, they confer on this law's provisions that call for human reason in the resolution of problems posed by social organization a certain quality of partaking in the nature of things. Here again it is hardly possible to be more precise if we keep to a formal characterization, as will be done presently. For this partaking in the nature of things is assured, in some kind of intuitive way, by that natural virtue of estimation, that sense of measure, that sense of the possible and impossible unable to be replaced by any rational construction. Political reasoning is natural when it is given form and predetermined by the natural virtues. Why would one reproach us for not saying more about it? We possess this good sense or we do not. If someone does not possess it, then reason legislates in the *a priori*, in a perfectly neutral speculative field where only the principle of contradiction comes into play. Everything is possible, nothing is real. Rousseau and Kant afford us an example of such a speculation. It is perfectly vain and perfectly dangerous: it is the alienation in these abstract mediations that our civilization is dying of today, because it offers the dreadful mirage of perfect solutions. This is a sin against the intellect, and this is why, even in the case of a purely natural interpretation of Christ's commandment, sociological or economic theories are disqualified *a priori* and unable to provide a more adequate means of action. In reality they provide only indefinitely alienating mediations.[9]

Therefore, it is clear not only that these words of Christ cannot be interpreted in the sense of a social action, but even that this 'social action' interpretation destroys their most obvious meaning, that of

---

9 Intending to keep to the plane of principles, we have not been concerned with elaborating, after these criticisms, an economic or social theory. We are opposed, as we have shown, to every theory of this kind. What is valid in this domain, when one truly cares for human happiness, is what has been called organized empiricism. The value of the Church's social doctrine is, in our eyes, precisely what makes for its weakness in the eyes of Marxists: it does not state a systematic theory ever belied by the facts, a theory making true action impossible. It brings to mind the moral principles that should preside over the practical organization of work and society. What remains is that the economic conditions of the modern world are such that they are opposed to every solution. Our civilization, like it or not, is abnormal. Man's normal economic state is that of a poor economy. The overdeveloped state in which we live is a direct effect of industrial mechanization, which is by essence alienating. It is not capitalism or liberalism that exploits man, and Socialism, the self-proclaimed remedy, can in reality only find a remedy for the imperfections of this exploitation, which is to say *organize things through rational planning*. The cause of evil lies with industrial society and all else flows from this. It is vain to attack effects while remaining ignorant of causes. In reality socialism is a product of mechanization. The 'leftist' or 'Marcusian' revolt against industrial civilization in the name of 'poetry' is vain and false. Let us turn to this text of the philosopher J. Lachelier: "The end of man and society is not here below, and justice and charity are themselves only means by which we prepare to realize our true nature in the City of which ours are only images . . . to seek to organize societies with a view to production and consumption is not only to depreciate *enormously* . . . the human condition, it is to go against the very end which is proposed and to destroy what one builds" (*Lettres* [1872], 99).

a human and natural charity, making it impossible. For human and natural relationships it substitutes theoretical and abstract ones as a function of a socialist or progressive construction. There lies in this mutation of the Christian mindset a theorizing of charity that completely subverts its nature. No longer even a love of neighbor, that is to say of an individual and concrete being, it is a sentimental oblation to a more-or-less rational philosophical system; it is a movement of the soul desperately offering itself to structural mediations, since the least human woe passes today through a revolution in the structures of an entire society. Formerly it was taught that the love of neighbor passed through the love of God. In our era men will have nothing to do with divine mediation. The price for the rejection of God and the natural virtues is structural alienation. The charity of the modern Christian is not the love of men, it is love for an abstract construction that is supposed to make men happy. But, while the desert of economic or social reason devours the heart, what abandonment for man, and what despair!

7

The Constitution of Man According to the Philosophical Method

WE COME NOW TO THE ANTHROPOLOGICAL determinations of charity. This involves showing how in man himself the psychic must be distinguished from the spiritual, a distinction which conditions the understanding and manifestation, in the human order, of the commandment to love. Love is, in fact, the privileged place for the meeting and cooperation of the psychic and the spiritual; therefore it can also be the privileged place for their confusion.

The anthropology to be set forth here is guided by an attention to the human being's spiritual destiny. But by no means does it relinquish, for all that, its claim to being objective and scientific in the strictest sense of these terms. This is because, in reality, man is not a machine to be described from the outside. And to be concerned about his spiritual destiny is not to add an ideological superstructure to a human structure putatively just scientific. But man is a being in becoming, like every creature, and the truth of this being is the truth which is realized in this becoming; it is the direction of becoming and the term toward which it tends, just as the most objective truth of the seed is the tree into which it will transform itself. And since, as it happens, it is man who undertakes to know himself in anthropology, it follows that there is no knowledge of man that is not at once a transformation and a realization of himself. According to the beautiful medieval expression, man on earth is said to be *in via*, on the way. Therefore how could he be validly studied while the end of his journey is systematically ignored?

This much is obvious, yet it seems to be completely ignored today. Modern theologians, even the greatest, turn to the social sciences to ask for instruction about man, after which they hope to 'theologically integrate' this objective data, that is add to natural man what they define as a spiritual dimension: "From the viewpoint of content, the great task of theology today is to incorporate anthropology," Father Congar declares.[1] Philosophical reflection shows that such an affirmation has hardly any meaning. One does not theologically integrate an anthropology formed not only outside of all theology, but opposed to all reference to God. This terribly naïve assertion endows the social sciences with an illusory objectivity. Marxism and psychoanalysis are not content to describe man; they also intend to construct man, to realize a project upon man: their theory is also a praxis. The same goes for all forms of sociology and psychology.[2] And this goal is not hidden but declared openly.

After all, it would be supernaturalism to wish to add a spiritual dimension to man if it lacked a root in his very being. Or else, conversely, we could lapse into a naturalization of the supernatural, as if it arised in response to the desires or needs of the human being. There is no autonomous profane anthropology to which the theologian could bring the spiritual complement that it lacks. There is no 'supplement of soul' (Bergson's formula) to be provided. More soul is not added to the human being like more sugar to cereal. The supernatural must be grasped inside nature itself as the destiny it bears within, a destiny it ought to realize. Man is precisely that 'denatured' being who, according to Amiel's expression, "is only what he becomes, a profound truth, but he only becomes what he is, an even more profound truth."[3] Now, if there is an objective datum of philosophical analysis, it is certainly this, namely that the present nature of man is not his true nature. As we will see in a later chapter, if Scholastic philosophy could integrate Aristotle's or Plato's anthropology, this was because it went straight to this indisputable datum.

The philosophical method therefore ought to interweave two themes: that of a search for the self which leads to the realization of being through its transformation — the alchemical theme — and that of an objective description of anthropological structure — the doctrinal theme. In a first section we will follow the path of self-knowledge. Arguing that it is impossible to follow this path without knowing

1 Arthème Fayard, *Sept problèmes capitaux de l'Église* (Paris: Fayard, 1969), 10.
2 Already with Comte sociology (the science of which he is the inventor) is a means to realize "Positive Politics" and the "Religion of Humanity."
3 Henri-Frédéric Amiel, *Grains de mil* (Paris: Joël Cherbuliez, 1854), 194.

72

the terrain which it crosses, we will broach the doctrinal theme. And, because man is first a being among all the other beings of the cosmos, the second section will be devoted to cosmological doctrine. Next, the third section will treat of anthropological doctrine. Finally, in a fourth section, returning to the initial alchemical theme, we will come to the end of the path of interior knowledge, to the mystery of the person.

I. MY-SELF AND MY-OTHER

1. The Self's First Otherness

Since we propose to study the constitution of the human being according to the philosophical method shortly, we will take as our point of departure that which the father of Western philosophy, Socrates, had adopted upon the order of the Oracle at Delphi: "Know thyself."

But, on this topic, we must forestall from the outset a misunderstanding as persistent as it is widespread: to see in 'know thyself' the inaugural maxim of psychological introspection. Does not such an "intelligent" and "cultured" European as André Gide reply to the Delphic oracle: "Know oneself? A maxim as pernicious as it is ugly. To observe oneself is to arrest one's development."[4] Now nothing is more foreign than such an interpretation to Socrates or to Plato, neither of whom would experience the least interest in this wholly modern thing that is introspective psychology. For both, to know oneself is to set out in search of the self, in search of one's true being. This search is understood to be inseparable from a true realization of one's self: to know what one is so as to be what one knows — that is the authentic meaning of the oracular maxim. However, let us admit this psychological interpretation on provisional grounds.

The first, most evident object of self-knowledge is our body. However, this not about the body as a purely 'physical' reality, as a molecular aggregation, since such a reality does not in fact exist — except in considering a corpse, but a corpse, a sheer molecular mass, is not a body by any standard.[5] The truth is that there is for a body only the

---

4 *Fruits of the Earth*, trans. D. Bussy (London: Secker & Warburg, 1962), 230.

5 There is no parallel between a body's growth and its dissolution. Embryological development requires a real duration, composed of qualitatively differentiated, intelligible and necessary phases. Dissolution is a process which calls for no

living body, and that a corpse, as Bousset writes, "has a name in no tongue."[6] We are speaking then of the psycho-corporeal reality, and this under a double heading: in itself and for us. In itself because the living body is a hierarchical and autonomous unity of synthesizing, overarching, and preserving activities impossible to account for in a 'materialist' or mechanistic fashion; for us because the living body is not *a* body but 'my' body, which is called 'one's own body'. Now one's own body is not a material object, but a system of integrated sensations, a pattern, an 'image'. However, even defined in this way, corporeal reality does not seem intrinsic to our most profound being. We have no difficulty — and perhaps we are wrong — in seeing here only a peripheral dimension of ourselves, for we commonly think that our true being will be encountered at the level of what is, in us, purely psychic: a thought, a feeling, an emotion, a memory.

We turn our attention now to the uninterrupted 'psychic melody' of our conscious states: memories, desires, movements of temperament, regrets, interior speech, and fears jostling each other, intertwining, chasing each other away, coming back, being transformed in an endless movement which appears as continual as the temporal flux itself, and which, besides, is not altogether inseparable from it. This remark is, after all, quite banal. If this is what introspection brings us — and who could doubt it? — it clearly seems that we should not title it 'myself'. This psychic flux is, in fact, essentially characterized by otherness: "From this evening I shall never more possess my soul," says Anna de Noailles: the term 'myself' is not appropriate then, but rather 'my-other'. This simple consideration is enough to definitely set aside the psychological interpretation. For whatever the most profound response to the Delphic injunction might be, one thing is certain: it is a search for my own identity. It is saying: know thy very self, and not: know thy other self. If then there is no other knowledge of myself than psychological introspection, this knowledge is deceptive.

For, as negative as it may be, the first result of our analysis is nevertheless of great value. By this, every attempt at self-knowledge upon

---

real duration — since it may vary from a few minutes (with a sulfuric acid bath) to several centuries (mummification or preservation in dry surroundings).

6 *The Funeral Orations of Bossuet*, ed. F. M. Warren (Boston: D. C. Heath, 1907), 144.

the psychological plane is discredited, and, at the same stroke, so too are all the methods (questionnaires, tests, surveys, etc.) offered us by modern science, yet with whose help we so stubbornly hope to discover at last the true face of our soul. A deceptive hope: we are seeking our identity upon the very plane of our otherness. And of course it is easier to expose this deception than to really detach ourselves from it. However, we must break with this fascination and turn a deaf ear to the appeals that our soul seems to cast at us: "By studying what I am, you will know what you are." If we respond, as surely we are able to do, for the social sciences have given us the means — we are not at all claiming that they yield only false knowledge — if we respond, we are only half-satisfied: "Yes indeed, that's me," we think, "but . . . I am also otherwise, or different, or contradictory." And we seek anew to 'fix' the face of our soul whose features, however, are perpetually changing.

As a matter of fact, the changeability of our psychic face is not total. The methods of the social sciences, or life experience, enable us to recognize in our behavior certain 'constants', either reactive or primitive, which seem to define a psychological profile, a certain structure, a certain character. This psychic architecture is at once innate and acquired. It is progressively built up out of the corporeal, humoral (temperamental), and psychic data[7] interacting with cultural, historical, and familial surroundings, under the effect of events encountered and experienced; a construction more or less harmonious, more or less successful, more or less equilibrated, to which psychoses and neuroses, which can always be viewed as architectural 'mistakes', bear witness. In addition, this psychic architecture has a tendency to consolidate more and more with time. After a more-or-less successful equilibrium of conflicting psychic tensions has been attained, it may even persist after the psychic tensions themselves have disappeared, or are

---

7 By psychic data we mean here the soul's natural tendencies and predispositions that spring in part from the parents, by virtue of a veritable psychic heredity. Kretschmer's works have shed light upon such heredity. As a result, contrary to an all-too-widespread opinion belied by the facts, the role of society, family environment, and events encountered in the formation of the 'personality' is less important than the role of psycho-corporeal data. But, in return, society 'conditions' the manifestation of innate tendencies. No society can give a genius for painting to a man devoid of it; but no painter of genius can manifest himself if the society is completely ignorant of what painting is.

exhausted, or have changed. However that may be, this architecture is ours and can be considered a good expression of our individual nature.

2. The Self's Second Otherness

Can we speak then of 'myself'? We have to say no. For even if our psychic architecture exhibits a relative unity, and even if this unity is distinctive for each individual, we could not truly identify ourselves with it. Actually, to the very extent that it is known, this architecture becomes an object. Without doubt we are indeed like an object, but precisely because we are, we are not strictly speaking an object. Our soul seems like a nature, a something that we have at our disposal and with which we must reckon; a certain manner of being, but one which, by the same token, is completely distinct from the knowing subject. This is not really then one's own self that is known in this manner, but always another self, in which the pure subject would not really recognize itself.

And so we have identified a second otherness, distinct from the preceding one, situated at a more profound ontological level. The first is the intrinsic otherness of the psychism which, in itself, in its temporal life, is always different and always changing. The second, which is discovered only by conscious reflection, is the extrinsic otherness of the psychism which, in relation to the conscious subject, presents itself in the consistency of its architecture as something other than the subject. However it is upon this psychic architecture that the subject fixes its gaze. It is of this that our consciousness is aware. Such is at least the ontological situation of ordinary man. This is 'me'. We grasp ourselves as an object, and since we possess ourselves, we identify ourselves with our possession — for what else could we be? Nevertheless, in the same measure that we recognize our individual nature as our self, we put it at a distance from ourselves: "I is another," Rimbaud has said. This analysis, which Sartre has developed systematically in *Being and Nothingness*, leads us therefore to define the ontological situation of man as a pure contradiction without any possible solution.

In an analysis of this kind, the consciousness of the Socratic seeker discovers then two dimensions of the human being that are relatively different by nature, with both of which it finds that it is in fact identified, without being able to rightly identify itself with either: on the one hand we have a psycho-corporeal dimension and, on the other, a purely psychic one. Is this the whole of man? Have we exhausted all dimensions of human nature? If yes, it being granted that the conscious subject can in no manner truly recognize itself, must we conclude that there is nothing in man which is truly 'himself'?

To know is always to know something, a nature. To know oneself is therefore to discover a nature which is also an 'itself'. Now consciousness is not of a psycho-corporeal nature (the living body proper), nor of a purely psychic nature (feelings, emotions, passion, memory, imagination). Is self-knowledge then impossible?

As we see, our research is developing according to two perspectives at once: that of self-consciousness, where a dialectic of subject and object is manifested, and that of the human being's constitution, which is concerned with the nature of things. We began with the first, and it has dominated our entire presentation thus far. But, if we are to pursue it, we must now consider the second. Man is also a being of nature, and therefore nature participates integrally in his constitution.

II. A COSMOLOGICAL DIGRESSION
Introduction: Faith's Need for a Cosmology

The following considerations pertain to cosmology. The reason for this is that there should be no anthropology that does not involve a certain conception of the world: man is a being of the world, his nature and constitution participate in the nature and constitution of the whole cosmos. Thus, contrary to the European idealism that began by isolating him from the rest of creation, man must be put back into his natural environment. Recall that for Aristotle psychology is a part of physics.

Interest in a cosmology is not rare today, not only from the anthropological viewpoint, but even from a religious viewpoint. Bultmannism, in many respects one of the most formidable threats to contemporary Christianity, is known to consist precisely in posing the question of the compatibility of modern science with the implicit or explicit cosmology of Judeo-Christian Revelation, and to pose it in all its rigor. The widespread conclusion is that it is no longer possible to sincerely and honestly believe in the near totality of events, miraculous or otherwise, related by the Scriptures.

This is how it is for the Resurrection or Ascension. Without even denying that God can do what He wants, raising His body above the earth for example, the question is what indeed the meaning of such an operation can be. Implied here is that the Kingdom of Heaven is not above, that space is indefinite, that there is moreover neither absolute high nor absolute low, and that the body of Christ, therefore, would not be able to 'leave' the created world. This criticism intends in this way to wrest the purity of Revelation (kerygma) from cosmological representations (mythology) by which the first Christians expressed it.

Now perhaps it is not impossible to object to Bultmann on the one hand for his incomprehension of traditional cosmology and on the other for his misreading of the results of contemporary science. He speaks in the name of a materialist scientism which already began to crumble seriously at the start of the twentieth century; surely this materialism still survives throughout the Western mentality, from biologists to sociologists and on through the philosophers (although much less among physicists), but this is actually only an ideological superstition. The most recent and most genuine science has made the very notion of matter burst into pieces.

On the other hand, in light of a traditional cosmology revived by the most recent cosmology, the texts of Revelation (Genesis as well as the Gospels) take on an altogether precise and perfectly objective meaning. These so-called naive images disclose in truth an altogether rigorous science and transcendent intelligence.

1. The Philosophical Distinction of the Three Worlds
A. The Corporeal State or the World Here and Now

Consider a tree, an oak for example. For modern man, distinguished by a secular, 'scientific' materialism, this tree is a body whose whole reality is physical in nature. What makes it differ from other trees is a certain organization of the material from which it is made. Now, if anyone analyzes this reality-matter according to the demands of current science, this material compactness, in which we place our trust to assure us of this body's reality, vanishes. Nothing is compact or self-consistent — ancient philosophy would say 'substantial' — in the 'matter' discovered by microphysics. In its recent development physics has gone from molecule to atom, then from atom to electron and the other particles that compose it, supported and guided by an unwavering plan: to explain the properties of a physical being (and first its very reality) through the nature and form of its component parts, these being considered the ontological foundations of all corporeal realities. These particles, as minute as they might be, are understood *a priori* to be bits of matter, and it is ultimately their spatial configuration (their geometric form) and the movements that stir them which should, in principle, explain everything else. Now, what quantum physics henceforth teaches us is that the material 'particles', the ultimate constituents of matter, are not 'material': they have no set spatial configuration and are not locatable, they are not isolated corporeal unities. "Do we have to," the physicist Frenkel asks, "consider material particles as the primary things in nature?" And he concludes that what is ontologically primary are not the corpuscles, but the electromagnetic field in which they appear and which produces them. This field is itself not produced by any material reality.[8] Will anyone be surprised to hear that the planetary model for atomic structure such as Niels Bohr imagined it — a nucleus around which revolve the peripheral electrons — is only a handy representation without any real value?[9] With this new conception, "it is not enough to say that it is impossible to know the exact position and velocity of a particle simultaneously. It must be maintained that, in general, there is no such thing as a well-determined position or velocity. Matter and light become fugitive indeed, and any hope of representing the world in terms of pictures and motions becomes nothing more than an empty dream."[10]

It is then the *material* consistency of corporeal reality that is today called into question, or sometimes even denied. Neither atoms nor

8   J. Frenkel, *Wave Mechanics*, vol. 2, *Advanced General Theory* (Oxford: Clarendon Press, 1934), 517.

9   Werner Heisenberg, *La nature dans la physique contemporaine* (Paris: Gallimard, 1962), 18. The concepts of Heisenberg, Bohr, and the Copenhagen School are accepted today by a majority of physicists. Louis de Broglie and his disciples are attempting, however, to achieve a realist description of nature. Such a description is not impossible, provided that one relearn the non-materialist language of traditional philosophy; cf. Wolfgang Smith, *The Wisdom of Ancient Cosmology* (Oakton, VA: Foundation for Traditional Studies, 2003). Raymond Ruyer's philosophy provides a modern formulation of this.

10   J. L. Andrade e Silva and G. Lochak, *Quanta, grains et champs* (Paris: Hachette, 1969), 164. The authors are students of Louis de Broglie.

particles are solid and stable structures. If, from particles and atoms, we turn now to molecules, and from molecules to the bodies they form, we again find a similar question: how do these molecules produce physical unities, how do they *hold* together so as to form *a* body? By what hooks are they fastened to one another? Why do the molecules out of which our oak is made not fly off in all directions? If intermolecular 'hooks' exist, it is therefore upon them that we must rely to assure the solidity of the whole, if not its unity. But out of what would these hooks be made? Atoms and elementary particles. Now, as we just saw, these particles are not physical individualities. What then? "The molecule as such — contrary to the atom — already has a structure. . . . But the bonding and interacting electrons are not locatable. For the formulas developed from a chemistry conceived of in geometrical fashion, chemists today substitute electronic density maps that represent, by contour lines, the means for a structuring behavior."[11]

Matter, like space (with which it is identified in certain respects), is indefinitely divisible. Never will we happen upon a speck of matter or shred of space that is indivisible. As a result we cannot find on this level the elementary 'tenon' to which is fastened the whole edifice of the corporeal world. If this elementary tenon is actually in space, it occupies a certain extension and therefore, like space, provides no end to its divisibility.

Space is exteriority. Its nature is to be *partes extra partes*. This means that space is composed not of points, which are without extension, but of the exteriority of every point with respect to every other: every point of space is the limit for every other one since it is 'exterior' to them.

---

11   R. Ruyer, *La Genèse des formes vivantes* (Paris: Flammarion, 1958), 59. The theses proposed here derive in part from this philosopher, one of the most important of the twentieth century, unfortunately a stranger to Christianity and to the light that it casts upon the real; cf. our book *Problèmes de gnose* (Paris: L'Harmattan, 2007), 113–41. What remains is that ignorance of the quantum revolution and the change it introduced into our view of reality disqualifies a major part of Bultmann's exegesis, which denies any reality, other than the purely symbolic, to the earthly manifestations of the divine spoken about in Scripture, for the sake of a long-outdated conception of physical reality, as was acknowledged in 1927 at the fifth Congress at Solvay: the entire world's leading experts officially dropped the realist character of the image of the world that the new physics was using (a temporary repudiation for some, Louis de Broglie and Einstein among them). But, in fact, philosophy like theology continued to function on a cosmological model entirely obsolete since the end of the nineteenth century and the advent of microphysics.

Space is then not a stable container, despite appearances, but rather, in this connection, a nearly realized 'explosion', 'nearly' because the actual realization of this explosion (paradoxical for a realization) would instantaneously exhaust the reality for which it is liable and obliterate it. Now the idea of a stability, of a material consistency, is the idea of corporeal elements that are in some manner *interior* to one another. Such an interiority, such a co-immanence, is necessarily non-spatial. The elementary tenon of the corporeal world not admitting of division (in order to assure its function), and every spatial admitting of infinite division, it follows that this tenon would not be in space. What keeps the parts of a body together, what causes its compactness and its consistency, its solidity, is not corporeal. It is a form-unity psychic in nature, immanent to corporeal reality, and therefore the latter is not able to be completely separated from it. The body is therefore as if a crystallization of a trans-spatial psychic substance, the last stage in a process of exteriorization, *the terminal mode of the psychic*, that is, the manner in which the psychic (understood in a not specifically human sense) stops or terminates its own movement of manifestation towards exteriority. It is a stop since, as we have seen, it is impossible for it to go farther in the *partes extra partes*, into sheer exteriority, without vanishing. If then we envision the corporeal world (or corporeal modality of created reality) in itself, from every vantage point it seems to be a world of limitation or a limit-world. This means that it imposes on all beings manifested within it limiting forms of existence, that is, on this side of its forms, existence disappears. We can, along with Ruyer, designate this merely corporeal world as the world of the 'here-and-now'. This is an altogether negative definition since, in reality, the here-and-now has a positive sense only with respect to a person-being through whom and for whom alone there is a spatial presence (*here*) and a temporal present (*now*); the being-person refers us to a reality spiritual in nature: no presence, if not by the spirit.[12] But if we set aside the ontological basis of the here-and-now's positive determination, Ruyer's designation is illuminating. *Here* and *now* are in fact the limiting modes of the corporeal presence of a thing or a being. To be *here* is to be absent from

---

12   Cf. *Problèmes de gnose*, 136–41. Ruyer, who does not believe in the transcendent reality of the person, has completely misunderstood this requirement.

space as a whole except for a single place which, geometrically, can be reduced to a point (consider the odd notion, in Galilean physics, of the center of gravity as a 'material point'). Likewise, the temporal presence of a being, its *now*, is an instant, a temporal point, the negative limit of the flow of time. The here-and-now is therefore reduced to a point of unicity, to a reality-limit, or rather to a limiting mode of reality. Far from establishing a being's reality, the corporeal world is its ultimate and continual limitation.

This point of unicity is as if the expression, in corporeal mode, of the formal unity required for a being to be real. As Leibniz has taught us: "What is not truly *a* being is not truly a *being*";[13] a pile of sand, a cloud, etc., are not beings but masses of beings. Real unity requires the actuality of a non-spatial form that is therefore psychic (or subtle) in nature, self-binding, in which a multiplicity of elements are immanent to one another. This mutual and trans-spatial imma-nence, which is the internal binding of corporeal elements and which makes *a* being of it, constitutes as it were a kind of brake which, from within, (relatively) slows and stops the process of centrifugal 'disper-sion' according to which the physical world is manifested. Preventing the corporeal forms from lapsing into nothingness, it is indeed then this — the formal unity itself, the individual form — that accounts for the substantiality of bodies, that is for their objective reality.

This is not then an acceptance of the idealist conclusions that cer-tain scholars thought they had to draw from their theories.[14] What is certain, as we have just seen, is that the reality and consistency of bodies cannot be accounted for in a materialist and mechanistic man-ner. Idealist physicists are in fact disappointed materialists: identifying reality and materiality, and being unable to verify this identification with quantum physics, they opted for the ideality of physical phenom-enon. One of the chief concerns of Ruyer's philosophy is precisely to show that there are consistent and objective modes of reality other

13 Letter to Arnaud of 4/30/1687; *Œuvres choisies*, ed. L. Prenant (Paris: Gar-nier, 1940), 202.
14 For example, Erwin Schrödinger, *My View of the World*, trans. C. Hastings (Woodbridge, CT: Ox Bow Press, 1983); cf. Ruyer, "Le petit chat est-il mort? ou: Trois types d'idéalisme," *Revue Philosophique* 160 (1970), 121–34, which shows the philosophic weakness of Schrödinger's subjective idealism.

than matter. One such mode of reality is already provided, for man, by the instance of a 'field of consciousness'. Within sight of my table there are clearly a multiplicity of objects (books, papers, etc.) that are joined in a single 'field of vision' and that do not coexist by juxtaposition in space. My consciousness does not actually wander through this 'field of vision'; it is conscious of each object without having any need to go from one to the other, it *is* the field of vision itself. Ruyer utilizes this model to show that something analogous should exist on the level of corporeal realities by which (or in which) these realities are in some manner present to themselves, that is to say real.[15]

B. The Psychic State or World of Life

In this way we are led to the second state of reality, namely the psychic state which is also called the 'subtle world', or the animic world.

By virtue of the materialist conditioning we have undergone for three centuries, we are disinclined to regard as real what is by nature psychic, at least when something other than the human *psyche* is involved. Still, even the manifestations of our soul do not seem to enjoy the objective reality of material beings, precisely because we have a direct and immediate knowledge of the former: we bathe in an environment of a subtle nature like a fish in water. Field of consciousness, memory, passion are so bound up with the conscious subject it seems impossible to distinguish them from it: they lack that independence, that autonomy, that resistance to the subject attested to by the objectivity of something. An object is first, in fact, an 'objection'. We are even much more hesitant when it comes to endowing non-human corporeal beings with a psychic modality, that is with a 'soul'. The material mode of their existence seems so obvious by itself that it seems to require nothing else to establish its reality. Quantum physics compels us, however. Save for falling into an untenable idealism, it obliges us to attribute a non-spatial subsistence to corporeal beings. Now, for the moment, we do not know about any other non-spatial mode than the 'psychic' or 'animic' mode.

The true reality of the psychic phenomena we experience in ourselves can be brought to light somewhat when we observe how a

15 *Néo-finalisme* (Paris: P. U. F, 1952), 94–104.

passion, for instance, or a memory is endowed with a self-consistent life and structure that withstand our will, are defined and assert themselves in spite of us. These are very real 'forms' that we have a share in and that 'give form' to our consciousness, organizing our behavior. In this respect we are captors caught. These forms enter into us just as we enter into them. The dream state is a striking confirmation — likewise the famous descriptions of Proust. Likewise a host of experiences in social life, for example, where, in thinking it over, we find that the events in which we participate are not only the contingent creations of human actors, but clearly seem to also possess a kind of almost objective identity: we quite rightly speak of a 'spirit' or 'soul' of a current of ideas, of *an* era, of *a* civilization. It is therefore possible, as surprising as this might be, to consider these as theme-forms, modulated no doubt according to the various cultures and their development, yet having an autonomous existence: art, politics, customs, dress, ideologies, and all the movements of ideas and sensibility, in a general manner, appear *on this level* as living and subsistent psychic forms.

As a result of this — we stress along with Ruyer — cultural and social forms are marked by a (relative) necessity and correspond to 'lasting possibilities'. Just as there are technical possibilities (and since the margin of freedom in engineering is quite limited, an angel or a 'Martian', wanting to construct a two-wheeled vehicle moved by muscular energy, will inevitably end up with a form of 'bicycle', with variations in the details), there are cultural and social possibilities for which the margin of freedom is unquestionably greater than for technical possibilities, but which no less retain enough of an identity throughout their historical development. This does not rule out the appearance of 'novelties'. But, rather than invent these novelties, the cultural or social creator puts himself in a position to pick the right shape as outlined *en creux* or in 'negative relief' on the general picture-matrix of culture or society at a given moment. It should be said, however, that these technical, cultural, or social possibilities refer in themselves to essences, that is, to trans-psychic realities.

If we return now to our initial oak, we will say that its growth and lifetime maturity manifest analogous phenomena. Considered strictly in its biological nature, an oak is an organization, a spatio-temporal structuring possessing not only its individual autonomy, but even its specific, perfectly identifiable genus. An acorn placed in the earth will never produce a pine tree. What do we start with, however? With soil — silica, clay, limestone, humus, organic residue — and with a shell enclosing a good quantity of starch — the acorn. And what is the end result? A living being of extremely differentiated structure with no longer anything to be seen of what it began with; a being that can maintain this form for more than five hundred years. This growth and this maintenance of the oak-individual happens not by molecular summation and juxtaposition, but always globally and synthetically, as if at each instant the oak 'knows' what it is doing and what it is accomplishing at every point of its being.

To this synthetic and unitary organization, we must add its genus. The oak is an oak in all of itself: its bark, its fibers, the texture of its wood, the habit of its branches, the form of its leaves, the arrangement of its bark — everything in it bears the mark of its 'oak' identity. And keep in mind that in each case this involves, in the last (physical) analysis, a 'cloud of electrons' that are ordered, structured, given form in oak bark, oakwood and fibers, oak leaves, and in the architecture specific to its branches; and remember that each of the structures just listed, all typical of an oak, differ nevertheless from all the others: the bark is neither wood nor leaves, etc. Lastly, it must be observed that structurings in space are, in reality, only the visible concretion of structurings in time. The oak 'knows how to' make an oak at every point of its body, but also at every moment of its duration. Time, here, is not a mere container, or an *a priori* form of sensibility; it is consubstantial with the very being of the oak. Thus the oak is an activity and the synthesis of an extraordinarily complex multitude of activities, from roots which analyze, decompose, recompose, and absorb elements from the soil necessary for the growth and life of the tree — those very elements and no others, as if the oak recognized them — right up to the chlorophyllous function of the leaves that utilize, through photosynthesis, the energy of certain luminous radiations to produce the carbonaceous food needed by the oak. To be a form or a structure on the one hand, to be a synthesis of activities and functions on the other, is for the oak and for every living being one and the same thing. A living being, whether man, animal, plant, microbe, or bacteria, is not first a machine comprised of components articulated with each other as needed and then set in motion: it is active structure and structuring activity inseparably. Structure does not precede activity (and therefore cannot account for it); it is exactly contemporaneous with it, it is its 'observable' trace.[16]

Modern biology is expected to answer all the questions we raise with the help of the famous DNA genetic 'code'. On the helical structures of desoxyribonucleic acid macromolecules is to be found inscribed all information necessary for the formation and functioning of a living being. We are not questioning the global relationship that can be established between a particular genetic 'code' and a particular living structure. But what a philosopher cannot help but notice is that it is impossible to explain in a materialistic manner the deterministic dependence between, for example, a particular genetic code and the form of a hand. What is unobservable, by definition, says Ruyer, "is the deterministic dependence of these [genetic] structures and the organic structuring that they are supposed to direct and contain *in nuce*."[17] We will make a comparison: let us suppose that the word *flour* is written (alphabetic code) in a cookbook. Between this word and the thing it designates there is indeed a relationship, but only for someone who knows how to read the code. For a cook ignorant of the written code, there is no deterministic relationship between these marks that are the letters on paper and the thing that is flour. Likewise, there is no deterministic relationship between the physical reality of genes and the physical reality of organs, the building-up of which genes are supposed to 'direct'. The genetic code (is this a metaphor?) is made up of sequences of four basic elements variously arranged in groups of three (inside the DNA macromolecule); the hand and eye, to the contrary, are built up through a form-activity that is an overall and unitary arrangement of space.[18] There is no scale model of a hand or eye in DNA. In other words, we are not denying that there might possibly exist a link between a particular gene and a

16   François Meyer, 'Épistémologie de la biologie', *Logique et Connaissance scientifique*, ed. J. Piaget (Paris: Encyclopédie de la Pléiade, 1962), 806.

17   *Les Études philosophiques* 3 (July 1960), 346.

18   Joël de Rosnay, *Les Origines de la Vie. De l'atome à la cellule* (Paris: Seuil, 1966), 62–77. For all its clarity and the precision of its information, this remarkable book nevertheless has a tendency to present as certainties what is only in the realm of hypothesis.

particular characteristic of a living being; but we are denying that anyone will ever discover in the gene the *reason* for the characteristic, that is to say that someone will be able to grasp an *intelligible* relationship between the one and the other in such a way that the latter would truly explain the former:[19] the form of a wheel explains the nature of its movement; the genetic code does not explain the structure of the eye. Such an explanation is impossible *a priori* because every living structure is first a whole, and not a sum of elements which, moreover, only have their existence through their mutual functional adaptation in a unitary organization. This unitary organization presupposes the existence of a 'plan' for the eye or the hand, but we do not see how this could be *materially* inscribed anywhere, and this for a number of reasons, the first of which is an embryological one: the formation of a hand is temporal and requires an 'embryological behavior' of a 'foresighted' kind.[20] Everything alive, from the cell to the tissues and the most complex organs, *is only making itself.*

We repeat: anything alive is not a material structure, a mechanical device of a physico-chemical nature which *in addition* is endowed with life, but it is a structuring and form-giving activity. True, a majority of epistemologists expect (in vain, according to us) in the more-or-less near future a solution to the serious gaps in the genetic account, but finally the most circumspect acknowledge it: "There is no way open yet for the deduction of manifest traits from the sequences of bases in the DNA molecule.... For that matter, no one can yet say precisely how the 'instructions' coded in the molecule are carried out in cell differentiation."[21]

---

19 Specialists have reacted against the 'metaphor' of the genetic code, which often seems quite inadequate; cf. C. H. Waddington, *New Patterns in Genetics and Development* (New York and London: Columbia University Press, 1962), cited by R. Ruyer, "Évolution et Cybernétique," *Année Biologique*, vol. 6, fasc. 9–10 (1967), 560. More recently, in a work with at times debatable conclusions, two scholars, Jean-Jacques Kupiec and Pierre Sonigo, have shown that "the notion of the gene insofar as a determiner of character has become extremely fragile, and even impossible to support" (*Ni Dieu ni gène. Pour une autre théorie de l'hérédité* [Paris: Seuil, 2000], 62–63).

20 Notwithstanding the possible excesses or gross simplifications of its advocates, the 'intelligent design' theory is the only rationally conceivable and scientifically acceptable one.

21 W. M. O'Neil, *Fact and Theory* (Sydney: Sydney University Press, 1969), 148–50; likewise Ruyer, "La quasi-information," *Revue Philosophique* 155 (1965), 285–302.

It is then the biological facts themselves that postulate, if we want to intelligibly account for their reality, the objective existence of a form-giving psychic, that is to say non-spatial, form, the formative activity of which develops over time. Non-spatial (or trans-spatial) does not mean here: above space — which would make no sense — but simply: not subject to the spatial condition and, for this very reason, able to be present or immanent then in the totality of organic space. This is precisely what the phenomenon of biological death shows. We (falsely) represent to ourselves the body as a solid and consistent reality and the (vegetal-animal) soul as a fragile and evanescent, impalpable reality. But the opposite is true. What makes for the reality and consistency of a body is the soul, since, from the time that the latter ceases to be active, the bodily substance decomposes and is undone. *It is the body that is 'in' the soul and not the soul in the body, and this is what preserves it.*

C. The Semantic State or Spiritual World

Although this structuring activity is carried out over time and thus includes an actual temporal dimension — time is inherent to the reality of living beings — it should also be mentioned that the structure as such avoids succession and change: the realized form is 'generic' and relatively immutable. The unexpected, marvelous thing is that the oak-form is always manifested anew in the world of space-time. Now, if this form is not reducible to a genetic code — the genome being only the 'means' according to which it is realized in space — neither is it purely reducible to a *'psyche'*, to a form-activity, to a temporal theme, to a specific incorporeal memory — this memory being, for the living, only the 'means' of realizing itself over time. Simply contemplating the oak is enough to convince us of this. We are not purely in the presence of a display of molecules, nor simply in that of an organo-energetic phenomenon. An oak is not solely rising sap, the peripheral growth of the sap-wood, sprouting leaves, respiration, chlorophyllous activity, etc. It is also, even above all, a certain 'meaning' of the universe, an 'expressiveness' that the poet tries to convey, an Idea in the Platonic sense. We are not dealing here with subjective impressions that the sight of an oak might awaken in us, with memory associations or states of the soul that literature can explain, but with the direct and essential perception of 'oak' reality. This is a quite common experience and yet one to which we hardly pay any attention: we will give this the name 'semantic experience'. When we are before a fir-tree we perceive another 'word' of the world, another meaning than when we are before an oak. This word and this meaning are perfectly objective, even though we cannot define them with concepts, except by approximate images. A perceived oak *tells* us something different than a perceived fir-tree, and to speak of a *telling* is hardly a metaphor. To ignore this dimension of our sensory existence, or reduce it to mere subjective impressions, is to render knowledge unintelligible, to amputate the reality of an essential and, in truth, obvious dimension. And we will equally qualify this reality as semantic, the adjective of the noun *meaning*. In its depths, this reality is identical to the Platonic essence: to see an oak is to see its oak-essence, its 'oakness', manifested in the perceived tree.

Now, a little reflection shows that this semantic reality constitutes the fundamental subsistence of the oak as 'perceived'. 'Before' subsisting in space-time, the oak subsists semantically as a constant possibility of meaning in the universe, actualized variously and innumerably according to its varied and innumerable corporeal realizations. For in the end the indestructible unity, the self-presence that establishes the most basic reality of the perceived oak, its irrefutable ontological solidity, is indeed of a semantic or, if one prefers, of an intelligible order: what is 'stoutest' in the oak is its essence. This reality is indeed a structure, an order, but an intelligible structure: the intelligibility of this structure is its very reality. This order is not only an organization, it is an inexhaustible fullness of meaning. To analyze an oak, to break it down as finely as one would like — this is always and indefinitely to discover something of order, of meaning, of the semantic; this is always and indefinitely to bring to light reality's continual discourse. And, actually, what is it that holds together a building's elements? Only mortar or cement? Is it not rather the structure, that is to say the order willed by the architect? But this order itself is not an invention of the architect, a fruit of his fantasy: it is a discovery. This order objectively exists, it is a technical possibility that imposes its law on our understanding which perceives its necessity. It is therefore the intellection of this possibility, objectively present in a ribbed vault, that holds the stones together and stops them from falling. And so it is for everything. Now, what is the unity of this order if not its meaning? What creates the unity in the order of words in a sentence, if not the meaning of this sentence, the order of which is only a consequence or manifestation? Whoever speaks about order is speaking about a system of intelligible relationships, but the unity of the system itself can only be the unity of a meaning. *There can be true unity only with semantic unity.*

The famous account of 'Milinda's chariot', although borrowed from a non-Western cultural sphere, will perhaps make it easier to grasp, as counter-proof, what we are trying to put forward.

Milinda is the Indian name for Menander, the Greek king of Punjab in the second century before Christ. He had philosophical conversations with the Buddhist monk Nagasena dealing in particular with the non-substantiality of the ego and everything in general. To persuade Milinda of this non-existence, Nagasena takes the chariot in which the king journeys as an example and asks him to declare what a chariot is: is it the pole, the axle, the wheels, the chariot body, the yoke, the reins, the goading-stick? No. Is it all these things unitedly? No, replies the king once more. And Nagasena's conclusion: "there is no chariot," "chariot is only a name." This line of argument, which the monk has already used in connection with the existence of his ego, does not seem very compelling.

Notice first that in posing the question: is the pole the chariot? one is presupposing that, if someone does not know what a chariot is, at least this person knows what a pole is, since it might possibly constitute the sought-for being. Now, we might just as well pose the question in connection with the pole, or axle or wheels, etc., which enjoy no ontological evidence superior to the chariot's. We will grant, however, that this is the case here. Another question arises: in asking what a chariot is, is not this to suppose that it is something? It would make no sense to ask someone what a thing is when it was known not to exist, a 'goat-stag' for example. True, Nagasena will counter, but this presupposition, the falsity of which being precisely what I wish to demonstrate, is clearly the very one that Milinda has in mind. However this may be, the chariot is presumed by him to be something, and this is rightly to lead him to realize that there is no answer to the question: what is it? It must be first conceded — provisionally — that it *is* something. That is true, and although this answer raises certain difficulties, we will accept it: the weakness of this line of argument does not lie here.

But here is the nearly unnoticed crux of the matter that constitutes the second phase of the argument. Nagasena does not just lead Milinda to agree that the chariot cannot be the pole, or axle, or wheels, etc., nor their assemblage; he also asks him to agree that he has listed all the possible identifiers of the chariot. Hence, it being given, he says, that there is nothing "else besides pole, axle, wheels . . . etc., which is the chariot," it must be concluded that "there is no chariot," that the chariot is merely a name.[22]

Assuredly, but on one condition: that Nagasena's list be exhaustive, that it exhaust all possible identifiers. Now, this is not the case, and this is what Plato's philosophy takes into account, and Aristotle's even more. For, although it is true that the chariot is neither pole nor axle nor wheels, this is not because it is nothing, this is because it is something else: there still remains, in fact, for the basis of its reality, what Aristotle calls the 'form' (*morphe, eidos*), that is to say not the spatial envelope (the *shape*), but the thing's intelligible structural unity. And this is no arbitrary metaphysical construction here, but to the contrary: for the form is such a truly objective reality that any craftsman, whether God, an angel, a 'Martian', or a man, wishing to build a land vehicle is only able to realize his work by being obedient to a 'chariot' form which is *essentially* invariable, whether we are dealing with a carriage, a cart, a coach, an automobile, or even a locomotive or wagon. And this is most exactly — and very rightly — what Scholastic philosophy calls a 'substantial form', that which constitutes the substance or reality of a thing. True, this form as such is not to be seen: only the intellect knows of it. But it is not because our eyes do not see it *in itself* (for they see it in the sensible chariot) that it does not exist, unless one supposes that only what is sensed corporeally has reality or existence. In other words, the Buddhist monk's argument rests on a strictly materialistic conception of the real, which is philosophically weak. We are not denying that Nagasena was right to show that it is not possible to attribute a material or corporeal substance to the

22 *Milindapanha* ('Questions of Milinda'), §15a; trans. Henry Clark Warren, in *Buddhism in Translations,* Harvard Oriental Series, III (Cambridge: Harvard University Press, 1896), 131.

chariot. Quite to the contrary, we affirm that beings and things have no purely material subsistence. But this means, not that beings and things have no ontological consistency, but that this consistency is of *another* order, another nature.

We have not recalled the account of Milinda's chariot with the intention of refuting Buddhism — which is altogether outside of our purpose and competence — but to better bring to light the reality of semantic subsistence by subjecting it to an especially strong negation. Moreover, it is possible that Nagasena's purpose essentially arises from a spiritual and not a philosophical pedagogy, even though he uses a line of argument incontestably philosophical. However that may be, what remains is that this account clearly illustrates the basically (and no doubt unconscious) materialistic nature of the presuppositions of Buddhist non-substantialism and idealisms in general.

We can now recapitulate the stages of our discovery of semantic subsistence. We started with the simultaneously psychic and intellectual experience of an oak's essence, of its 'semantic expressiveness'. This essence (this 'type') appears to be formed by an order, a structure, that is to say a characteristic system of intelligible relationships[23] that make up the entire reality of the oak. Finally, we have specified this reality as being semantic in nature, because only the unity of a meaning can account for the unity of a being without which there is no being. Unity of being requires, in fact, not only the intelligible assemblage of its elements, in such a fashion that each of them is in accord with all the others according to a hierarchical harmony and a mutual correspondence, but also an immanence of all the elements

---

23 Strictly speaking, we should say 'almost intelligible'. Having once allowed for an 'oak' structure, we grasp the perfect intelligibility of its arrangement. But what is the *raison d'être* of the 'oak' essence? Why is there an oak in reality? This question surely makes no sense in pure metaphysics. Like the rose, the 'oak' essence is without a 'why', a *supreme contingency* inseparable from the idea of creation. The *raison d'être* principle makes us ascend from the corporeal and sensible oak to the incorporeal and intelligible 'oak', and then to its Idea in God. If we then ask again: what is the *raison d'être* of the 'oak-Idea', that is: why is there the Idea of the oak in God, why does the Divine Essence settle upon the Idea of an oak? we cannot answer. Between the Divine Essence and the creative Ideas there is, for our understanding, a break in continuity. Received as a grace in an intellect "that knows how to close its eyes," this break in continuity delivers us from all the whys: the 'oak-Idea' is eternally just so, satisfying every search into the superintelligible evidence of the infinite Essence.

to each other in an indivisible unity, so that the intelligible structure will be, in a certain manner, only the 'unfolded' aspect of this unity. Otherwise, whatever might be the solidity of the assemblage, it would be open to divisibility, and we could not account for its irreducible reality. Now, how can the elements be immanent to each other if not in the unity of a meaning? This is what the analogy of language shows. Language is intelligible because the structure is one, because its elements are mutually comprehended, in the dual sense of the term: they compenetrate while being intelligible to each other.

Here, in the created order, we touch upon the absolute of being, for we cannot go back beyond the semantic, that is beyond meaning. Meaning is primary; we cannot define it except to recognize a meaning of meanings, purely metaphysical in nature, which is the divine *Logos*, or Supremely Intelligible. But, for a given being, what is absolutely indestructible in its reality is semantic in nature.[24]

2. Unity of the Three Worlds[25]
A. "The Seven Heavens are on Earth"

In closing, we must stress the unity of these three states or three worlds in order to avoid the most common error. This consists in representing them as superimposed planes. Such a representation is surely inevitable geometrically, and what is more, corresponds to an objective aspect of reality, as we will see in a moment when we study some examples of cosmological symbolism. However, it is rightly said that "the seven heavens are on earth": the corporeal world in no way hides the other two since, to the contrary, it attests to them and requires their reality.

The world of intelligible substance is the principle of the psychic or animic or subtle world, while this latter world is itself the principle of the corporeal or gross world. The animic world is the semantic world 'psychized' or vitalized, and the corporeal is the psychic spatialized. We find an indication of this doctrine in St. John's Prologue

---

24 The semantic experience, or experience of meaning, is direct, indecomposable, as is the perception of a color. It is for itself its own referent: this is an intellectual intuition.

25 Some of the views set forth here are inspired by, in addition to Ruyer, cosmological doctrines formulated by Guénon.

when he states: "the life was the light of men." Light is, in fact, a traditional symbol of the intelligible world; by penetrating into the human psycho-corporeal world, this 'light' becomes 'life'. In other words, 'life' in the human world fulfills the function that 'light' fulfills in the semantic (or spiritual) world.

We can also make the following observation. The corporeal world's objectivity seems self-evident because of the noticeably impenetrable character of certain bodies. The psychic world, to the contrary, seems more 'subjective' because we experience the human psyche from within.[26] At the same time, we cannot grasp it as a thing. It seems to escape our grip to the extent that, for us, to grasp is to grasp an object: but psychic realities possess us more than we possess them. The body's objectivity reaches us 'from without'; the objectivity of psychic realities is only revealed by being imposed as something lived, not as something perceived.

As for the intelligible world, we become aware of it — fragmentarily — in, for example, the purely intellectual activity of mathematical or philosophical knowledge. It is at once more penetrable than psychic realities — which, even when experienced, retain a certain opaqueness — and more unyielding than corporeal realities. More penetrable because it is luminous throughout: to grasp a philosophical truth, a mathematical being, is quite literally to be at the core of this truth or this being. More unyielding than bodies, on the other hand, because this truth is imposed on me in an absolute manner, since no exercise of the will can do anything to change it, and since it cannot be destroyed by happenstance, by a vicissitude: a triangle is 'eternal'. For these reasons intelligible substance can be symbolized by a snow crystal or diamond, which is as if a luminous crystallization of the Light of the Logos; psychic substance by water, which is as if a liquifying of the luminous crystallization of the Logos; corporeal reality by ice, which is as if a coagulation of the animic substance. Crystallization, dissolution, coagulation — these are the phases of cosmic alchemy.

A world is defined by a sum total of conditions, that is, by limitations. Whenever an intelligible reality enters into the subtle world it

---

26 This involves the psychic conscious or subconscious, not the psychic at work in the bodily processes, which is not specifically human, but common to all natural beings.

is subject to the determining conditions of this 'degree' of existence: life, duration and individual form. In this connection let us recall that an individual is a being that cannot be divided (etymological sense). A molecule, an oak, an ox, a man are individual beings: if I cut them in two, I will not obtain two molecules, two oaks, two oxen, or two men, whereas I can divide in two a mass of water, a cloud, a stone, a plank of wood: these are, says Ruyer, being-masses, not true beings like individual beings. We grasp here, fully, the reality of the individual form. This form might be described as the organization in autoelic circuit of a bioenergetic system, analogous to those whirlpools formed in flowing water, twisting about themselves; while semantic being, being one in the unity of its meaning, far from twisting about itself to individualize itself in a form, is open at the very core of its unity to the entirety of the intelligible light: it is a radiance of the light. Lastly, when the psychic enters into the corporeal, there are added to the limitations of the animic world those of quantified matter and space, thus opening it to indefinite divisibility. The passage from semantic to corporeal is, then, a passage from open interiority to closed exteriority. The individual form is already a first translation or expression of semantic unity, the quantitative and analytical unity of corporeal reality another, more distant expression of this unity. However, the corporeal, by the hardness and clarity of some of its forms, more directly reminds us of the purity and 'eternity' of the essence, as is precisely proven in the possibility of symbolizing the intelligible by what is most 'corporeal' among bodies: the diamond, the stone, the crystal.

B. The 'Seven Earths' are in Heaven

However, this alchemical process of exteriorization by dissolution and coagulation would not occur if it did not find its *raison d'être* in the very world of essences. The seven heavens are on the earth because the seven earths are in heaven as lasting and principial possibilities. Bodies possess then an intelligible (or semantic) modality, a psychic modality, and a strictly corporeal modality. Also, we might just as well regard the strictly corporeal modality as in reality not other than the intelligible or semantic modality of the corporeal, but perceived separately and as if abstracted from its intelligible environment: from this point of view, the corporeal is clearly an abstraction. We could likewise speak of an intelligible modality of the psychic, which is well illustrated by the symbolism of light and fire: the psychic is contained in the spiritual (or intelligible) as fire is contained in light as its dynamic and somewhat obscure aspect.

When we speak of the corporeal or psychic or intelligible modality of a being, we are no longer looking at things strictly from a cosmological viewpoint, from the viewpoint of worlds, but from that of the beings that inhabit them (the microcosmological viewpoint). As a matter of fact, these two viewpoints are inseparable. A world is defined by the sum total of conditions imposed on the beings that are part of it, conditions determined by the nature of the modality (corporeal, animic, or semantic) that each of these beings has assumed. We can therefore define a world starting with the beings found in it, or starting with the sum total of the conditions that define it. From the cosmological viewpoint, a world takes precedence over the beings that are subject to its conditions of existence. But, from the microcosmological viewpoint, beings take precedence over a world and summon it directly to the 'hypercosmic' transcendence of its ontological root, and this is why the primacy of beings is more important than the primacy of worlds. In a general manner, there is an intersecting of both, as we will see in the following chart which will make more explicit the doctrine of multiple modalities of one and the same being or one and the same thing. In particular, this chart will enable us to grasp how the body, by its three modalities — and this is not unconnected to the transfiguration and resurrection of Christ — reflects in its fashion the triple principial possibility of the semantic world.

		BEINGS		
		Essences	Souls	Bodies
WORLDS	Semantic	essences	spiritual souls	spiritual bodies
	Animic		souls	psychic bodies
	Corporeal			gross bodies

However, as for the corporeal deriving from the psychic and the psychic from the semantic, it does not follow that the semantic is nothing but the principle of the psychic, which would itself be in turn only the principle of the corporeal. In other words, the corporeal does not manifest the whole of the psychic, or the psychic the whole of the semantic, which besides is self-evident: every manifestation, in some respects, reduces what it manifests to the conditions of its plane of manifestation. Assuredly, by virtue of a being's unity, all its modalities symbolize each other and echo each other. Indeed, the total being is expressed in each of its modalities, and therefore the most limited modality, that is the corporeal, clearly reflects the entire being, but not as a whole. A comparison will make this more understandable. A circle on a plane can be considered the orthogonal projection of the *whole* sphere on this plane, but not its integral projection. And, just as the circle is contained in the sphere, which is its principle, as a possible determination of the latter, so the body is contained in the psychic form as a possible determination of the latter, that the body, this time in its sensible incarnation, manifests totally, but not integrally.

As a result of these somewhat abstract considerations — and leaving aside that which, being incorporeal, evidently arises only from the psychic life: ideas, memories, feelings, etc. — even on the strictly biological or microphysical level, there are functions (embryological, organic, homeostatic, etc.) for which no corporeal reality, no physico-chemical mechanism (through a determinism by degrees according to the punctal quality of the 'here and now') can account: the formation, building-up and subsistence of living things actually require an 'overall view', a 'unitary and domain-wide synopsis' of the living being by itself (for the living are *making themselves*), not only according to space, and therefore by correlation at a distance, but also according to time, and therefore by a finalized correlation. As for the corporeal modality properly so called, it is in no way being denied, but it is to the contrary established in this way in its *terminal* reality, the visible trace of a synergetic trans-spatial activity of a psychic nature, and even, in certain respects, the visible trace of a trans-temporal activity semantic in nature.

C. Geometric Synthesis of the Preceding Doctrine

We started out from the corporeal world to go towards the semantic world. Our quest was guided by a question: what is real in reality? What is required for something to exist? And, to answer this question, we have had to reach the semantic degree of reality, because the semantic alone possesses a sufficient ontological consistency.

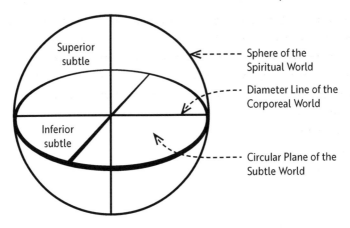

As we stressed at the beginning, we are obviously inclined to super-impose the three worlds as three hierarchized degrees. This is the case with numerous symbolic figurations, and it should not be denied that, from a certain point of view, such a representation is justified. How-ever, to the extent that the corporeal is less a proper degree of reality than the terminal mode of the psychic, according to the formula-tion we have used, it can be situated more exactly on the very degree of existence of the psychic. Strictly speaking, there is no corporeal existence: the indefinite divisibility of space-time is contrary to the requirements for true existence. It is the psychic which, by 'terminat-ing' in the corporeal, confers on the latter all the reality that accrues to it, that of a boundary short of which there is just nothingness. The corporeal is for us the most evident form of existence precisely because it distinguishes, in the final analysis, the psychic from the nothingness to which its expansive dynamism seems to consign it. This is also then, positively, what saves psychic beings from their fall into the darkness of infernal exteriority. The corporeal is heavy and opaque, but also stable and closed upon itself; the psychic is aerial and subtle, but also light, mutable, and dispersive.

If a geometric representation is adopted, the psychic, for a deter-mined being, will correspond to a plane, and the corporeal to a line on this plane showing the boundary of the plane figure contained there and which will represent the individual form of this being, say, for example, a circle. The semantic (or spiritual) will be symbolized by a vertical to the center of this plane, a vertical from which the plane is seen in its totality, without there being any need to actually cross it in order to know it. In such a representation, although the corporeal constitutes, for the psychic, a limit to exteriority, the spiritual constitutes a limit to interiority: this is why the term 'intermediate world' can be given to the psychic. With respect to the plane, the vertical is reduced to an unextended point, the foot of the perpendicular: this means that the psychic plane cannot by itself gain access to the vertical of the spirit ("no man hath ascended into heaven, but he that descended from heaven, the Son of man who is in heaven" [John 3:13]). The unextended point is indeed the limit of an interiorization of space.

If now, instead of considering a determined being, we consider reality as a whole — but still, and inevitably, from the corporeal human state — we could depict the sum of the psychic worlds by an indefinite multitude of concentric circles contained within a single plane, whereas the rise into the intelligible will be depicted, for the sum of the spiritual hierarchies (that is, chiefly the angelic hierarchies), by the non-quantitative multiplicity of points of the vertical axis. If, from the animic plane, the spiritual world makes its appearance as a point, and therefore as something of the transcendent, in reality, each point of the vertical seen in itself and no longer from the psychic plane should be seen as a sphere, and all of these spheres, by projecting themselves on the animic plane, mark out the indefinite multitude of circles depicting the psychic worlds. As for the corporeal world, it will be represented by the circumference of the most exterior circle. This representation shows that in fact the psychic realm comprises an indefinite multitude of different regions, while the spiritual realm possesses a still greater breadth since it is 'raised' to the 'third power': the corporeal world is unique; the psychic world is an indefinite multitude; the spiritual world is transcendental, that is to say a non-quantifiable multiplicity.[27]

This representation also enables us to approximately depict the mode of existence of these different realms. The circumference, by

---

27 In Scholastic philosophy one distinguishes between *numerical multiplicity*, that of a quantity formed by a 'material' division of unities, and *transcendental multiplicity*, which is the result of a distinction of 'forms', none of which is another (angels, for example). This multiplicity is not numerable: cf. St. Thomas, *Summa Theologiae* I, q. 30, a. 3.

limiting the extension of the circle, obviously corresponds to the corporeal as the terminal mode of the psychic, as boundary-world. The circle, which organizes space around an actually trans-spatial center-point, corresponds to the psychic mode of existence, which realizes its self-consistency by a looping-back upon itself, by an individualizing coiling, organically tying together vital forces around a center that they cannot truly reach. The circle thus presents two contrary movements that dynamize the psychism: a movement of centrifugal expansion proper to its subtle nature on the one hand, and on the other a movement of centripetal contraction proper to the circle's organization in individual form, which is, in the realm of life, the expression of semantic unity. As for the metaphysical equivalence of the point and the sphere, it symbolizes at once the presence of self to itself (represented by the central point) implied by every real existence, and the unity by mutual immanence of a system of intelligible relations. Every point of the sphere (volume or surface) is, in fact, directly present to the center from which it emanates, as to its origin. The circle turns about its center, imitating, as much as possible, the unity of the center by a near-closure upon itself (a total closure would be equivalent to its death). The animic world is one of individual forms that are only themselves by isolating themselves from each other, by mutually excluding each other, or by reducing the other forms by absorption into their own substance. The sphere to the contrary radiates from its center, thus signifying that the intelligible world is, by essence, the world of *participables*, an open and shining world where each reality is itself by comprehending all the others: the intelligibles are distinct — without opposing or excluding or absorbing one another — not by their 'external' limitation, their individualizing organization, but by their own nature, their intrinsic quality, as one color is distinct from another color and makes it 'sing'.

3. The Problem of 'Inferior Worlds'

In the adopted geometric representation, we have accounted for the ascending vertical symbolizing the angelic hierarchies and the spiritual states, as well as the 'heavens' that correspond to them. The horizontal plane depicts the human state upon which is traced the circle of the individual psychism, with the corporeal circumference limiting its centrifugal expansion. But one element of this diagram remains unmentioned: the inferior branch of the vertical that the logic of the geometrical figure invites us to trace and which must therefore be taken into consideration. This segment can only correspond to the inferior states of the human being, which Roman tradition calls the hells (*inferna*, neuter plural of *infernus*: 'the depths', the 'lower regions', which serve to designate the abode of the dead). In this sense, the Apostles' Creed tells us that Christ "descended into hell," that is, unquestionably, to the abode of the just of all the nations,[28] dead before having been able to benefit from salvation in Christ. This involves then a relatively peripheral continuation of the human state, which cannot directly participate in the active and free centrality of living men: in this sense it is inferior. The hells or rather hell, in the singular, is assuredly the world of rebel angels. But we should also include here a multitude of degrees and beings which do not rightly stem from the *demonic*, and which, for this reason, we can characterize as *demon-like*.[29] These are beings and forces spoken of in the traditions of every land: fairies, genies, elves, leprechauns, djinn, kobolds, goblins, phantoms, etc., among which we can establish a hierarchy according to their greater or lesser proximity to the centrality of the human state. However, the distinction between demonic and demon-like is not always easy to make. This is why techniques putting man in touch with these beings and forces of the subtle world, as neutral as they might be, always exhibit an ambiguous character about which we need to be wary: magic, as 'white' as it might be, is only a rather inferior kind of knowledge. Illusion arises when the

28 This what the enigmatic formula of the first epistle of St. Peter (3:19–20) seems to indicate. Speaking of the descent into hell, it declares that Christ "coming . . . preached to those spirits that were in prison: which had been some time incredulous, when they waited for the patience of God in the days of Noe." The 'days of Noe' designate the sum total of humanity of which Noe is the father, and therefore the salvation of Jews and non-Jews alike. The covenant with Noe precedes, in fact, the covenant with Abraham, founder of the Jewish religion.

29 *Demon* comes from the Greek *daimon* which designates a 'spirit', a 'genie', an intermediary between the divine and human orders. Thus Plato speaks of the *daimon* of Socrates, which guides and inspires him on certain occasions. Of interest is the treatise by Plutarch (first century) titled *A Discourse concerning Socrates' Daemon*, in *The Morals*, vol. 2 (trans. W.W. Goodwin [Boston: Little, Brown, and Co., 1878]). Latinized in the second century, under the *daemon* form (Apuleius), the term will be used by Christian authors to designate the rebel angels and evil 'spirits'.

visible effects of these techniques (when they are produced) exceed the ordinary laws of the corporeal world, especially anything having to do with its material and spatial conditions. Deriving from a causality of a subtle nature, these phenomena are in fact exempt from these conditions as well as from the *temporal* mode of duration. But then, if this is so, how is it possible to cosmologically situate the demonic below the human state, which is subject to a greater number of conditions, insofar as we have characterized the corporeal as the boundary-world of reality? How could there actually be an infra-corporeal dimension?

The psychic world, as we have seen, is a world of life, and therefore of energy, dynamism, and movement. It is pervaded by and takes its bearings from two major tensions: one aspires to the centrality of which the psychism is itself devoid, the other aspires to spread and disperse itself. The attraction exerted by the spiritual center, the person-being, on the psychic sphere is in principle enough for maintaining it in a state individual in form: this is Adam in the earthly paradise. When this attraction was weakened by original sin, the centrifugal dynamic tended to prevail over the interiorizing dynamic, the psyche hoping to find its truth in exteriority as a whole. The risk of disindividualization made its appearance. This is what corporification, the 'garments of skin' in which God clothed Adam and Eve (Gen. 3:21), came to remedy. The body, the terminal mode of the psychic, stops or rather (relatively) stabilizes its spontaneous process of expansion, not precisely by enclosing it as if in a shell or crust but by fixing and condensing it in a corporeal medium in such a manner that the world then corporified. To the very extent that it is a psychism 'freed' from the unifying attraction of the inner man, the body 'saves' the soul from a dispersal into the indefinite; it puts an end (relatively) to its potential straying. Surely this natural salvation exacts a price, that of mortality, but it also offers the soul the possibility of a return to itself, of a conversion, of a 'gathering into the heart' (Luke 2:19) of supernatural salvation through the grace of Christ's crucified Body.

Thus we glimpse that what of sensible reality is not the object of a fixating corporification is exposed, by virtue of its own dynamism, to the risk of an indefinite mobility. Where natural forces and beings (or near-beings) are involved, this spontaneous dynamism is governed and regulated by the natural ministry of angels, the cosmic rectors. By this is found justified the use that certain sciences or techniques (acupuncture, homeopathy, radiesthesia, mineralogy, etc.) make of these subtle energies, in correspondence with certain bodies or certain bodily tendencies. There exists then an order of realities that, all while exceeding the ordinary possibilities of nature as we know it, forms however a part of universal nature: theology gives it the name 'preternatural'. But there is also a demonic or near-demonic preternatural where these realities escape from the jurisdiction of the angels, or where they fall under the jurisdiction of the rebel angels. Withdrawn from their alignment above, they are delivered to their own dispersive and *blind* sphere of influence. This is the world of 'forces in motion', one of 'wandering influences' mentioned in Chinese tradition, of 'desiring forms' in quest of an indeterminate center, offering their gyrovague activity as needed to the domination of infernal powers and to their will destructive of all nature.

Cosmologically, this preternatural, devilish, or demonic realm retains its defining properties: form, life, duration. It is less limited than the corporeal world. But this lesser limitation, this greater freedom, if not directed above and governed by the spiritual realities it ought to serve, is degraded and dispersed. This is why there is a lower psychic world, a world less limited than the corporeal, but for this very reason less perfect. The corporification that occurred after the fall, and that affects the totality of the human world, is a punishment with mortality as its consequence, but also a benefit and a mercy.

4. About the Judeo-Christian Tradition's Cosmology

Up to this point we have followed, as much as possible, a philosophical, that is to say inductive course: it starts with the data of human experience and goes back to the metaphysical principles that can account for it. The conclusions we have reached are not at all original; we rediscover traces of them in many if not all cultural traditions. The sole merit of a philosophical account is to make possible a 'realist' and 'scientific' interpretation of the symbolic formulations of ancient cultures. Too often, in fact, only visions of an entirely outmoded world are seen in the cosmological indications of these cultures, which is certainly the case when we take them in their most literal sense. But this sense is foreign to the spirit of traditional civilizations, not because they attribute to these indications only a purely figurative value, but because, for them, cosmological phenomena are inseparably the manifestation of subtle or spiritual realities,[30] in conformity moreover with our spontaneous intuition, for example when we speak of 'heaven'.

As a reminder, let us recall that the tradition of India presents an especially clean formulation of a tripartite cosmology: this is the doctrine of the *tribhuvana*, a term that signifies 'three worlds': *bhu*, the 'earth'; *bhuvar*, the space that goes from the earth to the sun; and *svar* or *svarga*, 'heaven', which goes from the sun to the pole star, the summit of the universe[31]: from bottom to top, in brief, the 'earth', the 'atmosphere', and 'heaven'. The 'earth' corresponds to the corporeal—or 'crude', 'solid', *sthula*—state; the 'air' corresponds to the animic—or psychic, 'subtle', *sukshma*—state; and 'heaven' corresponds to the spiritual, luminous, semantic, or angelic state, that of pure intellects—the 'causal' state, *karana* in Sanskrit—where we have the root *kr*, 'to do' as in *creare*, but understood here in the sense of a secondary cause.[32]

The doctrine of a tripartite cosmology is less clearly affirmed in Plato, where the duality of the sensible and the intelligible seem to predominate. And yet it is incontestably there. Between the 'intelligible region'—*topos noetos* (*Republic* VI, 508c; Plato never speaks of an 'intelligible *world*')—and the sensible (*aistheten*), there is a World Soul—or the world as Soul—the function of which is to enable the intelligible to be present in the sensible and move it according to the intelligible order (*Timaeus*, 30b). This intermediate situation of the cosmic Psyche, which seems sometimes identified with the intelligible Model and sometimes with the sensible and its becoming, sufficiently explains how the cosmological tripartition can be presented, according to the case, as a bipartition. We will find this oscillation again in anthropology.[33]

---

30 Cf. Jean Borella, *The Crisis of Religious Symbolism*, op. cit.

31 Renou et Filliozat, *L'Inde classique. Manuel des Études indiennes*, vol. i, §1126 (Paris: Maisonneuve, 1985), 547.

32 Rene Guénon, *Man and His Becoming according to the Vedanta*, trans. R. C. Nicholson (Ghent, NY: Sophia Perennis, 2001), 89–94.

33 On this most complex question, hardly touched on here, Jean Brun's article "Platon et l'Âme du monde" provides a penetrating synthesis; cf. *Sophia et l'Âme du monde*, Cahiers de l'Hermétisme, ed. Antoine Faivre and Frédéric Tristan (Paris: Albin Michel, 1983), 53–67. In the *Epinomis* (the authenticity of which is no longer disputed) Plato distinguishes: living earthly beings, living beings of fire or the stars (981e), and transparent and invisible living beings made of air, called *daïmones*, to which are added living beings made of water and aether. This doctrine is taken up

The Old Testament books never had the formulation of a precise cosmological doctrine as an object. However, and to the extent that the revelatory events and the texts that relate them (narratives, divine words, prophecies, prayers, etc.) unfold in the human world, they imply a cosmological setting, about which they cannot help but speak, and involve a certain conception of the universe. The Greek idea of the cosmos, which signifies 'order' (the contrary of *chaos*), is often contrasted with the Jewish idea of a world entirely dependent on the will of God, and which therefore has no proper order. This is incontestable. But Scripture in no way disregards the order of the world, celebrated as the work and proof of God's wisdom — Job 38, for example. Speaking of creatures, Psalm 103/104, verse 24, declares: "Thou hast made all things in wisdom."

Overall, the Jewish conception of the created universe is tripartite, even though the 'heaven-earth' binary predominates. But do not forget that in Hebrew 'heaven' is always in the plural: 'the heavens', something most translations do not take into account (the Septuagint and Vulgate for instance). This plural can be interpreted as the translation of a plurality of degrees possibly in relation to the angelic hierarchies. Besides, heaven and earth imply the intermediate space of the atmosphere. The cosmological tripartition in the first chapter of Genesis is also presented under a different form when the text mentions the separation of the "waters above" from the "waters below." Here we should see the separation of the higher from the lower possibilities of creation; "between these two parts the earth forms a great plateau" covered by the starry dome of the firmament.[34] Once more we find here the three worlds, the heavens, the earth, and the hells, which the Bible sometimes calls 'abysses'.

It also happens that these three worlds are explicitly related to 'heaven', 'air', and 'earth'. If we reserve 'heaven' for the divine world (which contains then, in an uncreated state, the archetypes of creatures, their purely intelligible models), 'air' would correspond to the subtle world, and the earth to the corporeal world. In this case, angelic creatures will inhabit an aerial abode and, as a consequence, will be of

---

again by Philo of Alexandria; cf. E. Bréhier, *Les idées philosophiques et religieuses de Philon d'Alexandrie* (Paris: Vrin, 1950), 126–33.

34 Xavier Léon-Dufour, *Dictionnaire du Nouveau Testament* (Paris: Seuil, 1975), 46.

a subtle nature. There is hardly any doubt that this doctrine is widely represented in the Jewish thought of the last centuries before Christ, as well as in the early Christian centuries. The *Book of Jubilees*, an Old Testament pseudepigraph (third century before Christ?), relates the creation of the angels on Day One; it tells us of "the angels of the presence, and the angels of sanctification, and the angels of the spirit of fire, and the angels of the spirit of the winds, and the angels of the spirit of the clouds and darkness and snow and hail and frost, and the angels of resoundings and thunder and lightning, and the angels of the spirits of cold and heat," etc.[35]

A text from Philo of Alexandria (20 before–50 after Christ) perfectly illustrates this point of view. In *De Somniis*, he comments on the vision of 'Jacob's ladder':

> By the ladder in this thing, which is called the world, is figuratively understood the air, the foundation of which is the earth, and the head is the heaven; for the large interior space, which being extended in every direction, reaches from the orb of the moon, which is described as the most remote of the order in heaven, but the nearest to us by those who contemplate sublime objects, down to the earth, which is the lowest of such bodies, is the air. This air is the abode of incorporeal souls.... Now philosophers in general are wont to call these demons, but the sacred scripture calls them angels, using a name more in accordance with nature.[36]

35 *The Old Testament Pseudepigrapha*, vol. 2, ed. J. H. Charlesworth (Garden City, NY: Doubleday, 1985), 55.

36 *De Somniis*, 134–35, 141, in *The Works of Philo Judæus*, vol. 2, trans. C. D. Yonge (London: Henry G. Bohn, 1854), 320–22. In *De Gigantibus* 2 (ibid., vol. 1, p. 331) Philo likewise teaches: "Those beings, whom other philosophers call demons, Moses usually calls angels; and they are souls hovering in the air." For the Kabbalah it seems that angels are also of a subtle nature. Indeed this doctrine envisions three worlds: the 'world of creation' (*Olam ha-Beriyah*), purely spiritual in nature; the 'world of formation' (*Olam ha-Yetsirah*), subtle in nature; and the 'world of fact' (*Olam ha-Asiyah*), corporeal in nature. However, the 'world of creation', that is to say of 'creative causes', analogous to *karana*, the 'causal state' of Hinduism, is not part of the created, but of the uncreated; cf. Leo Schaya, *The Universal Meaning of the Kabbalah*, trans. N. Pearson (Baltimore: Penguin Books, 1971), 69–70, 78, etc. Contrary to

This doctrine seems to identify purely and simply the Greek *daimones* and the angels of the Bible. Do we conclude from this that in reality, as many exegetes affirm, we cannot find in the Old Testament any attestation of the existence of beings intermediate between angels and men? Those beings we have called here demonic beings, "who are to be classed neither with the demons, the subjects of Satan, nor with the angels, the servants of God"?[37] The question is not easy to resolve. In the text cited from the *Book of Jubilees* — true, this is an apocryphal book — it is hard to rank 'angels of the presence' and 'angels of sanctification' in the same category as the 'angels of the spirit of the clouds', or those 'of snow and hail'. The very expression 'angels of the spirits' seems to refer to a category other than that of angels strictly speaking. Moreover, the term 'spirit' is found again in other Old Testament apocrypha, in *Enoch* for example (60:15–21) which attributes angels or spirits to the different elements of nature.[38]

The cosmology of the New Testament does not basically differ from that of first-century Judaism. It is therefore tripartite according to the two ternaries we have marked out: heaven, earth, subterranean, or: heaven, air, earth. Christ Himself generally keeps to the binary: heaven-earth. In Mark 13:27, however, He announces that He will gather the "elect from the four winds, from the uttermost part of the earth to the uttermost part of heaven": the four winds define the horizontal cross of the cardinal points with reference to the 'air' element, and "from the uttermost part of the earth to the uttermost part of heaven" raises the vertical of redemption.

We read of the ternary heaven-earth-hell in St. Paul in Philippians 2:10: "in the name of Jesus every knee should bow, of those that are in heaven, on earth, and under the earth"; likewise in St. John in

---

what Guénon suggests (*Man and His Becoming according to the Vedanta*, 49n7), the doctrine of the Kabbalah does not exactly coincide with that of the Vedanta. From the Catholic point of view (St. Augustine), there are essences *in divinis*, in the Word, the place of the possibles, and essences in the angelic world, as the 'seminal reasons' of psycho-corporeal creatures: essential continuity, ontological discontinuity: this is the doctrine to which we subscribe; cf. *Un homme une femme au Paradis* (Geneva: Ad Solem, 2008), 101.

37 Ferdinand Prat, *The Theology of Saint Paul*, 2 vols., trans. J. L. Stoddard (Westminster MD: Newman, 1946); here, 2:410.

38 *The Old Testament Pseudepigrapha*, vol. 1 (1983), 41; likewise: *2 Enoch*, 19:5, ibid., 132.

Apocalypse 5:3: "no man was able, neither in heaven nor on earth nor under the earth, to open the book." The ternary heaven-air-earth seems implied in Ephesians 2:2 when St. Paul speaks of "the prince of the power of this air." A little further on (6:12), he specifies that we have to struggle "not against flesh and blood," but "against the spirits of wickedness in the high places [*epouraniois*]."[39]

The world of the air is not inhabited solely by evil spirits. One might also see therein, we think, the realm of cosmic forces of an actually subtle natural. This is the sense we give to the much-debated expression 'elements of the world' in Colossians 2:8: "Beware lest any man cheat you by philosophy and vain deceit: according to the tradition of men according to the elements of the world [*stoikeia tou kosmou*] and not according to Christ." It is taken up again in 2:20–21: "If then you be dead with Christ from the elements of this world, why do you yet decree as though living in the world? Touch not: taste not: handle not." This has to do with more or less magical or superstitious practices that utilize corporeal elements — stones, diamonds, plants, etc. — or which obey numerological rules, astral observations — phases of the moon, lucky or unlucky days, etc. — so as to be in accord with the beings that inhabit them or control them, or again so as to be preserved from them. Galatians 4:3 and above all 4:9 seem to confirm this: "You served them who, by nature, are not gods. But now, after that you have known God, or rather are known by God: how turn you again to the weak and needy elements?"[40] These gods who are not so in reality, on whom Christ's coming and the taking of sides it imposes confer the quality of wicked beings, spirits of darkness, these are the '*cosmocratores*', the 'cosmic rulers' (Ephesians 6:12), who seem to us hard to purely and simply identify with rebel angels, and who surely must be situated between angels and men. But are we sure there is no scriptural evidence for this kind of being? In Luke 24:37, in the presence of the risen Jesus, the apostles "supposed that they saw a spirit." Christ tells

---

39 *Epouraniois* signifies 'that which is in heaven'. St. Augustine, in *De natura boni*, 33, specifies: This "is not that heaven in which there are stars, but this lower heaven by the smoke of which the clouds are conglobulated, and where the birds fly"; cf. *Cité de Dieu*, VI–IX (Paris: Desclée De Brouwer, 1959), 600, additional note 56.

40 Simon Légasse, *L'Épître de Paul aux Galates* (Paris: Cerf, 2000), 293 and 312ff., discusses at length the meaning of these expressions.

them: "Handle, and see: for a spirit hath not flesh and bones." The existence of such spirits is not then denied by Christ. And, in Acts of the Apostles 23:8–9, the category of spirits is distinguished from that of angels. And in Hebrews 1:14 'spirit' defines the genus of which the angel is a 'ministerial' species dedicated to serving God.

We can dwell no further on a question that it is easier to cautiously disentangle than to treat to its full extent. Beyond all doubt the category of the demonic, which Jews and Christians found in Greek culture, was a source of embarrassment for them.

This is why, in the first and second centuries, the general trend is to simply classify the 'demon-like' with the demonic.[41] However, philosophy attests to the existence of 'good demons', of 'good genies' intervening in the lives of famous and virtuous men, like Socrates. Speculating on a text from Apocalypse 20:1–3, revealing that God has chained the devil for a thousand years in the abyss, some Doctors have concluded that, although the intermediate region is the ordinary abode of demons,[42] at the end of the world they will be cast into the infernal abyss beneath the earth. Both cosmological ternaries are thus combined. This is because this aerial abode poses a problem for the Christian theologian. The air being above the earth, the beings abiding there are superior to mankind, which inhabits an earthly abode; moreover, these beings are endowed with properties not possessed by men. We must then at once account for the superiority that their subtle nature confers on them and for their 'moral' inferiority with respect to good and virtuous men. It was towards this notion that St. Augustine, who devotes almost the entirety of books 8 and 9 of the *City of God* to the question of demons, was working.[43] Far from denying their reality, or even that 'good demons' might exist,[44] he strives to establish that they can in no manner be regarded as

---

41 Cf. Jean Daniélou, *Gospel Message and Hellenistic Culture*, trans. J. A. Baker (London/Philadelphia: Darton, Longman & Todd/Westminster Press, 1973), 427–41; also: *Les origines du christianisme latin* (Paris: Cerf, 1978), 323–40.

42 St. Jerome, in connection with Ephesians 6:12, writes: "The opinion of all the Doctors is that this air separating heaven and earth is found in the middle, and what is called empty is filled with hostile powers"; cited (in Latin) by Dom Augustin Calmet, *Dictionnaire de la Bible*, vol. 2 (Paris, 1730), 265.

43 Trans. H. Bettenson (New York: Penguin Books, 1972), 298–370.

44 *City of God*, IX, 13, 3; Bettenson, 358–59.

mediators to whom a Christian might have recourse, Christ being the sole Mediator. On the other hand, the role played by demons in magic keeps them from serving as intermediaries between men and God.[45] What remains is that God "permitted [them] to occupy not the pure realm of air above, but the misty air near earth, and this is a sort of prison house for them, in keeping with their nature, until the day of judgment."[46] At the end of the world all creatures will occupy the rank and the place that is their due.

5. The Cosmic Order and the 'Christ' Event

The doctrinal development carried out by St. Augustine and several other Christian writers during the early centuries, with the intention of matching, as much as possible, the teachings of revelation with those of Platonism — Plato's as well as the Neoplatonists': Plotinus, Porphyry, Apuleius, etc. — very nearly ended up with the following conception. There was first the heaven of the stars (sun, moon, stars) to possibly set in rapport with the angels, the beings of light. The stars being for Plato living fiery beings identified with the 'gods',[47] the outcome is that the gods of the Platonic religion — what some call his 'astral theology' — these living, immortal, blessed and always good beings in reality correspond, according to St. Augustine, to the angels spoken of in Scripture: "The fact that they gave the name 'gods' to creatures who are immortal and blessed in the above sense, there is here no dispute between us [and the Platonists], simply because we can find in our sacred Scriptures such quotations as: 'The Lord, the lord of gods, has spoken' (Psalm 49:1)."[48] The world of the air

---

45   Ibid., VIII, 19; Bettenson, 325ff.

46   *The Literal Meaning of Genesis*, Bk. 3, ch. 10; trans. J. H. Taylor (Mahwah, NJ: Paulist Press, 1982), 84.

47   *Laws* X, 899a; *Epinomis* 982a, etc.

48   *City of God* IX, 23; Bettenson, 368–69. A difficulty presents itself here. The stars are 'visible gods', just as Plato notes in *Laws* as well as *Epinomis*, as opposed to the *daimones*, whereas angels are invisible creatures. However, of these 'visible gods' we only see the body, which is composed of æther. Must this body be joined to a soul? It seems that Augustine's thinking remained undecided on the point; cf. 'Les âmes des astres', note 13 in *La Genèse au sens littéral*, Oeuvres de saint Augustin 48, 1 (Paris: Desclée De Brouwer, 1972), 612–14. Do not forget, though, that in having the star-gods of Plato correspond to the angels of Scripture, Augustine is proposing an interpretation correcting astral theology and not saying that the two are identical.

comes next—the temporary abode of the demons—and lastly the world of humanity's earth.

There is much that remains obscure in this pairing between the Judeo-Christian and Platonic cosmological traditions. Might it be brought to a good conclusion? It does not seem so. The question was obviously not posed for the sacred writers who, under the guidance of the Holy Spirit, have written down the texts of the First Testament: they have, as regards cosmology, and to the extent they were led to make mention of it, only that one common to the whole Middle East, however completely reoriented according to the demands of strict monotheism and creationism. They have no concern for an unknown or poorly known philosophical tradition, and little interest, if any, in cosmology as such. This perhaps explains why, when a Jewish philosopher such as Philo of Alexandria, however faithful and profoundly 'biblical' he might be, elaborates a philosophical interpretation of Judaism, he seems to experience no difficulty in espousing the cosmological concepts of Platonism which do not come into conflict with those non-existent, or very nearly so, cosmological concepts of his Jewish faith. In addition, this cosmology, where Stoic and Neopythagorean terms are combined with a Platonic substratum, had grown so widespread at this time, at Alexandria especially, that it was quite commonplace and implied no particular commitment on the part of those who adopted it.[49]

For a Christian, the question is posed differently because of the incarnation of Christ. Greek cosmology is essentially (at least in its guiding intention) a representation of the *order* of the world. This entails that everything found there is ruled according to this order and defined, as to its nature and its function, by considerations of order, especially within the cosmic 'situation'. Christ's incarnation, to the contrary, is a unique, transcendent *event*, an unforeseeable and 'anomalous' divine story that introduces a radical break in continuity into the cosmic order, and which, by this very fact, disrupts the cosmos and changes the nature of beings and things, or at least modifies it. *We* do

---

49 We are following Father A. J. Festugière: *La Révélation d'Hermès Trimégiste*, vol. 2, *Le Dieu cosmique* (Paris: Les Belles Lettres, 1986), 518–85; "in this great cosmopolitan city [Alexandria] . . . a Jew could preserve the pure monotheism of his faith while employing the language of astral polytheism" (585). In the proper sense of the term, the stars and heaven are ranked by Philo in the category of 'false gods'; Festugière, 569n3.

not say this; it is St. Paul and the entire New Testament. We have here something remarkable in the history of religions. The divine descents (*avatara*) spoken of by eastern traditions concern the human world and, far from disrupting the cosmic order, have for a function its reestablishment: the *Bhagavad Gita* teaches that the Lord manifests himself when "the Dharma totters," or, according to another translation, "each time *order* falters."[50] Whereas, in His redemptive and transforming manifestation, Christ traverses all worlds, from empyrean heaven to the depths of hell. This cosmic traversal is an 'event' for all worlds and reorders the organization of all creation with respect to itself: nothing is any longer as before, everything changes meaning. In a certain manner, the incarnation of the Word in the flesh of Christ, in whom "dwelleth all the fulness of the Godhead *corporeally*" (Col. 2:9), is the end of the world: all the angelic hierarchies, all aerial and earthly beings no longer have their significance in themselves, according to the neutrality of their topological situation, but are called to enter the service of the sole Mediator, for "heaven and earth will pass away." In this way a certain 'diabolizing' of the aerial spirits is justified; surely a relative diabolization, and one which a cosmology concerned for the nature of things can only relativize,[51] but clearly one which should also have its significance. The order of things in their natural consistency surely continues to have its validity, and accounting for this is cosmology's duty, but, at the same time, creation as a whole is wounded with a salutary wound by the cross of Christ.

This is why there cannot be, it seems, a complete cosmology in the Christian order of things. Within itself the cosmos has been signed with the cross of Christ and broken asunder with an eye to its redemption, with an eye to the new heavens and the new earth. An entirely systematized doctrine of the world cannot be found then in Christian tradition. However, as incomplete and imperfect as our explanation might be, perhaps it will be of help in understanding that this is a real and relevant question, and not just a scholarly point concerning the

50   *La Bhagavad-Gita* IV, 7; trans. A. M. Esnoul and O. Lacombe (Paris: Seuil, 1976), 54.

51   There are two points to stress: the traditional sciences cannot be denied either their high degree of development or the possible reality of the effects of their application; on the other hand, as proven by the example of St. Hildegard of Bingen, their use is not solely derived from diabolism.

history of Judeo-Christian doctrines. This is because in truth (and we will come back to this point in Part 5 of this work), we can have no authentic cosmology without taking angelology into account. Even more, it is the mode of angelic knowledge that 'defines' creation as cosmos.[52] Moreover it is the angels who, as secondary causes, are the basis for the possibility of intra-cosmic causations. This is what St. Paul affirms when, as we have noted, he speaks of the 'rulers of the world'. We do not in fact encounter, on the corporeal level, anything to account for causality: all we find there is a step-by-step determinism. Now the causal power implies the passage of the action of one being on to another, and an action consistent in the transmission of a structuring and organizing form to a sum total of indefinitely multiplied material unities. Its efficacy would be inexplicable if it were to be reduced to the contact, at a particular instant, of a particular unity with another one. Being necessarily trans-spatial and trans-temporal, because finalized, causal action therefore requires the assistance of an agent equally superior to space and time, at least in the earthly mode of duration. The angel is this agent.

And yet it is not only angels that are required in a true cosmology as 'semantic beings' and 'cosmic rulers', it is also and more radically the *Logos*, the place of the possibles, the principle of semantics and the absolute unity of all things, as St. Paul teaches in Colossians 1:15–17: Christ "is the image of the invisible God, *the firstborn of every creature*: for in him were all things created in heaven and on earth, visible and invisible, whether thrones, or dominations, or principalities, or powers. All things were created by him and in him. And he is before all: and by him all things subsist." The "firstborn of every creature" means the *Logos* is the prototype of all the created that pre-exists in Him, the Word, the place of the possibles; "all things were created by him and in him" means that creation, in its totality and each one of its beings, is appointed to Christ as to its true end: "by him all things subsist" means "without him all creatures would be scattered, crumble to pieces."[53] The Word is the ontological bond, the principle of unity, the principle of 'internal cohesion' (this is

---

52 This proposition is explained especially in *Un homme une femme au paradis* (ch. 10) — and has, we think, a decisive *philosophical* importance.

53 Prat, *Theology of Paul*, 1:291.

the meaning of the word *sunestheken* translated here by 'subsist').

However, even though the 'Christ-event' marks the universe as a whole with the disruptive sign of its transcendence, it does not fundamentally abolish its tripartite structure. This ordering still forms the cosmological setting for the Christian soul's spiritual ascension, as we see in St. Paul when he tells of his rapture "to the third heaven" identical to "paradise" (2 Cor 12:2–4), that is to the divine world. He is referring to the 'celestial' tripartition of ancient Judaism[54] which distinguishes between a first aerial heaven, next a second heaven, that of the stars, and lastly the heaven of God. This celestial tripartition is as if the matrix for the cosmic tripartition, which is itself as if its consequence, which is repeated harmonically at the core of each world, and in which we can see the reflection of the trinitarian structure of the Divine Essence: the Father corresponding to the divine heaven, the Son-Logos to the heaven of the stars, symbol of the intelligible, and the Holy Spirit to the aerial heaven where the birds — and the dove — fly. And now we will rediscover this universal vibratory structure of creation, which "sings the glory of God," in anthropology, in this microcosm that is man, in whom is summarized the order of things, but in whom also resides a mystery greater than the world.

III. THE ANTHROPOLOGICAL TRIPARTITION[55]

1. The Primordial State of Man

The preceding considerations seemed to draw us away from our subject. Yet this detour was needed to explain anthropological doctrine

---

54 Cf. *The Testament of Levi*, 3:1–8; *The Old Testament Pseudepigraphia*, vol. 1, 788–9, where we find a rather clumsy attempt to combine the tradition of the three heavens with a more recent one (it does not date back further than the second century after Christ) of the seven heavens (likewise to be met with in the Kabbalah). For a more extensive treatment, see our annotation on the *Commentary on the Second Epistle to the Corinthians* by St. Thomas Aquinas (Paris: Cerf, 2005), 266.

55 Since first publishing these pages on the 'body-soul-spirit' ternary, the issue has been taken up again and considerably developed by Michel Fromaget in a series of remarkable and very incisive works. We will cite *Corps, Âme, Esprit: Introduction à l'anthropologie ternaire* (Paris: Albin Michel, 1991); *L'homme tridimensionnel* (Paris: Albin Michel, 1996); *Dix essais sur la conception anthropologique "Corps, Âme, Esprit"* (Paris: L'Harmatan, 2000); *La drachme perdue* (Paris: Éditions Grégoriennes, 2010); *Modernité et Désarroi, ou l'âme privée d'esprit* (Paris: Le Mercure Dauphinois, 2007).

objectively. Man is a being of nature and therefore exhibits a structure analogous to that of all created beings. In him there is a corporeal, psychic, and spiritual reality. We shall call these three 'parts' of man body, soul, and spirit; in Latin: *corpus, anima,* and *spiritus.* This involves, as we stated, three realities of a different nature, or better put, one and the same reality, spiritual in nature, the animic and corporeal modalities of which, originally included in it as possibilities, are actualized as such in a separated state (or nearly separated state, for a total separation would be equivalent to non-existence pure and simple).

If we wish to represent this principial state of man, we could picture it under the form of a sphere, that of the spirit, including another smaller sphere within itself, that of the psychism, closing itself about a point, the center of the two preceding spheres and corresponding to the body. Thus the body appears as an infinitesimal modality of principial man's spiritual reality. But it also appears as what is most interior and most secret in the spirit.

This principial man corresponds to the first Adam of the first account of the creation, the Adam created in the image and likeness of God. The second account of man's creation already represents a cosmic descent to the properly subtle level. The pneumatic sphere no longer envelops the animic and corporeal spheres. On the contrary, the *pneuma* (the spiritual) is breathed *into* the body, and man, by this insufflation, becomes a 'living soul'. This clearly signifies that the pneumatic is the principle of the psychic (which is therefore its effect), but also that the psychic becomes the general form of humanity. Finally Original Sin is the cause of a second cosmic descent, this time to the corporeal level: "their eyes were opened and they saw that they were naked." The body is no longer clothed with the soul, nor is it only a subtle modality, but is corporified and envelops the soul: "And God made for Adam and his wife *tunics of skin* and He clothed them with them." This is the actualization of the corporeal modality properly so-called, such as we presently know it, the tunics of skin symbolizing the corporeal form which envelops the subtle form.[56] At the time of

---

56 This interpretation, which seems 'preposterous' to our contemporaries, is however traditional for the Greek Fathers, particularly St. Gregory of Nyssa. The strictly anthropological texts of the Old Testament will be studied later (in ch. 9), but it is obviously impossible not to make any allusion to it, even in a purely

this process of progressive externalization, the order of the anthropological spheres is therefore reversed; the corporeal sphere envelops the animic sphere which in turn envelops the pneumatic sphere. The latter appears then in its turn as an infinitesimal point, and, if these spheres are projected onto a horizontal plane, two concentric circles are obtained (the corporeal surrounding the psychic), with the spiritual point at the center corresponding to the trace of the ascending vertical. Also, notice how the animic sphere always occupies an intermediate situation, whereas, the corporeal and the spiritual having exchanged their respective positions, we grasp the direct relationship that unites them and thus understand how the body is truly the visible symbol of the invisible spirit. Restoring the principial Adam will consist then in rendering the spirit corporeal and the body spiritual. This is the teaching of numerous mystical schools.

2. Anima-Corpus

However, as total as this reversal might be, it would not go as far as a complete negation of normal relationships among these three spheres. The spiritual dimension of man which envelops him like a nimbus of glory, that is to say which irradiates the deiformity of his nature — this dimension has not disappeared; it is reduced to a pinpoint trace, to a germ then, or even to a virtual state: man no longer possesses its actuality (the coming of Christ will be necessary for the door of our interior heaven to be opened). Man is by nature then a living soul, and it is this actual nature which he transmits to his descendants; everything that transcends this psychic nature belongs to the supernatural. Furthermore, although the body envelops the soul, it has not ceased, and for good reason, being only a modality of it. Rather than body, we should speak of a psychic body or even a soul-body.

The Latin language offers us an interesting possibility in this respect. The word *soul* possesses two Latin equivalents: *anima* and *animus*. It seems that the word *anima* encompasses rather well the sum total of psychic functions connected by themselves, directly or indirectly, to the body, and from which the body, as a matter of fact,

---

philosophical process, at least by way of illustration. The image of material tunics to designate the body is likewise encountered in the Platonic tradition: cf. Proclus, *Eléments de Théologie*, intro. and trans. J. Trouillard (Paris: Aubier, 1964), 187 n209.

is not completely separable. Basically this is what, in Western tradition, is called the vegetative soul (symbolized in the Bible by the belt of fig-leaves) and the animal or sensitive soul (symbolized by the tunics of skin). We shall take up, then, this topic of the *anima-corpus* pair.

However, even though the *anima* is more or less directly linked to the body, it includes functions that are, in themselves, purely psychic. These are the affective functions: sentiments, passions, emotions. They arise from the sensitive (or animal) soul — there is also an affectivity among the higher mammals — and are linked to the body, or rather the body participates in their manifestation while actualizing them symbolically on its own plane; but they are not corporeal. Even more, they constitute for man what is most truly psychic; they bring to awareness the psychism in its most essential activity. In its primary nature the psychism is in fact tension, tendency towards, movement, impulse, life. This dynamic nature of the psychism is not however sheer activity. To the contrary: this activity is a reactivity, this action is a reaction. Animic substance is thus defined by tensions oriented according to an action-passion bi-polarity; its very activity presupposes a former passivity; the soul only acts because it has been first *touched*, *struck*. True, it reacts in conformity with the nature of the forces that are in it, but these forces are only moved or unleashed because the soul first experiences itself as preeminently 'touchable', threatened, exposed, excitable, submissive, in other words as able to be "affected."[57] Therefore, the soul being essentially affectivity, it follows that rest, peace, or serenity, would not be found at this level.[58]

57 Psychologists think that fear is the basic emotion. There is some truth to this thesis in the sense that, for man, the soul becomes aware of itself as something which is 'affectable'. The response to this awareness is anger, which is the original form of psychic dynamics. The corresponding virtue, which is to say the successful response, the soul controlled in its first impulse by a specifically human effort, is courage. In fact, each time there is an effort to control a natural movement, there is man. We therefore have the triad: fear, anger, and courage, which defines man on his most natural level. Remarkably enough then, what we call affectivity, Plato calls irascible soul, and the word for courage in Greek is *andreia*. Now *andreia* is pre-eminently the virtue of man (*aner, andros* in Greek), a little like saying 'manness'; cf. *vir* in Latin (man in the masculine) and 'virility' in English.

58 When we say that the soul is tension, this should be understood of the fallen soul. The Fall being an inversion in many respects, it follows that the animic substance of principial man is not tension but peace, symbolized by the surface of tranquil water, which is to say the reabsorption of tensions in an undifferentiated equilibrium.

3. Self-conviction

As we shall soon see more directly, the affective soul is the realm of
'self'. But one may have understood already that the self is 'engendered' by the conviction of being affected or, if one likes, 'concerned':
what is 'self' is what is 'touched'. The self arises from the wound-
ing of the soul. In fact, when something reaches the soul, the soul
finds itself something pursued, and therefore different from whatever
comes towards it, a center of interiority facing an environment of
exteriority. Such is 'self-conviction'. A totally unaffected soul would
have no self-conviction and would in no way distinguish between an
interior and an exterior. This is probably the case with the soul of a
tree. To the contrary, if we for example endure mockeries, sarcasms,
or reproaches, or if something threatens us, then a point in our chest
becomes suddenly sensitive, we are 'struck to the heart', a feeling of
self bursts out painfully within us and our hand is brought to the
center of our chest to startle or accuse us.[59]

Yet the simple fact that the soul is 'affectable' is not enough to
explain the advent of the self. Knowledge of this 'affectability' is necessary. This knowledge is, moreover, presupposed throughout the
course of the preceding description. Affectivity is not only felt, it is
also known and thought, and without this it could not even be spoken of. A merely felt affectivity would be a simple fact, incapable of
engendering self-conviction, and would seem just as 'objective and
natural' as a chemical process within a cell. Not only is affectivity
needed as 'matter' for the self, but also the *idea* of this affectivity in
order to give it 'form'. The self is a thinking affectivity, that is to say
no longer a fact but a structure. In fact, to think about affectivity
is to do what we have just done, is to formulate the intelligible (or
conceivable) structure subjacent to affective experience: in thinking
about affective experience, the soul 'thinks about itself' as interior
center opposed to an exterior environment, and there is the self. The
idea of a center of interiority does not come from affectivity as such,
but from thinking, which alone is truly 'interior' with respect to the
world of psychic energies, because it alone is truly distinct, being not

59 Not without reason is the affective soul related to the chest (in Plato, for
example) and the vegetative soul to the stomach.

a force but a light. This then is its true 'situation' which it projects in some manner on any thinking about experience. And yet pure thought, reduced to itself, could not engender self-conviction either. Such a thought is actually not in itself 'subjective', it does not posit itself as a subject; it is simply awareness (or knowledge) and, as such, is objective, transparent, neutral: the thought of a triangle or the thought about a feeling does not, by itself, harbor any self-affirmation. At this level awareness is nothing but the property that the human psychism has of knowing itself — so that, paradoxically, the object of awareness, the affective psychism, seems to be, under the light of our consciousness, a subjectivity. Thus our description sheds light upon the ambiguity of the self; our awareness being unable to separate itself from the object known, the self arising from their union sometimes presents itself as a thinking subject (awareness), sometimes as an existing subject (the affective soul). Subjectivity is to be seen at once as the *conscious pole* of our being and as the *being pole* of our consciousness.

4. The 'Animus' or Mental Soul

If we represent the psychism as water, thinking consciousness could be depicted as light reflected in the water and penetrating it, at least to a certain degree of depth. This image has the merit of showing that thought is immanent to the psychism, but yet distinguished from it since it is not water. To us this psychic light seems to correspond to the Latin term *animus*, and we shall call it the mental soul. This soul characterizes man as such and distinguishes him from all other beings.

It is not easy to define the mental soul, but it involves the psychism's cognitive modality. To describe it we shall use the image of the mirror, for the specific nature of this knowledge seems to be its indirect character. The mentality 'reflects' what it knows, or again, to know for it is to reflect its object of knowledge. Our mentality (or thinking) does not penetrate the object in its own essence, but it is rather the object that 'penetrates' our mentality, not as such but as an abstraction. The object 'informs' the cognitive soul, but, by receiving this information within itself, the soul clothes it with its own subtle nature. What is known is, of course, not the abstraction, it is the object; but this object is known by way of abstraction. If one prefers, the mentality is the 'refracting medium' through which the object is known.

Knowledge is achieved then by 'mental impression'; the mentality is a mirror reflecting the world. Thus, as already observed in connection with culture, this indirect or reflecting character of human knowledge introduces between man and the world what Ruyer calls a 'psychic distance'[60] which establishes the possibility of the symbol. The intelligible, or rather at this level we would have to say the conceivable, does not only exist in things but also, in some way, 'in itself', thanks to human knowledge, about which it might be said that in a certain manner it actualizes, in a separated state, the intelligible modality of things. This is not only a 'thinking about something', but a thinking *at* or *on* something. This possibility of the symbol is realized essentially in language, which does not consist chiefly in expressing something, which the animal does, but in speaking *about* something, which no animal is able to do.[61] And, since to speak *about* something is to speak of something that is 'absent' and which, for this reason, is represented, we see that mental awareness implies not only conceptual thought, but also memory and imagination, a function of absence in time and space. All of this is the *animus*.

5. Reason is Obedience

However, mental knowledge not only receives and elaborates 'impressions', it organizes them among themselves by connecting them according to set relationships imposed as rules on our mental world.[62] Altogether these rules constitute the very architecture of our mentality: this is what reason is. In fact, reason originally meant 'relationship'. Notice that even in this activity our mental state remains, if not passive, at least submissive. Actually, and this is a very important point, the mind's rational structure seems, to the mind itself, an inexplicable 'foreign' presence. If turned toward its object — even if this object is our own soul — our mind reflects those exterior or interior

60 Cf. R. Ruyer, *L'Animal, l'Homme et la Function symbolique* (Paris: Gallimard, 1964).

61 Ibid., 95. This fundamental principle of every true philosophy of language is explained in *Histoire et théorie du symbole* (Lausanne: l'Âge d'Homme, 2004), 123–28. All discussions of animal language rest either on a misunderstanding or on the desire to amaze the ignorant.

62 This distinction is not unconnected to that between *vasanas* and *samskaras*; cf. O. Lacombe, *L'Absolu selon le Vedanta* (Paris, Guethner, 1966), 134–35.

worlds imposed on it; when it turns towards its own internal structure, it discovers — and experiences — another demand, imposed on it with equal authority: reason, that is to say the coherent set of logical principles governing all human knowledge.

Our mental world is thus situated between two demands, one external and the other internal, between two objectivities, that of things — even psychic substance — and that of logical relationships. True, this dual obedience is hardly conscious, and therefore hardly voluntary. And yet it does not proceed without will altogether. It can be interrupted; the mentality can be in revolt, in the depths of itself, against this submission to logical principles as well as against the nature of things. Reason is *obedience* first; folly is *denial* and *insurrection* first. Reason, in its most precise definition, is first the relationship of mental subordination to the logical principles within it. But sometimes the rational 'propensity' becomes burdensome, the mental soul tires of obeying what it does not altogether understand, and, breaking the original pact with its own internal structure, which education had helped to form, develop, and maintain, it unbinds itself with and abandons itself to the chaotic multiplicity of its own contents.[63]

6. The Intellect or Intuitive Knowledge

In its ordinary exercise, mental knowledge is subject to reason; the mental soul could just as well be termed then the rational soul. As we have seen, this knowledge proceeds according to a double need: it goes from the order of the world to reason and from the order of reason to the world. These two directions are bound up with the concept which is the means, the mediation of this knowledge. As a result, this approach can be characterized as discursive, discursion signifying a process subject to duality, to division. Actually, knowledge itself is not discursive, but rather its process is, a process that perpetually confronts the demands of things with the demands for reason and vice-versa. For knowledge in itself, considered at whatever level, can only be intuitive in the end, that is to say 'vision' (or hearing), a direct and unitive perception of its object.

63 Obviously this doctrine concerns a good number of psychic illnesses; but we cannot develop these applications.

That knowledge is only intuitive, and not the conclusion of some reasoning process, is clear. To know is to 'see what is'. Besides, it is impossible to define knowledge; it is primary, irreducible, and ungenerated. We must be content with metaphors such as vision. Still, such a metaphor is only adequate because vision is itself a knowledge, or rather one of the sensible modes of knowledge. What is not intuitive is the process of gaining knowledge, as well as the establishment of its validity. The mind proceeds discursively, by inquiry, reasoning, deduction, only for what it does not know. But knowledge, in its own activity, can only be a direct reception of intelligible data. Discursive inquiry can last as long as one likes; it can be supported by every possible guarantee of the most rational criteriology. After all, we have to have confidence in this cognitive act by which a known object is directly united with a knowing subject in a kind of mutual transparency. This is the very experience of the intelligible. Otherwise, and whatever the philosophy professed, we do not see how we could gain any knowledge whatsoever, even of the most elementary kind.

We give to that which knows in us the name of intelligence, or intellect. Now, with the intellect, we enter a realm not yet encountered, whose nature seems to differ greatly from psycho-corporeal reality. In the psycho-corporeal realm individuality and existence are on equal footing. Unquestionably the psycho-corporeal exists; it moves, acts, reacts, desires for the same reason as all natural beings, like a distinct being among all of the distinct beings, making up an organization closed upon itself. This existence is life for an individual.[64] With knowledge we seem to be outside of existence because outside of the individual. We said that knowledge, the activity of the intellect, was a direct and unitive perception of being. This implies a near-absolute transparency of the intellect to all it receives into itself, that is to say a near-absolute openness, and not the closure upon itself realized by individual existence. From the side of the known object, on the other hand, it is clear that what is received into the intellect is not its own being, but the intelligible modality of its own being, stripped of its own individual existence,[65] which by definition remains impenetrable. The act of knowledge is therefore realized only at the price of a kind of derealization.

64 At this level, to exist = to live.
65 It would be more accurate to say: of its own individual *act* of existence.

And yet knowledge is indeed real, even a pre-eminent function of the real. There is being only for knowledge. If we had to give a definition for the intellect we would say it is the sense of the real. Just as 'sugared' and 'salted' are only meaningful to the tongue, just as 'visible' and 'audible' are only meaningful to the eye and ear, so the 'real' is only meaningful to the intellect—and therefore the intellect is the faculty for distinguishing real from unreal.[66] It is hardly possible to account for this paradoxical situation of the intellect—at once outside of the real and bound up with it—other than by admitting that the light illuminating it comes from elsewhere, that it is of another nature and of another degree of reality than the plane on which it is manifested. This is why it can be represented as a point, found at the center of the mental soul, indicating the trace of the vertical axis.

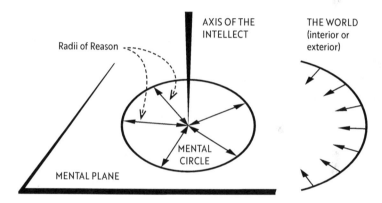

The cognitive content of the intellect exceeds the degree of reality of its manifestation; in other words, its content is transcendent of it. We end up then with the following representation: the mentality is figured by the surface of a circle whose center is the intellect, while the

---

66 This statement represents an irrefutable 'proof' of supreme divine Reality: the existence of intelligence proves God because, in the last analysis, God or the absolutely Real is the true content implicit in all our intellectual acts. This argument might also be formulated in the following manner: no one can deny, without contradiction, the existence of empirical natural reality. Now this reality, being relative, lacks reality; therefore there is an absolute Reality both transcendent to nature and its basis. Do not be fooled by this 'syllogistic' form: what we have here is intellectual evidence that language can only express anything discursively. This is not a demonstration of the existence of God; it is a statement intended to make everyone aware of how he is constantly affirming God.

radii which emanate from it correspond to reason. This image clearly illustrates the respective nature of each of these cognitive functions. In conformity with the architectonic and regulating role of reason, the radii order and measure the mental circle, and join the periphery to the center (*ratio* = relation). On the other hand they are the emanation of the center, or the reflection on the surface of the mental waters (the *animus*) of the intellect's vertical axis, whose meeting-point with the psychic domain is the center of the circle. By this may be grasped why the principles of reason are imposed non-discursively upon the mental soul: this is because they reflect, in fact, a supra-mental light, whose evidence will manifest itself then as a constraint.[67] Lastly, the characteristic mental function shown by the surface of the circle is the formation of an appropriately human 'environment' where all knowledge is refracted, an environment which invests this knowledge with an abstract form. But the content of knowledge taken in itself is of the intelligible order: it is realized when the external intelligible (the world) enters into contact with the internal intelligible (the intellect) and wherein both are mutually actualized in the common act of knowledge.

7. Intellect and Reason

By the above we see what distinguishes reason from intellect (in Greek: *dianoia* from *nous*). True, this distinction does not go as far as a total separation, since *ratio* is the broken and fragmented light of *intellectus*. But they should not be confused, nor should we deny either mode of cognitive activity. This is just what many philosophers have done, however. And, although in the present chapter we only intend to follow the thread of philosophical analysis without reference to particular doctrines, nevertheless, because we are steeped in a profoundly deformed culture and because our vocabulary is affected by this, some historical allusions are necessary here.

The non-distinction between *intellectus* and *ratio* seems to come from Descartes. In the *Second Metaphysical Meditation*, where he undertakes to prove that the soul's nature is more easily known than

---

67 Modern mathematics, for example, has demonstrated the impossibility of demonstrating the principle of non-contradiction (Gödel's theorem). This principle is therefore an intuitively imposed truth.

the body's, Descartes, after establishing the existence of this former nature, asks in what it consists and he answers: *Sum igitur res cogitans, id est mens, sive animus, sive intellectus, sive ratio*, that is: "therefore I am a thinking thing, or again a spirit, or again a soul, or again an intellect, or again reason." The problem with this text is not the equivalence established between *mens* and *animus*, for there is a long tradition of using such an equivalence and it is to be met with in various cultures.[68] But it is otherwise for *intellectus* and *ratio*, terms almost constantly distinguished in prior philosophical tradition.

As for the negation of *intellectus*, or the intuitive intellect, this is the work of Kantian philosophy. Endeavoring to assume a critical consciousness of reason (*The Critique of Pure Reason*), Kant did not perceive in it this power of intuitive knowledge (*intellectus intuitivus*) with which Descartes endowed it (*sive intellectus, sive ratio*). And since there is no *intellectus*, no metaphysics is possible: "Intellectual intuition . . . is not ours, and [its] possibility . . . is precluded from our insight."[69] Reason (*Vernunft*) becoming then the higher faculty of knowledge, Kant is led to invert the relationship which the whole prior philosophical tradition had accepted and to call understanding (*Verstand, intellectus*) the lower cognitive activity, that is, the activity that invests sensible knowledge with a conceptual or, in our terms, mental form. From an initial confusion to negationist inversion, this is the path followed by the West's intellectual decadence.

8. Intellectus *and* Ratio *in* St. Augustine *and* St. Thomas Aquinas

To grasp the true distinction between *intellectus* and *ratio* and the just subordination which ought to be established between them, a quick look at the more than one-thousand-year-old philosophical tradition of the Latin West will suffice.

St. Augustine is quite clear about this distinction. His doctrine is simple: although human knowledge begins with the reason which

---

68   In Sanskrit, for example, the word *manas* can designate: 1. mentality (thinking activity, the internal sense); 2. individual consciousness; 3. spirit or intellect (which is rather expressed by *buddhi*, however).

69   *The Critique of Pure Reason*, trans. W. Schwarz (Aalen: Scientia Verlag Aalen, 1982), 98.

seeks, it ends with the intellect which finds. "Reason is a movement capable of distinguishing and connecting our knowings among themselves."[70] But: "distinct is the intellect, distinct is the reason."[71] The *intellectus* or *intelligentia* ('the intellect or intelligence'[72]) is in fact the higher faculty of the human soul, directly illuminated by the divine light: "Thus there is in our soul something which is called intellect. And this part of the soul, which is called intellect or spirit, is itself illuminated with a higher light. Now this light by which the spirit is illuminated is God."[73]

Sometimes St. Augustine distinguishes a lower reason and a higher reason. The latter is then another name for intellect. This designation is justified because, as we stated, reason is not separated from intellect, as reason receives the light of the first principles from it. On the other hand, just as reason is subject to the intellect, so intellect is subject to the divine light. However, it would be more fitting to say that reason is actively subject to the intellect, which means that there is reason when mental activity is subject to the principles of knowledge — although it can disobey — while the intellect is, by nature, passively subject to the truth, which it cannot help but reflect. "The exercise of superior reason is essentially the submission of the individual to something beyond him, and the adherence of the mind to the source of light which illumines every mind."[74] On the whole, reason is distinguished from intellect as science (with a view to action) is distinguished from wisdom (with a view to contemplation): "If therefore an exact distinction exists for wisdom and science, namely, that to wisdom belongs the intellective knowledge of eternal things, while to reason belongs the rational knowledge of temporal things, it is not difficult to judge which is the first and which is the second."[75]

The doctrine of St. Thomas Aquinas hardly differs from that of St. Augustine. At least the terminological distinctions are identical on

70 *De ordine* II, 30; *Patrologia Latina* [=PL] 32:1009.
71 *Sermo* 43, II, 3; PL 38:255.
72 *Ennar. in Ps.* 31, 9; PL 39:263.
73 *In Joan. Evang.*, tract XV, 4, 19; PL 35:1516–17.
74 E. Gilson, *The Christian Philosophy of Saint Augustine*, trans. L. E. M. Lynch (New York: Random House, 1960), 119.
75 *De Trinitate*, XII, 15, 25; PL 42:1012.

both sides.[76] "Reason differs from intellect as multitude does from unity. Thus Boethius says [in Book IV of *De consolatione*] that reasoning is related to understanding as time to eternity and as a circle to its center. For it is distinctive of reason to disperse itself in the consideration of many things, and then to gather one simple truth from them.... Conversely, intellect first contemplates a truth one and undivided and in that truth comprehends a whole multitude, as God, by knowing his essence, knows all things."[77]

Not only does this intellect *qua* passive receive into itself knowledge coming from without, but *qua* active it also illuminates the knowledge received to reveal its intelligible dimension to itself, like an eye enlightening what it sees.[78] Now this light by which the intellect actualizes the intelligible nature of the known is of divine origin: it is a "light derived from God" which is thus the (pre-eminent) cause of our science.[79]

Proceeding further: the supreme happiness for man is of an intellective nature: with respect to its very essence, "happiness consists in an act of the intellect."[80] The intellect is in fact what man has in common with God and the angels — not practical intelligence, but speculative or contemplative or all-knowing intelligence:

> The asserted likeness of the practical intellect to God is one of proportion; that is to say, by reason of its standing in relation to what it knows, as God does to what He knows. But the likeness of the speculative intellect to God is one of union and "information" [that is: in the knowledge the speculative intellect has of God, it is God himself who informs the intellect]; which is a much greater likeness. And yet it may be answered that, in regard

76 Thomists challenge such an affirmation. For our part we believe that, for St. Thomas, Augustinianism remains more fundamental than Aristotelianism.

77 *In Boet. de Trin.*, q. 6, a. 1, sol. 3, trans. A. Maurer (Toronto: Pontifical Institute of Mediaeval Studies, 1953).

78 *Contra Gentiles* II, ch. 76, trans. J. F. Anderson (New York: Doubleday, 1956), 239–45.

79 *De Verit.*, q. XI, a. 3.

80 *Summa Theologiae* I-II, q. 3, a. 4.

to the principal thing known, which is His Essence, God
has not practical but merely speculative knowledge.[81]

Even if reason in its cognitive principle can be reduced to the intellect, what remains is that "intelligence takes its name from being an
intimate penetration of the truth, while reason is so called from being
inquisitive and discursive."[82] And this intimate penetration is not
only objective knowledge, but also 'subjective' assimilation and divine
life: "This [intellective] vision is perfected in a sort of participation
in eternity. Moreover, this vision is a kind of life, for the action of
the intellect is a kind of life. Therefore, the created intellect becomes
a partaker in eternal life through this vision."[83] It follows that the
beatific state thus obtained by the intellect's vision cannot be lost and
participates in the immutability of its object:

> The created intellect sees God by virtue of being united
> to Him in some way, as is clear from what we have said.
> So, if this vision were to cease, bringing this union to an
> end, it would have to be done by a change in the divine
> substance, or in the intellect of the one who sees it. Both
> of these changes are impossible: for the divine substance is
> immutable ... and, also, the intellectual substance is raised
> above all change when it sees God's substance.... No
> creature can come closer to God than the one who sees
> His substance. So, the intellectual creature that sees God's
> substance attains the highest immutability.[84]

81 Ibid., I-II, q. 3, a. 5.

82 Ibid., II-II, q. 49, a. 5.

83 *Contra Gentiles* III, ch. 61 [2], trans. V. J. Bourke (New York: Doubleday,
1956), 200.

84 *Contra Gentiles* III, ch. 62, 10 and 11. Some major Thomists assert that there is
no intellectual intuition for St. Thomas (see, for example, Sertillanges, *Saint Thomas
d'Aquin*, vol. 1 [Paris: Alcan, 1912], 134). This is even the generally held thesis. We have
explained why this seems quite incomplete (see our article: "La notion d'intellect chez
saint Thomas d'Aquin," in *Philosophia perennis* 3 [Jan.–Feb. 1970]). Here let us only
recall that for St. Thomas, "intellect and reason differ as to their manner of knowing;
because the intellect knows by simple intuition (*simplici intuitu*), while reason knows
by a process of discursion . . . " (*Summa Theologiae* I, q. 59, a. 1, ad 1). On the other hand,
as we mentioned, it is the intellect that is beatified and united with the Divine Essence.

9. Intellect and Spirit

With these few references we see at what height the notion of intellect was situated in the Latin tradition, a tradition that Descartes seems to ignore completely. This height is such that it puts us at the border between natural and supernatural, between the human and the divine. The intellect is thus naturally supernatural. It testifies, in man himself, to something surpassing all that we have encountered so far, particularly the limits of our individual nature. This something, the trace of which is the intellect at the center of the mental soul, must be called *spirit*.

As a matter of fact, it has become increasingly clear that it is the cognitive activity of the intellect, natural to man, that has revealed the presence in man of a reality that transcends the human in the ordinary sense of the term. Without it we would not have been aware of it; in other words, the spirit (in Latin *spiritus*, in Greek *pneuma*) would seem to belong completely to the realm of grace, and only by means of grace would we have access to it. But there is within us a properly spiritual light, that is to say not subject to the limiting conditions of individual existence, and this light is the intellect. The very existence of knowledge — and certainly there *is* knowledge — is an irrefutable proof of that, since within it individual realities cease being impenetrable and become communicable, which is only possible by means of a higher reality: the spirit. However, it must be pointed out that the intellect is envisaged then as a cognitive function of the spirit, but in itself it is not the spirit. In reality we do not have, in the order of nature, a true awareness of our spiritual being. A spiritual way is nothing but the sum of divine (the grace of the sacraments) and human (prayer and the virtues) means which religion offers us so that we might really attain to a degree of spiritual awareness. This spiritual awareness alone will enable us to gain access to the awareness of the divine, the divine that is pure Spirit. But in our ordinary state the only experience we have naturally of our spiritual reality is an experience of the intellect, a cognitive act emanating from the spirit.

We understand then that spirit and intellect may be viewed at times as synonymous, since the intellect is nothing but the cognitive aspect of the spirit and therefore is essentially identical to it. This is, it seems, the case with St. Thomas Aquinas and certain Scholastics like Meister

Eckhart.[85] However, keeping to the terms of our analysis, such a synonymy is only possible at the price of a transposition of the intellect, we say a veritable pneumatization of the intellect. And we will come back to this pneumatization of the intellect, one of the fundamental themes of our book.

For the moment it seems, to the contrary, extremely important to mark well the differences between spirit and intellect. As we have said, and as we shall see again, the intellect can receive into itself the knowledge of all things only because it is none of the things it knows. From our standpoint, this intellect clearly merits the name 'speculative intellect' because it is a mirror (*speculum* in Latin) that reflects the world. The price to be paid for its lucidity is a kind of distancing from reality, by which reality as such is revealed to man but man is also set apart from being in his very being. Knowledge is clearly an intelligible communion of the knowing and the known, but this is in some manner a communion at a distance. With cognitive activity, everything transpires as if man had retained the memory of an ontological communion between himself and the world, but he can achieve this — by his merely natural powers — only in speculative mode. Knowledge is this very possibility, this ultimate possibility, this memory of a lost paradise. It is an anticipated fusion of subject and object, but anticipated only because unrealized.

10. Intellect and Will, the Two Modes of the Spirit

We discover then, at the intellect's core, a desire to realize what it knows: this desire is the will. The intellect is a sense of being and speaks only of being. But it is vision only on condition of not being what it sees, which is however reality itself. This is why desire for this reality, born of a 'vision' of being, is yet found to be necessarily 'blind'. Since to see being is to hold it at a distance, this vision, which withdraws us from being at the very instant that it is given to us, must

---

85   Realizing in some manner the synthesis of Thomism and Augustinianism, Meister Eckhart identifies *spiritus* with *intellectus*, and, since the light which illuminates the latter is God himself, he identifies the intellect with its luminous content and declares it 'uncreatable': "the intellect is uncreatable as such" (*Quaestiones parisienses, rationes Eckardi*, 6; ed. Klibansky [Leipzig: F. Meiner, 1936], 18). "As such" means: in its pure essence. Such a formula implies no pantheism.

be renounced if we are *willing* to attain that which is communicated to us by desire. There is an obscure side to a mirror, or else there is no reflection. Likewise there is an obscure side to the intellect, and this is the will, which is basically the desire for being, just as the intellect is a perception of being. The will then seems to be another mode of the spirit. Let us say this: the human being is polarized into two opposed but inseparable and complementary modes: intellect and will, with the intellect being the spirit's cognitive pole and the will its ontological pole. And so we realize that the will has a share in the transcendence of the spirit when we see that, not only does the source of the will evade us, but there is something of the unintelligible in its very nature. To the intellect, the will is like a power rising from the depths of its being, and this being cannot be grasped by the intellect: it is its own 'other side', the backing of the mirror thanks to which it is not simply transparent.

11. The Human Being as Intelligence and Will

The fable of the blind man and the lame man expresses the complementarity of intellect and will, or even knowledge and action, quite well: intellect without will is powerless; will without intellect is blind. This complementarity, that of the two poles of the spirit, is found again at all levels of the human being, but in various proportions according to whether we draw away from or approach one pole or the other. Before examining this point we should observe that it is indeed the spirit that forms the unity of the human being. In reality everything in man is spirit, and this is normal, since only spiritual reality includes the subtle and the corporeal within itself. 'Everything is spirit' means that in man everything is an aspect of the spirit, a particular mode of spiritual reality. And since these modes are structured according to the two poles of intellect and will, or knowledge and being, each of them can be considered as a mode of knowledge or a mode of being, according to the viewpoint adopted. Intelligence is itself a mode of being and will a mode of knowledge.

At each level of the human tripartition (spiritual, animic, and corporeal) we should thus be able to examine the knowledge aspects and the being aspects of all functions of our lives. Desire, for example, which seems to be on the being and will side, is also evidently a mode of knowledge. Likewise the biological functions (cardiac rhythm, respiration, etc.) testify to a phenomenal intelligence. Conversely, what seems *a priori* to be knowledge, reason, and intellect, for example, conceals a profound dimension of will, as we have just seen.

With this interweaving of intelligence and will, there is nevertheless a level where they seem in equilibrium, if not truly united. This is the affective level, and the form in which they are in equilibrium is love: to love is in fact to desire what the intelligence makes known to us as good. Consequently, in love both intellect and will cooperate in the same task, in one same work, but are not truly united. They tend towards their unity, that is towards the spirit. And yet, at the core of this love, all the being's energies and powers are bound together to attain their unique source. Superior to intellection as to being, superior to desire and instinct as to knowing, love is the most central and most noble act of which the individual being is capable, the act through which the psycho-corporeal substance aspires to its own surpassing. As the act of a self that assembles and gathers itself together in order to sacrifice and renounce itself, love is then essentially spiritual, it is essentially love of the spirit. This aspiration might be defined as a tension between will and intelligence. Will is the impulsive movement arising from the being's depths; intelligence is the axis defining the direction and term of movement, pointing toward the heights of being. In love the ego discovers it is not the true center of being, since this center seems at once, in the will's impulse, to be more profound than it, and, in the intellect's attraction, loftier than it.

12. The Person, the Spiritual Unity of the Human Being

All we have said up until now clearly shows that the intellect forms the human being's unity of nature. Thus we come back to the traditional account of human unity: the soul is the form of the body. But the intellective soul — and not only the affective or vegetative soul — is involved here. There is a unity of nature because the nature of all elements making up a human being, that is to say their intelligible structure, is revealed to be a particular mode of the intellect. In the traditional definition of the soul as the form of the body, that is to say as that which structures and animates the body, by soul we therefore need to understand *spiritus* and *animus* or else by body *anima* and *corpus*; as long as only the individual man is envisaged, that is to say man as an indivisible natural reality, and not personal man, that is to say man as spiritual unity.[86]

But this unity of nature requires a unity of being, a true ontological subject which, in order to be the human being's principle of unity, must in a certain manner be transcendent to everything we experience naturally. Obviously we also experience this transcendence, but as a limited and somewhat negative experience given to us in the experience of the will. Not that the person, since this is what we are concerned with here, is identified with the will, but it is the will's existence that most directly manifests to our awareness the transcendence of the person.

In other words the person, the human being's principle of unity, must be at once, like every principle of unity, both immanent and transcendent to what it unifies. Its immanence is made possible by the intellect, which is everywhere present in the human being; its transcendence is manifested by the will, which 'reveals' most directly to our awareness the transcendence of the person.

The intellect is not, for all that, devoid of transcendence, nor the will of immanence. By his intellective awareness, as we stated, man is a universal reader. He is then the world's consciousness, the mirror in which the world is reflected. Far from isolating or separating man from the world — as is too often the case with modern philosophers, Kant in particular — this situation makes of man a being of the world, the being through which knowledge comes into the world, or again the being through which the world becomes knowledge: the world is seen, felt, known by one of its parts, human awareness. Just as the world realizes photosynthesis thanks to the chlorophyllous function, so it realizes knowledge of itself thanks to human awareness, and in just as objective and impersonal a manner. Awareness is a property of the cosmic fabric for the same reason the chlorophyllous function is. However, this property displays a characteristic unique among the innumerable properties of cosmic substance: it is universal and valid for all forms of the cosmos. *A priori*, knowledge can know everything,

86   Individuality is the quality of a reality that cannot be divided (*in-dividu*); if someone is cut in half, we do not have two men, we no longer have anything. Personality is the quality of a reality that is freely and consciously grasped as a principle of unity.

whereas the world's other beings (the root of a tree, for example) know only what strictly conforms to the nature of their being. Therefore when man, a being of nature, reflects upon his own ability to know, he perceives that human knowledge, by its universality, testifies in the world to the existence of something surpassing the world by its very being. It is the awareness of this transcendence, grasped negatively as what is not the world, that man can call his person. One might say the intellect is objectively immanent and 'subjectively' transcendent.

Conversely, the will, which is objectively transcendent since it is free, since it appears objectively to awareness as independent of all nature, as objectively different ("to truly want," it is said, "is to want what one does not want")—the will has power over us only insofar as it is subjectively immanent to our most intimate heart, only insofar as it is our very being in its most radical affirmation.[87]

Such is the person, at least what we can negatively grasp of it in our present state. It is a union of intelligence and will, or rather the nucleus of knowledge and freedom, that is to say a spiritual reality, the image of which on the plane of psycho-corporeal reality is love, and the true principle of which—from the viewpoint of its ontological foundation—is God. The person is the upper limit of the created, where it touches God by humbling itself to an infinitesimal point, and this is also identically at the center of the created, the door through which God opens Himself to man to realize him: the person, the unutterable secret between the relative and the Absolute, where God communicates to each one of us a Name unknown to the whole of creation.

Truly, these two infinitesimal points can be viewed synthetically as being only one. But it is also useful to consider them as the upper and lower limits of the vertical perpendicular that unites them, the upper center corresponding then to the divine root of the person—the immortal soul in God—and the lower center to its encounter with the horizontal plane of natural individuality—God in the soul. To identify the person with a vertical—and not with a point—not only enables us to break with the illusion of egoic punctuality, but above all to show that the person is a deepening mystery, a process of personalization, and not something to be acquired and possessed. Being the central unity of all states a being traverses in order to go towards God, in some

87 "The will," said Karl Jaspers, "is the eternal in the instant."

manner it is always further on, until the moment when it is fulfilled in the Divine Person who, being the preeminent personality, the very essence of each person, finally bestows on it its true identity. This is a wondrous mystery, since here the maximum of identity of all souls with God is also the maximum of distinctiveness for each one of them.[88]

Finally, it is not unimportant to ask why the lower infinitesimal point is symbolically situated in the heart, at the center of the body. We are in fact spontaneously inclined to place the spirit, or at least the intellect, in the head. As for the will, it seems to us in some way diffused through the whole body. However, as we have said, the body is also, by itself, a manifestation of the spirit. The center of the body, the heart,[89] corresponds then to the center of the spirit, to the immortal person, that is to say to the point where the Uncreated touches the created.[90] In this sense it is at once intelligence and will and, hence, love. When our hand is brought to the center of our chest in concert with the thought of oneself, it shows itself a better judge than our mental soul, for our hearts are more really ourselves than our mentality. But it is also this immanence of the divine in ourselves that makes possible the illusion of the self, which would not even exist if there were not, at the core of our psycho-corporeal individuality, a mysterious place where a presence greater than all of creation dwells.[91] To realize our immortal person requires then that the scattered will be reassembled from the periphery to the center, that the intelligence be made to 'descend' from the brain into the heart. To gain access to the person is at once to leave behind the individuality and reabsorb it into its center.

88   The person is at once being and relationship. As being, it is the center of human reality, the ontological support of all its attributes. But this being is defined by an onto-pneumatic relationship that unites it with God: the unique and founding relationship of its unicity.

89   This is not necessarily the anatomical heart, but the center of the chest where we situate, prior to all reflection, the presence of the self, not the self as an act of appropriation, which we will now describe, but the ontological principle of pure subjectivity.

90   There is a kind of intellect (or spirit)-heart duality, which is basically nothing but the nature-person or even knowledge-being duality.

91   If the heart is the point through which the created touches the Uncreated, it is also, by this very fact, the point at which the created illusorily limits the Uncreated, and is therefore the source of the egoic coagulation. This is why Scripture speaks of a hardening of the heart.

IV. THE SELF AND THE 'I'. NEGATIVE EGOLOGY

I. Anthropological Doctrine governs the Understanding of Charity

We return now to the Socratic question of self-knowledge. Before undertaking a journey, is it not first necessary to study the map of the countryside through which one wishes to travel? We have drawn up this map. Of what we would seek out, the self to be known, we henceforth know on what level it is situated. What remains, then, is to attempt to describe in its basic vicissitudes the voyage that leads to the true homeland of our reality.

So we are not immediately and naturally given access to the person. To achieve this a veritable conversion to oneself, that is to say to our spiritual being, is needed. But to be converted to oneself is to turn away from what illusorily presents itself as spirit. To distinguish the true from the false self is equally to distinguish the spiritual from the psychic with which we instinctively confuse it. And even more, it is precisely with the ordinary self that this confusion occurs. Now this confusion is, as we have amply demonstrated, the very one that perverts Christian charity. We have identified its social and collective aspects and can now understand it in its subjective root; we can see this perversion being accomplished in the individual himself and implicating all of Christianity in his fall. Such are the stakes of our analysis. Perhaps it will be better understood now why we have made so long a detour, why we have appeared to digress from this principal point of our theme.

To say it quite plainly: if Christ's commandment to love is addressed to the empirical self, to the individual ego, then the commandment is in vain, for the individual self is the very negation of all love. And still more seriously, this ego is perfectly apt at playing the comedy of charity, not only in the eyes of others, but even in its own eyes, in its own estimation, which destroys all of love's truth. Under these conditions, why would we want to do without a reflection upon the nature of man and an anthropological doctrine? An arduous meditation, some will say. Unquestionably, but the love of God — who is so poorly loved — demands all of our intelligence. And we will not think ourselves too lightly repaid for our efforts if this meditation enables us to better *understand* what Christ asks of us. The saints and the ages of great faith knew this by instinct, but we are wide of the mark today. Only our good will and intelligence remain: let us therefore strive to think well.

2. *The Self is not a Being*

We will begin with a terminological distinction offered by our language itself, that of the 'I' and the 'me'.[92] Our analysis will consist in highlighting the following thesis: the self (*moi*) is not a reality, an entity, a being, but an act of appropriation: to say *me* is not to say: "I am myself" but: "*I* am *my own* (à moi)," "*I* belong to myself"; or perhaps it would be more exact to say "I *is* my own." From such a perspective, 'I' and 'me' are moreover two correlative terms, for if the 'I' designates the person in such a case, the subject in its unable-to-be-objectivized reality, the 'me' designates the relationship of the 'I' to the psycho-corporeal individuality, and marks it as a relationship of appropriation or possession. But in such a relationship the 'I' is actually a possessed possessor. Captured by the psycho-corporeal individuality, it momentarily confers on this capture, that is to say on the 'me', the consistency of a unity: momentarily, for ultimately, nothing can fetter the transcendence of the 'I'.

This 'I-and-me' distinction is relatively common in Western thought. We find it in Kant under the form of a transcendental 'I' opposed to an empirical 'me', also in Husserl and William James. However, not having a religious anthropology in view, none of these thinkers seems to have grasped with enough precision the lie of the 'me', which is to ascribe being to itself, whereas it is only a having. To the contrary, the very words of Christ himself have compelled our philosophical analysis to unmask the ruse of the individual 'me', to expose its basic unreality.

Consider the numerous texts where Christ enjoins his disciples to renounce their soul (or their life), for a living soul is clearly involved here, the soul which Christ also calls their 'possession': "Who would find his life will lose it, but the one who loses his life *for My sake* will find it" (Matt. 10:39, 16:25); "who wishes to save his soul will lose it, but the one who loses his soul *for My sake* will save it" (Mark 8:35);

92 (In French *moi* is both noun, 'self', as used previously, and pronoun, 'me', as used here. — *Trans.*)

"if someone comes to Me and does not hate his father, his mother, his brothers and sisters, and even his own soul, he cannot be my disciple.... So then whoever among you does not renounce everything he possesses cannot be my disciple" (Luke 14:26 and 33). These texts put a dynamic structure with three elements into play: a natural human 'me', a divine 'Me', the pole of spiritual pilgrimage which endows us with a new supernatural human 'me' if we abandon the old one. Translated into our anthropological language this means: in order to pass from the individual me to the personal 'I', it is first necessary to gain access to the divine Me and through this to the unspeakable secret which God has reserved, from all eternity, for my immortal soul: that face of God which I alone see, that face of God unknown to all other creatures, uniquely visible to my spiritual being, or rather which is that being itself;[93] the true person, that secret which constitutes the personal being as such, which establishes the person in being (metaphors are not involved here; this is about circumscribing with language a perfectly evident reality, but a reality beyond language). So, in order to gain access to the divine Me, we need to renounce the natural me or self. And now we pose the following question: how can a human self renounce its human self? Two conditions are required, which are moreover only one: on the one hand that there is in man another more radical and more profound self, and, on the other, that what is renounced is not truly real. Nothing of what is real can be abolished. Clearly, the *self* renounced is not the self we seek to know; the *I* that renounces is not really that which is renounced, even though it identifies with it through natural illusion.

3. The Genesis of the Self

As natural as this illusion might be, it nevertheless does not correspond to a fundamental structure of the human being. This illusion is acquired, it has a history. Less than a being, the self is a *habitude*, and it is fitting that that the word *habitude* comes from the Latin *habere* which means: to have, to possess, for it actually involves an act of possession which is progressively consolidated until it is able to pass for a substantial reality.

93 This reality being at once being and vision, we understand how only in the person is that unity of being and knowing realized.

Surely this history could be told in several ways. It is not even foreign to each of our own histories, and it might be rediscovered especially in what the psychologists call the formation of the self, a formation carried out from birth to around the third year. But here we will view it in a more general manner.

We begin with the remark of an ancient teacher who said: "We want to possess what we were." Now, clearly, to want to possess what we are is only possible on condition of being distinct from it. Therefore separation and division must be introduced into the unity of being, with possessor and possession contraposed to each other. But, at the same time, we are condemned to never being joined back together again, since the very act by which we wish to be ourselves supposes that we remain at a distance and always separated from ourselves. Such is the contradiction of the desire for self-possession. To wish to possess oneself is to wish to be possessively united to oneself, but this very desire forever separates us from its realization.

It is spirit and soul that are thus contraposed to each other, the spiritual person and the psycho-corporeal reality. In its primary nature (which is never truly abolished), the spirit is the whole of man: the soul and body are its own modalities included within itself. But this state implies that the spiritual sphere is wholly oriented toward its Principle from which it receives being and light: in such a case man is in the image *and* likeness of God. Actually, to be in the image — or to be the image — of God does not only define a nature acquired once and for all; it also defines an act which it must accomplish (this is likeness) — for in God alone being and act are only one, God being pure act of being. This nature given to primordial man is also therefore an order and a Commandment.[94] In Adam, then, the body is turned toward the soul, the soul toward the spirit, and the spirit toward God. In this primordial orientation the spirit does not 'look behind itself', does not 'go back on itself', but is open to God who contemplates

---

94 There was then a religion in the Earthly Paradise, that is to say an act through which man bound himself to God. Adam was the priest of this religion, and what was sacred was his own nature: he rendered his worship to God in realizing his the-omorphic nature and by his dominion over creation, whose crown and synthesis he was. Through him the whole cosmos participated in divine worship. The commentary of Lanza del Vasto on Genesis (*La Montée des Âmes vivantes* [Paris: Denoël, 1968]) denies the existence of this primordial religion (227).

Himself in it. Man does not possess or know himself (with a dualist knowledge), but he is known, penetrated by the divine light, because he is turned toward his Principle.[95]

On the contrary, the movement by which the spirit—under its aspect of freedom, not under its aspect of knowledge[96]—turns away from God, becomes disoriented, is also that movement by which it is turned towards itself and hence towards the world, whose ruler man effectively (but not virtually) ceases to be. Master of himself and therefore of the universe to the extent of his ontological submission to God—man is in the image of God—he loses this double mastery the instant he turns towards his soul in order to possess self and world, which become objects to conquer, that is to say: enemies.

What we have is disoriented man, turning the glance of his consciousness towards the animic waters of his interior world. What he perceives upon the surface of these waters is the shadow projected from his own person which seems to come to him from the psychic depths. Narcissus, leaning over the banks of himself, is fascinated by the mirror of his own psyche. He becomes his own illusion, and the act by which he wishes to abolish this illusion, that is, to conjoin the model and its reflection, is also the act by which this illusion is engendered and which leads to his loss. Such is the self, the reflection of my personal being on the bosom of the psychic waters, and which

95 Fallen man can regain this state of primordial man through the grace of Christ and become once more, to the extent that he turns to Him, that 'recipient' of divine light. "Yes, down to this very day, when Moses is read, a veil covers their hearts; but when they turn in repentance to God, the veil shall be taken away. Now the Lord is the spirit [*pneuma*]; and where the Spirit of the Lord is, there is freedom. But all of us, with faces unveiled, reflecting as in a mirror the glory of the Lord, are being transformed into his very image from glory to glory, according to the action of the Lord who is spirit" (2 Cor 3:15–18). Glory, in the metaphysical sense, always designates the irradiation of the Principle, its presence through radiance, outside of the divine sphere. To the extent that he is the image of God, man is a mode of glory, since he is the image of God only insofar as he reflects the cosmic irradiation of the divine. The expression 'from glory to glory' indicates different degrees of divine irradiation, corresponding to so many spiritual stations which man, in the course of his transformation into the image of God, passes through under the action of God who, being Spirit, pneumatizes him more and more integrally, even as far as the almost total identification of the image with its Model.

96 The spirit, we have said, is knowledge and freedom; this is why it can 'disobey' God (who is its *raison d'être*), but it cannot cease being knowledge. A mirror, plunged in darkness, retains its reflecting power.

they seem to disclose like a secret that beckons us to discover it. Now the psychic waters are ungraspable. Hardly have we touched them when they are troubled and distort the face we perceive there. But this perpetual change is an even more pressing invitation to possession. Our soul ceaselessly tells us: "Come, possess me, it is yourself you will grasp. Do not tire of pursuing me. And if I change forms, this is so that you advance towards your truest form. Who knows, perhaps the face you catch sight of in me tomorrow will be the one you have sought since your birth, the one in which you will recognize yourself? O my love, lie down in my waters, wed me forever; you will finally be who you are."[97]

The me, the lie of the I, is thus as much a fascination suffered as a desired possession. What justifies the original fall of the I into the psyche consisting of the me is the memory of a lost being. Possessor possessed, we think we find ourselves again wherever we lose ourselves. How could we cease our avid vigil over our psychic reflection, how could we accept *losing sight* of ourselves, since no one else watches over us, since no one but ourselves would know how to recognize us? We appoint ourselves as our own guardian, usurping in this way the place of our guardian angel. However, what Christ asks is precisely to renounce this usurpation: "to lose one's self" does not simply mean "don't be an egotist," but also to achieve that conversion through which the I is turned away from the captivating psyche, that is to say breaks the illusion of the me in order to turn towards the Divine Me, the unique basis of our person. This really and truly involves losing

---

97   We cannot cover here all of the forms under which the holy war between *I* and *psyche* is expressed. Folklore in particular is very rich in this respect. It seems that many fairytales and songs can be interpreted in this sense. Among others, we will mention a song like "Magali" in which a woman, whom a man wishes to seize, successively takes on all kinds of forms, which oblige her pursuer to take on the corresponding predatory forms. In the same way, in several tales, a cruel queen kills those who desire her until the day when her true master survives the deadly tests which she imposes. He pursues her then and strikes her each time she takes on a deceiving form until, finally exhausted, she becomes herself. These works symbolically retrace a spiritual process. The soul is the trap by which the I is caught. In order to seize it and possess it, it would have to be identical to it. Now the soul is capable of all identities because it owns none of them. The pitiless lucidity of knowledge foils all of its ruses and forces the soul to be nothing, to renounce all identifications, to make itself poor — virgin. Only then can it receive its master, the I, which is also its spouse and its father, for Adam is the father of Eve.

sight of oneself, of not looking over oneself. In such a case we are on a whole other level than that of the altruism-egoism alternative which is the concern of action. We are at the level of the human being's fundamental structures, of an attitude so habitual and so basic that it has become 'second nature', from which without a higher grace we would not have the ability to detach ourselves. Altruism enjoys no privilege in this respect, and if, in itself, it may be regarded as preferable to egoism, it does not make us relinquish the self's illusion. It is only a 'transposed egoism' and includes no spiritual dimension.

To summarize, whether desired or hated the captivating psyche retains its power. To hate the possessive me and to give oneself to others in the hope of renouncing the ego means only ineffectively simulating its abolition. One's me is delivered up to others in a kind of indefinite passion, and in this is seen a radical means of dying to oneself, of finally breaking out of the charmed circle of an egotistic mindset. However, altruism by no means differs from egoism. It is situated strictly on the same plane. To deliver one's ego up as fodder to other *egos* is still, for the ego, a way of existing and indeed the most formidable of all, because the most justified in appearance. There is no fascination greater than this last one. Far from dying, the ego, parceled out in its passional sacrifice, grows from its own parceling. It is reflected, replicated, and extended. The true solution is to understand that "without Me" man can do nothing. "Without Me," that is to say without the supreme and transcendent Me, he cannot escape from the fruits of the Tree of Good and Evil. But, in order to gain access to charity's spiritual dimension, man needs to break away from the captivation of the passional soul. And to break with the psyche is to accept that the left hand (the consciousness) does not know what the right hand (the soul in a state of charity) is doing. It is the supreme Me who knows in secret the passion of the psyche. But the relative me steals this fruit of the knowledge of Good and Evil and pretends to have the fruit and eat it too.

4. Original Sin: History and Symbol

The preceding analysis of the dialectic of the I and the psyche, out of which the me is formed, has brought in extra-philosophical elements, borrowed in particular from the account of original sin given in Genesis. For such borrowings are inevitable to the very extent that the me derives from an historical explanation. It would be useless, impossible, and even deceitful to rest content with a purely abstract language here. Use of symbols is absolutely necessary, not only because they advantageously replace lengthy dissertations, but also because we live this dialectic in a symbolic fashion. However, that the account of Genesis is symbolic does not at all mean that it corresponds to no historical reality. To the contrary, it is to the extent that an event considered as historical has a symbolic significance that it is real. All degrees of reality being in analogical correspondence with each other, and this by virtue of the necessary unity of creation, it follows that what takes place at a certain level has its correspondence at a higher level and is its symbol. Although impossible, if some modality of a lower level did not have its correspondence on a higher level, that is to say if it was not its symbol, this modality would thus be separated from the totality of creation and would be purely and simply then non-existent. By this we see that the historical reality of an event is based on an archetype, with this event being its symbol. As for the language of Scripture, it includes two planes in one and the same expression ('symbol' comes from *sumballein*, which means: to *relate*). To speak of a tree, of a fruit, of its being eaten, of a serpent, is to speak at the same time then about an interior archetypal reality and of an exterior reality, its manifestation.

From all that we have said about the cosmic descent of the degrees of reality, moreover, it is easy to understand that the closer one is to the origins, the closer is the sensible world to the intelligible. In the Adamic age "the seven earths are in heaven," the sensible is only a modality included in the intelligible. This means, for example, that when primordial man breathes, he prays; when he names things, he contemplates their essences; when he eats a fruit, he knows and is united to the known essence, since eating — assimilation of a foreign body by the body — is nothing but the corporeal translation of the cognitive process — assimilation of a foreign intelligible by the intellect. In that age the unity of the cosmic degrees is actual. This unity is reestablished by Christ only in the sacramental order, since a sacrament is a sensible sign that actually produces what it signifies: the Eucharistic bread is, substantially, the *corpus Christi*. Thus, in Paradise, all things have an analogically sacramental dimension. The tree is a symbol of the cosmic intellect, that is to say the intelligible structure of the world, or rather it is this intellect under a certain mode because of its verticality and immobility: the intellect is the ray that unites all cosmic degrees among themselves in passing through their center (the tree of Paradise is planted at its center); also because of its mode of nutrition: the tree is nourished with light and transforms into light what comes from darkness. The serpent is a symbol of the subtle world, or rather it is the subtle world under a certain mode, because of its horizontality and movement: "the reptile which moves itself without feet and by a continuous rhythm of its entire body is, as it were, the incorporation of a subtle 'vibration'";[98] it thus represents the expansive and dissolving energy of subtle forces. To summarize, we deem the mention of Adam, Eve, the tree, its fruit, the serpent, and the eating to be 'scientifically exact'. And if anyone has a little 'cosmological imagination' he will understand that this event, in its historical reality, had to be something extraordinary.

We will only consider what relates to our topic in this Genesis account.

5. The Story of Original Sin tells of the Fall of the I into the Psyche

Man is created in the *image* of God and according to His *likeness*. These two terms do not have the same meaning. Man is the image of God: this defines the cosmic function of the human being. In this world, and for this world, he is the image of God. This indicates a horizontal relationship. On the other hand this image is a likeness. This no longer concerns the relationship of one human being to other beings but the content of the image, which is in conformity with its Model—that is to say, in his nature, man resembles God. What we have here is a vertical relationship to the Principle. Man is therefore not only God for the world, but even in himself. To say that he is God for the world is to say that he is a central being, and that he cannot but be so. To say that he is God in himself is to say that man is a center for himself, that he is aware of being a center and

---

98   Titus Burckhardt, *Alchemy* (Baltimore: Penguin Books, 1971), 130.

therefore of participating in a single Center, which is God in Himself. Likeness indicates then the spiritual person. It is named in second place because it is as if a consequence of the image, it is implied by the image. This is also why sometimes only the image is mentioned. But this consequence of man's iconic situation may not always be actualized. The human mirror can cease reflecting the Divine Face without, for all that, losing its quality as mirror.

Thus, the fall of the I into the psychism might be described as an attempt of the image to possess the likeness. The serpent affirms that, in eating the fruit, Adam and Eve will be 'as gods'. Now they are already 'like God'. But, under the figure of the fruit, the interior theomorphism of the subject opened to God is presented as an exterior and closed object, which it is necessary to open and eat in order to possess its secret. To desire to possess what one is already: this is *ipso facto* to lose this nature, to introduce duality and division into oneself. The image is separated from the likeness in order to better possess it. The mirror is turned back upon its own content, but, doing this, it interposes itself between this content and the Model which it reflects: it 'covers' its own theomorphism 'with its shadow', thus realizing the reverse of the paracletic overshadowing by which, in covering Mary with His shadow, the Holy Spirit signs the original purity of the human mirror and brings about the manifestation of the Son, the image of the Father, the New Adam. The Virgin, the symbol and prototype of the human soul, is the pure mirror where God can be reflected, the 'Mirror of Justice' who is also the 'Gate of Heaven'.

The sinful eating of the forbidden fruit brings about an inversion of the anthropological structure. What was interior becomes exterior, what was higher becomes lower and *vice-versa*, an inversion that presupposes the actualization of the distinction between within and without, high and low, that is to say duality. In the original state all cosmic dualities, and therefore all limitations and oppositions, were as if covered over by the splendor, the 'glory' of the spiritual world that mercifully enveloped them. Here is the key of the mystery of the two trees which occupy the center of Paradise or, again, the center of the properly human degree of creation.

Paradise represents the perfection and crowning of the psycho-corporeal human world. It is also therefore its synthesis and contains within itself, in a virtual state, all the lower possibilities of this world, down to the most sinister. These possibilities are symbolized by the tree of the knowledge of good and evil, and are contained at the center of Paradise as the germ of all duality. But these possibilities are also hidden and covered over by the light of the spiritual world that irradiates Paradise: Heaven, here, touches earth. This direct communication with the spiritual world is symbolized by the Tree of Life whose roots — say, certain traditions — were in Heaven. The tree of life envelops the tree of the knowledge of good and evil, or, if one wishes, the tree of the knowledge of good and evil is an aspect, a possibility (or a sum of possibilities) of the tree of life; as such, the good/evil duality is maintained in a state of undifferentiated equilibrium. If we reduce the tree of life to the vertical, we see that this vertical virtually contains two directions, which are actualized if one traces a horizontal line determining two branches, an upper one toward the top, the lower one toward the bottom. The serpent, the power deployed from the lower possibilities of the terrestrial state, is coiled around the vertical axis like the spiral of the cycles of human history. In eating the forbidden fruit, Adam, because he is master of the earthly cosmos, involves the cosmos in his fall: he gives to the serpent the possibility of uncoiling itself, that is to say of *being attracted to the periphery*, of letting itself be drawn towards the outside instead of being focused on the heights. The serpent unloops its coils and becomes horizontal ("you will walk upon your belly"). Adam himself then, at the entreaty of Eve (who represents his psychism), traces the horizontal line separating the vertical into two parts, and therefore separates the tree of life from the tree of the knowledge of good and evil whose roots are 'below'. Hence life, that is to say communication with the spirit, is lost. Of that only a theoretical knowledge remains. To the contrary, the knowledge of good and evil, which was purely speculative in Paradise, has become the life of fallen man. Man has become as God, knowing good and evil — for God 'knows' all relativities, but He knows them within Himself, without ceasing to be the Absolute — while man, in gaining access to the knowledge of lower possibilities virtually contained within the paradisal state, ceases being what he was, the actualization of these possibilities being incompatible with the living conditions of the primordial state.

146

At the same time, by virtue of the correlation between man and the world, the actualization of cosmic dualities is accompanied by the actualization of a dualist consciousness: one that separates subject from the object in every act of knowledge, and for which all actions to be accomplished, as well as all things to be transformed, present two faces, one good and the other bad, inseparably linked. "Their eyes were opened," the Bible says. The plural clearly indicates birth to dualist and separative consciousness. But, as a consequence, their unique and inner eye, the eye of the heart, is closed. Man then becomes an object for himself, he is cast outside himself: "and they saw that they were naked."

The nakedness for which Adam had no shame is an interior nakedness, the nakedness of being entirely stripped of himself, which is then covered over by divine light. The primordial Adam was clothed with glory. This is the state to which Mary's virginity, through the grace of Christ, will enable us to gain access once more. Through the Virgin humanity will find again that interior nakedness we cannot be ashamed of because it is the very reality of our being willed by God. But exterior nakedness—for which the body's nakedness is only a symbol—makes us ashamed because it is the very reality of our being willed by ourselves, that is to say imperfection and ugliness; it is the nakedness of nothingness: it objectively bears witness to our fault. Exterior nakedness is, on the whole, the exteriorization of nakedness. The body appears then 'on the outside', which is symbolized by the 'tunics of skin' with which God clothes Adam and Eve,[99] that is to

---

99 The original fall separates the visible from the invisible. But it could not abolish the relationship that unites them; the exterior remains the symbol of the interior. The tunics of skin, designating the corporification of the subtle body, also exteriorly signifies the actualization of the animal soul in the human soul. Man becomes a reasonable animal, while originally he was an animated reason, a spirit, just as previously the aprons of figleaves (vegetal) designated the actualization of the vegetative soul, situated symbolically in the stomach (aprons). The fact that it is the work of man, while the tunics of skin are the work of God, perhaps signifies that the fallen body remains capable, by itself, of the most elementary vital functions (respiration, cardiac rhythm, metabolism, etc.), while the noblest functions (movements, walking, nutrition, etc.) necessitate the concurrence of the will and consciousness and are therefore subject to moral and religious law: the vegetative soul does not sin, it is still innocent; the animal soul can sin. But it is equally capable of serving the good: this is why the tunic of skin is also a gift of God. To clearly state once more: the passage from the subtle body to the gross body changes nothing in the essential structure

say our corporeal appearance as known today. And, since it is our appearance, let us understand that exteriorly our humanity is invisible, only our animality is manifested.

The original fall is the origin of every fall: it is the fall of the I into the psyche of which the self consists. This is the passage from a unitive consciousness of being to a distinctive consciousness of having. The 'common' interpretation which sees in the Fall a sin of the flesh includes a symbolic meaning identical to the one we have explained. The woman represents then the *anima-corpus*: she is in fact drawn from Adam (she is a part of the man) while he is in a state of profound sleep, that is to say rapt beyond Paradise, having in some manner abandoned the subtle modality of his being to itself. This is also what the open side indicates, since the chest (the thorax) is the symbolic seat of the *anima-corpus*. In desiring to possess Eve, Adam (the I) desires to possess his own soul and not be united with it.[100]

6. Negative Egology and the Divine Self

However that may be, it seems that all interpretations can be reduced to the one we have attempted to explain. It follows that the search for oneself, for the true person, can be accomplished only through an interior conversion, a change of knowing and awareness that takes us back beyond original sin. As we see, such a search cannot be described in a purely theoretical manner. Since the true person is unitive knowledge of being, what can a being inhabiting the plane of a dualist consciousness be told about it? Basically the I cannot be grasped in any manner. Only a single possibility then remains, that of a negative understanding. This is why we speak of a *negative egology*, just as we speak of a negative theology to designate the intellectual process that denies that anything can be affirmed about God, because God is beyond every concept and even being. Unquestionably, we

---

of the body; it is the same body, but manifested under different living conditions. The body forms a part of primordial human nature, but not the body under its present-day modality. Our true body is the glorious body, that of Christ transfigured and risen, that of the Virgin Mary 'assumed' completely by God.

100   Tradition relates the birth of Eve and the birth of the Church accomplished on Calvary when the centurion's lance opened Christ's side; the Church of Christ is also flesh of His flesh, His beloved spouse, a new Eve rectifying the misfortune that came from the old one.

have not actually arrived at the state of personality, at pure and interior knowledge. But we have at least become aware of our spiritual unconsciousness. Now this is a very important point. If the me is the illusion of knowledge, as for the I, it seems to be the awareness of our ontological ignorance, like a blind spot at the very heart of our consciousness; all we can do is identify ourselves with it. Surely this still has to do with an 'appearance' and not the I in itself. But this last appearance is also the first true face of our immortal person, the one that God loves and contemplates in secret.

Proceeding further, to become our self we then need to renounce all that we are not, all possessive and alienating identifications, to make room for the sole spiritual reality. How then do we undertake this path? The last and most fundamental paradox of all, in this search for the I, is that we should not be aiming for the I, but for God Himself, not at the human person, but the Divine Person who alone knows our true I, because our I is nothing but this very knowledge. "Seek ye first the kingdom of God and his justice: and the rest shall be added unto you" (Luke 12:31), the rest, that is the interior person, "for the kingdom of God is within you" (Luke 17:21).[101] God alone will give us to ourselves, because there is no other identity than His. God alone being identical to Himself, God alone being the center and sole Center, all identity, all centrality is participation in the Supreme Identity, or it is not identity, centrality. It is by the grace of the Supreme Identity that each one realizes his own identity. The Kingdom of Heaven synthetically integrates all possible identity into its own, pure Identity that is not the identity of someone but pure and simple Identity, Identity in Itself.

We understand then how the path to self-knowledge leads well beyond philosophical analysis and brings us to religion. Doubtlessly our immortal person is virtually within us, but we could only actualize it by starting from a supernatural reality in act. Now, for a Christian, there is no other supernatural reality in act than that of the sacraments communicated by the Church. In eating of the Eucharist, the salvific antithesis of the sinful eating, we are in reality

---

101 Today *entos humon* is translated by 'among you', which is one possibility. But the primary meaning of *entos* (*intra* in Latin) is indeed 'within', 'inside'.

absorbed by Christ. It is He who effects the return of the prodigal son to the Divine Self that has engendered him. In the Eucharist we commune with the Divine Person. Next, the human response to divine grace is realized in prayer, especially that of the Name of Jesus, for in saying 'Jesus' we cease saying 'me', since "no one can say 'Jesus is Lord'" except under the action of the Holy Spirit (1 Cor 12:3). For the Christian way, to set out on a search for self-knowledge is then in a practical way going to Mass and participating in the Holy Sacrifice on the one hand, and on the other returning home and, in secret, reciting the Rosary.

We could summarize in this way: the essence of the human person is spiritual and not psychic. The alienation of the I resides in an identification of itself with what is not itself. The alchemy of the person, true personalization, consists then in detaching us from ourselves, by refusing every illusory identification with what is not the spiritual center of the human being, in breaking with the comedy of the ego that binds us to a having instead of liberating us into being. To cease binding ourselves to incessant psychic changes out of which our daily life is made is to pass through death; but, if what ought to die were a reality, the commandment of Christ would make no sense, for what is cannot, cease being. In return, if the self is only an illusion of appropriation, a flight from existence, then to die to illusion is to be born to knowledge.

Bent over ourselves in pursuit of our soul, we are like someone who wants to jump beyond his shadow. "Madman, they will say, are you going to jump beyond your shadow?,"[102] and the discouraged madman 'resolutely' abandons himself to despair. The answer, however, is of an admirable simplicity: TO LEAP BEYOND OUR SHADOWS, WE HAVE TO TURN TOWARDS THE SUN.

102   Del Vasto, *La Montée des Âmes vivantes*, 159.

The Constitution of Man According to the Philosophical Method

The Anthropological Caduceus

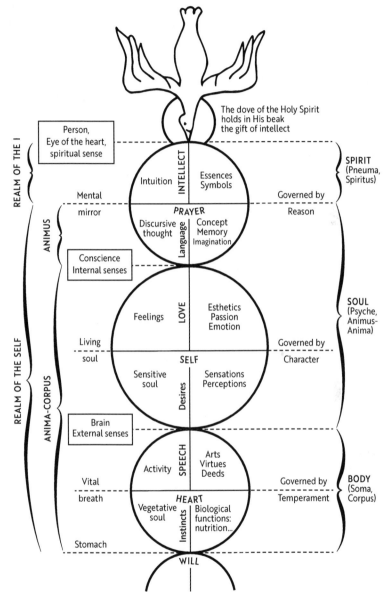

What is a man, that thou shouldst magnify him or why dost thou set thy heart upon him?
Job 7:17

Note: This diagram shows only one possible synthesis among others

8

The Constitution of Man According to the New Testament

THE DOCTRINE JUST EXAMINED IS A KEY TO New Testament anthropology. But only a concise demonstration will be useful, since an exhaustive study is obviously impossible. To do so would mean entering into quite lengthy debates, as well as justifying our interpretations each time before the tribunal—in frequent disagreement with itself—of all the exegetes who have dealt with these questions.

Now we contend that most exegetes we have read do not draw their anthropological interpretation from the text studied, but rather interpret the scriptural texts as a function of their own anthropological bias, that is to say: either that of the Catholic Church — this is the best case; or that of our own time — and that is not worth much; or that which, *in their opinion*, the evangelists must have had — and that is the worst case. There are, however, anthropological ideas about which they do not have the slightest clue, ideas that will, we think, clarify the texts.

Knowing what the sacred text says about man is without interest if it is only to satisfy cultural or ethnological curiosity. What matters is knowing what the constitution of man is (structural anthropology) and if Revelation is indeed speaking to us about it (exegesis). Undoubtedly Revelation passes through cultural contingencies. But, in reality, this culture reflects a universal doctrine to be found again and again under various forms in all civilizations, except in the modern West. Perhaps it is time to credit the scientific objectivity of Holy Scriptures' anthropological concepts, and to question those of the modern West, whether the implicit anthropology of an ordinary person or, which is worse, the explicit and fundamentally anti-religious anthropology of the social sciences, psychoanalysis for example.[1]

---

1   The human sciences may touch upon the truth in a great many points of detail. But the intention that presides over their birth and continues to animate them is, essentially, antireligious and delights in debasing man by reducing him to

Viewed as a whole, New Testament anthropology is tripartite. This is obviously contested by the majority of exegetes, for it either seems to contradict the Church's teaching or is unintelligible to the modern mind. And yet numerous texts incontestably express a tripartite anthropology. Why should they have less value than the equally numerous texts that attest to a bipartite anthropology? And so it seems of the utmost importance for theology to take both into consideration.[2]

This question is easily resolved, for once the contents of the previous chapter are clearly grasped, it will be understood that whatever is not body can be called 'soul'. Now this being perfectly admissible and verified for all cultures, what remains is that tripartition and bipartition do not correspond to the same context. When Scripture calls upon man to gather together all the elements of his being in order to venture toward God, it generally articulates a tripartition of elements. Conversely, when it calls upon man to divide himself, to renounce what—within himself—is not truly himself, it generally articulates a bipartition, and simply opposes the soul to the body. The first point of view has a more doctrinal value, while the second has, rather, a methodical or ascetic value. Man is in fact more truly himself when standing lovingly recollected before God, in the perfection of his nature, than when struggling sorrowfully in the world to conquer the imperfections of his sinful condition. Doctrinal tripartition/methodical bipartition: this principle is a major reference point, and we will come back to it as the need arises.

---

any number of determinisms: unconscious, biological, psychological, sociological, and so forth. Thus, Freud declares that man has been subject to three great humiliations: with Copernicus he learned that he was not at the center of the universe; a biological humiliation is added to the cosmological one with Darwin—man descends from the ape; with Freud himself a psychological humiliation, the most serious one, makes its appearance—man is not his own master. Cf. Freud, 'Papers on Applied Psychoanalysis', in *Collected Papers* (London: Hogarth Press, 1925), 4:350–52.

   2   One theological expert speaks of an "alleged *biblical* trichotomism" (Mgr. B. Bartmann, *Précis de théologie dogmatique* [Mulhouse: Ed. Salvator, 1938], 1:305). But one scholar, mentioning the ternary: intelligence, sensibility, corporeal activity, comments: "Here we have an unalloyed diagram of Hebraic psychology" (A. Guillaumont, 'Le sens des Noms du coeur dans l'Antiquité', in *Études carmélitaines: Le Coeur* [Bruges, Belgium: Desclée de Brouwer, 1950], 63). To our knowledge, this article is one of the most important contributions to the study of the anthropological question. We shall come back to this biblical 'trichotomism' in the next chapter.

In the present study we leave aside the question of Old Testament anthropological vocabulary. Given the abundance of texts, this is a more difficult question. For the moment, we chiefly wish to extract some basic points. First we will study the anthropology of the Gospels, then St. Paul's.

I. GOSPEL ANTHROPOLOGY ACCORDING TO THE SUPREME COMMANDMENT

If there is a central moment in Christian Revelation, it is when Christ pronounces (or causes to be pronounced) the Supreme Commandment summed up in the love of God. Now this love involves the whole man, and this is why Eternal Wisdom, opening its mouth in Jesus Christ, enumerates the basic elements of the human being that should share in this love and which, as a consequence, 'consume' human nature. To do this, Christ refers to a saying transmitted by Moses to the Jewish people on behalf of God, and that became (it is still so today) the preeminent Jewish prayer, the '*Shema Israel*' (Hear O Israel). This saying, in the Hebrew text of the Old Testament, is as follows: "Hear O Israel, the Lord our God; the Lord our God is One. You will love the Lord your God with all your heart, with all your soul, with all your strength" (Deut. 6:5).

The texts of the Gospels return to this pronouncement, but with some slight changes. Given the importance of these texts we have set up a table for them:

		You shall love the Lord your God with all your	WITH ALL	WITH ALL	WITH ALL
References	Deuteronomy 6:5	Heart	your soul (*psyche-anima*)	your strength	
	Matthew 22:37	Heart	your soul (*psyche-anima*)		your thought (*dianoïa-mens*)
	Mark 12:30 (Jesus)	Heart	your soul (*psyche-anima*)	your strength	your thought (*dianoïa-mens*)
	Mark 12:33 (the scribe)	Heart	your mind (*synesis-intellectus*)	your strength	
	Luke 10:27	Heart	your soul (*psyche-anima*)	your strength	your thought (*dianoïa-mens*)

155

A first observation to be drawn from this table is this: the anthropological structure of New Testament texts is, on the whole, identical to that of the Old Testament text. However — and this is our second observation — Matthew does not name 'strength' (present in Mark and Luke), while he adds 'thought' (which Mark and Luke also do). Why does Matthew not name the body? And why do the three synoptics add 'thought' to the traditional ternary?

To the first question we answer: since 'soul' is not used in isolation (in which case it would designate the entire person), it is endowed with a specific sense — the 'living' soul. It therefore indicates the vegetative and animal psychism. As, in reality, the body is inseparable from the soul, its presence is assumed implicitly, and this is why Matthew does not speak of it explicitly. For Matthew, then, the soul is the *anima-corpus*. Also notice how the other formulations do not speak of the body either, but of 'strength' or 'might'. This means that the body is viewed under its dynamic aspect, that very aspect by which it is most closely related to the psychism properly so-called.

As for the second question, notice that we have translated *dianoia* and *mens* as 'thought' rather than 'mind' as is usually done. Many commentators think[3] that the introduction of this fourth term proves that the authors of these texts no longer understand the word *heart* as designating one's intelligence, the intellectual intuition, and that for them it simply means affectivity. We remain unconvinced for several reasons.

The Gospels do not ignore the profound meaning of *heart*. However, to be brief, we cannot examine all uses of this term. As we have demonstrated, the heart can designate the 'me', the center of the psycho-corporeal individuality, just as well as a person's spiritual center. And the Gospels exhibit this duality of meaning. But, as a matter of fact, there are two quite essential texts that attest to the 'heart-intellect' meaning, to a direct and unitive heart-knowledge. The first is also the one in which Matthew uses the word *heart* for the first time, the sixth Beatitude of the Sermon on the Mount: "Blessed are the pure in heart, for they shall *see* God" (Matt. 5:8). If the pure heart sees God, this is because there is an 'eye of the heart', which is the spiritual intelligence.

3 This is so for A. Guillaumont in his article from *Le Coeur* ('Le sens des Noms du coeur dans l'Antiquité', 64).

Besides, the Church has interpreted the text in just this way. Connecting the sixth Beatitude with the sixth gift of the Holy Spirit, the Church sees in the 'pure heart' the gift of understanding: "The sixth operation of the Holy Spirit, which is the intellect," writes St. Augustine, "comes to those who have a pure heart, to those whose purified eye can see what the eye does not see."[4] And St. Thomas, who quotes this passage from St. Augustine, concludes by saying here "the perfect vision of the intellect causing us to see God in his Essence."[5]

The second passage is the following: "But Mary kept all these things, pondering them in her heart" (Luke 2:19). The Greek verb—translated as 'ponder'—is *symballein* (to connect or join together), already encountered with respect to symbols: Mary connected, joined together all these things in her heart. This is the founding verse of Christian theology, since its goal is not so much to render each truth of faith intelligible in itself as to clarify one truth in the light of all the others; in short, to demonstrate the *coherence* of dogma: "Theology supposes the objective unity and the logical relatedness of Revelation," through which it provides "a scientific exposition of supernatural truths and facts concerning salvation . . . an exposition presented as an organic whole and a systematic unity."[6] The systematic coherence of dogma, the theological endeavor, was formulated for the first time by Mary, in her heart, and she can be seen as teaching it to the first theologians, the Evangelists and Apostles (St. John in particular). Mary's heart is the source of theological knowledge.

It is uncertain, then, if the 'heart' mentioned in the Greek of the New Testament's *Shema Israel* had lost its intellectual and spiritual dimension. Nor is it certain, on the other hand, that the word *dianoia*, added to the biblical ternary, designates spiritual intelligence. We would rather, in conformity with its etymology *(dia-noia* = knowledge through...), see it as the discursive faculty, thought, the mentality. This is its meaning, for example, in the following passage from the Magnificat: "[God] has scattered the proud in the imagination [thought] of their heart" (Luke 1:51)[7]—an example that is so much the more

4 *De. Serm. Dom.*, I:9.
5 *Summa Theologiae* II-II, q. 8, a. 7.
6 Bartmann, *Précis de théologie dogmatique*, 20.
7 With the same meaning, cf. Eph 2:3, 4:18, 2 Pet 3:1, and Col 1:21.

interesting since it brings together *cardia* (heart) and *dianoia* (thought), and therefore makes a distinction: the heart is the center of the being, the person involved, while thought is a faculty belonging to the person. Surely, *dianoia* used alone can designate intelligence and spirit,[8] but when juxtaposed with 'heart' it seems to designate something analogous to what we have called the 'reflective' or 'speculative intellect' belonging to the *animus* but reflecting the intellectual light. More particularly, the heart represents, then, the *being* pole of the spirit and thought the *knowledge* pole. The Gospel quaternary, then, is no less basic than the Mosaic ternary; it is even, alchemically, more precise, since it allows for the polarization, in fallen man, of spirit into being and knowledge (or, from a slightly different point of view, into will and intellect).[9]

Lastly, there is another Gospel text that implicitly attests to the anthropological tripartition, the first verse of the Magnificat. In it Mary sings: "My soul (*psyche*) doth glorify the Lord. And my spirit (*pneuma*) hath rejoiced in God my Savior." This text differentiates between the soul, which glorifies the Lord, and the spirit, which is plunged into God. Mary's soul 'glorifies' because perfectly pure and virginal; her soul reflects the Divine Light integrally, and the Divine Light is the light of glory. But the spirit exults in God himself because it is encompassed by the Divine: the soul's perfection is its virginal annihilation, its status of being a pure mirror; the perfection of the spirit is its exultation, its deifying participation in the eternal dance of Divine Love.

Something remains to be said on the theme of a person identified principially with the Divine Self. The I is not the Divine Self, and yet, outside of this Self, it is nothing: this is a mystery of both absolute identity and radical distinction that language can hardly formulate.

---

8 Cf. 1 John 5:20. This is one of the rare indisputable examples (along with 1 Pet 1:13).

9 Likewise we need to examine, in the same order of ideas, the Greek word *nous*, which means 'intellect'. Outside of St. Paul *nous* is used three times: once in Luke and twice in the Apocalypse (13:18, 17:9). All three situations involve spiritual intelligence: "Then he opened their intellect (Latin: *sensus*) to understand the scriptures" (Luke 24:45). "Let him that has intellect (Latin: *intellectum*) reckon the number of the beast." "This calls for an intellect (Latin: *sensus*) with wisdom" (Apoc 13:18, 17:9). To translate *nous* by 'reason', as is often done, is obviously not false, for we can speak of intuitive reason. We can also speak of the intellective soul or the spiritual sense. But, as is the case nowadays, rational knowledge designates the discursive train of rational thought exclusively, which exposes us to indefinite misunderstandings.

This mystery is, however, expressed by Christ in several comparisons, the clearest of which is that of the vine and the branches in St. John's Gospel. There we find every theme of our analysis clustered around the central affirmation: "I am the vine, you are the branches. He who abides in Me and I in him [in the I], he it is that bears much fruit [of love and knowledge], for apart from Me [without the Divine Self] you can do nothing. If a man does not abide in Me, he is cast forth [outside the Divine Self there is only exteriority]" (John 15:1–6). The basis for negative egology is likewise to be found there: "I am the true vine, and my Father is the vinedresser. Every branch of mine which bears no fruit [original sin], he takes away [paradise lost], and every branch that does bear fruit [the soul intent upon divine love], he prunes [negative egology] that it may bear more fruit [perfect sanctity].... Abide in Me, and I will abide in you."

2. ST. PAUL'S ANTHROPOLOGY: THE HUMAN TERNARY

St. Paul's text displays the richest palette of terms applicable to man's constitution.[10] But we will only draw attention to a few essential points, most particularly to the distinction between the psychic and the spiritual; or again, from a cognitive point of view, to the distinction between mentality and intellect, since it is their confusion that leads to the aberrations of modern pseudotheology. Now, for St. Paul, this distinction is altogether essential. But when this is not understood, or forgotten, the entirety of Christianity lapses into naturalism. The work of scholars is not without interest, but they do not always understand that the 'providential dissonances' in the language of Revelation betray the inadequacy of every formulation regarding the Formless, and this is one means by which the spirit can surpass scriptural data. Both the problems posed by scholars and the difficulties they encounter generally stem from analyzing scriptural anthropology with modern concepts.

10 Cf. Prat, *Theology of Paul*. For the question that we are treating see Father Festugière, *L'Idéal religieux des grecs et l'Evangile* (Paris: Gabalda, 1932), especially Excursus B, 196–220. We have also consulted Dom Jacques Dupont's *Gnosis, La connaissance religieuse dans les Epîtres de saint Paul* (Paris: Desclee de Brouwer, 1949), 604–59.

The ternary conception of man is clearly stated in this passage from the first letter to the Thessalonians: "May the God of peace himself sanctify you wholly; and may your whole spirit [*pneuma*], and soul [*psyche*], and body [*soma*], be kept sound and blameless in the parousia of our Lord Jesus Christ" (5:23). We will totally disregard the problems raised by historians over the Platonic, neo-Platonic, or Jewish origin of this formula.[11] Certainly it is Jewish for St. Paul, but, under one form or another, it is also universal.

However, to retain the human ternary in its virginal state, to preserve it blameless or immaculate, the grace of Christ is first needed, a grace that regenerates it by making a distinction between the psychic and the spiritual—a distinction which, of itself, incurs the death of the ego. Next we will quote another famous text: "The natural man [*psychikos anthropos*, *animalis homo*] does not perceive the gifts of the Spirit of God, for they are folly to him, and he is not able to have a gnosis of them because they are spiritually discerned. The spiritual man [*pneumatikos anthropos*, *spiritalis homo*] judges all things, but is himself to be judged of no one" (1 Cor. 2:14–15). Truly an altogether extraordinary text, it confers a near absolute superiority on the spirit. But, at the end of this same letter, there is a no less astounding text, a text where St. Paul makes a distinction between the psychic body and the spiritual one (either pneumatic or heavenly): "The body is sown a psychic body, it is raised a pneumatic body.... Thus it is written: 'The first man Adam became a living soul [*psyche*]'; the last Adam became a life-giving spirit [*pneuma*]. But it is not the pneumatic which is first but the psychic, and then the pneumatic. The first man was from the earth, a man of dust; the second man is from heaven" (1 Cor. 15:44–47).[12]

11 Cf. E. van Dobschutz, *Meyer's Kommentar*, 7th ed. (Goettingen: Vandenhoeck & Ruprecht, 1909), 230–32; cited by Prat, *Theology of Paul*, 2:54.

12 This text evidently solves the 'problem of the Resurrection', while anthropological doctrine provides a basis for this solution. What the Resurrection reveals is the semantic modality of the body of Christ, which is also its total reality. This is why it would be more exact to say, after all, that the 'gross', 'material' modality of the *corpus natum* (the body born of the Virgin) ceases to be manifest: it is reabsorbed into its psychic principle, which is in turn reabsorbed into its spiritual principle. This is why the tomb is empty of a corpse. Let us add, however, that by itself the pneumatic body cannot be sensed. To be seen and touched, it has to put on a psychic form, which it is perfectly capable of doing since, having passed beyond the world of forms, it is no longer passively subject to form, and so becomes its master. What

This teaching is echoed, it seems, in the letters of Saints James and Jude. St. James writes, speaking of those who lie against the truth: "This wisdom is not such as comes down from above, but is earthly, beastly [*psychike*], devilish" (James 3:15). And St. Jude, speaking of men of the last times, states: "It is these who set up divisions, worldly [*psychikoi*] people, devoid of the Spirit" (Jude 19).

We are confronted not only with this distinction between *pneuma* and *psyche*, but also with a real opposition. Either a man is dominated by his animic nature, and in such a case is unable to acquire a 'gnosis' of the Christian mysteries, or he becomes identified with his spiritual reality, and in such a case he judges everything and is not himself judged by anyone.

For the origin of this distinction, we turn to the scholarly discussion of it in Dom Jacques Dupont's *Gnosis*[13] and make his conclusion our own: "In speaking about psychics and pneumatics, all that we can say is that St. Paul makes use of biblical terminology." Besides, St. Paul himself indicates this by referring to the creation of Adam.[14]

This distinction between the psychic and the spiritual is quite clearly asserted by St. Paul, and yet has almost no effect on modern theological reflection. And yet everything we have said about this demonstrates its significance and importance. What we are being taught here is a rule of spiritual alchemy. Just as in alchemy a noble metal has to be separated from those vile substances with which it is alloyed, so by the grace of the Word Incarnate the pure gold of the spirit must be separated from its lethal alloy with psychic substances. St. Paul himself teaches this alchemical rule in his letter to the Hebrews: "The word of God [the *Logos*] is living and active, sharper than any two-edged sword, piercing to the division of soul and spirit" (Heb 4:12).[15]

---

must be clearly understood is that, on the one hand, there is nothing lacking in the body of the Resurrected One—to the contrary, this body is indeed truer than all other mortal bodies—and that, on the other hand, all of these facts obey perfectly objective and rigorous laws.

13   Dupont, *Gnosis*, 151–80.

14   The text of Genesis will be studied in the next chapter.

15   In keeping with Origen and the main Christian tradition, we will consider the letter to the Hebrews as being essentially from Paul. Father Prat thinks that Origen has too vague an idea of authorship (*Theology of Paul,* 1:355–6). To the contrary, it could be said that modern people, imbued as they are with individualism, have no idea of the traditional notion of authorship.

Reading these texts, it becomes perfectly clear how impossible it is to approach them with modern concepts; also how dangerous it is to have recourse to a strictly systematic terminology, or else, by a contrary excess, to see only the stutterings of a primitive form of psychology. St. Paul is certainly not concerned with the social sciences, and in no way does he seek to describe man from without. But neither does he speak just to say something — the words used are just as precise as can be. What he does say is simply this: to know oneself is to become oneself. In other words, the objective viewpoint of doctrine is inseparable from the 'subjective' viewpoint of spiritual alchemy. And it is precisely the *pneuma* that obliges us to join the one to the other. For the *pneuma* is not *naturally* at our disposal. We need to know *which* man we are speaking about: if it is about fallen man, then it is useless to have grace intervene; but if it is about the true man, then we cannot rest content with a description; we must be transformed. And yet this spirit given to us in grace is also a part of our nature, but a nature somehow supernatural. The *pneuma* is only actualized in us by *metanoia*, 'inner conversion', which is for the *psyche* purification and for the *ego* death.

This is where knowledge comes into being. And this conversion, this transformation, this alchemy is only the human dimension or human aspect of the transforming and alchemical action of divine grace. This is why the Pauline *pneuma* is sometimes the Holy Spirit and sometimes the spiritual man, without it always being possible to discern which one is involved. This is because the spirit of man is inhabited by the Spirit of God that renews him (Eph 4:23) and unites with him (Rom 8:16), so that "he who is united to the Lord becomes one *pneuma* with him" (1 Cor 6:17).[16]

16   Recall that this human *pneuma* is the very breath of God with which he has 'inspired' us (Gen 2:17). Philo of Alexandria writes: "While non-reasoning beings are directed at all times by divine eternal reason, each one of us share directly in divine life through the communication which he has received at birth from the divine *pneuma*. And this *pneuma* is not the air in motion, but a certain imprint and replication of the divine power which, with a fitting word, Moses names 'image' (icon), to signify that God is the archetype of the 'logical' nature, man being His resemblance and effigy — man, not one who lives with a dual nature, but the best part of the soul which is called intellect [*nous*] and *logos*." *Quod deter. potiori insidiari soleat,* 80–84, cited and translated by Festugière, *L'Idéal religieux,* 216. And Festugière concludes: through the *pneuma* "the human soul, alone among all creatures, is really more than a creature, is something of God himself" (219).

3. PNEUMATIZATION OF THE INTELLECT

St. Paul's text also poses the problem of the relationship between spirit (*pneuma*) and intellect (*nous*). We have already dealt with this question from a philosophical point of view and, at that time, indicated that such a problem was likewise posed in other cultures.[17]

Many commentators think there is an opposition between spirit and intellect in St. Paul.[18] Others are confronted by a difficulty. "The supernatural," writes Father Prat in regard to the intellect, "is outside of its sphere, and the mysteries of faith are beyond it."[19] But later he recognizes: "It is certain that St. Paul sometimes employs *pneuma* as a synonym of *nous*";[20] to which should be added: and conversely.

Faithful to the conclusions of our anthropology, we propose that matters be viewed in the following way — once marginal variations in vocabulary are admitted. The spirit designates the Divine Life in a creature, life according to its inmost dimension, the actualization of which is strictly dependent upon the grace of Christ. *Intellect* designates a 'naturally supernatural' faculty of knowledge which knows — or can know — spiritual truth, but which, being passive by definition — the price of its objectivity — is also powerless to move the will of a being in its entirety. However, being natural, being that capacity for pure knowledge that sin has not abolished — but only obscured — the intellect enables the human being, in its present state, to enter *intelligibly* into contact with or have a clear awareness of realities that surpass it *ontologically*: by the naturally supernatural intellect, supernatural realities are meaningful for a natural being; otherwise they would remain all but nonexistent. As extraordinary as manifestations of spiritual power may be, they are strictly unimportant for a being that is their momentary support if it is incapable of grasping them intelligibly, of having a true and effective awareness of them, and also of assimilating them into its own being. There is no salvation for man as a conscious being outside of this awareness.

17 Cf. Guénon, 'Spirit and Intellect', in *Miscellanea*, trans. H. D. Fohr, C. Bethel, P. Moore, H. Schiff (Hillsdale, NY: Sophia Perennis, 2001), 24–28.

18 Dupont, *Gnosis*, 154.

19 Prat, *Theology of Paul*, 2:51.

20 Ibid., 2:54, note 4.

And so we come to a dual relationship between *nous* and *pneuma*: to really understand the mysteries of the Spirit, man needs to proceed with an *intellectualization of the spiritual*; but, to give life and reality to what is only speculative and therefore impotent knowledge, he also needs to proceed with a *pneumatization of the intellect*. By itself, natural knowledge is able to set our being in motion: if we know that our house is burning, we save ourselves because, for our natural being, life and death have an immediate and existential significance. But when in the same way we know that without Divine Grace we will not escape the fire of hell (or, let us say, the deadly irreality in the very fabric of the created), this knowledge is without effect on our being because it has only a theoretical significance: our natural being does not have the sense of its own salvation. The spirit (the sense of spiritual *reality*) awakens once intellective knowledge begins to have a life-or-death significance as existential as burning is for the body.

The intellectualization of the *pneuma* is taught in the famous passage from First Corinthians where St. Paul alludes to phenomena, probably spiritual in origin, produced in certain Christian communities. These charismatic phenomena were manifested above all in the utterance of unintelligible words, 'speaking in tongues'. St. Paul writes: "For if I pray in a tongue, my spirit prays but my intellect [*nous*] is unfruitful. What am I to do? I will pray with the spirit and I will pray with the intellect also; I will sing with the spirit and I will sing with the intellect also.... I would rather speak five words with my intellect, in order to instruct others, than ten thousand words in a tongue" (1 Cor 14:14–19). As we see, the intellect should intervene, if only to 'interpret', as St. Paul says, what the Spirit reveals.

Likewise, we see by this that the realm of the supernatural is in no way forbidden to the intellect, since, to the contrary, it is the intellect's duty to penetrate it. But, even though the intellect is able to 'interpret' the pneumatic and is truly the hermeneut of the spiritual, nevertheless it remains powerless by itself alone to make a human being enter into the life of the Spirit: "For I delight in the law of God, according to the inward man, but I see in my members another law.... Wretched man that I am! Who will deliver me from the body of this death? Thanks be to God through Jesus Christ our Lord! So

164

then, I of myself serve the law of God with my intellect, but with my flesh I serve the law of sin" (Rom 7:22–25).

In this celebrated text the intellect appears in its true nature: it is, by essence, divine knowledge; like a mirror it cannot but reflect the light that it receives: "I of myself serve the law of God with my intellect," a submission in some way inevitable, a submission of nature, and yet a submission powerless, because of "the body of this death," to enable a being to enter wholly into Divine Reality. Surely this does not involve the body as such, but the flesh, the fascinating and captivating *anima-corpus* of the person, that which makes us feel another law, another will: the law of its members. We need, then, to disentangle the spiritual from the psychic, to alchemically extract man (the inward one) from his mortal body, and this is truly the pneumatization of the intellect, that which transforms the speculative intellect into the operative intellect. This process is explicitly taught by St. Paul, who writes in the continuation of our text: "I appeal to you therefore, brethren, by the mercies of God, to present your bodies as a living sacrifice, holy and acceptable to God, which is your spiritual worship. Do not be conformed to this world, but be transformed by the renewal of your intellect, that you may prove what is the will of God" (Rom 12:1–2).[21]

The 'renewal' of the intellect thus results from the change of the ego's attitude with respect to the body (the *anima-corpus*), which stops wanting to possess the body since it, the body, is offered in sacrifice to God. The same alchemical separation, the condition for the pneumatization of the intellect, is taught even more explicitly in the letter to the Ephesians, but formulated with a more striking analogy: "Now this I affirm and testify in the Lord, that you must no longer live as the Gentiles do, in the futility of their intellect . . . you did not so learn Christ!—assuming that you have heard about him and were taught in him, as the truth is in Jesus. Put off the old man which belongs to your former manner of life and is corrupt through deceitful lusts, and be renewed in the *pneuma* of your intellect, and put on the new man, created after the likeness of God (*kata Theon*) in true righteousness and holiness" (Eph 4:17–24).

21 This text marks the limit of Conciliar *aggiornamento*.

In the old man, corrupted by deceptive lusts, we easily recognize the self, a prisoner to its illusory desire to possess. As for the formula 'the *pneuma* of the intellect', in which we find the New Man, it admirably conveys how the intellect is imbued with the *pneuma* that 'renews' it, transforms it — 'metamorphoses' in the Greek text — or even leads it beyond the world of forms, the world of psycho-corporeal reality. We have access, then, to the true intellect that is the Divine Intellect: "O depth of the riches and wisdom and gnosis of God! How unsearchable are his judgments and how inscrutable his ways! For *who has known the Intellect of the Lord?*" (Rom 11:33).[22] And St. Paul answers Isaiah: "The pneumatic man judges all things; but is himself to be judged by no one. For who has known the intellect of the Lord so as to instruct him? But we have the Intellect of Christ" (1 Cor 2:16).

4. THE PERSON: THE INWARD MAN

The goal of the pneumatization of the intellect is access to the inward man, the immortal person. That the intellect, in its true nature, is identical to the inward man is implied in the text quoted from the letter to the Romans. Let us reread this text: "For I delight in the law of God, according to the inward man.... So then, I of myself serve the law of God with my intellect" (Rom 7:22–5).

This inward man is our true self, the one no longer a prisoner to the deceptive lusts of the ego desiring to possess its psycho-corporeal substance, that is to say, the flesh. First, we need to recognize this dialectic of the I and the me, and become aware of the duality of wills: "For I do not do what I want, but I do the very thing I hate. Now if I do what I do not want, I agree that the law is good.... So then it is no longer I [the true I] that do it, but sin which dwells within me. For I know that nothing good dwells within me, *that is, in my flesh*" (Rom 7:15–18). Thus, the possessive illusion of the natural self, the illusion of the flesh, of the outward man, is decried. And, at the same time, the restoration of the new man is effected, he who is also primordial man, he who was created "in the likeness of God" under the action of the divine *pneuma*, which is united with the human *pneuma*

---

22   The question in italics is a citation from Isaiah (40:13).

in the grace of Jesus Christ: "But if ... you, a wild olive shoot, were grafted ... to share the rich root of the olive tree, do not boast over the branches. If you do boast, remember it is not you that support the root, but the root that supports you" (Rom 11:17–18). Sprung from the root of the Christic olive tree, the initiate to the mysteries of baptismal illumination sees the outer man perish and the inner man grow: "For it is the God who said, 'Let light shine out of darkness', who has shone in our hearts to give the light of the gnosis of the glory of God in the face of Christ.... Though our outward man is wasting away [with tribulations, sickness, and death], our inward man is being renewed day by day" (2 Cor 4:6–16).

This is the (never-ending) goal of our long journey. And some will say: "What bearing does all this have on charity?" Listen to St. Paul's answer:

> For this reason I bow my knees before the Father, from whom all paternity in heaven and on earth is named, that according to the riches of his glory he may grant you to be strengthened with might through his Spirit in the *inner man*, and that Christ may dwell in your hearts through faith; that you, being rooted and grounded in charity, may have power to comprehend with all the saints what is the breadth and length and height and depth, and to know the Love of Christ which surpasses all knowledge, that you may be filled with all the fulness of God. (Eph 3:14–19)

And this is why God would reveal this anthropology to man. But Christians have turned toward the secular sciences, and the Love of Christ is no longer known.

9

Concerning Anthropology
in the Greek, Jewish, and
Christian Traditions

INTRODUCTION

Under the term 'trichotomism', coined by later theologians, the Catholic Church has condemned in several instances a conception of man that would divide him into three different principles and would 'cut in three' (trichotomism) the human being. "Man's nature is composed of body and soul. To this anthropological dualism is opposed *trichotomism* according to which man is composed of three substances: body, soul and spirit"[1] — the very three terms of our anthropology. In general (but not always), this doctrine is attributed to Plato. In giving a divine origin to the soul, Plato, it is believed, establishes its immortality. But he destroys the unity of the human being by having this soul descend into a body which is by nature foreign to it. This is also why he needs to suppose another soul, intermediate between the immortal soul and the body. Actually, theologians sometimes rank Plato among the trichotomists, and sometimes among the extreme dualists![2]

This question is quite complicated, and we do not intend to deal with it exhaustively. But obviously it cannot be avoided, given the doctrine we have set out. The most important point seems to be the following: the Church essentially upholds the unity of the human being. The soul being the principle of unity (the soul is the form of the body), to allow for two souls is to allow for two principles of

---

1 Mgr. Bartmann, *Théologie dogmatique*, vol. 1:303. The term 'trichotomism' is, moreover, not very satisfactory, since it literally means 'cut in three'. We prefer to speak of an anthropological tripartition.

2 In general, theologians think that the Magisterium has condemned trichotomism, at least implicitly, in several declarations; cf. Denziger 148, 255, 338, 480–81, 738, and 1655 (numeration according to Eng. ed., *Sources of Dogma* — Trans.), which date from the years 451, 870, 1312, 1513, and 1857.

unity. If such is the Catholic doctrine, surely it defines an incontestable truth that disqualifies every contrary doctrine.

Now, whether the errors condemned by the Church were actually those of the people to whom they were attributed, that is another matter eliciting countless questions, some of which we should pose.

On the first point, the reading of magisterial texts indeed seems to confirm that, for the Church, this essentially involves affirming the unity of the human being: "While the Old and the New Testament teach that man has only one reasonable and intellective soul, and while all of the Fathers and God-inspired doctors in the Church affirm the same doctrine, some, heeding perverse intentions, have come to such a degree of impiety as to imprudently teach that man has two souls...."[3] Such is the declaration of the first Council of Constantinople (the Eighth Ecumenical Council, 870) condemning Photius. The most important magisterial text is that of the Council of Vienne and dates from 1312. It condemns, without naming him, a Franciscan theologian Pierre-Jean Olieu, also called Olivi:[4] "we reprove as erroneous and opposed to the truth of the Catholic faith every doctrine and every thesis rashly affirming that the substance of the rational and intellective soul is not truly and by itself the form of the human body, or placing such in doubt; ... let whoever will nevertheless dare to obstinately affirm, defend, or support that the rational or intellective soul is not by itself and essentially the form of the human body, be considered as a heretic."[5]

As for the second point, which concerns the crux of the problem, we only wish to pose some questions and make some remarks.

From the outset, and whatever the anthropology adopted, one truth is universally recognized by particular doctrines as well as philosophical analysis in general, and this is that *the spiritual and the psychic are not realities of the same nature,* any more than nerve impulses and blood are. Not only does neither Holy Scripture nor reason teach the contrary of this truth, but they both even affirm it quite positively. Between a biological process, an emotion, and the understanding of

3 Dumeige, *La Foi catholique* (Paris: Éditions de l'Orante, 1961), noum. 264.
4 About Olivi, cf. David Flood's article "Le projet franciscain de Pierre Olivi," in the review *Études franciscaines* 23, no. 3-4 (1973), 367-79.
5 Dumeige, noum. 265.

a metaphysical truth, there is a difference not only of degree but of nature, just as what the last two terms have in common is to be 'invisible' in themselves.

Secondly, when it is specified that the intellective soul is — by *itself* and without intermediary — the form of the body, that is to say the principle of its unity and activity, a truth is taught that in no way contradicts our anthropology, since, as we have seen to the contrary, intellect and will (that is to say the spirit) form the unity and activity of the whole human being, and are without intermediary — which would hardly have any meaning. But, the line of demarcation being able to pass to different levels, what is understood by body and what by soul must therefore be made explicit. If by body is understood the living organic matter of the body actually present, then it would be necessary to speak of giving a form not to the *corpus*, but to the *anima-corpus* by the *animus-spiritus*, for, as we have shown, the body, the notion of a purely material reality (*partes extra partes*) is devoid of meaning.[6] If, on the other hand, by soul is designated, in a more vague manner, the human being viewed in its internal principle, prior to every distinction of function or nature, in this case the soul is posited as the synthetic reality of everything invisible in man, and is therefore opposed to the visible body. To distinguish several souls is then, from this perspective, to cut man up into several realities, and this is actually unacceptable. Surely it is in this broad sense that the word *soul* is used in canonical texts.

But whether it is a question of the pair *anima-corpus/animus-spiritus* or of the pair *corpus/anima* (*animus-spiritus*), the solution remains the same: it is clearly the intellect (or the spirit) that is, without intermediary, the principle of unity and corporeal activity, — our whole anthropology shows this — but it is not so under its properly intellective or spiritual modality, under its purest form. The error of Father Olivi, if it is indeed his, is to conceive of the animal soul as a principle other than the spiritual one and exterior to it, thanks to which the intellect would become the principle of the body. Olivi objected, they say,

---

6 We shall soon see that such is indeed the Thomist solution (which certain Thomists have a tendency to obscure): the intellective soul comes to give form to a corporeal matter, itself *already* given form by the vegetative soul and the animal soul; in short, the intellect gives form to the *anima-corpus*.

that if the intellect were formally the principle of the body, the body would be spiritual. Now the body is indeed actually spiritual, even if this modality is not presently manifested (although it can be among the saints),[7] while the psychic modality of the corporeal is altogether perceptible, and perhaps commonly observed, if one is not blinded by a narrowly materialist prejudice. In pervading the body the spirit assumes a psychic modality: this is apparently what the Bible teaches when it says that God formed the human body from the earth, then breathed a breath of life — the spirit — and Adam became a 'living soul'. We would abandon this view only if someone would explain how there is no difference between cellular metabolism and metaphysical contemplation. We do not deny that this metabolism is, at last resort, intelligible in nature, and we even affirm this explicitly. But we do not encounter here *actual* universality, timelessness, or transparency (since, to the contrary, it actually involves a particular process, temporal in its very reality, and carried out by being closed upon itself). Now universality, timelessness, and transparency are surely features of intellective activity, such as we know it, viewed, certainly not in its physiological concomitances, but in itself. Short of proof to the contrary, to understand a truth means that a universal, timeless reality, without any opaqueness or closure, comes to exist in our mind.[8]

On the other hand, it is not at all certain that the doctrine of the soul as 'form of the body' preserves the unity of the human being. Descartes in fact, who is credited with having pushed the dualism and the mutual exclusion of soul and body to their extreme consequences, was not loath to use this expression. And yet it is quite clearly Aristotelian.[9]

7 Cf., for example, St. Seraphim of Sarov.

8 By universal we understand that which is valid for every being; it is true for God, for the angel, for man, for the cat, for the 'Martian', as, in Euclidian geometry, the sum of the angles of a triangle is equal to two right angles. By timeless we mean that which has no need of time to exist, that which, of itself, is outside time; a geometric relationship proceeds in fact from the timeless nature of the triangle. By transparent we mean perfectly understandable, and therefore able to be partaken of, open to the totality of the real; this proposition does not exclude any other one (in a general way, transparency is the quality of non-individual realities, realities that have no need of being individuals — closed upon themselves — to be real).

9 Cf. the two letters to Father Mesland, *Œuvres* (Paris: Gallimard, 1937), 1174 and 1224. Recall, however, that there is also for Descartes a substantial union of

Finally, it should be asked whether the handbooks and dictionaries of theology, even the most serious, always make the effort necessary to understand anthropological doctrine clearly, Plato's as well as Aristotle's. One often has the impression that, far from reading the texts, the authors of these works are content to repeat certain oversimplified statements that are, in reality, only dealing with a caricature of Platonism. How far the imaginary Plato of Jacques Maritain is from the real Plato of Simone Weil! Will it be said that for St. Paul there are two souls, or two selves, because the Apostle declares with one and the same breath: "It is no longer *I* who do [evil], but the sin which dwells in *me*. Yes, I know that nothing good lives in me, that is in my flesh"? What may be thought of this dualism of the carnal self and the spiritual self? And how do we not find the Pauline opposition between inner and outer man excessive? How do we not qualify as hatred of the body the celebrated cry: "Who will deliver me from the body of this death?" (Rom 7:24) That it might be concluded from a cursory reading that St. Paul is denying the unity of man, that for him the body is a tomb — this is what will provoke the liveliest reactions of theologians and exegetes. Yet it is exactly in this way that they proceed with regard to Plato and the Platonists, and even Aristotle, for Aristotle himself said that the intellect was not the form of the body.

It seems that we need to supply then, in a first section, some texts and references which will afford a better grasp of the doctrines of Plato and Aristotle.

In a second section of this report we examine Old Testament anthropological doctrine, the 'trichotomist' character of which is not in doubt.

Lastly, in a third section, we attempt to locate the thread of a tripartite anthropological conception in the Christian tradition. Texts are not lacking, they abound. The difficulty is to choose the most significant.

---

soul and body, and that the 'animal spirits' in particular are charged with assuring the communication of thinking substance and extended substance, of knowledge and action.

I. THE DOCTRINES OF THE SOUL
IN PLATO AND ARISTOTLE

1. Plato or the Unification of the Multiple Soul

We see in Plato the one responsible for an almost Manichean dualism of soul and body leading to a scorn for the latter. The soul is divine by nature, the body is a tomb: *soma-sema* in Greek.[10] There must be then an intermediary element between the two that participates in both and puts them into communication. The 'part' in man that is turned towards the upper regions and the intelligible is the intellect (*nous*); the 'part' turned towards the lower regions and the corporeal is the concupiscible (*epithumetikon*), the object of desire (*epithumia*); the intermediate 'part' is the irascible (*thumoeides*), the seat of which is the *thumos*, the noble heart. However different in nature, these three 'parts' yet form a single whole in man.[11]

How is this possible? To show how one same reality can present contrary aspects, Plato borrows the (traditional) image of a spinning top.[12] We in fact distinguish in this object an immobile vertical axis at its center and a circular surface in motion, perpendicular to this axis, the circumference of which is moving with the greatest speed: there is at once, then, rest and motion in one and the same thing. One will recognize here our previously sketched geometric diagram: the circumference corresponds to the body, the circular surface to the psychism, the circle's center to the intellect, and the vertical axis to the radius that unites the human immortal to the Divine Immortal.

This unity is not only expressed in an abstract and geometric manner. It is equally and quite concretely represented in the famous image of the man presented by the *Republic*[13] as a 'chimerical animal' whose belly is formed by a many-headed Hydra, its heads regrowing as they are cut off—a symbol of the concupiscible with its manifold and ceaselessly renewed desires; the chest by a lion—a symbol of the irascible, at once courageously noble and prone to fits of hot temper; and lastly the head by a human body—a symbol of the intellect—with

10   *Gorgias* 493a.
11   *Republic* IV, 435d–441c; IX, 58b–e; *Phaedrus* 245c–246d, 253c–254b; *Timaeus* 34c–37c, 41a–44d, 69c–71a, 77b.
12   *Republic* IV, 436d–e.
13   *Republic* IX, 588c–e.

the whole enveloped in a greater human body — the unity of the composite. We can relate the three parts of this Chimera to the anthropological localizations of the *Timaeus*,[14] which places the intellective soul in the head, the irascible soul in the chest, above the diaphragm, and the concupiscible soul in the belly. The head is then seen to be a kind of summary of the body when we discover that the mouth corresponds to the belly, the nose to the chest, and the eyes and brow to the head itself. The head is therefore a summary of man, and this is why the mythical animal of the *Republic* is itself represented by man: in some fashion it is 'the man within man'. The human body in its totality is therefore raised to the dignity of a symbol of the intellect and, by that very fact, visibly manifests the unity realized invisibly among all elements of the human being. Inner man is symbolized by outer man; he is to himself his own symbol, in a kind of 'scene within a scene', where the one is echoed within the many and prolongs its ontological vibration up to the unity of the first Source.

Simply reading these texts we can gauge how absurd it is to see in this identification of man with the intellect a kind of 'angelist' mutilation of the human being. Besides, such an interpretation expressly contradicts the role that Plato has the body — and music — play in the education of the city's guardians (and apprentice philosophers): in Book IV of the *Republic* we are being invited to practice a veritable 'yoga'.

Although Plato's anthropological tripartition is not a trichotomism, that is to say a cutting of man in three, is there a certain 'orphic' dualism in it that seems inspired by a scorn for the body? Is there a contradiction? Is not the body a tomb for the soul? Now, far from being evil by nature, the body can also, for Plato, belong to the gods: "our fancy pictures," he says, "the god whom we have never seen, nor fully conceived, as an immortal living being, possessed of a soul and body united for all time."[15] The body falls, then, under no curse. But, for man, the possibility of evil resides in the soul itself, to the extent that the exterior world, through the sensory appearance effected by its corporeal medium, *can* become for the soul an object of covetousness. Once more we find here, under a somewhat different form, what we call the possessive illusion of the self and what Scripture calls the *flesh*:

14 *Timaeus* 69c–d.
15 *Phaedrus* 246d.

"the soul," says Plato, "is a helpless prisoner, chained hand and foot in the body, compelled to view reality not directly but only through its prison bars"; but "philosophy can see that the imprisonment is ingeniously effected by the prisoner's own active desire, *which makes him first accessory to his own confinement.*"[16] As Paul Ricœur writes, "the evil influence of the body does not reside in what today we would call its materiality, nor in its power to make contact with things; rather, what is blamed in that contact is the 'spell' that bewitches it and thus rivets the soul to the body, making it captive to the 'contact.'"[17] For the desiring soul, the body is the possibility of an opening towards an indefinite and dispersive multiplicity; this is so not in itself, but because it offers the soul an occasion to actualize the 'vertigo' within itself.

As already noted, the opposition of body and soul therefore has, with Plato, an essentially 'alchemical' and spiritual significance, even though this 'separation' is itself only a phase of this alchemy. The other phase is that of unification of the soul's parts by a hierarchizing of them: the concupiscible soul subjects itself to the irascible soul which in turn subjects itself to the intellective or noetic soul, which only realizes its true nature by gaining access to the 'beatific vision'.[18] Now this hierarchical unification is not a stopgap measure for a doctrine which, unable to be rid of a foreign element, namely the body, would resolve matters by neutralizing it: this is an integration of the lower elements of the soul which *makes use of their energies in its ascent to God.*

These are not minor or latent themes that might go unnoticed with a cursory reading. Without speaking of the *Phaedrus* where these themes are evident in all their 'exultation', we will just recall that they are a fundamental topic in the *Republic*, Plato's longest and most important dialogue. One can obviously 'trichotomize' Plato by taking literally an almost always symbolic manner of speaking, or by being content with a summary of second- and third-hand information from a history-of-philosophy handbook, especially 'Scholastic' handbooks. Such an interpretation is more difficult to support when a text brimming at once with freshness and the sublime is read attentively.

---

16 *Phaedo* 82e.

17 *The Symbolism of Evil* (Boston: Beacon Press, 1969), 338.

18 *Phaedrus* 250b. The expression 'blessed vision' or 'beatific vision' is actually in the Greek text: *makarian opsin.*

We think that Plato would hardly recognize himself either in the trichotomism ascribed to him or in the scorn of the body attributed to him. Defining what justice is, no longer in the city this time but in the individual, in that interior city that is the wise man, he writes: "These two [the intellective and affective parts], thus reared and having learned and been educated to do their own work in the true sense of the phrase, will preside over the appetitive part which is the mass of the soul in each of us."[19] A little after, as to the just man, he affirms both the unity of the soul and the place set aside for the body: the just man

> must not suffer the [three] principles in his soul to do each the work of some other and interfere and meddle with one another; but he should dispose well of what in the true sense of the word is properly his own, and having first attained to self-mastery and beautiful order within himself, and having harmonized these three principles [of his soul], the notes or intervals of three terms [of a musical scale] . . . and made of himself a unit, one man instead of many, self-controlled and in unison, he should then and only then turn to practice if he find aught to do either in the getting of wealth or the tendency of the body or it may be in political action or private business — in all such doings believing and naming the just and honorable action to be that which preserves and helps to produce this condition of soul, and wisdom the science that presides over such conduct.[20]

The difficulty with this doctrine, for Christians or simply anyone heir to a vision of man marked by Christianity, is not so much the problem of the unity of the soul — which, by itself, is a unifying principle — as that of the unity of a 'man-being' and his soul. In some respects the soul, or rather the intellect that is the 'soul's pilot',[21] makes its appearance in Plato as a transcendent principle that sometimes seems to pass through the human form while remaining ontologically foreign to it. Should we

19 *Republic* IV, 442a.
20 Ibid., 433d–e.
21 *Phaedrus* 247c.

stop at this conclusion? Or else is the question we raise only meaningful for a Judeo-Christian perspective that sees first in man his *being as a creature*, regardless of the properties defining his essence? We readily lean in this direction, seeing that it is not easy to understand exactly what Plato 'thought' about man-beings, or even if he thought anything at all about them — for want of a radical (*ex nihilo*) conception about creation — which also prevents us from interpreting this in a basically non-Christian sense. But there is no doubt that he saw the way of wisdom as the realization of inner unity, and Paul Valéry is right to place on the lips of Socrates the words: "I was born several . . . I died *one*."[22]

2. Aristotle or the Mystery of the Intellect

To go from Plato to Aristotle is to change intellective climate. Plato is a 'mystical' metaphysician, Aristotle is a scientific philosopher. This difference in thinking 'styles' must never be lost sight of if one values the pertinence of certain comparisons.

Aristotle defines the soul as the 'form of the body', or, more exactly, as "the completed form [*entelekheia*] of a natural body having life potentially within it."[23] 'Form' does not just mean 'shape' or 'spatial envelope', but more generally 'whatever informs', that is, gives some 'material' a specific organization. Thus Apollo's form informs the material of marble, conferring on it not only a spatial envelope, but even a set 'cultural identity': that of Apollo, who might just as well inform bronze or wood. For Aristotle, the pure form of Apollo does not exist all by itself, in a separated state, like Plato's Ideas. It is only real by being actualized in matter, which does not have moreover an exclusively 'materialist' sense, nor does it exist in a separated state.

To speak of the soul as the form of the body therefore means that it is the principle and cause of everything that is organization, structure, order, and activity in the body. From the tiniest cell to the differentiated structuring of bone, muscle, and nervous tissue, etc., right up to the structure of the most complex organs, everything is the work

22 *Eupalinos*, in *Dialogues*, ed. Jackson Mathews (Princeton: Princeton University Press, 1989), 109.

23 *On the Soul* II, 1, 412a2. With some exceptions we will cite Aristotle in the Smith translation (Oxford: Clarendon Press, 1931); we venture to translate here the untranslatable *entelekheia* (entelechy) as 'completed form'.

of the informing soul; or rather, because the soul does not act *on* the body, the corporeal organization is the soul as the form of the body, a unity immanent to matter, as inseparable from the body as the blade is from the axe. It is then that which actualizes the life that is potentially in the body, or rather it is the very act of life, life in act, the living being insofar as it lives. This is not a static structure but a continual activity. In other words, there is no other body than an animated body, a living body: at the very instant the soul vanishes the body deconstructs, loses its organization, becomes undone; its 'solidity' and permanence are the soul's, not its own.

Quite briefly summarized, such is Aristotle's doctrine.[24] Body and soul being inseparable, the problem of their union is not posed: they are aspects, distinguished by a well-justified abstraction, of one and the same reality. But it does not follow that the study of the soul is in this case a part of *physics*, in Aristotle's sense, that is, as the study of everything that forms a part of nature (*physis*). The soul being the form of the body, and the body being wholly nature, soul is body's 'naturing' principle, the principle of everything that is living structure and physiological functioning. This is true for the vegetative and animal souls. But is this true for the whole soul? No, Aristotle replies, "for it is not the whole soul that constitutes the animal nature."[25] There is something difficult or obscure here, bound up with what we have called the 'mystery of the intellect'.

The human soul is, in fact, capable of thinking. Now this intellective activity is, in itself, unrelated to any bodily movement, to any particular biological function, such as the digestive or visual functions.[26] The intellective — or noetic — soul is 'naturing' from nothing of the corporeal: in this sense it is not the 'form of the body', the 'entelechy of the natural body'. Whereas the vegetative and animal soul is always the naturing principle of a set activity — the stomach digests and does not see, the eye sees and does not digest — the thinking soul can think or comprehend no matter what: it is, one might say, a universal

24 Ibid., II, 1.

25 *On the Parts of Animals* I, 641b10 (trans. Ogle).

26 *On the Soul* III, 4, 429b24. Contrary to Plato, Aristotle does not tie the activity of common sense to cerebral activity but to the physiology of the heart: *On the Parts of Animals* III, 3, 665a.

function. It can perceive in itself all possible forms and therefore, by itself, is none of them — it *can be* every being. The human soul is not, then, the form of the body; its study does not spring entirely from the physical; there is something in it that springs from the metaphysical.

The soul's varied functions led Aristotle to distinguish several 'souls' in a single human soul and, by this, rediscover a kind of anthropological tripartition. Thus he identified a vegetative or nutritive soul common to all living beings — plants, animals, and humans — as well as an animal or sensitive soul common to animals and humans and lastly a thinking or intellective — or noetic — soul proper to humans.[27] Such a tripartition, Aristotle asserts,[28] does not call into question the unity of the human being. However, what poses problems as to this unity is the existence of the intellect, for, he says, "if the whole soul holds together the whole body, we should expect each part of the soul to hold together a part of the body. But this seems an impossibility; it is difficult even to imagine what sort of bodily part mind will hold together, or how it will do this."[29]

What about this intellect then? Without being identical to the body, the nutritive and sensitive souls are yet 'something of the body';[30] they truly are the natural soul and correspond to what we have named the *anima-corpus*. This soul is so very much the form of the body that it disappears with it: "when the soul departs the body disintegrates and decays."[31] But the intellect is itself "a widely different kind of soul,"[32] for "it cannot reasonably be regarded as blended with the body."[33] It is immaterial, incorporeal, since it performs immaterial operations and since the nature of a being is revealed in the operations it is able to do. It should be said to be then 'distinct and separable' from other souls: "the faculty of sensation is dependent upon the body, mind is separable from it."[34] Being separable, immaterial and impassible, the intellective soul is distinct from the soul as a whole, "must be pure of all admixture."[35]

27 *On the Soul* II, 2, 413a20–b29.
28 Ibid., I, 5, 411b5–13.
29 Ibid., I, 5, 411b15–18.
30 Ibid., II, 2, 414b21; *On the Generation of Animals*, II, 4, 738b25.
31 Ibid., I, 5, 411b29.
32 Ibid., II, 2, 413b24.
33 Ibid., III, 4, 429a24–25.
34 Ibid., III, 4, 429b5.
35 Ibid., III, 4, 429a28.

Now man alone possesses intellect, and therefore it alone characterizes man. As a result the *human* soul is not, for Aristotle, uniquely and exclusively the 'form of the body', for "when mind is set free from its present conditions it appears as just what it is and nothing more: this alone is immortal and eternal."[36] After all, the origin of the intellect is in conformity with its supra-physical nature: the intellect, Aristotle tells us, comes "from outside," literally "through the door," *thurathen*.[37] As for this *thurathen*, we will shed some perhaps unexpected light on it in the next section. But for the moment we will just observe that in some respects Aristotle's doctrine is even more problematic than the unity of the human being in Plato's doctrine, contrary to a rather widespread theological opinion that sees in the concept of the soul as form of the body the firm principle of this unity. As for the psychobiological being of man, this opinion should be indisputable. But, by that very fact, the psychobiological unity so strongly marked by Aristotle accentuates just as much the extraneousness of his noetic soul, the one by which man is truly man. The history of philosophy is here an undeniable witness to this problematic unity in Aristotle's system. Many commentators on his work, in antiquity as well as the middle ages, have interpreted pure intellect either by identifying it with God — "God thinking within us" according to Alexander of Aphrodisias[38] — a thesis partially taken up again by certain Augustinians as well as Franciscans such as Roger Bacon, or with an angel (Avicenna), or again by supposing that there is only one sole and unique active intellect for all men (Averroes), which casts doubt on the immortality of each particular human being. St. Thomas will mobilize all the power of his dialectic to show, against the Averroists and (especially) Siger of Brabant, that it is not the intellect that thinks but man through his intellect and that this is the true doctrine of Aristotle.[39] Recall as well that the noetic in philosophy was, not directly but through deviations caused by an Averroism more or less faithful to the doctrine of Averroes, at the origin of the most serious intellective crisis known to the Middle Ages and, in 1277, was struck with the condemnation

36 Ibid., III, 5, 430a23–24.
37 *On the Generation of Animals* II, 3, 736b28 (trans. Platt).
38 J. Chevalier, *Histoire de la Pensée*, vol. 1 (Paris: Flammarion, 1955), 362.
39 *The Unicity of the Intellect, Against the Averroists of Paris*, in *Two Opuscula by St. Thomas Aquinas*, trans. Sister R. E. Brennan (St. Louis/London: B. Herder Book Co., 1946).

of Aristotelian philosophism by Etienne Tempier, Bishop of Paris, a condemnation that affected St. Thomas Aquinas himself.

We are not going to enter into this vast debate.[40] We will only observe that its difficulty is not just related to the supposed imprecisions of the formulations of Aristotle (perhaps the greatest philosopher the world has known): it is also related to the very nature of the intellect. Our contemporaries are less sensitive than ancient and medieval people to the extraordinary character of 'thinking', to its 'naturally supernatural' character which, by itself, manifests in the world something of the supra-cosmic, the non-spatial, the immaterial, something that is in the individual human and yet, in itself, surpasses it, a transcendence that miraculously includes us. For, truly, it is man that thinks, and the personal reality of each intellect should not be doubted.[41] But here also, just as previously for Plato (to whom Aristotle is connected through his doctrine of the intellect), what is lacking for uniting the intellective with the natural psychobiological is a firm notion of the being-person, which antiquity had probably not known (even if it was not very far from it) and which, tied to a strictly understood idea of creation, could only be developed by Judeo-Christian thinking.[42]

II. THE HUMAN TERNARY AND THE OPENING OF THE HEART IN THE OLD TESTAMENT[43]

Not only will the following remarks validate our anthropological conclusions; they will also refute some recent statements by those Christian philosophers who think that they can biblically deny the immortality of the soul.

40 J. Chevalier, *Histoire de la Pensée*, vol. 2 (Paris: Flammarion, 1956), 354–79.

41 Far from denying that "the substance of the rational or intellective soul truly and in itself is a form of the human body," according to the Council of Vienne (1312, *Sources of Christian Doctrine*, 481) — which Aristotle did not say — our anthropology seeks to the contrary to show how this is possible.

42 Bernard Meunier (ed.), *La personne et le christianisme ancien* (Paris: Cerf, 2006) — decisive; Philippe Cormier, *Généalogie de 'Personne'* (Paris: Critérion, 1994) — a penetrating philosophical analysis.

43 These pages have been read by Abbé Jean Carmignac, a scholar expert in Hebrew, who has approved of them, even urging us to develop them further, though this was not possible.

Matters are sometimes presented as follows. Many biblical passages show that the Jews were long unaware of the soul's immortality. At death the soul passed away to Sheol, a place of darkness where the soul is absorbed into a kind of larval state while awaiting the resurrection of the body. Likewise St. Paul speaks of the resurrection of the body and not of the immortality of the soul. So much for Scripture. On the other hand, the Church theologically defines the soul as the form of the body.[44] When the body disappears, the soul no longer has a role to play and the form of the body likewise disappears. The immortality of the soul (without the body) is therefore a Platonic survival contrary to revelation as well as to theology.

Now, as we have just seen, it is doubtful that in defining the soul as the form of the body Aristotle saw the animation of the body as the soul's only function. Quite the contrary, when it comes to the intellect he explicitly states that it is something *not* of the body. On the other hand, it is beyond question that Christ very clearly teaches the life of the soul after bodily death. But, foremost in these controversies, one never asks what is understood by 'soul': whether it has to do with the psychic or the spiritual soul. And this is precisely the distinction that the Old Testament always makes in a quite obvious way: the extreme variability of the Bible's anthropological vocabulary is significant to the very extent that it is incomplete, even though some invariable distinctions do appear.

I. The Human Ternary

Surely the trend in the Old Testament is toward a tripartite division of the human being, and most dictionaries of biblical theology admit it (without saying so explicitly).[45] This tripartite division is expressed in the following Hebrew terms: *nefesh*, *ruah*, and *neshamah*. To which the Kabbalah adds two others: *hayah* and *yehidah*, "the eternally living soul" and "the unique soul respectively."[46]

---

44 Cf. Dumeige, *La Foi catholique*, 141.

45 Cf., for example, 'Homme' by Ed. Jacob in *Vocabulaire biblique* (ed. J. van Allmen [Lausanne: Ed. Rencontre, 1969], 124–26), and "Ame" by X. L. Dufour in *Vocabulaire de théologie biblique* (published under the direction of Dufour [Paris: Ed. du Cerf, 1962], cols. 29–33). The comparisons with the Greeks put forward by Dufour are altogether conventional and, in other words, false.

46 Cf. Leo Schaya, *Universal Meaning of the Kabbalah*, 123. We are transcribing

All three—*nefesh*, *ruah*, and *neshamah*—evoke the idea of breath and life. In this sense, all three can be rendered by the word *soul*, which in the various Romance languages possesses the same meaning and the same indeterminacy: the soul is that which 'animates'. Their respective uses are quite specific, however: *nefesh* (literally 'vitality') designates the animal soul (both the nutritive and sensitive souls of Aristotle), while *ruah* (literally 'wind' or 'air') designates the 'mental' soul—which we have called "*animus*"—and finally *neshamah* designates rather the sacred or spiritual soul. Thus *nefesh* is seen to include both the nutritive and sensitive souls of Aristotle. These definitions can be illustrated by numerous quotations.

A. *Nefesh.* The dual meaning of *nefesh*, almost always translated as *psyche* in Greek and *anima* in Latin, is apparent in the following examples where it sometimes denotes life as a biologic reality, linked to the blood in particular: "for the life of every creature is the blood of it" (Lev 17:14); or again: "the blood is the life" (Deut 12:23)[47]; and sometimes life in a clearly more 'inward', psychological sense, the principle of the feelings and passions, desire and fear: "O Lord thy name, and thy remembrance are the desire of the soul" (Isa 26:8); or again: "the day when I take from them their stronghold, their joy and glory, the delight of their eyes and their soul's desire" (Ezek 24:25); and even: "Why are you cast down, O my soul, and why are you disquieted within me?" (Psalm 42:6). In accordance with what we have shown, *nefesh* can also designate the complete human individuality: "The king of Sodom said to Abram, 'Give me the persons (literally *souls*), but take the goods for yourself'" (Gen 14:21);[48] while such cases as the following pertain to the natural empirical self: "Jonathan made a covenant with David, because he loved him as his own soul" (1 Sam 18:3).

Now, although *nefesh* conveys all of these meanings, it never, remarkably enough, designates the immortal soul! To the contrary, *nefesh* dies and disappears with the body: "Let my soul die the death of

---

Hebrew terms according to whether or not they must be pronounced according to scientific transliteration.

47 These indications are in complete agreement with Hindu tradition, where blood is likewise viewed as the support of life; cf. Guénon, *Man and His Becoming according to the Vedanta* (London: Luzac, 1945), 96–97. All of this is, moreover, closely connected to the meaning of the Eucharistic Blood.

48 In the Vulgate.

the righteous" (Num 23:10). Disappearing, the soul is reduced to nothing, to pure and simple nonexistence: "When you chastise man because of his iniquity, you condemn his soul to dissolution" (Psalm 39:12). The soul is no longer anything in the abode of the dead: "For the living know that they will die, but the dead know nothing ... and they have no more forever any share in all that is done under the sun" (Eccles 9:5–6). And this is why any number of modern exegetes assert that the Old Testament is unaware of the immortality of the soul, and hence that there is no immortality beyond the resurrection of the body. But this thesis is altogether inexact. We need to consider, in fact, not only *nefesh*, but even *ruah*, and above all *neshamah*.[49]

B. Ruah. The uses of *ruah*,[50] which might be translated as 'mental soul', are many and often nearly indistinguishable from those of *nefesh*. It is generally translated as *pneuma* in Greek and *spiritus* in Latin. Thus, with respect to the idea of breath and wind, it can express, like *nefesh*, the principle of animal life. Yet even in its nearly biologic meaning, *ruah* is much less 'individualized' than *nefesh*. It does not designate a living being in its concrete and enumerable individuality, but what is alive in this living individuality. *Ruah* has a somewhat 'impersonal' connotation, in agreement with the physical reality that symbolizes it: it is *the* breath, *the* wind, and "you do not know whence it come or whither it goes." Although *ruah* and *nefesh* are not always presented as different realities, still they are at times clearly distinguishable: "O ye spirits and souls of the just, bless the Lord" (Dan 3:86).[51] Yet we have to say that, except for those cases in which *ruah* means breath (in the physical sense), this term is never applied to animals, but only to God or man. And the opposition between *ruah* and *nefesh*

49 These conclusions are also those of Daniel Lys (*Nephès, Histoire de l'Âme dans la révélation d'Israël: Études d'Histoire et de Philosophie religieuses* [Paris: PUF, 1959]), who writes: "Thus *nephesh*, which basically expresses life, does not designate the divine potentiality of a being, but the animated and individually enumerated creature" (201). We must likewise remark, along with J. Pedersen (*Israel, Its Life and Culture*, 2 vols. [London: Oxford University Press, 1926], 466), that *sheol* designates not only the sojourn of the dead and nothingness, but also the lower limit of vitality (34).

50 Here we are just considering the anthropological sense of the term and not any designating the Divine Spirit. But there are — and this is inevitable — some ambiguous occurrences.

51 We see in this verse a fine scriptural witness to the anthropological tripartition.

even serves to distinguish man from animal: "In his hand is the soul [*nefesh*] of every living thing [animals and men] and the breath [*ruah*] of all flesh of man" (Job 12:10). This is why *ruah* has a more intellective and inward sense. In such cases it designates the principle of wisdom and understanding, but also 'spirit' as the essential principle of any reality whatsoever, as, for instance, when one speaks of the spirit of a doctrine. A principle of understanding, the mental soul (and therefore that which can become 'insane') is the meaning given to it by Isaiah: "And those who err in spirit [*ruah*] will come to understanding, and those who murmur will accept the law" (Isa 29:24). In many places *ruah* is also found to designate the essential principle, the inspiration for a behavior: it is the "spirit of jealousy" that overmasters the bridegroom (Num 5:14–30), the "spirit of wisdom" which guides the sacred artist (Exod 28:3), the "spirit of judgment" that inspires the judge in his decisions (Isa 28:6), and so forth.

For all of these reasons *ruah* seems to indicate a certain immanence of the divine in man, corresponding to what theologians call the "presence of immensity." With *ruah* we have passed beyond the individual level properly speaking, without for all that having access to a truly personal degree. In the terminology we have adopted, *ruah* is no longer *anima* but not yet *spiritus*, at least in its deepest and most intimate reality. It corresponds, then, to the *animus-spiritus*. *Ruah* is immanence, the descent of the divine life-light into the human *anima* (*nefesh*), its reflection on the surface of the animic mirror. And this is why *ruah* does not die, but returns at death to God who is its source. Is a personal immortality or the immortality of the life-light principle involved here? Exegetes argue about it endlessly. Let us say we are dealing with a principle transpersonal in itself, but personalized by its infusion into the human being: "The dust returns to the earth as it was, and the spirit returns to God, who gave it" (Eccles 12:7)—words actually designating not the immortality of the personal being, but surely *what* there is of the immortal in man.

Will it be said that theology does not believe in a personal immortality from the fact that it does not speak of man's immortality, but of the soul's? Why demand what is considered scientific precision from the sacred text, a precision that no anthropological treatise can support? But how deny that a personalized use of *ruah* is to be seen in the following verse: "Into thy hand I commit my spirit, O Lord" (Psalm 31:5)? And is not this beautiful prayer to be found in Tobit: "Command my *spirit* to be taken up, that I may depart and become dust [as to my natural reality] ... Lord, command that I may be now released from my distress to go to the eternal abode" (Tob 3:6)? If personal immortality is to be understood as an individual appropriation of the spirit, then such an appropriation is self-contradictory; as our philosophical analysis has shown, it is anti-spiritual since it is the fruit of sin and death destroys it. The whole error of the exegetes comes from seeking the person where there is none, at the level of *nefesh*.

Lastly, we turn to some texts from Wisdom (written originally in Greek) which, contrary to the assertions of the exegetes, clearly distinguish, when necessary, between *psyche* and *nous* or *pneuma*. Certainly *psyche* designates all that is not body (*soma*) in man, but when these terms are used in one and the same verse, *pneuma* designates solely the spiritual and immortal element: "A man in his wickedness kills another, but he cannot bring back the departed *pneuma*, it shall not return, nor set free the imprisoned *psyche* [imprisoned, that is, in Hades]" (Wisdom of Solomon 16:14). Now Hades cannot be the posthumous sojourn of the human being, since an earlier portion of the text states that after death, the soul is established before God: "the righteous live for ever, and their reward is with the Lord" (Wisdom of Solomon 5:15).[52] Hades must therefore be understood as what René Guénon calls the 'inferior psychic world', where those peripheral psychic elements that have not been 'pneumatized' are 'collected'. But you might well ask why, if there is no difference between *pneuma* and *psyche*, the text uses two different terms to recall the creation of man according to Genesis: "the one who formed him and inspired him with an active *psyche*, and breathed into him a living *pnoe* [spirit]" (Wisdom of Solomon 15:11).

C. *Neshamah*. And so we have drawn increasingly near to *neshamah* while distancing ourselves from *nefesh*. Difficult to translate, this term is rendered in Greek by *pneuma* or *pnoe*, and in Latin by *spiritus, spiraculum,* and *habitus*. With *neshamah* we touch upon what is most profound in man, upon what is truly divine, by grace

52 Immortality involves a belief common among the Palestinian Jewish milieu of the second century BC. Cf. Bonsirven, *Le judaisme palestinien* (Paris: Beauchesne, 1950), 1:322–24.

assuredly, but also by nature. This is indeed, then, the spirit such as we have characterized it in our anthropological analysis.

The first occurrence of *neshamah* in a biblical text is of supreme importance, since it involves the creation of man. In this founding text, not of man's metaphysical nature defined as 'image and likeness' in the first Creation narrative, but of his own structure, we find irrefutable evidence of the anthropological tripartition: "God formed man of dust from the ground [the body], and breathed into his face the 'spiracle' of life [spirit], and man became a living being [soul]" (Gen 2:7). To correctly follow the biblical text we need to admit — once more confirming the results of our anthropology — that the living (or animal) soul is as if the product of the meeting of the spiritual and the corporeal. Clearly, then, it is intermediate between spirit and body, not in the manner of a different instrument of the spirit, by which it would be the animating principle for the corporeal, but as the form assumed by the spirit when it penetrates the body. The psychic (or living) aspect is, so to speak and in this regard, the natural synthesis of the spiritual and the corporeal, or rather the 'milieu' in which the spiritual gives form to the corporeal. As for spiracle (from the Latin *spiraculum*, as suggested by Lanza del Vasto), it is a translation of the Hebrew *neshamah*. Assuredly this term signifies the 'breath of life', as can be seen in any number of places.[53] It is to be distinguished from *ruah* on several accounts, showing that from *ruah* to *neshamah* there is an internalization of one and the same spiritual breath. It is the same reality, but if, with *ruah*, this reality is immanent to the human being as one of its potentials (and not indicative of the person), with *neshamah* this reality is regarded as penetrating the human subject. This means several things. First of all, through *neshamah* man is connected to God, since the breath that penetrates man is God's very own. On the other hand, since this breath comes 'from without', it supposes a 'within' for man that it delineates by its very penetration: it is that which engenders human inwardness, because this inwardness — a *secret* between God and man — is precisely the point through which this being is open to God. What is most intimate to myself is that side of myself that is an escape from myself (the natural being), and through which I am in contact with

53 Job 32:8, 33:4, 34:14.

God. That which is closest to man is that which is most open to God. *Neshamah* is not itself this inwardness, but rather an opening of the human being through which it receives its reality from God's creative act—it is the transcendent root of our inwardness.[54]

This interpretation, simply inferred from the text of Genesis, is confirmed by the majority of the uses of *neshamah*. Since we receive our reality from God through *neshamah*, it is through *neshamah* that we must also return to him; most especially in prayer, where our entire being actively gives itself (and not only passively as in death) to God. This is why the sacred author, in the last verse of the last Psalm (which summarizes all prayer), uses *neshamah* to designate man in his highest sacred function, that of Divine Praise: "Let everything that breathes praise Yahweh. Hallelu-Ya" (Psalm 150:5). The breath that ascends toward God then is the same one that descends from him in Genesis. Therefore *neshamah* is also the intellect, not directly in its human exercise, but in its Divine Origin: "Whose spirit [*neshamah*; from the Latin *spiramentum*] has come forth from you?" asks Job of Bildad the Shuhite, who comes to him to speak with great wisdom (Job 26:4). And Solomon declares: "The spirit [*neshamah*, *spiraculum*] of man is the lamp of the Lord, searching all his innermost parts" (Prov 20:27).

2. *The Opening of the Heart*

All of these meanings can be grouped around the theme of 'opening' as understood in the active sense, the act of opening by intimate penetration. Is not this the primary meaning of *spiraculum* and *spiramentum*, which designate first the 'nostril', before designating the breath that passes through this opening? But is not this also its sense in several places in Job?[55] And why 'opening'?

Here we would like to speak of the unexpected relationship just mentioned with the intellect of Aristotle: is not the secret of '*thurathen*' (through the door), which points to the mysterious origin of the intellect, contained in the mystery of *neshamah?* This door of the human being is the spiracle of life through which we spirate

---

54 Surely we should relate *neshamah* to *sutratma*, which in Sanskrit designates the thread of the Self *(sutra-Atma)* which joins the being to God.

55 Job 32:19: "My heart is like wine which has no vent *(spiraculum)*"; likewise, Job 41:16: "One is so near to another, that no air *(spiraculum)* can come between them."

and breathe the Divine Being, eternal Light and Life. Now what is an opening if not a hole, an interruption of closure? In other words, 'in' this hole of the human being, which is the spiracle of Genesis, the human being ceases; it is interrupted. But where man ceases, God begins. Man is enclosed in his own nature as in a shell (and this also includes, in a certain way, all of creation). Beyond this shell suddenly begins the ocean of divine light. God pierces a hole in this shell that is immediately invaded by divine light. Insofar as this light comes from elsewhere, it is divine; but insofar as it wholly occupies the place of the orifice, it is part of human nature. From this point of view there is a profound analogy between microcosm and macrocosm, as is sometimes represented in medieval iconography: the stars are not so much luminous bodies fixed to the celestial vault as openings in the firmament through which the sparkling of the divine light is glimpsed. Once we know what a close relationship there is, for Plato and Aristotle, between the stars and the essences of the intelligible world, this analogy is seen in all of its profundity. Are Plato's essences intelligible 'things'? In a certain sense, yes. But, in another, they are holes in the sensory cosmos which, by their very 'inlets', delineate or cut out distinct luminous unities in that ocean of infinite light that is Divine Reality — how else could we withstand its brightness?

To conclude we will just add that, if the immutable essences are macrocosmic doorways to the divine, if *neshamah* is the microcosmic doorway, then the Most Holy Virgin is its spiritual doorway, the *Janua Coeli*, which makes of her "the Mother of fair love, and of fear, and of knowledge, and of holy hope" (Eccles 24:24). Yes, spiritual intelligence comes into us through the doorway of Heaven.[56]

One last term of biblical anthropology remains to be examined: the heart.[57]

With the heart we reach the very center of the human being, for such is indeed the most consistent meaning that the Bible attributes

---

56 There is a direct connection between what Aristotle says about the possible intellect, which remains virgin with respect to all of the knowledge received within itself (*On the Soul* III, 429a15–25), and the virginal substance of Mary, who receives within herself the Logos.

57 Antoine Guillaumont has collected the biblical and extra-biblical references to this term in his 'Le sens des Noms du coeur dans l'Antiquité'.

to it: it designates man in his most profound reality, it is truly identical with what we have called the 'I'. All commentators have remarked that, for the Semites, the heart is the organ not only of affectivity but also of knowledge. There are numerous examples: it is the heart that rejoices (Psalm 33:21) and leaps in the breast (1 Sam 2:1).[58] It is also that which hates or is saddened (Psalm 109:22). And yet "we discern among the ancient Semites a tendency towards differentiating the faculties of the soul, at least towards making the intellect distinct from the other phenomena of the psychic life; they tend to assign a particular location to the intellect, and this place is the heart, the emotions and feelings being localized then in the other viscera."[59] In Job, Elihu says to those whom he first called "wise" and "understanding": "Hear me, you men of heart" (Job 34:10). Quite clearly, this has to do with intuitive understanding. On the other hand, since the heart (of flesh) is also the vital center of the body's activity, we see how the heart can be identified with the three basic aspects of the human being.

This triplicity of uses has led us to a somewhat unusual conclusion. We do not think that one can simply say that the heart is the life of the body; it is also the affective life as well as the intellective life; otherwise it would be a useless repetition of either the vital soul or the mental soul. It is better to say that the heart is not *in itself* the life of the body, but only insofar as a person identifies himself with his feelings, emotions, and passions. And it is the same for the intellective life. However, the more we ascend in the hierarchy of the human being's powers, the more the heart — the *I*, the pure selfhood, or the person — recognizes itself in that power with which it becomes identified. This is why it can expressly designate the spirit-intellect, as is seen in this fundamental passage from Deuteronomy: "You shall love the Lord your God with all your heart, and with all your soul, and with all your might" (Deut 6:5), which declares the essential tripartition of biblical anthropology in the clearest possible way.

Previously, we saw the analogy between the microcosmic spiracle and the macrocosmic celestial doorway, an analogy so much more meaningful when related to the doctrine of the 'Universal Man' who

58   Cf. Guillaumont, 43.
59   Ibid., 45.

is, in reality, identical to Adam.[60] But consideration of another symbolism must be interjected here, a symbolism in some way intermediate between those of microcosm and macrocosm: the symbolism of the temple, which is either an architectural translation of the body of the Second Adam or a version of the entire cosmos in miniature. The analogy between the human head, pierced by the spiracle, and the celestial vault, pierced by a doorway, is thus to be found again in the church dome that corresponds simultaneously to the firmament (it is sometimes decorated with stars) and to the human skull. Now this dome is often pierced with an opening, the 'eye of the dome', which represents a veritable celestial doorway through which the ray of divine grace descends, but also a kind of chimney through which the 'smoke of sacrifice' ascends: this is, then, the way by which the priest returns to God the breath of life that he has bestowed on us. The ray of divine grace (or the spiration of the spiracle of life in the head of Adam), passing through the eye of the dome, intersects with the horizontal plane of the temple at a point where we find the altar of sacrifice. This point, in its microcosmic correspondence, is the heart.

For a confirmation of this symbolism, recall that this divine ray, or world-axis, is also the cross of Christ, or rather the cross of Christ forms the ascending part of the divine ray, since it is actually through this that communication with Heaven has been reestablished. Now this cross, which passes through the dome of the world, is planted on *Golgotha*, an Aramean word meaning 'skull'.[61] This is significant for two reasons: first, history thinks Golgotha a classical toponym designating, in many languages, a small eminence that is actually skull-shaped — but universal symbolism shows, to the contrary, that there is a profound meaning in the comparison of a mountain, a hill, a tumulus, or a dome to a skull; second, tradition teaches that this skull buried on Golgotha is Adam's. Having been driven into the skull of Adam, the Universal Man, the Cross therefore reopens the doorway of Heaven for all.[62]

60   This is how Fabre d'Olivet translates *Adam*; cf. *The Hebraic Tongue Restored*, trans. N. L. Redfield (New York and London: G. P. Putnam's Sons, 1921), 69.

61   The French word *calvaire* (from the Latin *calvaria*) has the same meaning (cf. likewise the French word *chauve* = 'bald', 'bare').

62   To all of these analogies to the Adamic spiracle should be added the ritual trepanation of skulls in very ancient civilizations, the tonsure for priests and religious, and the crowning of kings. Also, in Jewish metaphysics, the first *sefirah*, that

The heart is therefore the internal end-point of the axial descent of *neshamah*, which is itself nothing but the Divine Spirit. But if *neshamah* is the divine gift as such, the heart is rather like its effect, its end. And what is this end? Why does God send forth his breath? To create a human being, which is to say a central being, a being who exercises the act of existing for himself, a being who says '*I myself*', an autonomous center of existence. The generative act of the Divine Spirator is of such perfection that it endows its own quality of center on the product of this spiration: whoever understands this is contemplating the very secret of Creation. By *neshamah* the human creature, as if by an umbilical cord, receives its being from the Divine Being. But, *at the same time*, this being is made a person and able to face its Principle. This being is received into a heart, and this heart does not exist before the being it receives within itself, but is its exact contemporary. Wherever the spiracular ray stops, there is a heart to receive it.

The heart is, then, the profound center of the being, the location of its ontological root, the point through which God touches it, where it can meet God and find the way out of the cosmos. This infinitesimal point, which we have spoken about previously, also contains in a certain manner the very One who contains the world — such is the mystery of the person.

A famous Hindu text puts it this way: "This *Atma* [Self], which dwells in the heart, is smaller than a grain of rice, smaller than a grain of barley, smaller than a grain of mustard, smaller than a grain of millet, smaller than the germ which is in the grain of millet; this *Atma*, which dwells in the heart, is also greater than the earth [the corporeal world], greater than the atmosphere [the subtle world], greater than the sky [the intelligible world], greater than all the worlds together."[63]

---

is to say, the first determination of the Divine Essence, is called crown (*Kether*); for all of these questions, cf. Guénon, *Symbols of Sacred Science*, trans. H. Fohr and S. Fohr (Hillsdale NY: Sophia Perennis, 2001), 247–59. The Adamic spiracle is analogous to the *brahma-randrha* of the Hindus, the 'orifice' of the skull "by which the spirit of the being on the way to liberation escapes" (ibid., 259). Cf. likewise A. K. Coomaraswamy, "Eckstein," in *What Is Civilization?* (Ipswich, Great Britain: Golgonooza, 1989), 168–77.

63 *Chandogya Upanishad* III, 14, 3. We use Guénon's translation of this text as given in *Man and His Becoming according to the Vedanta* (Hillsdale, NY: Sophia Perennis, 2001), 33–34.

And, now, this is what Mechthild of Magdeburg tells of a mystical dialogue with Christ. The Lord says:

" — See how she ascends, the one who has wounded me [with love]. She comes with a great rush, like an eagle from the great deep of the sky.... Tell me, my queen, what do you bring?"

" — Lord, I bring you my joy. It is greater than the mountains, larger than the world, deeper than the sea, higher than the clouds, more beautiful than the sun, more numerous than the stars, it weighs more than the entire earth."

" — O thou image of my divinity, honored by my humanity, adorned with my Holy Spirit, what is your joy called?"

" — Lord, it is called: Joy of my heart."[64]

III. THE HUMAN TERNARY IN CHRISTIAN TRADITION

Before briefly addressing the anthropological thinking of Christianity among a few of its authors, we must draw attention to one major fact, a fact well known but little 'recognized' by standard handbooks of theology. Our insisting on the presence of a tripartite anthropology in Christianity will be judged non-traditional in the face of the teaching that the soul is the form of the body — a teaching we do not deny. However, as we have seen, this formulation comes from Aristotle. Now here is the major fact to be taken into account: for 1,250 years theology was done without Aristotle and with Platonism. Did it only produce mere babblings while awaiting the scholastic developments at the end of the twelfth century?

1. In the Texts of the Church

The text we will cite is not among the dogmatic definitions of the Church in the proper sense of the term. Neither is it the work of a council or a pope, but of a bishop of Salamis, named Epiphanius, who lived in the fourth century. St. Epiphanius is not in the opinion of historians an original thinker. But he is a scholar and a man of tradition. The Christians of Pamphylia "wished to have a summary of

---

64   Quoted from *Le Coeur*, 165.

the Christian faith."[65] Responding to this wish, St. Epiphanius drew up a treatise in 374, *The Ancoratus*,[66] accompanied by two creeds (two professions of faith as we would say today), which are perhaps from his hand (or which were in use in the Church), but to which in any case Catholic tradition attributes "a great dogmatic value."[67]

His era was devoted to Christological debates. After the Arian heresy, orthodox theologians had a tendency to insist upon the oneness of Christ. The Council of Chalcedon had not yet specified a vocabulary — the nature/person distinction — enabling the duality of natures — divine and human — to be defined in the unity of a single person or hypostasis — hypostatic union. Among these theologians we have to include Apollinaris and his disciples.

Apollinaris thought that the Word did not assume a complete human nature, for otherwise there would be a duality of persons: "If there exists in the same being two intelligent and free principles, it is fatal when these two principles enter into conflict and each one follows its own direction."[68]

Now the intelligent and free principle is the *nous* or *pneuma*, identical to the person. It follows that Christ does not possess a human *nous*, he only possesses, as man, a body and an animal soul. As for the *nous* in Christ — this is how the trichotomism of Apollinaris resolves this Christological difficulty — it is the Word itself: "The humanity of Jesus Christ is composed of a body (*soma*) and an animal soul (*psyche*), the Word itself being its *nous* and its *pneuma*."[69] Or again, according to a formula of Apollinaris himself: "Christ, having God for *pneuma*, which is to say for *nous*, with a *psyche* and a body, is for good reason called the man from heaven."[70]

The whole difficulty of the question is clear and, for anyone who follows our account of anthropology, it will be understood that there is perhaps a way to view the Apollinarian doctrine that is not frankly

65 Cf. F. Cayré, *Précis de patrologie*, vol. 1 (Paris and Tournai: Desclée, 1930), 387.
66 "The Well-Anchored."
67 Dumeige, *La Foi catholique*, 7.
68 *Epist. ad Dyonisium*, fragment 2; ed. H. Lietzmann, *Apollinaris von Laodicea und seine Schule*, vol. 1 (Tübingen: J. C. B. Mohr, 1904), 257. Cited from J. Tixeront, *Histoire des Dogmes dans l'Antiquité chrétienne*, vol. 2 (Paris: Gabalda, 1912), 96.
69 Tixeront, *Histoire*, 97.
70 Ibid.

heretical: if the spirit is what there is of the divine in man, can it not be admitted that in Jesus Christ it is God himself? In fact, on the one hand, it should be said that the *nous* (or *pneuma*) is not as such identical to the person (which is the *pneuma* viewed in its transcendent ontological root, and not as a faculty or power defining a human nature), and on the other hand that the *nous* is indeed what there is of the divine, not in the Word Incarnate, but in the man Jesus.[71] Apollinarism is therefore indeed a heresy since it mutilates the human nature of Jesus Christ. But, for all that, this does not make the anthropological tripartition itself heretical as a result.

Actually, when St. Epiphanius, who was a friend of Apollinaris, broke with him and undertook to oppose truth to error, that is, to affirm the integrity of human nature in the Incarnation, far from rejecting the anthropological tripartition, he enunciates it in the most express manner possible, to signify by this that the Eternal Word assumed human nature in its totality. This was done in a text which, as we stated, was given as a creed, and which the Church has almost dogmatized by taking it as the basis for the draft of the Creed of Constantinople (Second Ecumenical Council). Here then is St. Epiphanius's text: "We believe ... in Jesus Christ, the Son of God ... who was made man, that is, has taken on a *perfect human nature, soul, body, spirit* and all that is of man, except for sin."[72]

Finally we will give a text which clearly illustrates another aspect of our anthropology, namely, the analogy of microcosm and macrocosm: man is viewed in this as a summary of the universe, and so it is the entire universe that is evangelized and saved in him. Formerly the Church recommended this text (we do not know what has happened to it today) to priests and faithful by placing it in the breviary for the feast of the Ascension, which actually shows that man summarizes and surpasses the universe. This text is from St. Gregory the Great: "Man has something in common with all levels of creation. He has

71 Every human being is made in the image and likeness of God. Therefore the man Jesus, he as well, is in the image of the Deity. He is pre-eminently this very image, since he comes to once more make its realization possible in everyone. And since it is essentially by the spirit/intellect that man is like to God, the humanity of Christ necessarily includes a pneumatic-intellective soul.

72 Dumeige, *La Foi catholique*, noum. 5.

existence in common with stones, life in common with trees, sensation in common with animals, intelligence in common with angels. If, then, man has something in common with all ranks of creation, in a certain sense all creation is summed up in man. And so the Gospel is preached to every creature, when it is preached to man alone." In the three words *life, sensation,* and *intelligence* will be recognized the three 'parts' of the human being.[73]

2. Among the Church Fathers

St. Irenaeus of Lyons. St. Irenaeus is not counted among the greatest geniuses of Christian theology. However, he is of the utmost importance on more grounds than one. First, he is a man profoundly attached to tradition, that is, to that sum total of theological, ecclesiological, and liturgical conceptions which Scripture does not expressly contain, but which form a part of apostolic Revelation and which were transmitted orally by the Apostles to the first Christians. He is also a man of great knowledge. Finally, and above all, his historical situation confers on him an altogether exceptional and perhaps unique value: St. Irenaeus, who lived in the second half of the second century, had in his youth followed the teaching of St. Polycarp, a direct disciple of St. John the Evangelist, who had installed Polycarp as bishop himself. "Also, at the end of his life he had great authority. Numerous disciples thronged about him to gather from his lips the last living echo of the apostolic word."[74] Whatever we might think about this, we are very close here to that wondrous event which was the Revelation of

---

73 Today some deny the historical (physical) reality of the Ascension of Jesus Christ. This denial would be unimportant if it were not officially accepted by some bishops and taught to the faithful. To deny the Ascension is to deny the Incarnation. To pretend, as do so many exegetes, that the Evangelists meant 'something else' in relating this event is to trifle with the world. When the Evangelists speak figuratively — "is seated at the right hand of God," for example — we completely understand it; when they speak historically we also understand it, particularly when they tell us that Jesus has been "raised up *beneath their gaze*" and that "a cloud removed him *from their sight,*" and that then "they continued to *gaze intently* [*atenizo* means: to be intent] toward the sky, as he was going" (Acts 1:9–10). If this event did not take place, then the Evangelists are either liars or fools. As for the basic problem, it must be understood that verticality constitutes the mode according to which space realizes its own surpassing. A *body* can "actively leave the spatial condition" only in accordance with the vertical. A cloud that 'obliterates the visible' displays the same character of rigor and necessity.

74 Cf. Cayré, *Précis de patrologie,* 72.

Christ. What St. Irenaeus says, he holds from St. John himself through the intermediary of a single man. St Irenaeus speaks about very recent history, the last witnesses of which had just died. The teaching to which he is connected, as if by a living voice, is that of the first and highest of Christian metaphysicians, John, the Son of Thunder.

The major work of St. Irenaeus, *Adversus Haereses*, is directed against Valentinian gnosticism, which was very widespread at the time in Gaul. The gnostics, schematicizing to excess the Pauline categories, distinguished three kinds of men, the 'hylics', the 'psychics', and the 'pneumatics', according to their predominant tendency, in such a way that the salvation of a being no longer depended upon divine grace and its good will, but upon its nature.[75]

St. Irenaeus contests this classification. He does not, for all that, reject a tripartite conception of man. Certain historians, Gilson in particular, find[76] his anthropology too confused. Ecclesiastic historians seek rather to cleanse him of all suspicion of trichotomism.[77] These judgments, we think, attest to a poor understanding of the anthropological tripartition. Cayré seems to sum up the thought of our author quite clearly when he writes: "the spirit is presented as an element inherent to the perfect man. The latter includes, beside the body and soul, the *spirit*, the gift of God, in which must be simultaneously recognized the created gift of grace made to the human person and the Person of the Giver, inseparable from the Gift."[78]

"The soul and the spirit," writes St. Irenaeus (who therefore distinguishes one from the other), "are parts of man, they are not man himself; for the perfect man consists in the commingling and the union of the *soul* receiving the *spirit* of the Father and the admixture of that

75 The difficulty with the study of Gnosticism stems, in our opinion, not from the complexity of errors professed, but from the close connection presented by its theses to the most profound truth of the Christian Revelation. This heresy has weighed, perhaps more than any other, upon the destiny of Christianity: its excesses have discredited for all time the royal way of sacred knowledge. On gnosis, cf. *infra.*, ch. 22 and our *Problèmes de gnose*.

76 Etienne Gilson, *Christian Philosophy in the Middle Ages* (New York: Random House, 1955), 23.

77 *Dictionnaire de théologie catholique* [=DTC], Vacant-Mangenot, vol. 1, part 1 (Paris: Letouzey et Ané, 1909), col. 983–86.

78 Cayré, *Précis de patrologie*, 145–46.

fleshly nature which was molded after the image of God."[79] But is the spirit of the Father the created spirit of man or the Holy Spirit? To tell the truth it is both, and, we say, one is created by the grace of the other. St. Irenaeus himself specifies this, showing clearly that the spirit is the third principle of his anthropology. "For if any one take away the substance of flesh, that is, of the handiwork [of God], and understand that which is purely spiritual, such then would not be a spiritual man but would be the spirit of a man, or the Spirit of God.... But if the Spirit be wanting to the soul, he who is such is indeed of an animal nature and ... carnal."[80] In this case, St. Irenaeus actually thinks that man clearly remains the image of God (natural order), but has lost his likeness (supernatural order). "For that flesh which has been molded is not a perfect man in itself, but the body of a man, and part of a man. Neither is the soul itself, considered apart by itself, the man; but it is the soul of a man, and part of a man. Neither is the spirit a man, for it is called the spirit, and not a man; but the commingling and union of all these constitutes the perfect man."[81] Therefore "there are three things," concludes St. Irenaeus, "out of which, as I have shown, the complete man is composed — flesh, soul, and spirit. One of these does indeed preserve and fashion [the man] — this is the spirit; while as to another it is united and formed — that is the flesh; then [comes] that which is between these two — that is the soul, which sometimes indeed, when it follows the spirit, is raised up by it, but sometimes it sympathizes with the flesh, and falls into carnal lusts."[82]

Likewise the notion of the psychic body, the validity and necessity of which we have shown, is to be found again in St. Irenaeus. More-over, everything he says about the soul (the *psyche*) and its posthumous condition can only be explained if we admit that this is indeed that reality of the subtle world we attempted to describe earlier.

St. Clement of Alexandria.[83] With St. Clement of Alexandria — why not give back to the author of such a sublime and fundamentally Christian doctrine his title of saint? — we are dealing with a veritable

79 *Adversus haereses*, Book V, 6, n. 1; *Patrologia Graeca* [=PG] 7:1137–38.
80 Ibid.
81 Ibid.
82 Ibid., Book V, 9; PG 7:1144.
83 On St. Clement of Alexandria, see also *infra*, ch. 22, second section.

intellective genius, probably the first up to that time in the history of Christian thought, since he lived at the same time as St. Irenaeus. A man of prodigious learning, wholly imbued with Greek and biblical culture, his anthropology is basically tripartite. We will cite only one text from the great Alexandrian.

St. Clement comments upon a passage from St. Matthew's Gospel where it is said: "For there where two or three are reunited in my Name, I am in the midst of them" (Matt 18:20). And St. Clement, asking himself who these three are, after having passed in review the more exterior meanings, writes:

> In another sense the three are passion (*thymos*), desire and reason, the flesh, the soul and the spirit according to another denomination.... When, having surpassed *thymos* and desire, man will love in deed the creation of God and the Creator of everything, he will live as a gnostic ... already 'one' here below in his judgment and truly spiritual, inaccessible in everything and everywhere to the reasonings of passion and desire, completed in the image of the Lord by the Craftsman himself, a perfect man, worthy of being called brother by the Lord, and friend and son at the same time. In this way the two and the three are reunited in the gnostic man.[84]

And this tripartition, A. Méhat notes, may be traced back to Plato as well as St. Paul.[85]

St. Gregory of Nyssa. We are unable to do justice, even succinctly, to the anthropology of St. Gregory of Nyssa, the 'father of mystical theology', for it holds a considerable place in his work.[86] As we have

---

84 Cf. *Stromateis*, III, 68,5–69,4; we follow the translation provided by A. Méhat for this text in *Étude sur les "Stromates" de Clément d'Alexandrie* (Paris: Seuil, 1966), 460, which to our knowledge is the most complete and most penetrating work published on this author. It comes as no surprise that, after Clement, we do not speak of Origen, whose anthropology is clearly tripartite: we would only be repeating what we have said elsewhere. Cf. H. Crouzel, *Origen*, trans. A. S. Worrall (San Francisco: Harper & Row, 1989), 87–91.

85 Cf. *Stromateis*, III, 68,5–69,4.

86 In this regard it is necessary to read ch. II, "La structure de l'âme et les

said in many places, it is impossible to imagine an anthropology that is not at the same time a spiritual alchemy. To speak of man is already to begin doing this. Knowledge of self requires a conversion. And this is exactly how St. Gregory views this question. Human nature, for him, is the perfect man such as God had wished him and, therefore, the spiritual man living the divine life. This inseparable union of natural and supernatural is implied in the very notion of the image of God. "The image," explains Cardinal Daniélou, "includes at once what we call the intellective life, the *nous*, and the supernatural life, the *pneuma*; the sum total of these realities constitutes nature, in contrast to the animal life [*psyche*] which is added on to it."[87]

This added-on animal nature is signified by the tunics of skin with which God clothed our first parents.[88] They not only signify the body then, but indeed the 'corporeal condition' and, even more precisely, the mortal condition: "So, we too, when we have cast off that dead unsightly tunic made from the skins of brutes and put upon us — for I take the 'coats of skins' to mean a conformity to an animal nature with which we were clothed when we became familiar with passionate indulgence — shall, along with the casting-off of that tunic, fling from us all the accretions that were round us of that skin of an animal."[89] A consequence of sin, the mortal condition is also however a gift from God, since it prevents our ruin from being perpetual. "But since all skin, after it is separated from the animal, is dead, I am convinced that this mortal condition, up to that time reserved for creatures devoid of reason, was henceforth applied to men by the Physician, who treated this inclination to evil without meaning to have it last forever."[90]

Moreover it must be pointed out that these tunics may assume a more technical meaning. In that case they designate what we have called the subtle body and the pneumatic body. The subtle body is

---

passions," in Father Daniélou's classic work *Platonisme et Théologie mystique* (Paris: Aubier, 1944), 46–83, from which we draw our documentation. St. Gregory of Nyssa, one of the Cappadocian Fathers, lived between 335 and 395.

87 Ibid., 50.

88 We must point out here the striking similarity of the doctrine of the 'tunics' to that of the *koshas* or envelopes (sheaths) of the person in the *Vedanta*.

89 *On the Soul and the Resurrection*; PG 46:148c–149a (cited in Daniélou, 56).

90 *Catechetical Discourse*, VIII, 4, ed. Meridier (cited in Daniélou, 59).

that with which we were clothed in Paradise. We think this is how Gregory likewise understood it when he said, for example, that "we see each and all of these garments of skin round our nature, and also the transitory fig leaves of this material life which we have badly sewn together for ourselves after being stripped of our own resplendent garments."[91] As for the pneumatic body, this is what we will be clothed with in the heavenly Paradise: "the corporeal lining, dissolved [by death], is woven anew, not in this gross nature, but in a light and airy fashion."[92]

We see with what clarity Gregory distinguishes between the spiritual/intellective and the psycho-corporeal. This distinction implies a tripartite structure of the soul. In this respect the thought of St. Gregory is fundamentally Platonic; we mean that it expresses the depth of Platonism, more authentically, no doubt, than many university studies:[93] "What constitutes the image of God, and therefore what belongs to man by nature, is the faculty of pure knowledge, discrimination and supreme illumination, in other words the intellect [*nous*]; the rest, the desiring soul and the affective soul, is added."[94] This is a very clear affirmation of the anthropological tripartition. St. Gregory, in *The Life of Moses*, comes to the scriptural passage where God orders the Jews to put the blood of the lamb upon the lintel and the two doorposts (Exod 12:7), and asks himself what is the spiritual meaning of this gesture:

> In this way Scripture gives us in figure a teaching about the nature of the soul, which profane philosophy has discovered for its part, dividing the soul into reasonable [intellective soul], concupiscible [desiring soul] and irascible

91 *On the Lord's Prayer*, fifth petition, PG 44:1184B; trans. H. C. Graef (New York/Ramsey, NJ: Newman Press, 1954), 76.

92 *On the Soul and the Resurrection*, PG 46:108A.

93 To be clear on a subject close to our heart, St. Gregory is not a Platonist in the sense of adhering to an individual school of thought. He is a Platonist because Plato has expressed the truth.

94 *On the Soul and the Resurrection*, PG 46:57B (cited in Daniélou, 62); we have translated the quote which Father Daniélou gives in Greek; "supreme illumination" translates *epopteia*, a technical term which, in the Greek mysteries, designated the highest degree of the initiatic way.

[affective soul]: these last two parts are subordinate, we say, and hence support on each side the reasonable part of the soul above them; the latter holds them by the reins, governs them and is *carried* by them [the spiritual integration of the psychic and corporeal elements], the irascible appetite animating it with courage and the concupiscible appetite raising it towards participation in the Good.[95]

St. Augustine. Born in 354 and died in 430, he could have known St. Gregory of Nyssa, who died in 394. He has merited being called the greatest doctor of the Church. Here as well, Church historians have been at work clearing him of the taint of trichotomism. St. Augustine is, however, a Platonist, and we have already seen what distinction he established between lower and higher reason. And, unless every trichotomism is understood only in the most caricatured and crude way, the anthropological tripartition surely constitutes the basis of his doctrine of man.[96] Besides, in this respect there are hard-to-impugn formulations by St. Augustine himself.

In a text probably dating from 393 (St. Augustine was then 40 years old), he writes: "There are three things of which man consists — namely, spirit, soul, and body [*spiritus, anima, corpus*] — which again are spoken of as two, because frequently the soul is named along with the spirit; for a certain rational portion of the same, of which beasts are devoid, is called spirit: the principal part in us is the spirit;

---

95   *Vie de Moïse*, trans. Jean Daniélou (Paris: Cerf, 1941), 83. We have reprinted the Cardinal's translation while commenting upon it in brackets. The adjective *reasonable* (*logikon*) should not mislead us. St. Gregory distinguishes clearly between intellect and mental activity, and indeed the latter is for him, as in our anthropology, a reflection (a memory) of the former: "Divinity is intelligence [*nous*] and reason [*logos*]: 'you also see in yourself reason and thought, the imitation of the first reason'" (Daniélou, 49). In the same way he shows that the intellect "is knowledge of the realities" (Daniélou, 50).

96   This is also the case with geniuses of lesser breadth, St. Ambrose for example, who are ranked among the dichotomists, but who clearly distinguish two parts in the soul, one animal and the other spiritual and divine *(De Noe et arca,* 92; PL 14:403–4); or again St. Jerome, who comments on the parable of the leaven mixed with *three measures* of flour (Matt. 13:33) by explaining that these three measures represent the three parts of the human soul according to Plato: the rational (*logikon*), the affective (the irascible, *thymikon*) and the desiring (the concupiscible, *epithymikon*). Cf. *Commentary upon the Gospel of St. Matthew,* L. II, c. 13, PL 26:94.

next, the life whereby we are united with the body is called the soul; finally, the body itself, as it is visible, is the last part in us."[97]

But, from our viewpoint, what is most interesting in Augustine is his doctrine of inner illumination and of the divine Master at the heart of our heart. On this theme he has provided some definitive formulations which illustrate well all that we have expressed on the person and its mystery. "Enter again into yourself," he says; "within the interior man dwells the truth."[98] Thus the truth of self-knowledge is the truth of the knowledge of God: "in knowing Thee, I will know myself."[99] For it is God who seeks our soul in our trying to find ourselves: "O God, light of my heart, and bread of the inner mouth of my soul, and the power that weddest my mind with my innermost thoughts."[100]

To conclude, let us recall the famous formula wherein St. Augustine so clearly expresses the radical immanence and radical transcendence of God conjoined in the mystery of the person. God, we say, is at once the center of the person and beyond it, totally identical to it and totally other, and it is here, we should think, that the key to this head/heart (or intellect/heart) duality is to be found, a duality that makes one or the other, according to the case, the symbolic seat of the person, the intellect-head rather indicating transcendence and the heart-center rather indicating immanence: "You were more inward to me than my most inward part; and higher than my highest."[101]

3. Among the theologians of the Middle Ages

The notion of the Church Fathers is not strictly defined in time.[102] There is agreement however in applying it to the great writers of

---

97 *De fide et symbolo* X, 23; PL 40:193–94 (S. D. F. Salmond translation). St. Augustine's vocabulary is fluid. Outside the symbolic language of mathematical formalism (which means nothing), what language is not? Nevertheless there are constants. If, in the controversies with the Manicheans, St. Augustine, accommodating himself to his adversaries, frequently employs *anima* to designate the vital soul and also the spiritual soul, in the *Confessions* the latter is always called *animus*, clearly proving that for him there is a difference between the one and the other.

98 *De vera religione* 72; PL 34:154.

99 *Soliloquies* II, 1; PL 32:885.

100 *Confessions* I, 13 (Pilkington translation).

101 Ibid., III, 6.

102 In itself it is defined by the four following marks: orthodoxy, holiness, approbation of the Church, antiquity.

Christian antiquity, from the beginning to about the eighth century. The texts we will cite now belong to another era, that of the great medieval theologians. In no way are we claiming to study medieval anthropology here. It will be enough to provide a few testimonies to the preservation of the tripartite conception of man under varied forms, testimonies met with in some twelfth-century authors on the one hand and in St. Thomas Aquinas on the other.

William of Saint-Thierry. We would have to cite quite lengthy passages from the great mystic that was William of Liège, abbot of Saint-Thierry and friend of St. Bernard of Clairvaux (called the 'last of the Fathers'), to show what place Platonic anthropology holds in his work and spiritual experience.[103] In his writings we come across a remark altogether analogous to the one cited from St. Augustine: "Such is the spirit [*animus*], or again the soul [*anima*] which God gives us. But," he remarks, "it is from the soul that our natural life comes."[104] He undeniably recognizes then the ambiguity of the vocabulary and is forced to make it precise in the direction of a very clear distinction between the psychic and the spiritual. This distinction occupies a large part of William's treatise on the nature of the body and the soul, where he describes the different functions of the vegetative and animal life, identifying in particular, under the term 'spirits', the notion of psychic (or subtle) elements. But, says William, "All else is the spirit (*spiritus, pneuma*) of man,"[105] to which, some lines further, he gives the name animus (*nous*).

Thus we see his terminology becoming progressively more precise in the direction of a very clear anthropological tripartition. And Father Déchanet gives us this remarkable summary: "William tends to distinguish the *anima* from the *animus*, the *anima* designating

103 *Œuvres choisies de Guillaume de Saint-Thierry*, introduction, French translation, and notes by Father J. M. Déchanet (Paris: Aubier, 1944). The notes and commentaries of Father Dechanet are valuable and illuminating. We deplore however his systematic anti-Platonism which, under the circumstances, seems unwarranted, bearing witness to a misunderstanding of Plato's doctrine. To speak of Plato's 'flights of fancy', in connection with the psycho-physiology of the *Timaeus* (op. cit., p. 248), is inaccurate.

104 *On the Nature of the Body and the Soul*, Bk. II, part I, in *Œuvres choisies*, 121–22.

105 *Œuvres choisies*, 104.

the soul in as much as the body's principle of life, the *animus* that same soul inasmuch as intelligent and free. Thus a first trichotomy is heralded, the *corpus-anima-animus*, which, under Origen's influence, will become in the *Golden Epistle*: *corpus, anima-animus, spiritus*, and will end up being reduced to the following formula: *corpus-anima, animus-spiritus*; the body and the soul, inasmuch as animating principle and lower reason; the spirit, receiver of grace, and the soul, inasmuch as intellective power."[106]

Such an anthropology is not however presented as a gratuitous speculation. It conditions the whole spiritual life. And we should not forget that William was the intimate friend of one of the greatest Christian mystics. "From all evidence, prayers and those who pray are classified according to three states of soul: *animal, reasonable*, and *spiritual*. Each one builds or represents in its own way the Lord his God."[107] Later he successively describes the prayer of the animal man, that of the reasonable man, and finally that of the spiritual man, each being of course the same man. "This man, it has been said already, inasmuch as he works for his purification, is *reasonable*; purified, he becomes *spiritual*."[108] Then, "bounding, as it were, out of a hiding-place, without the least thing held back, without declaring either his name or origin," this man enters finally into the order of Divine Love: "O Love, from which all love, even carnal, even degenerated love, takes its name; holy and sanctifying Love, pure and purifying, vivifying life, open to us then your Holy Canticle, unveil the mystery of your kiss, the profound meaning of your slight murmur by which you modulate the heart of your children, your virtue and the delights of your sweetness."[109]

The Victorines. By this term is designated a school of theology and spirituality founded at the beginning of the twelfth century by William of Champeaux. The latter, tired of the dialectical battles which he had undertaken against Abelard in particular, resigned from his official functions and retired to a hermitage situated in Paris — today the Halle aux Vins quarter — a hermitage dedicated to St. Victor. Some

---

106 Ibid., 33n34. *The Golden Epistle*, or *Letter to the Brethren of Mont Dieu*, about struggling Carthusians, is the most famous of the author's writings.
107 *On the Song of Songs*, in *Œuvres choisies*, 221.
108 Ibid., 229.
109 Ibid., 231.

disciples joined him. Soon this spiritual center shone with a lively brilliance and was elevated to the status of abbey of Saint Victor. Its most illustrious masters were Hugh, Richard, and Adam of Saint Victor.

A dominant feature of this school (and of twelfth-century authors in general) is the attention they devoted to the study of man. A great quantity of anthropological treatises are numbered among their works.[110] We will quote only a few texts from Hugh and Richard of Saint Victor.

We have seen William of Saint-Thierry identify, under the term 'spirits' — the 'animal spirits' of Descartes — the notion of a subtle (psychic) substance actually inseparable from the *anima*, the life-principle, making of the soul (*psyche*) a veritable intermediary between spirit and body. The same conception is found again with Hugh of Saint Victor in his treatise *On the Union of Soul and Body*: "Although spirit, the soul *in its nature* shares in a certain mutability as it approaches the body in vivifying it."[111] Insofar as the principle that fixes the human being within the sphere of the truly real, the soul is *spiritus*; insofar as the animating principle of the body, it is *anima*.[112]

But the background of this anthropology is mystical and only makes sense in terms of God: man is essentially the one who knows God. In his most celebrated work, *De Sacramentis*, Hugh writes: "The soul had the world outside of itself and God within. It had received an eye to see the world outside and that which is found in the world: this is the eye of the flesh. It had received another eye to see within itself: this is the eye of reason. It had received yet another eye to see God within itself and that which is in God: and this is the eye of contemplation."[113]

The intermediate position of the soul corresponds therefore to a properly spiritual situation, to which its religious destiny is committed.

---

110   Cf. the informative list given by Father Déchanet, 51. For this question we have drawn our documentation from two works by Father Robert Javelet, works of an exceptional quality, as much for the knowledge communicated as for their spirit: it is on the one hand a question of *Psychologie des auteurs spirituels du XIIe siècle* (Strasbourg: Muh-Le Roux, 1959) as well as a doctoral thesis in two volumes: *Image et Ressemblance au XIIe siècle, de saint Anselme à Alain de Lille* (Strasbourg: Université de Strasbourg, 1967).

111   PL 177:288C.

112   *In cant. B. M. V.*, PL 175:420; cited by Javelet, *Psychologie*, 5.

113   PL 176:329CD; Javelet, 9.

"Through Origen, through St. Jerome," writes Father Javelet, "a *scriptural trichotomy* (chiefly Pauline) has reached as far as Hugh, as far as the spiritual authors of the twelfth century, and it must be understood that it is integrated with an original vision of man: carnal man, rational man, spiritual man . . . all three forming only one same person, although sometimes, according to the predominance of one or the other, the person may be considered as carnal (hylic), psychic or pneumatic."[114]

From this perspective the word *mens*, so often translated as 'spirit', acquires a more specific sense, echoing in a surprising way the terminology we have proposed adopting. This sense is that of mental and rational knowledge, and makes of *mens* a synonym for *animus*, the mental soul—"the *animus* sees by the eye of reason," says Hugh[115]—while *pneuma* is better translated as *spiritus*.

We have seen Hugh speak of the eye of the soul. He also speaks of the eye of the heart or of the spirit. This is a matter of direct and intuitive knowledge of divine realities. Employed universally, this metaphor is likewise found again with Richard of Saint Victor, who, distinguishing the carnal eye, the rational eye, and the eye of the heart-intellect, sees in this last one the highest power of the soul. He writes: "This intellective sense grasps invisible things, in invisible ways certainly, but in their presence, in their essence."[116] This intellect, which is also the spirit, is freedom and corresponds to the person, to the inner man. This is what Richard sets forth in *On the State of the Inner Man*, where he connects the person and freedom, and in *Benjamin Major*, where he relates the intellect to the spiritual person.[117]

Benjamin Minor and *Benjamin Major* illustrate moreover the two fundamental stages of this pilgrimage towards oneself, which is in reality a pilgrimage towards God. It is the pilgrimage of the Jewish people in march towards the Promised Land, a pilgrimage accomplished in two stages: "first the leaving of Egypt, then the crossing of

114 Ibid.
115 *In Hierarchium*, in PL 175:975–76; Javelet, 10.
116 PL 196:119.
117 Javelet, 13. We also find some remarks on Richard's anthropological vocabulary in *Richard de Saint-Victor, Les quatre degrés de la violente charité* (Paris: Vrin, 1955), 192–99.

the desert. Passing therefore from the world to yourself, then from yourself to God."[118]

In this way we are led toward a metaphysics of the person which implies, at the same time, a veritable process of self-dispossession. In the description of this mystical way, to which we have given the name of *negative egology*, Richard attained unsurpassed heights, earning the title of greatest doctor of medieval mysticism.[119] His doctrine culminates in particular in the notion of *alienatio mentis* or *excessus mentis*, which can be translated as transport or ravishment of the spirit. The expression *excessus mentis* has been traditional in Latin mysticism for a long time. It is borrowed from the Vulgate, which speaks of *"Benjamin adolescentulus in mentis excessu . . .* Young Benjamin in a transport of the spirit . . . "* (Psalm 67:28). Interesting to note is how the Vulgate here translates a Hebrew term that designates the state of deep sleep.[120] This *excessus mentis*, this transport of the spirit that is also a laying-bare of the mental soul, in reality uncovers the intellect at the center of the mentality, hidden in its depths, for, "through the intellect, the inmost 'receptacle' of the spirit (*sinus mentis*) is opened to the Infinite. . . . "[121]

St. Thomas Aquinas. Not from any taste for paradox are we including St. Thomas in a study devoted to medieval witnesses of anthropological tripartition, and this will surely incite annoyed disbelief with a majority of Thomists — and non-Thomists. Everyone knows that the Thomist doctrine of the soul is, by itself, a refutation of 'trichotomism'. Yet we ask them to consider two already-made remarks: on the one hand, it is uncertain if the Aristotelian doctrine of the soul as form of the body, to which St. Thomas unquestionably subscribes, is by itself the negation of every tripartition; on the other hand, no philosopher worthy of this name (and above all not Plato) has cut man into two or three.

---

118 *Benjamin Major*, PL 196:1076D. An analysis and excerpts from *Benjamin Minor*, with translations and commentaries by Hélène Merle, have been published in the review *Études Traditionnelles* from January to June 1963, numbers 375, 377, 378, 379. These two texts constitute an immense work.

119 Cayré, *Précis de patrologie*, vol. 2, 448.

120 *Rodem*: participle of *radam*. Modern Bible editors evidently see a scribal error here.

121 *Benjamin Major*, PL 196:67.

There is at least one text of St. Thomas where the human ternary seems evident under a slightly different but recognizable form: this is the commentary on the Supreme Commandment as formulated in St. Luke. "Love is an act of the will which is denoted here by 'heart', because just as the bodily heart is the principle of all the movements of the body, so too the will, especially as regards the intention of the last end which is the object of charity, is the principle of all the movements of the soul. Now there are three principles of action that are moved by the will, namely, the intellect which is signified by 'the *mind*', the lower appetitive power, signified by 'the *soul*', and the exterior executive power, signified by 'strength.'"[122]

But, to this text of a religious tenor, we would like to add other more technical ones which prove, quite clearly, that for St. Thomas the intellective soul can give form to a body only if it has already been given form by the vegetative and animal soul. For St. Thomas then there is indeed in man, at least for a certain time, an animal soul differing by nature from the intellective soul. In other words man, in the embryonic state, begins by being an animal before being a man. Father Sertillanges, hardly to be suspected of Platonism, writes:

> Prior to its basic organization, the body does not admit of a soul because, at the beginning, it is not a body, because at later stages (of embryological development) it is not a body for *this* soul.
>
> Do we not know that the soul is to the body what sight is to the eye? No more than the sight can exist before the eye, can the soul exist before the body, nor the properly human soul before the properly human body, which is to say the body organized in a way able to lead a human life.

122 *Summa Theologiae* II-II, q. 44, a. 5. In the course of the article St. Thomas recalls other, equally acceptable interpretations of the Fathers, in particular those that identify the heart with the intellect. In his commentary on the parallel passage in Matthew 22:37 (*Catena Aurea*, vol. 1 [Turin: Typographia Pontificia, 1912], 296), St. Thomas returns to the same citations and adds that, according to Origen, "but there is a difference between spirit (*mens*) and heart: The mentality (*mens*) is so called because it measures [estimates, evaluates]; the heart is taken here to signify the simplicity of the intellect."

> ...Philosophically, to place a (human) soul in an
> embryo of a body or, so much the more, in *semen* is, for
> St. Thomas, a clear heresy: one does not confide the art
> of building to flutists.[123]

Therefore the human embryo is first given form by the vegetative
soul, next by the animal soul, finally by the intellective soul, each
one of these successive forms moreover destroying the previous one
and assuming its function: "Thus the vegetative soul, which is present first (when the embryo lives the life of a plant), perishes and is
succeeded by a more perfect soul, both nutritive and sensitive in character, and then the embryo lives an animal life; and when that passes
away it is succeeded by the rational soul introduced from without,
while the preceding souls existed in virtue of the semen."[124] This text
from the *Contra Gentiles* is taken up again under an identical form
in the *Summa Theologiae*, except that the expression 'rational soul'
is replaced by 'intellective soul': "The embryo first possesses a purely
sensitive soul that disappears to make room for a more perfect soul,
sensitive and intellective at the same time."[125]

This distinction between animal and intellective souls is so much
more interesting since, for St. Thomas, only the second one is created
by God, the first one being produced by the very act of generation.
This thesis is so important that St. Thomas devotes lengthy pages to
it in several of his treatises.[126] It follows that, in its origin, the sensitive soul is distinct from the intellective soul as the natural is from
the supernatural.

However, it is no less true that St. Thomas intends to oppose himself to Plato—a Plato whom he reads through Aristotle—and that he
deploys all his dialectical might to establish the unity of the intellective soul.[127] Yet how can the intellect assume the vegetative and sensitive functions assumed by the animal soul? St. Thomas's response

123   *Saint Thomas d'Aquin*, vol. 2 (Paris: Alcan, 1912), 154.
124   *Summa Contra Gentiles*, Bk. II, ch. 89 [11], p. 304.
125   *Summa Theologiae* I, q. 76, a. 3, ad 3. The moment when the embryo
receives a human soul is not specified in these texts.
126   *Contra Gentiles*, Bk. II, chs. 88 and 89; *Summa Theologiae* I, q. 118, aa. 1 & 2.
127   *Summa Theologiae* I, q. 76, aa. 2–4.

is inspired by Aristotle and rests on the principle: whatever can do more can do less. The intellect, being ontologically more perfect and more noble than the vegetative or animal soul, therefore contains, by reason of its perfection and nobility, the virtualities of both: "the intellectual soul contains virtually whatever belongs to the sensitive soul of brute animals, and to the nutritive souls of plants. Therefore, as a surface which is of a pentagonal shape, is not tetragonal by one shape, and pentagonal by another — since a tetragonal shape would be superfluous as contained in the pentagonal — so neither is Socrates a man by one soul, and animal by another; but by one and the same soul he is both animal and man."[128] This is an important image, since it basically means that the intellective soul is the integrating principle, we could almost say the integral principle, of a human being. But yet, as St. Thomas himself says, "A body is not necessary to the intellectual soul by reason of its intellectual operation considered as such; but on account of the sensitive power."[129] Is this not once again a kind of human ternary: body, intellective soul in its sensitive faculty, and intellective soul properly speaking? We are integrally Thomist in affirming the ontological unity of a human being and his soul, but it is now altogether obvious that between the two operations of animation of the body and intellection of divine truth there is a difference of an irreducible nature (at least in the sinful human state), since it is not by virtue of its properly intellective nature that the human soul is the form of the body.

This is why we have focused so long on this question. It is the first key to the spiritual way: to begin to distinguish in ourselves what is a movement of the natural soul and what is the awakening of a truly spiritual awareness. We can enter now into the way of love.

---

128 *Summa Theologiae* I, q. 76, a. 3; Aristotle, *On the Soul*, II, 3, 414b.
129 *Summa Theologiae* I, q. 76, a. 5, ad 2.

PART III

The Metaphysical Structure of Charity in Its Human Order

INTRODUCTION: SPIRITUAL CHARITY
AND THE TWO COMMANDMENTS

IN THE FIRST PART WE HAVE SHOWN HOW CHAR-
ity, insofar as it is a virtue, was the choice motivation for confusing the
psychic and the spiritual. Next we saw the different aspects of this confusion. In the second part we examined the limits and determinations
imposed on charity by the setting of traditional culture, on the one hand,
and the ternary composition of human nature, on the other, establishing in this way an anthropological basis for the distinction between the
psychic and the spiritual. Now we shall try to describe the metaphysical
structure of charity in its three orders: human, divine, and cosmic.

How are we to understand that charity is the pre-eminent spiritual
way, or even simply that it is a spiritual path, when its given as well
as assumed meaning is always and inevitably identified with altruism
and philanthropy and their different modalities, such as socialism,
progressivism, pacifism, etc. — that is, with something purely human,
or even at times infra-human? Or again: what is the content of the
message of love? What do we understand about it? If the highest
spirituality consists in doing what atheists and even the most implacable enemies of all spirituality can do, is there not at least a contradiction here? If charity's contents are fraternity and humanitarianism,
as the *near totality* of clergy and laity now overwhelmingly suppose,
then in what does this pre-eminent spiritual way consist? The question is not whether human mutual aid is good or bad under all its
forms, for such a question is not being posed and never has been.[1]

---

1   It is only posed from a Marxist perspective since for it, every man being
obliged to sacrifice everything for the good of humanity, the absolute character of
fraternal mutual aid transforms it into a utopia.

The question is whether or not that is charity. If yes, then there is no longer any spiritual charity, that is to say charity in the proper sense of the term, nor any Revelation either, and we do not see why Christ should be incarnated if His only goal was to teach us, as a supreme secret, what everyone accepts without difficulty. If those Christians who identify charity and socialism, charity and revolution, and lastly charity and universal earthly happiness were not Christians, basically there would be no problem. They would not adorn their human activity with a sacred epithet. On the whole they would be much more modest and, in a certain manner, much more lucid. Faced with this naturalist and sentimental 'understanding' of charity, which could be quite precisely defined as triumphalist charity and which could be talked about indefinitely without convincing anyone, we therefore need to recall the true metaphysical understanding of the charity of Christ.[2]

Charity is the favored locus for confusion between the psychic and the spiritual. This means that the truth of charity resides in the distinction between the psychic and the spiritual, and that to realize charity is to realize this distinction. The realization of this distinction consists in the death of the ego, which is self-love, or in other words the possessive desire of self. What was an illusory center must accept becoming the periphery with respect to the Supreme Center as well as to those other illusory centers that are other selves, *alter egos*. To say 'myself', whether one is aware of it or not, is to deny God and others. Certainly this negation is in some manner inevitable, but nonetheless it introduces a separative illusion between God and man, between man and man, and between man and himself. Now love is union. To say that love sums up the Law and the Prophets is to say that it is an abolition of separative illusion and therefore of the ego. Or again, to say that we need to love God and neighbor as ourselves means that we need to renounce the ego. And again: to renounce the ego is to love

---

2   Christ enjoins us to love our enemies and pray for those who persecute us. If one adopts the viewpoint of triumphalist charity, which is wholly imbued with Marxism, in good logic the poor would need to love the rich, the oppressed their oppressors, the exploited workers their exploiting bosses, the colonized their imperialist states, etc.; for it is a question each time of their enemy. And so we do not understand how the Gospel can justify class conflict.

God and neighbor as another 'oneself'. But not by its own powers can the ego renounce itself. Only Divine Love can love to the point of dissipating the illusion of separativity. Only Love can give to the ego, not the power to annihilate itself, but a working knowledge of its own nothingness, which is at the same time knowledge of Being. The ego is nothing but this self-illusion that characterizes it; for it to be anything else is an outright impossibility, but it can become cognizant of its own status. For awareness or speculative knowledge is, by essence, the anticipation of what is not yet realized. In this it is more than being or will. Divine Love transforms the speculative knowledge of anticipation into the working knowledge of realization. This is why, as the Greek Fathers and Scripture say, charity is the doorway to Gnosis.

The human order of charity is composed of two dimensions, one horizontal and the other vertical: love of neighbor and love of God. These two dimensions intersect in love of self. And this is the blueprint followed here. In a first chapter (10) we study the love of neighbor, and then, in a second chapter (11), the love of self and the love of God.

10

Love of Neighbor

THE SECOND COMMANDMENT IS INSEPARABLE from the first; all Scripture teaches this. Love of God is not achieved without love of neighbor, nor love of neighbor without love of God. This unique love has then two dimensions; to separate them is to destroy them, that is, destroy the love which is their crucifying union.

But to confuse them is also to destroy them both by ruining their *raison d'être*. Love is not just anything. I do not — ought not — love God as I love my neighbor. Therefore we need to love God with all of ourselves (body, soul and spirit), that is to say more than ourselves, because He is more myself than I am. We need to love our neighbor as ourselves, which supposes that we love ourselves. But to love ourselves we need to love God. The love of self, which is the measure of the love of neighbor, is founded and possible only through the love of God, which is measureless. The cause for which I love God, St. Bernard said, is God Himself; the measure of this love is to be without measure. Indeed, love of oneself is always love of a creature, therefore of a limitation and an imperfection. Love of self is only possible then if this imperfection is as if wiped away, pardoned, ransomed by the Divine All-Perfection into which the love of God makes me enter. If not there can only be self-hatred, of which self-respect (*amour-propre*), that is to say love of appropriation, is then only a modality.

I. FRATERNAL CHARITY
IN ITS OBJECTIVE ORDER

1. Active Charity

There are two commandments: the first and the second. The second is not the first; it is similar to it, its image, the projection or exterior manifestation. Let us say that the first can be related to the vertical branch of the Cross and the second to the horizontal. The first commandment is also the greatest, Jesus says in St. Matthew. This means that it comprehends or includes the second, but not vice versa. The second 'expresses' the first, but does not exist without it and has no meaning outside of it. As a result, the second does not replace the first. However, this is what modern Christianity explicitly or implicitly asserts. But, seeing that the second commandment is set in the place of the first, the former has to completely assume its exalted station, so that then it becomes: you will love your neighbor more than yourself. This assertion necessarily supposes that the love of self be conceived of only under the form of egoism — in other words, that the second commandment is not the love of others first, but hatred of the ego. Conversely, it follows that love of others becomes love of their egos, and that what is despised in the self is adored in the other. Thus love of neighbor is only a transposed egoism, an alibi allowing us to egotistically love ourselves through others. This attitude is particularly evident in all that concerns the rich/poor relationship. To regard things objectively, and without taking other considerations into account, the destitution of those who have nothing seems to authorize them to reclaim all the wealth despised with so much arrogance when it belongs to the bourgeoisie. The consumer society is justified when 'workers' and 'under-developed countries' demand a share in it, but violently condemned in the person of those who enjoy it.

There is, however, a natural duty for mutual aid arising out of necessity; it forms a part of a certain kind of charity, but as its external and objective dimension. This objective charity is a kind of love without love, for it is not directly addressed to the other's person and, consequently, it does not effect charity. It is not love of the person, but the objective perception of a disequilibrium of injustice or misfortune of which the person is the victim and which reason intends to redress. This active charity, says St. Bernard, belongs to the order of truth: it is "dry but strong."[1] This objective charity does not constitute then what is essential to the second commandment, otherwise, as we have shown, such charity is only the farce of an egoism disguised as altruism. And the awareness of this objective character alone permits escape from the *ego-alter* dialectic, certainly not by abolishing or surpassing it, but, to the extent possible, by not being

---

1   Cf. St. Bernard, Sermon 50, in *On the Song of Songs*, vol. III (Kalamazoo: Cistercian Publishing, 1979), 33.

its victim or neighbor. From a certain point of view, to do good is the most dangerous thing there is, objectively as much as subjectively — subjectively because, at this level, it is always the ego which acts and risks finding itself reinforced; objectively because, in order to reduce a disequilibrium, it is necessary to introduce a disequilibrium in the opposite direction whose consequences will inevitably provoke a 'backlash'. Thus, in this realm, there is no perfect solution. Neither is abstaining from all active charity an option at all, since this is quite strictly impossible. Indeed, nobody is normally lacking in active charity towards himself. Hence this abstention would be sheer hypocrisy. One must simply carry one's cross.

Consider this assertion of St. Paul in his hymn to charity: "Even if I distribute all my goods as alms, and if I deliver my body up to be burned, but if I have not charity, this is of no profit to me" (1 Cor 13:3). "What hyperbole," St. John Chrysostom exclaims! "Paul does not say: if I give half my goods to the poor, nor two or three parts . . . but all that I possess. He does not say: if I die, but specifies the most painful kind of death: to be burned alive!"[2] This saying of St. Paul, extraordinary as it might be for modern man, seems altogether apt for making the contents of the commandment of charity explicit, even if only negatively. Charity is, in its essence, neither social action nor fraternal mutual aid, nor the most generous philanthropy. Although works are its exterior mark, they are not its principle. Interior charity necessarily manifests itself in objective charity. But every social action is not automatically the manifestation of interior charity, even though it is impossible to distinguish one from the other exteriorly. To conceive of and live exterior works, whether for collective or individual purposes, as an expression of interior charity — *this is the true spiritual meaning of charitable work*. On the contrary, to make of the consequence a principle is to destroy charity as such and make it impossible. In the end, this also destroys social action itself, for — and we think that we have shown this sufficiently — if this activity has solely rational criteria, it engenders the most monstrous and inhumane of necessitarisms.

2 Cited in *La Sainte Bible*, Pirot-Clamer, vol. 9, Part 2 (Paris: Letouzey et Ané, 1950), 263.

Nihil mihi prodest, "this is of no profit to me," says St. Paul. A modernist would say: "What spiritual egoism!" Thus the work of charity is viewed solely with regard to the spiritual end which it realizes in me! I have only one soul which must be saved. But St. Thomas Aquinas already affirms that it is necessary to love oneself more than one's neighbor in view of salvation,[3] for "holiness is incommunicable." It could be objected that Christ's injunctions have a universal and absolute bearing, since it is necessary to love one's enemies, turn the left cheek, and do good to those who hate us. However, Christ's point of view, if one may dare to say, is the same as St. Paul's. "Love your enemies and pray for those who persecute you, *so that you may become children of your Father who is in heaven*" (Matt. 5:44–5). These reactions to evil do not have a moral objective but a spiritual one, for Christ concludes His injunction by saying: "Be you perfect as your heavenly Father is perfect."

2. *Under what Conditions is Objective Charity a Spiritual Way?*

There are then two orders of the love of neighbor: an objective and a subjective order. The objective order is founded on the objective reality of love. To the question whether the acts of an atheist have a charitable value, the answer must be in the affirmative. They possess this value 'objectively'. All existence is the fruit of Divine Love. Every act of love participates in Divine Love. But, in a certain manner, this objective dimension of charity does not concern *me* precisely because it is objective. There is no essential difference, as regards objectivity, between the charity of a tree giving its shade or fruits and the charity of any man whatsoever who alleviates some misery or makes good an injustice without showing any partiality. The atheist may see here the perfection of human love and therefore commit his entire self to it, in this way undertaking a subjectivization of objective charity. The

---

3 *Summa Theologiae* II-II, q. 26, a. 4. "The spiritual nature and the corporeal nature have to be distinguished in man. Now man is said to love himself in that he loves himself in his spiritual nature; . . . and under this rapport man should love himself, after God, more than any other." But, in article 5, the Doctor shows that it is necessary to love one's body less than the neighbor: "Our body is more united to our soul than the neighbor as regards what is of our natural constitution, but, relative to participation in beatitude, there is a closer union between the soul of the neighbor and our own than between the latter and our own body."

modern Christian does the same. And both ruin the very order of objective charity by destroying its *raison d'être* and the condition for its validity. The ego, relating the act of charity to itself, introduces disorder and negation. It appropriates charity to itself, whether it wants to or not, only insofar as it is objective. Returning to Matthew's text, we will see that Christ says nothing else:

> You have heard it said: You will love your neighbor and hate your enemy. But I say to you: Love your enemies and pray for those who persecute you, so that you may become sons of your heavenly Father, who makes his sun to rise upon the wicked and upon the good, and makes it rain upon the just and upon the unjust. For if you love those who love you, what recompense will you have? Do not the publicans do as much? And if you greet only your brothers, what more do you do? Do not the pagans do as much? Be therefore perfect, as your heavenly Father is perfect.

"You will love your neighbor and hate your enemies. But I say to you: Love your enemies." Christ is not saying that the enemy is my neighbor; otherwise there would be no enemy, and the paradoxical character of Christ's injunction would disappear. Besides, how do we abolish, on the plane of relativity, this same relativity? The radical imperfection of every human society, a manifestation of which is the existence of the enemy, cannot be avoided on the very plane of imperfection. But He says that if I have to love my neighbor, I should also love my enemy. With what sort of love? With that objective love which we have described, for the reason provided by Christ, for this love is directly dependent upon the objectivity of the cosmic order manifesting the objective Love of God for His creation, or rather, is dependent upon the objectivity of the cosmic order which *is* the Love of God as creation: "become children of your heavenly Father who makes his sun rise upon the wicked and the good, and makes it rain upon the just and the unjust." Christ does not say that there is no difference between the just and the unjust, the good and the wicked. On the contrary, for Him there are just and unjust, good and wicked. And the unjust and the wicked are the enemies of the friends of God,

as the commandment to pray "for those who persecute you" sufficiently proves.[4] But He tells us to take cosmic phenomena, the sun
and rain — the symbolic meaning of which we leave aside here — as
models for this love so to imitate their indifference or, again, their
objectivity. To become perfect does not mean to abolish imperfection
upon its own plane. God Himself does not do this.

Christ enjoins on us an attitude of withdrawal from, not negation
of, the inevitable contradictions of fallen creation.[5] This attitude of
withdrawal with respect to cosmic contradictions is at first that of the
ego which retires from its charitable activity. This is the impersonality of a charity refusing to know or own itself. This is the left hand
that does not know what the right hand is doing. For this charitable
work is pure objectivity, it is a work of justice. To be convinced, let
us continue with our text:

> Keep yourselves from practicing your justice in public in
> order to be seen by men. Otherwise you will not have

4 On this subject we will point out that the traditional interpretations of the
Gospel texts relative to the love of enemies — and, we add, the honest interpretations — have always distinguished *inimicus* and *hostis*, namely the personal enemy
and the enemy of war. When Christ speaks of the love of enemies, it is impossible to
see here a condemnation of war, for the Vulgate text like the Greek always, in such
instances, translates this by *inimicus* and not by *hostis*. Besides, such a condemnation
would be something quite modern. It is not a part of the Gospel's 'mental horizon',
even if certain contemporary thinkers imagine they can — incorrectly — deduce this.

5 Again we will say this: the most extreme assertions of Christ concerning this
attitude with regard to others cannot be considered, unless by the most complete
hypocrisy, as foundations for a social and worldly order; rather they clearly signify
withdrawal from the world, and are to be understood only if we acknowledge along
with Christ the world's radical imperfection. Basically they signify that a disciple of
Christ must never enter into disputes with the world, for the world is not worth the
trouble. Let us admit for a moment that these injunctions have a social and purely
horizontal character. Consequently, when Christ says in St. Luke 6:29: "To the one
who takes your cloak, do not refuse your tunic," or "do not reclaim your property from
whoever takes it," we are obliged to admit that Christ is enjoining us to encourage
theft, pillage, and lying (for example in accepting yet not believing in the promises of
restitution of those to whom one has lent money), in short to assure everywhere and in
all things impunity for malefactors. If one claims that the only way out of the difficulty
is to understand that Christ is able to implicitly envisage the negation of the right to
property in a Proudhonian or Marxist style, we ask then why He could take as a symbol
of the perfect man, in His eschatological parables, the master who carefully watches
over his possessions all night if necessary (cf. Matt 24:43, Mark 13:34, Luke 12:39).

any reward with your heavenly Father. Therefore when you give alms, do not sound the trumpet before yourself, as the hypocrites do in the synagogue and the streets, in order to be praised by men. Truly, I say to you, they have their reward. For yourselves, when you give alms, do not let your left hand know what your right hand is doing so that your alms remain in secret and your Father, who sees in secret, will reward you. (Matt 6:1–4)

Christ's commandment can just as well have a more interior sense, but one that does not enter into contradiction with the previous interpretation and that to the contrary even implies it. From the necessary love, which sees in the enemy a man and that which is due to human nature, we can proceed to love for the person who hates us. But this love is only possible on one condition, that this hate have only an objective reality from now on: in other words, that my enemy is no longer such for me, even if I remain so in his eyes. For to love with true friendship the one I hate — that, being nonsensical, is not within anyone's power. Therefore this love requires that I withdraw from this hostile relationship, that I consider him as not affecting me and in no way concerned with me: in short, that I practice this withdrawal of the ego from the cosmic contradictions previously mentioned, but withdraw inward, since it is not within my power to exteriorly prevent others from hating me. One then gains access to the spiritual order of charity, but this cannot be completely confused with the objective order as such. Quite the contrary, Christ's formulas teach us how to distinguish the two orders. All too often the modern Christian is prone to confuse the two; what centuries of faith and holiness would consider to be the summit of perfection,[6] he makes a precept obligatory for all. Drunk with a confused charity, it seems he no longer has any hate for anyone; amazed, he basks in his own goodness. But this love is purely sentimental and corresponds to no objective possibility. Naturally I can love someone for his natural qualities, if they are lovable. I can love human nature objectively in everyone, even the one in whom it is degraded. Finally,

6 *Summa Theologiae* II-II, q. 25, aa. 8 & 9.

I can love his immortal person supernaturally, here as well on the condition of distinguishing this person from the psychic accidents through which he manifests himself, and in spite of them — such is the supreme sense of love of the enemy. But I do not have the right to desecrate the charitable power by loving in the enemy what is objectively to be hated, or else I destroy with the same stroke the very reality of love. "He who loves nothing merely human loves all men."[7] To accept such a distinction clearly requires a very high degree of spirituality. However, this degree is as if prefigured in the most exterior objective charity, because, as we have said, this charity, in order to be integrated with the spiritual way of Christ, has to be treated objectively. It is presented to the Christian as the most immediate occasion for withdrawing the *ego* from its charitable activity, by which is realized a first mode of the death to oneself.

To be altogether clear in this respect, we will say then that charity, in its objective order, presents a dual aspect. It can be viewed in its concrete reality, but also in its relation to the human agent. Outwardly, nothing distinguishes the charitable activity of an atheist from that of a Christian. Inwardly the difference is great. Only in the first case can we speak of a natural or 'profane' charity. In the second case objective charity is already of the supernatural order, and we can speak of a 'sacred' charity. Consequently, when we speak of natural charity, it is exclusively of the first kind. Besides, this natural charity is not reserved for atheists; Christians also practice it each time — and obviously this is a frequent situation — they forget the theological dimension of this virtue, or again, each time they 'egoically' commit themselves to the activity it inspires. Objective charity does not belong of *itself* to the spiritual order. And it is best that its conditions be made explicit.

3. The Universality and Limit of Charity in its Objective Order

So the work of charity, that is to say active charity, represented by the mention of *hands* (what your hand is doing) and defined by its objectivity, already implies, if not a renunciation of the ego, at least a renunciation *by* the ego and even a double renunciation: renunciation

---

7 St. Maximus the Confessor, *Texts on Love* III, 37; *The Philokalia*, vol. 2, trans. Palmer, Sherrard, Ware (London and Boston: Faber & Faber, 1981), 89.

of exterior recognition ("do not sound the trumpet before yourself") and, more profoundly, renunciation of interior recognition ("may your left hand not know..."). In its universal dimensions, Christ's commandment demands the blotting-out of every egoic singularity, as much in my own person as in that of others. *A priori*, the work of justice does not consider the neighbor but man in his cosmic situation, and does not exempt itself from this objective order.

Being universal, this commandment is by definition and *a priori* applied to every man, but its realization does not require, for it to be accomplished in perfection and for us to be perfect, that we apply it successively to all men. A similar interpretation is implied, however, in the manner in which our contemporaries have become intoxicated with a quantitatively unlimited charity. Besides, why limit the import of this commandment to humanity? Does not the cosmic order concern the whole of creation, and has not Christ ordained the teaching of the Gospel to every creature and not to man alone? And on the other hand, imperfection, misery, and injustice being by definition inexhaustible, the work of justice claims the totality of my time and therefore the totality of my life.

Consequently, everything not directly an individual or social work of justice is mortal sin. Prayer and liturgy, momentarily requiring the whole man and the cessation of every action for the sake of the collectivity, become mortal sins themselves. For to pray, we must withdraw from the world. It is not we ourselves but Christ who is saying this, and we only need state that the commandment on prayer comes immediately after the just-quoted passage, as if the Gospel wished to forestall the modern errors of interpretation: "For yourself when you wish to pray enter into your chamber, close the door and pray to your Father who dwells in secret, and your Father who sees in secret will reward you" (Matt 6:6).[8] The *hic* and *nunc* of our existential situation implies a unicity of acting. We cannot do several things at once. The act of prayer and the liturgy concretely exclude the social act and vice versa. If active charity is to absorb the totality of the charitable

8 Without wishing to enter into the problem of the logical succession of Gospel pericopes, we will confine ourselves to remarking that likewise in St. Luke the preeminence of contemplation (Martha and Mary) immediately follows the parable of the Good Samaritan.

power, everything opposing it should be eliminated. And this is why we think the modern conception leads directly and logically to the elimination of liturgical worship and the spiritual life, that is to say ultimately of the Church and theism, for their opposition, *in concreto*, is strictly inevitable. There are moments, then, when time for the love of God is taken from time for the love of men, as if there were an appointed limit to this love and therefore a time when I do not love men in deed. But did not St. John say: "The one who does not love his brother whom he sees, how can he love God whom he does not see" (1 John 4:20)? St. Thomas Aquinas has already anticipated the objection which can be drawn from this verse. He first shows that, in order to take a just measure of this verse, it must be compared with this saying of Christ: "If someone comes to me and hates not his mother and father, and his spouse and his children, and his brothers and sisters, he cannot be my disciple" (Luke 14:26). There is need for a break with respect to created love inasmuch as it necessarily includes a tendency that estranges us from God.

It is this estranging tendency that must be hated, because what God loves is proximity or reconciliation — an important remark we will come back to later. We must become alienated from that which alienates. Moreover, in the assertion of St. John, if the love for my visible brother proves that I am not lying in affirming love for the invisible God, this is necessarily because the visible is considered as a manifestation, a symbol of the invisible. The visible love of my visible brother is the visible testimony of Love for the Invisible. It therefore presupposes this as its cause. Or, as St. Thomas says: "The likeness we have to God precedes and causes the likeness we have to our neighbor."[9] Conversely the human being, which is an effect, can only go back towards its cause. This is why, "the neighbor being more visible" as effect than his invisible Cause, we learn to love the Cause from its effects.

Thus we are introduced to the subjective order of the love of neighbor, through which a second, more interior mode of the death of the ego is realized.

---

9 *Summa Theologiae* II-II, q. 26, a. 2.

II. FRATERNAL CHARITY
IN ITS SUBJECTIVE ORDER

1. The Golden Rule

"You shall love your neighbor as yourself." This commandment, which together with that of the love of God sums up the Law and the Prophets, has a more particular formulation, a formulation which, without defining its essence, in some way traces its limits — or is its limits, for anyone who would like a rule for practical application. This rule has traditionally received the name 'Golden Rule': "Therefore, all which you wish that men do to you, do it to them also yourselves: for this is the Law and the Prophets" (Matt 7:12, cf. Luke 6:31).[10] As we have said before, for man objective charity does not exhaust the commandment to love. According to an expression of St. Thomas Aquinas, "Charity likens us to God by uniting us to Him in the bond of love: wherefore it surpasses mercy, which likens us to God as regards similarity of works."[11] Mercy, in the sense of exterior charity, therefore constitutes an objective perfection, but one we are not yet able to interiorize, one we do not really understand, one that might and should leave our individual soul outside the circuit of sanctifying Love. Now Christ does not enjoin us to only love the neighbor as God loves His creation from beyond good and evil,[12] he also enjoins

10 The Golden Rule is in introduction for St. Luke and in conclusion for St. Matthew to the discourse on charity towards the neighbor. In some manner it constitutes its beginning and end. Now where the beginning coincides with the end, there is perfection (the symbolism of the circle). And likewise we read in St. Matthew: "Be perfect as your heavenly Father is perfect." And in St. Luke: "Be merciful as your Father is merciful." This means then that it is charity or mercy that realizes perfection, because charity connects the beginning to the end, and this is why St. Paul says of charity that it is the 'bond' of perfection (*vinculum perfectionis*), Col 3:14.

11 *Summa Theologiae* II-II, q. 30, a. 4. We interject briefly here, but will come back to it: this remark denounces the angelist or prideful character of triumphalist charity.

12 Yes, active charity, exterior charity, objective charity, and justice are in a certain manner this side of good and evil. This is the lowest degree of charity, that which reflects then, by virtue of the principle of inverse analogy, the highest degree of charity, which is beyond good and evil. This is why, within its order, it can appear to be the most perfect and the most authentic. But anyone who, instead of treating this objective order objectively, becomes passionately attached to it and sinks his charitable power into it assumes a function and claims a responsibility to which he has no right. Doing this, he destroys the objective order and is himself destroyed.

us to love him as ourselves. If the 'Golden Rule' defines the love of neighbor exteriorly according to a measure of reciprocity, the 'second commandment' defines it according to a measure of interiority and proximity. It is the love I bear myself which furnishes the rule of Charity toward my neighbor.

At least three questions are posed: Who is the neighbor? What is it to love oneself? And what does "as oneself" mean?

2. Who is the Neighbor?

This question was already posed two thousand years ago, and it was answered in a strange fashion by the parable of the Good Samaritan.

Christ had just recalled that the essential rule for believing resides in the love of God and the love of neighbor. The doctor of the Law, who recognized this rule himself, posed one last question: "Who is my neighbor?"—which is to say, since the neighbor is the one who must be loved, "whom must I love?" Let us keep to the spirit of this question and listen to Christ's reply. It is given under the form of a parable: the story of a man, a Samaritan, who saved the life of a traveler robbed, wounded, and abandoned—the last by a priest and a Levite—successively. Let us suppose that the story ends here. The conclusion directly stemming from it would be that my neighbor, the one whom I must love, is the wounded man. The neighbor is the one I must attend to because he is in need, that is the one I should love 'as myself'. The text, however, has a surprise in store. Christ does not say: "Who was the neighbor to this abandoned man?," which would seem the normal question, but: "which of these three [priest, Levite, Samaritan] seems to you to have been *this man's neighbor*?" At the beginning of the episode the neighbor is the *one I should love*, although I do not know who it is: "love your neighbor as yourself." Now Christ leads the doctor to designate as neighbor the *one who loves*. If, therefore, we compare the question "who is my neighbor?" with the reply "it is the Samaritan," it must be concluded that to love one's neighbor means to love the one who has cared for us and saved us from death. This is why the traditional interpretation, which sees Christ Himself in the Samaritan, is perfectly justified. The wounded traveler is fallen man, the man of sin. Jerusalem, a city elevated above sea level, the holy city, and Jericho, situated below sea level, the debased city, respectively represent the Earthly Paradise and the world here below. The Good Samaritan — this is the revelation of Christ, differing from the laws of Israel as do the Samaritans from the Jews. This man, half-dead, had been abandoned. This is in fact because sin (the traveller despoiled by robbers = Adam's nakedness after Original Sin) does not destroy Adamic nature but wounds it. The wine and oil poured out upon the wounds are the sacraments instituted by Christ. The inn is the Church and the money given to the innkeeper is the treasure of grace which Christ has confided to His Church. So our neighbor, the one we must love, is Christ the Savior, and in this way the second commandment is truly like the first.

However, if such is the most direct and loftiest sense of this parable, there remains that it also carries instruction about the love of men among themselves. Must we then continue to see the neighbor in the Samaritan? And since the neighbor is here the one who has loved, must we conclude that the love of neighbor consists in loving the one who loves us? But the doctor of the Law has never doubted this, for the Mosaic Law has always taught it; therefore Christ's reply has another meaning, even though it agrees quite well with that natural love which we bear for those who are our friends and brothers. Christ has actually carried out a reversal, a conversion of perspective. It is this reversal we must now study.

The doctor's question rests on a previous affirmation not in itself called into question: the neighbor is someone. Or again: who is the individual subject to whom the term 'neighbor' can be applied (which supposes that this term is actually applied to an individual)? Now this determining of the question beforehand makes a response impossible. Either Christ replies by identifying the neighbor with a determinate category of individual, and hence this determination needs to be justified anew, that is, shown to be a fitting definition of *neighbor*... Are we being given the run-around? Or does Christ reply by identifying the neighbor with just anyone? If so, the commandment no longer makes any sense, for to love just anyone is to love no one, love being a particular personal relationship. Moreover, Jewish law determined the neighbor as contrasted to the stranger, at least practically, for Sacred Scripture in principle nowhere prescribes hatred of the stranger, not even a wartime enemy. The doctor's question is therefore a question of scriptural exegesis and theology at the same time. As always Christ's reply transcends the plane of oppositions from which the question is posed, by revealing what it was presupposing and negating it: *the neighbor is not someone, an individual determination; the neighbor is a relationship*, or again a bringing-together—*et appropians*, and a drawing-near, according to the Vulgate. This is why, in two places, it is indicated that the priest and Levite "pass beyond," "swerving away." But whoever speaks of 'relationship' is saying two things: if I am relating to someone, it is just as much that person who is relating to me. The neighbor is neither I nor he, it is both together. If someone is my neighbor, this is because I am his. Thus we come to the notion of a relation of proximity which gives us the key to reciprocity. To love the neighbor means to have access through love to a reciprocating relation of proximity.

Achieved in this way, the notion of proximity is going to play a major role in our reflections. We will make an altogether 'technical' use of it, conferring on it a very precise meaning that will emerge progressively. For us, this is one of the key notions of the doctrine of charity. Its introduction into theology might be surprising, for it is certain that the chief expressions of the Christian faith have never made use of it. The novelty is only apparent, however. In reality this notion is encountered in the Old and New Testaments with a very particular meaning about which we will now say a word or two.

When we read in Isaiah: "Peace! Peace to him who is far and to him who is near! says Yahweh" (57:19), clearly these two expressions—to be near and to be far—are understood not only as manners of speaking, but also as almost technical designations for two categories of men: those in a state of estrangement and those in a state of proximity. This technical usage is confirmed and consecrated moreover by the Talmud. The term *proselyte*, when first encountered, rightly designates those of an origin foreign to Israel who accept the authority of the Mosaic faith and draw near to the true God. In Greek the word actually means "one who draws nigh." It is employed by the Septuagint to translate the word *stranger* (convert).[13] And since that time the term *proselutos* "connotes a religious reality."[14] Finally, at the time of Christ and above

13 Joshua 8:33.
14 *La Sainte Bible*, Pirot-Clamer, vol. 3, 59.

all in the New Testament, the term proselyte has an altogether technical usage.[15] But after the one who draws nigh, there is the one who
is brought nigh and who has therefore attained to a state of 'nearness'.
It is in this way that the Talmud presents the 'just ones' as the 'near
ones' (*qerobim*) of God. The *qerobim* represent the spiritual class of
men who have attained the perfection of holiness — *qerobim*, despite a
great literal similarity, does not seem to have any connection with the
Kheroubim, the Cherubim, a word whose etymology is contested, even
unknown. However, such a symbolic kinship justifies the interpretation that sees in the Cherubim those who are in proximity to the divine.

As for the New Testament, it is at least as rich, if not more so, in
references to the theological theme of proximity. We are speaking here
of a theme, for it is difficult in New Testament Greek to tie the idea of
proximity to a single term. First to be cited are texts about the proximity of the Kingdom of God, the pattern of which is furnished by this
saying: "Repent for the kingdom of God is *very near*."[16] The repentance in question here is not of a moral order, but of a spiritual one. It
translates a Greek word, itself translating an Aramaic expression, which
means a change of knowledge. This change of knowledge is that very
one defined in our anthropology when we spoke of the return of the *I*
to its divine source. As for the expression 'the Kingdom of God is near',
it is so fundamental that good commentators see in it the synthesis
of the *totality* of Christ's message, the quintessence of the kerygma.[17]

We are somewhat surprised then that the theme of proximity
(which is kerygmatically paired with the theme of spiritual conversion,
that is to say of the passage from psychic to pneumatic) has not been
the object of more abundant exegetical studies. In all of these texts it
is not just a spatial or temporal proximity, but, since this Kingdom
is Jesus Christ, God incarnate, it is also a relationship of proximity
that is simply Jesus Christ as perfect mediator: "The Lord is near,"[18]
writes St. Paul. Elsewhere, echoing Isaiah, he declares: "You were formerly far off, you have become near, thanks to the blood of Christ...

15   Acts 2:11.
16   Matt 3:2, 4:17, 10:7, etc.; Mark 1:15; Luke 10:9, etc.
17   Cf. C. H. Dodd, *The Founder of Christianity* (New York: Macmillan, 1970), 56.
18   Phil 4:5. We are stressing that the adjective 'near' translates a Greek adverb:
engus, 'close', 'beside', which expresses Christ's 'manner of being': Christ stands 'in
proximity'.

And he has come to announce peace for you who were far and peace for those who are near."[19] A divino-human proximity, as St. James affirms: "Approach God and he will approach you" (5:8). All these examples cited employ the same Greek term *engys* or its derivatives. But is it not the same idea expressed in other terms when St. Paul writes, continuing the just-quoted text from Ephesians: "for through him we both have access close to the Father in one single and same Spirit"? These few remarks will be enough, we think, to indicate the scriptural foundations for the notion of proximity.

3. Love does not create the Relation of Proximity

However, to define Charity as a pure motion, a dynamism of love, a creator of proximity, a pure act by which the entire being consists in this very act, exposes one to a relapse into that very triumphalist charity we have denounced, that charity without truth. Charity becomes for itself its own truth, and we return then to the deadly confusion between the psychic and spiritual, a confusion at work in the intoxication of a charitable power that supposes itself infinite. We might also ask why it is said: "Love your neighbor," for if it is love that creates the neighbor, that is to say proximity, there is a pleonasm in the commandment. Christ should have said: "Love others" or "Love man." But what He did say is "love your neighbor," and if the neighbor is such only because I love him, then there is again a tautology and the Pharisee's question is posed anew: "Who is my neighbor?" To this question Christ answers: "Which of these three, *in your eyes*, has been the neighbor...?," that is: which *appeared* so to you, which is *shown* to be, or again which has *revealed* the proximity tying him to the wounded man? It is clearly indicated in this way that love does not create proximity, it only causes a *pre-existing* proximity to be revealed; for Christ would have been able to say more simply — and the simplicity of the evangelic style is not an empty phrase — "which has been the neighbor?"

Charity is therefore the realization of an ontological proximity, or, if one prefers, its actualization, that is, the very passage from potency to act. It does not create the neighbor *ex nihilo*, as triumphalist charity implicitly affirms; it achieves that which determines it from all eternity. And this is why there is a commandment, and this is why this

19 Eph 2:13–17.

commandment can only be a commandment of love. For one might ask: "Why did Christ celestially command what is inscribed in the nature of earthly things?" St. Thomas himself poses the question,[20] and likewise St. Bernard.[21] And why is there a commandment to love when one cannot be commanded to love?

But a commandment defines what is *to be done, to be realized*, and it is by the ministry of man that what is the ontological foundation and commandment *in* the nature of things issues from these things themselves in order to be completed and become awareness and spiritual life, and, in the supernaturally human, finality. Now this commandment is one of love, for love is nothing but realization itself, the preeminent actualization, the movement which goes from beginning to end, from center to periphery and from periphery to center, since love is union and there is only union of the Alpha and the Omega, of the Beginning and the End, of the Same and the Other, the *means* of perfection, the *vinculum perfectionis*; for by it we *become* perfect as our heavenly Father *is* perfect. The command to love is thus given to our very existence. What is being in God seems only a possibility to us because of our ontological relativity, and this is why we should realize it. But we can only do so because there is metaphysical identity between the possible and the real. Through love we realize the truth of our existence and save ourselves from the abysses of existential separateness, that is from our own unreality. Of the fundamentally *real* there is only what we *realize*. Now God wants to lead us to Reality. The act of love does not therefore go only from what is in potency to what is in act, but, yet more profoundly, it is the revelation that what was in potency has never ceased being eternally in act. The love of neighbor indeed consists in the realization of a relationship, but of a *relationship pre-existent to its very realization*, of an ontological relationship, or again we might almost say, using a term we will come back to later, of a 'subsistent relation'. Such is, it seems to us, the most obvious significance of the reversal of the question posed by the doctor of the Law: not "who is my neighbor?," but "who has shown himself to be the neighbor?" This makes sense only if the relation

20 "It would seem that no precept should be given about charity." *Summa Theologiae* II-II, q. 44, a. 1.

21 St. Bernard, *Œuvres* (Paris: Ed. du Seuil, 1963), 530.

of proximity can be *shown*, revealed, by a loving act, this being its essential function. This relationship therefore 'pre-exists' the act. The Samaritan is not the creator of proximity, he is its servant.

4. Love of Neighbor presupposes Love of Self

Since the love of neighbor is based upon a pre-existing proximity, it follows that the love of neighbor is the love of proximity. We must therefore ask ourselves about the essence of this proximity. Now, under the reign of fallen matter, the other is not the neighbor. Every ego is negated by the *alter-ego*. The coexistence of egos is certainly a fact, but is none the less contradiction. The corporeal object denies the ego *ad extra*. Outside myself no object of the world is 'me'. But other people deny the ego *ab intra*, for all men are 'me' and yet none are. Anyone else is not a *not*-me, but *another* me. Otherness defines this; not pure dissimilarity, but dissimilarity through similitude: he has a self like my own. If to love the neighbor means to love proximity, that is to love what is neighbor or proximity in everyone, it is necessarily a reversal of the previous relationship, that is to say a similitude by dissimilarity. In the fallen natural order it is our similarity that separates us. In the order of love it is our dissimilarity that must unite us. But for dissimilarity to reunite us, it must become interior instead of exterior; we must become dissimilar to ourselves.

By no means can we abolish on its own plane the existential contradiction of a plurality of egos which are other than us because they are as we are; or again, I differ from other people because I am myself. But we can also understand and realize that "I am not myself," and so, in a certain way, "I am another," since, in the *fallen ego*, I am other than my true self. To interiorize dissimilarity is to exteriorize similitude at the same stroke, is to become one's own neighbor, is to establish within oneself the relation of proximity, and is finally to love oneself as another. We understand then why Christ has said: "You will love your neighbor *as yourself*," and why, to the question of the Pharisee, He replies by returning the question. To say: you will love the neighbor as yourself, is to say: you will love yourself as the neighbor, you will cease identifying yourself with the fallen ego — interiorization of dissimilarity — and, distancing yourself from the possessive self, you will be able to love your true identity.

II

Love of Self and Love of God

THE DEADLY ILLUSION OF A NATURAL LOVE for others appears now in all its clarity. Just as the other is 'other', so it is impossible for me to truly love someone without an inner conversion. The warmth, power, and breadth of natural love can in fact change nothing about the plurality of egos. Indeed, charitable power may hide existential separateness behind a veil of unitive affection, but it is unable to abolish it on its own level: it can only lie about reality. Natural love for others is a falsehood, perhaps not subjectively and intentionally, but objectively and despite all of our efforts.

I. LOVE OF SELF, REMORSE, AND INNER NAKEDNESS

Love of one's neighbor can only be realized, therefore, by an interiorization of proximity. In order to become the other, which the commandment implies in a certain manner — you will love your neighbor as if he were yourself — one needs to become other than oneself; which means that I am not myself. By this we see how all we have said about Christian anthropology conditions true charity: I am not myself because the *me* is not the *I*.

Thus, true love of self implies a conversion from natural love of self or self-respect. Indeed, it might even seem paradoxical to present the interiorization of dissimilarity as identical to the interiorization of proximity, since dissimilarity is estrangement and ultimately seems to amount to self-love while appearing to oppose it. But proximity supposes difference and love, which is a desire and search for union; it supposes duality. For want of acquiescing to this interior distance, the love of appropriation is consumed by suffering, remorse, bitterness, and finally self-hatred. Fallen man, by the coagulation of the ego, is bewitched by himself. Having lost God, all he retains is his own imperfection. To renounce this imperfection, which constitutes his whole reality, is to renounce all that remains to him of himself.

235

However, unable to rest within himself and to find joy in his own ego, he disguises this *shameful* passion for himself as a punishment, and, by that, justifies the passion. Such is the nearly invincible illusion of remorse. Since I know, judge, and accuse myself in my own unbearable imperfection, to my own eyes I am justified in my desire for it. Original sin, the fall of the I into the *psyche*, usurping the function of the guardian angel, appoints us guardians of ourselves. The basis of the ego is remorse for the ontological fault. Remorse is even, in a certain way, a poor imitation of a perfection that has become inaccessible through an amorous returning to one's own imperfection. As guardian of myself, far from protecting and guiding myself like the angelic guardian, I appoint myself as tormentor to punish and justify myself for not being more beautiful than my desire. Man spends his life in this way: his past is remorse, his present vile, his future an illusion. In remorse he takes for his desire's end the imperfection that was at the beginning; in vileness he abandons himself and consents to its ugliness; in illusion he hopes, ineradicably, to surprise in himself the blossoming of an impossible perfection — as if I might, by chance, become what I will never be. There is a moment in love when a man and woman must stand naked before each other. Without doubt nakedness is clothed by desire and also, later, by habit. But this nakedness is part of love's destiny. To love, to commit oneself to the destiny of love, is to accept one day this encounter with nakedness. Now to stand naked is also to be stood naked, to offer oneself such as one is, in objectivity, and therefore to somehow renounce oneself; we never know in advance if our nakedness will be saved and clothed again with the grace of desire. In nakedness there is necessarily a moment of sacrifice and vice versa: nakedness, under one mode or another, is an integral part of sacrifice.[1]

---

1 This is seen in the nakedness of the God-Man on the cross. To set up nakedness as an ideology within a Christian world — as is done in atheist nudism — amounts to a profanation, whether conscious or unconscious, for it cannot but allude to that of Christ's. The nakedness of a couple in love is an exteriorization with a view to interiorization. In atheist nudism, exteriorization opens directly onto exteriority. The means becomes an end and loses its *raison d'être*. To be more exact, the symbolism of Christ's nakedness on the cross means both the total stripping-off of the ego and the restoration of Adamic purity, *the former being the pre-condition of the latter*. As already mentioned, if the body should be clothed and hidden, this is because it has become, through the Fall, an object; it belongs to exteriority and is no longer

It cannot happen otherwise for the love of self. In a certain manner, we need to be exposed to ourselves, to renounce our imperfection, that is to accept it as such. Fallen man no longer has any other 'property' than his decadence. He also refuses to be separated from it and watches over it *jealously*, free to accuse and condemn himself indefinitely so as to justify this jealous vigil. This is remorse and this is illusion.

We will not conceal the fact that our analysis is demanding, but this stems from how we spontaneously think about the ego. All too easily the renunciation of one's own imperfections seems to imply a prideful desire for an inaccessible perfection, or to be the effect of too scrupulous a conscience. In reality, by virtue of the ego's illusory subjectivity, to renounce one's imperfection and to see oneself objectively, such as one is, are the two faces of one and the same conversion. Humility is objectivity first. It should not be humiliation, even and above all when it is ourselves whom we humiliate. So we need to stand naked in ourselves, to strip ourselves of egoic garments, to accept no longer watching over ourselves, to lose sight of ourselves. Surely, we cannot leave and turn our back on ourselves so as to finally face the sun without shivering and dying, because then we would no longer be there to cover ourselves.

---

clothed with the soul. Indeed, the Fall is nothing but a process of objectification for the sake of possession. Or we can also say that the fallen body is an overturned soul. What is hidden and secret by essence is disclosed and prostituted. Having become an object, the body in its nakedness *incarnates* transgression, transgression congealed. It becomes an object of shame because it is shame become an object; it testifies against the ego, by its objectivity it 'accuses' the illusion of egoic subjectivity, it 'betrays' the soul because the soul betrayed it. Ever since then, having become obscene in the etymological sense of the term, the body craves a new garment to replace the psychic one. And by this we can understand how, in a normal civilization, clothing symbolizes the animic quality of a whole humanity: clothing of animal skin betokens an animal soul, clothing derived from plants a vegetative soul, while nylon and synthetic materials denote a mineral soul. In any case clothing falls under the jurisdiction of divine mercy since, by veiling the body, it attenuates the effects of the Fall. To reject the wearing of clothes means either that one has sacrificially renounced the ego through death and the Cross, or that one has laid claim to a purity that he is incapable of sustaining and, leaving behind the mantle of mercy, has pridefully exposed himself to naked rigor. Such an attitude cannot be without danger, and its consequences have unsuspected repercussions upon our ordinary psychism. However, and so as to include all possibilities, we will add that an ascetic naturism, accompanied by a profound spiritual intention, is in certain instances Christianly acceptable.

2. THE REALIZATION OF INNER NAKEDNESS
IN ITS CHRISTIC PROTOTYPE

The symbolism of the respective positions of the Virgin and Christ, both in Christ's holy Infancy and in the Crucifixion, in this regard seems of utmost importance. In many respects the Virgin represents the human psyche and Christ the intellect, and therefore the true I. The Virgin, the denuded and liberated soul, humility-made-creature, is always situated in Christian art behind the child Jesus who never looks at her. Only at the Crucifixion does Christ turn towards his Mother in the nakedness of his sacrifice. This means that the egoic illusion is the nakedness and the crucifixion of God within us; within us at every moment a God dies naked upon the cross of our ego. And yet it is at every moment and within ourselves that we must welcome him, clothe him, feed him, and quench his thirst, just as he has commanded in the words of the Last Judgment. Gazing upon the Cross, the human soul contemplates both the ultimate consequence of its sin, which is nothing less than the death of God, and the chief image of its destiny, which is nothing less than its own death. This is why the sacrifice of Christ prefigures and renders inevitable our own sacrifice, so that, according to a certain perspective, the story of Jesus retraces the human story in reverse order. What is at the beginning of Christ's life, the birth of the Word in the pure Marian substance, is at the end of our spiritual destiny in the grace of filial adoption (*theosis* or 'deification').[2] What is

2 *Theosis* or deification — a topic dealt with in the last part of this book — is the term used by the Greek Fathers to designate the reception and actualization of the grace of filial adoption, in conformity with the words of St. John's Prologue: "To all who . . . believed in his name, he gave power to become children of God" (John 1:12). This grace, connected to the Holy Spirit, is bestowed in Baptism, a sacrament that "communicates the divine gnosis" (Basil of Caesarea, *Treatise on the Holy Spirit*, 32). In this respect, read ch. 4 of the introduction to *Traité du Saint-Esprit* by Fr. B. Pruche (Paris: Ed. du Cerf, 1947), 64–76. According to all of the Greek Fathers, the distinctive mark of the Christian doctrine of deifying gnosis is that it has been actually *confided* to all the baptized. But its actualization pertains only to those worthy of the Holy Spirit, those "capable of the intelligible light," writes Basil of Caesarea. This presence in Christianity of a deifying gnosis entrusted to all of the baptized, which defines the style peculiar to the Christian perspective and which is its 'scandal' or 'folly', spoils the thesis of those who assert the existence of an esoteric Christianity, institutionally distinguished from an exoteric Christianity and having its own rites and means of grace. An attentive reading of the German and Latin works of a gnostic as exceptional

at the end of His humanity, in His death on the Cross, is our birth to the truth of our nothingness. The birth of the Word is death for the ego; Christ's death upon the Cross is our birth to the Spirit.

From the viewpoint of temporal flow, this reversal shows that the end of our spiritual destiny is really an origin and, therefore, that spirituality is a return to the beginning, a veritable ascent of time back to its atemporal source.[3]

3. ACCESS TO INNER PROXIMITY

In just such a way a relation of proximity can be established in the human soul, a way by which man becomes a neighbor to himself,

---

as Meister Eckhart offers no example of this kind. But, even more, St. Dionysius the Areopagite — whose work is one of the loftiest doctrinal expressions of Christian gnosis — explicitly affirms the contrary by speaking simultaneously of the 'celestial' and 'legal' (of the esoteric and exoteric) character of Christian initiation or, in other words, of the Church and Sacraments (cf. *The Ecclesiastical Hierarchy*, V, I, 501C). Also Gandillac (Introduction to *OEuvres du Pseudo-Denys* [Paris: Aubier Montaigne, 1943], 33) writes: "By substituting sonship for servitude, the sacral order of the New Testament forms a step midway between text and allegory (i.e., sensory understanding and gnosis). And out of this arises its at once exoteric and esoteric character." Finally, I have spoken of an esoteric Christianity so to exclude even its possibility, but not of a Christian esoterism; for an esoteric understanding of Christianity does exist, an understanding of its most inward and mysterious dimensions. Moreover, the historical existence of a *de facto* quasi-esoterism in the Middle Ages is undeniable. But these are particular developments inherent in the general possibility of Christianity, and in no way admit of sacraments or rites being superimposed over the ordinary sacraments and rites, as superior over inferior. If we accept the expression 'Christian esoterism' but not 'esoteric Christianity', this is for the same reason that we can speak of a Christian metaphysics or theology; whereas a theological or metaphysical Christianity would not make much sense, for Christianity is precisely and altogether both esoteric and exoteric. However indispensable, we recognize that these distinctions are all too concise. They are clarified and explained in their own right, both historically and theologically, in our *Christ the Original Mystery* (Brooklyn, NY: Angelico Press, 2018).

3   This reversal is depicted in the Rosary. In certain respects there is a reversal between the order of the mysteries of the Rosary and the order of the mysteries of the *Ave Maria*. The *Ave Maria* goes from Mary to Jesus, the Rosary from Jesus to Mary. Thus the recitation of the Rosary is similar to a river whose water, always the same (the *Ave Maria*), would rise back to its source. And surely this is one reason why the Rosary is considered an especially sanctifying form of prayer, a prayer in which is realized the movement of all spirituality. In this respect the *Ave Maria*, the first part of which — the only revealed part — we are considering here, is basically identified with the human soul, while the stations of the mysteries are the essential stages of our spiritual destiny.

the only way in which a man can truly love himself. The basis of this relation is figured by the founding words of Christ to the Virgin Mary: "Woman, behold thy son," and to St. John: "Behold thy Mother." Inasmuch as Christ mercifully and objectively incarnates the denuded and crucified ego, so too Mary is the human soul liberated from possessive decadence and St. John the human intellect brought to birth at last. They stand on either side of the Cross: this is what separates and unites them. It is the crucifixion of the ego that breaks through the confusion between the psychic and the spiritual, and separates them from each other. But separation creates distance and, ultimately, makes love possible. For this love to be no longer self-love, a love of appropriation or possession, but a renunciation of oneself for another's sake; or, even more profoundly, for one not so much to give oneself to the other as not to give the other to oneself, the Word of Christ is needed. In giving the Mother to the son and the son to the Mother, he at once gives the Mother to herself and the son to himself.

Only by the Cross can the confusion between psychic and spiritual be abolished; only then can they be distinguished from each other; for this confusion is inherent to the illusion and corruption of the charitable power, and in this distinction abides the realization of true charity. But here we also understand why this distinction defines the truth of charity. For if it is true, as we have shown, that love of neighbor, which is the love of proximity, implies love of self, then clearly this love of self, rendered impossible by egoic appropriation, also implies proximity and therefore distinction. However the crucifixion of the ego, the precondition of charity, cannot be effected by oneself, cannot be effected by a desire of the will. Although the ego finds its true I in realizing its desire for death, yet it is not for this that it is searching. This will not give oneself to oneself, since what one especially needs to do is lose oneself. Only by giving ourselves do we lose ourselves.

Let us reconsider Christ on the cross: "Father, into thy hands I commend my spirit." Or more precisely: "Father, into thy hands I commend my *pneuma*" (Luke 23:46). The Son of Man renounces all of himself: body, soul, and spirit, for one needs to love God with all of one's body, soul, and spirit. And so, through an oblative renunciation to spirit, spirit is recovered; through ex-spiration, in-spiration is made possible. Through love of God, love of self and neighbor is made possible. Through the first commandment we can have access to the second, access to the spiritual degree of proximity. "And from that hour, the disciple took her to his own," *Et ex hora illa accepit eam discipulus in sua* (John 19:27). As Mary is taken *"in sua"* by the holy disciple, so the human soul is received into the dwelling-place of the intellect. Through this love of self the body is received within the soul and the soul is received within the spirit. The alchemical distinction of a human being's 'elements' introduces them to the degree of proximity. The body becomes neighbor to the soul and the soul neighbor to the spirit. Being no longer either *my* body, *my* soul, or *my* spirit, they become the terms of the relation of proximity in the circumincession of charity. Christ's saving Passion abolishes the "useless passion"[4] of man by fulfilling it. *Solve et coagula*. To dissolve the ego is to realize the unity of man and his perfection, and to make possible the circulation of charity, charity the 'bond of perfection', that which links everything to everything else according to the perfection of its order.

4. THE ALCHEMICAL CRUCIFIXION

This is what the Cross itself, which both separates and unites, also represents. From this perspective it can be said that the horizontal branch, where the ego dies, represents the separation of the *pneuma* from the *psyche*. But the vertical axis reestablishes and realizes their union. *Si exaltatus omnia ad Me traham*. "If I am lifted up [exalted], I shall draw all things to myself" (John 12:32). This means that exaltation realizes and gives its own direction to the horizontal plane, or width. Or again, transcendence is the key to immanence. The identity of transcendence and immanence resides in the Divine Self (*ad Me*), the supreme point from whence the cross of transcendence-immanence bursts forth like a sun of glory. But this radiance is also an attraction (*traham*: "I shall draw"). What issues from God leads back to Him: the Cross is both centrifugal and centripetal. It is simultaneously the irradiation of Divine Love and the absorption of all exteriority through the interiorizing vibrations of this same Love. This is why

---

4 Jean-Paul Sartre, *Being and Nothingness*, trans. H. E. Barnes (New York: Philosophical Library, 1956), 784.

love is the bond of perfection, since through it the perfection of the entire Divine Work is accomplished.

This dual function of the Cross is apparent in a reversal of symbolic directions: When Mary and St. John are represented standing on either side of the Cross, they symbolize, respectively, the soul and the intellect on the same horizontal plane extending from the axis. When a second representation is adopted, *pneuma* and *psyche* are formed into a hierarchy with respect to a horizontal distinction and are therefore seen vertically. Each point of view expresses in its own way the mystery of immanence and transcendence, the center alone being immobile and immutable. The horizontal representation of Mary and St. John is at once inferior and superior to the second. In fallen man, the ego's confusion situates the spiritual and animic upon the same plane. Only a single plane exists then: the vertical tree of good and evil bisects reality, deceptively opposing realities which in truth, being hierarchically subordinated, cannot be opposed.

At the same time, in the human microcosm, the ego's confusion destroys the separation of the "upper and lower waters" through which God enacts the alchemy of macrocosmic creation. This separation must then be reestablished, and this is the work of the Cross's horizontal branch, which manifests the macrocosmic division between heaven and earth and the microcosmic distinction between *pneuma* and *psyche*. Here are the extended arms of God, crucified from East to West, his transpierced hands tearing apart universal existence. Here is our Divine Horizon — shoulders true, arms strong, hands blessing — bearing the weight of the intelligible Ocean until the end of time, until the Last Day when the upper waters will pour down in cataracts to engulf the world beneath the eternal Mercy.

With the horizontal branch reabsorbed at the atemporal instant of Judgment, the axis of transcendence will divide the elect and the reprobate to the right and left of the Father until the *apocatastasis*,[5]

---

5   The Greek word *apocatastasis* means 'restoration', 'reestablishment'. In the language of the Church Fathers it designates the doctrine according to which all beings, the damned and the demons included, will be reestablished 'one day' in the Divine Love; Satan will be restored to his initial state of the heavenly Lucifer. This doctrine has been attributed to Origen and to St. Gregory of Nyssa, and has been rejected by the Church which, in conformity with Christ's word, teaches the eternity of the pains of hell.

when the Divine Axis will be reabsorbed in its turn into the Supreme
Point from which, in truth, it never left.

The macrocosmic process just described is repeated on the microcosmic level, within the human being, by what Orthodox tradition
calls "the descent of the mind into the heart." This descent is figured
in the Gospel when it is said: "Now there was leaning on Jesus' bosom
one of his disciples, whom Jesus loved" (John 13:23),[6] and again at

---

But what does *eternity* signify? The word can have two meanings: either non-time,
non-duration, Pure Being in contrast to becoming (*aeternitas* in the proper sense);
or indefinite duration, perpetuity (what St. Thomas Aquinas calls *aeviternitas*). Now
hell cannot be eternal in the first sense, since this would involve an attribute of Pure
Being, of God: if hell were eternal (in the first sense), it would no longer be hell.
Therefore it can only be eternal in the second sense, that of an indefinite duration.

How can we understand such a possibility? Guénon provides an answer when he
explains that the indefinite is analytically inexhaustible. Hell is perpetual for those
(angels or men) who have fixed their wills on analytically exhausting the created. In
other words, hell is perpetual for those who, while rejecting that Eternal Love which
incites us toward the Infinite, want to remain within the finiteness of the created and
pretend that they can reach their goal by division and fragmentation. This however
leaves us with the paradox of an eternity of Being and a perpetuity of duration. Will
this perpetuity come to an end some day? Or else will Divine Love be eternally held
in check by the refusal of Satan? It is not easy to answer these questions. We would
have to escape the created conditioning of our intellect in order to reply; we would
have to recognize that, in reality, there is no coexistence. It is from the creature's
point of view that the Uncreated is outside of the world; from God's point of view
the created is within the Uncreated: God sees the world within Himself. For those
in hell, hell is perpetual. For those in God, hell is eternally abolished, and here we
have the truth of the Apocatastasis. The paradox of the unintelligible coexistence of
the eternity of Being and the perpetuity of hell (the lack of Being) expresses the need
we have for a change of state to understand certain things: the plain is only visible
from the peak of the mountain; the relative is intelligible only from the viewpoint
of the Absolute: "Seek ye first the kingdom of God and his justice, and all these
things shall be added unto you" (Luke 12:31). Let us truly realize that it is not we
who understand God, but God who understands us and envelops us on all sides with
His infinite Love. What burns in hell is the fire of Divine Love.

6   The descent of the mind into the heart requires a renunciation of the mentality, whch corresponds to the crowning with thorns. We find this descent indicated
in the *Veni Creator Spiritus:*

Mentes *tuorum visita*	Visit the minds that are yours;
Imple superna gratia	fill with heavenly grace
Quae tu creasti pectora.	the hearts that you created.

The Holy Spirit first pervades the mind, then fills the breast and heart. This
descent can be related to Christ's descent from the Cross. Inasmuch as Christ is
man, inasmuch as man is defined specifically by the mind, and inasmuch as Christ is
crucified in his humanity, the Body of Christ corresponds to human mentality. The
Body is buried in a tomb hollowed in a rock — in a cave. The cave corresponds then

Christ's death: *Et inclinato capito, tradidit spiritum*, "And bowing his head, he delivered up the spirit [to his Father]" (John 19:30). The symbolism of these moments teaches a very precise spiritual science, and we venture to say that what the ear of St. John perceived upon the bosom of God was the very vibrations of the primordial Sound by which "all things were made."

But we can understand the words of St. Paul in the same way: "I bow my knees to the Father . . . so that Christ may dwell by faith in your *hearts*; that being rooted and founded in charity, you may be able to comprehend with all the saints, what is the Breadth, and Length, and Height, and Depth: to know also the charity of Christ which surpasseth all knowledge, that you may be filled with all the fullness of God" (Eph 3:17–19). This text, the meaning of which is rightly infinite, shows the connection between charity, the Cross, and gnosis. To know the charity of Christ is to comprehend the mystery of the Cross. The text sets out two charities: "rooted and founded in charity . . . you may be able to know also the charity of Christ." Between the two charities — charity in man (or, even more profoundly, man in charity) and the charity of Christ — the Cross is interpolated, because it forms the bond of perfection, establishing the ontological relation between heaven and earth. The Cross connects us to love *in divinis*, introducing us to the spiritual degree of proximity. To be rooted and founded in charity is to *trace the Cross*, which distinguishes and unites, discerns and concentrates, which is both proximity and ontological relationship. We

---

to the 'cave of the heart', to the *absconditus*, the 'secret': *et clauso ostio ora Patrem tuum in abscondito, et Pater tuus, qui videt in abscondito, reddit tibi*, "and shut the door, and pray to your Father who is in secret; and your Father who sees in secret will reward you" (Matt 6:6). The *absconditus* is the center of the heart, and the eye of God, "who sees in secret," is to be found there. This is the eye of the heart spoken of by St. Paul (Eph 1:18). The heart, illumined by the Spirit, joins love to knowledge: the intellect descends into the heart (Rom 1:21, 10:10). This eye of the heart is also the eye of deified man, his veritable transcendent person, his immortal Self, the source of his most intimate being, his true identity. This prayer *in abscondito* is the prayer of the heart that realizes divine gnosis through invocation of the saving Name: "For man believes with his heart and so is justified; and he confesses with his lips and so is saved . . . for the same Lord is Lord over all and bestows his riches upon all who call upon (*invocant*) him. For, 'every one who calls upon [*invocaverit*] the name of the Lord will be saved'" (Rom 10:10, 12–13). When Christ Jesus "dwells [in this way] in the heart" (Eph 3:17), "the Spirit of the Son cries 'Abba, Father'" (Gal 4:6) and grants us gnosis of the divine *Pleroma* (Eph 3:19).

will begin with St. Paul's first three terms: breadth, length, and height.[7] Then we will look at the fourth, depth, which poses a problem.

Breadth, length, and height trace a three-dimensional cross. The first two are confined to a horizontal plane, breadth being defined as a straight line 'in front', parallel to the eyes of an observer, and length as a line 'straight ahead', perpendicular to the observer. Height, then, is defined as a vertical line perpendicular to this horizontal plane. Breadth and length trace a horizontal cross, the cross of our earthly life. Thus, we normally relate breadth to space and length to time, for breadth, like the space that surrounds us, swells and overflows to the right and left, while length implies that we 'travel through' this space, that we enter into it and leave there an enduring trace. A road is long only because it continues. To comprehend breadth an instantaneous glance is enough. But we need time to comprehend length; space has to be *'lived'* in, advanced into, which is what length invites us to do. It is 'before' us like the span of our lives, plunging on towards a point of inaccessible flight: our death and immortality "on the confines of the indefinite." With breadth symbolizing the order of existences, since beings coexist in space, we can understand (as St. Paul invites us to do) that, through breadth, we have access to a *spiritual degree of proximity with the 'spatial' multiplicity of egos.* To understand the breadth of charity is to realize the true nature of loving one's neighbor, which provides the structural model for all charity, and this is why it is possible to give a *spatial* figuration for every mode of charity, whereas this figuration is only appropriate for the love of one's neighbor. St. Paul himself says that access to the spiritual degree of proximity is the prototype of all modes of charity when he writes: "in Jesus Christ

7 This text has given rise to copious exegesis. The interpretations of the Fathers are often extremely suggestive; modern discussions are sometimes very deceiving. St. Paul does not say to what these dimensions are related, but in this context it seems to involve the dimensions of Christic charity set forth according to a cruciform symbolism. With such a symbolism space corresponds to reality in general, to being. The cross that delineates this space symbolizes the knowledge of being, since it determines its potentialities and reveals them. Here this reality is the charity of Christ, for it has to do with knowledge. Basically this mode of expression is simple enough, once one has the key to traditional symbolism given by Guénon in his various works. Concerning the passage upon which we are commenting, consult Dom Jacques Dupont, *Gnosis*, 479–89. Dupont gives numerous references but, in our opinion, does not accord the four dimensions the attention they deserve.

we have the boldness to approach God" (Eph 3:12). Thus the love of God itself can be figured by the love of one's neighbor: Christ says that the latter is "similar," image of the former.

Length, as we have remarked, is more directly involved with time, and therefore with life and the soul. *To understand length is to have access to proximity with ourselves*: it is the spiritual axis of our lives that unifies the moments of our temporal existence. Length refers, in fact, to the order of successions, since succession characterizes time. But length is not a pure succession in Bergsonian fashion, which is to say a succession of moments completely heterogeneous to each other. Inasmuch as length is the *tracing* of a course, it unifies these different moments; it establishes them in a spiritual and mutual proximity; it establishes a certain contemporaneity within them. This contemporaneity of life's moments rests on a more profound contemporaneity: that of man with himself. With spiritual length man is no longer at a temporal distance from himself. Consciousness is no longer 'temporalizing', no longer aware of something (the self) that temporally precedes the awareness one has of it and therefore introduces, through an effect of original sin, a temporal distancing into the heart of man. But, by this length, man has access to the true love of self—he finds himself borne along and transpierced by a dimension that goes from eternity to eternity.

Now we come to height. And we can actually see that one passes from breadth to height through length, which is as it were a 'horizontal' translation of the vertical. Height, on the one hand, is projected onto the horizontal plane in a point. But, on the other hand and for the being who has not yet attained to this central point where one can ascend toward the heights, height is *reflected* upon the surface of the horizontal plane according to a length that joins the observer to the central point. Length is like a luminous ray which, being reflected in the water, traces a golden path uniting our gaze to the meeting-point of the celestial ray with the earthly plane. Only inasmuch as it is a reflection of height (proximity to God) does length possess the power to unify successiveness and to present an image of eternity in time.

But here is the complementary relationship: we have seen height lower itself and come to us on the surface of the existential waters in the form of a fiery flash; now it is length that raises up and becomes height. We pass from breadth to height through length: we pass from earth to heaven through a lifetime *oriented* towards God Incarnate. This transit can be described as a reabsorption of length back to the crucial point from whence it emanated, or even as a rotation of the horizontal cross around the immobile axis of breadth. Length there-fore rightly becomes height: thus Jesus Christ is first nailed to the hor-izontal cross of earthly existence, which is then raised vertically. Only then do we have access to proximity with God, in that lightning-flash of love in which Man and God are wedded to death and to life.

As for depth, it can refer either to the lower branch of the cross or to its crossing-point and center. According to the first point of view, which is static, depth symbolizes, in conformity with the descending direction of the lower branch, the Word's descent, the Incarnation of Jesus Christ and hence the revelation of God's love for men. It is a saving catabasis. As a result, depth also symbolizes doctrine and truth, since the truth is revealed by Jesus Christ, the Word-made-flesh. This truth *fixes and determines* charity, which, being volatile or pneumatic in essence, "knows not from whence it comes or where it is going." Furthermore, the lower branch supports the cross as an immobile pivot that roots it in the earth: a truth-stem on which flowers the 'cross of charity'. According to an allied and concordant interpreta-tion, we can likewise consider the vertical formed by the reunion of height and depth synthetically. Such a vertical would depict, then, the doctrine-truth axis 'determining' the horizontal plane of charity, with the lower branch symbolizing doctrine properly so-called and the upper branch representing, not exclusively our love for God as above, but the realization of Divine Truth, the fulfilling of charity in supreme gnosis. According to the second point of view, now, depth connected to the crossing-point designates the inwardness of the charitable mystery, for all other dimensions are reabsorbed there; in this case it is height, and it alone, which indicates the whole vertical direction: St. Paul in fact enumerates only four terms, and so, if the last one, depth, designates a 'nonspatial' or intensive direction, the other three necessarily designate the three extensive directions of space, an immediate symbol of 'reality' or being; basically, a symbol of God himself. Consequently, when the vertical is figured by height alone, we are dealing with a dynamic and hence spiritual perspective, with an elevation or deifying anabasis. Height clearly symbolizes, then, our love for God — as just stated, the preeminent way to deification. But the depth-point reveals that this love-elevation, instead of simply being exalted into the wholly other, should also and finally be brought back and converted into its own essence that is God-Love, come back once more to the unique Center, should 'enter' mystically into Divine Charity, like the lance of the centurion Longinus that 'opens' the interior dimension of Christ. The mystery of elevation is accomplished 'in depth' by the mystery of the transpierced Heart, the mystery of the Sacred Heart.

The mystery of the Cross now yields to the mystery of the sphere. Entry into this transpierced Heart is an immersion within Divine Love itself, the infinite sphere in which all crucial determinations are reabsorbed and abolished. And this is just what St. Paul's text indicates: "may you be able . . . to know the charity of Christ, which surpasseth all knowledge, that you may be filled unto all the fullness [*pleroma* in the Greek text] of God" (Eph 3:17–19). The fullness of God, the divine *Pleroma*, is the infinite sphere of Divine Reality. The *pleroma* is not God as envisaged in his pure Ipseity, but is rather the infinite 'place' needed for His unlimited deployment,[8] the uncreated matrix within which God conceives his Word, and that is thus a matrix filled with God, a matrix mysteriously identified with all created matrices, once they have been 'plenified' by the knowledge of love's cross.

A cube, a cross, and a sphere: the alchemy of love and knowledge. A cube, the earth, the intelligible structure of which is represented by the Cross. And, thanks to the sacrificial mediation of the Cross, the earthly cube — having been reabsorbed within the crossing-point — is integrated within the *Pleroma*, the universal sphere of the Absolute. *In divinis* the Cross determines this infinite sphere principially, for the Cross *determines* the knowledge of the Absolute, the knowledge that the Absolute has of itself and that "surpasseth all knowledge." Thus the Cross, integrated within the sphere, expresses the mystery of supreme gnosis. Here, in this mystery of supreme gnosis, love gains access to the perfection of its most profound essence that is pure knowledge: the cross within the sphere, the mystery of the Eternal Star.

---

8 On this subject cf. Dupont, *Gnosis*, 419–93. The author concludes an in-depth philological inquiry through Jewish and Hellenistic (above all, Stoic) literature by saying: "The term *pleroma* always has a passive meaning; it designates 'that which is filled,' not 'that which fills'" (473).

5. REMARKS ON LOVE AND GNOSIS

In the course of this study we have not referred to the theses of Anders
Nygren's famous book *Eros and Agape*.[9] That he refuses to establish
a basis for love is well-known, for he sees such an exercise as contrary
to the unmotivated nature of charity. But such a position is based
upon a particularly narrow and rationalistic approach to the idea of
establishing a basis. And this is why he denounces the alleged impre-
cision of the Johannine concept of love:[10] "The Johannine idea of
Agape thus actually occupies a somewhat uncertain position between
unmotivated and motivated love" — an assertion that passes for commentary. Its author, lacking all sense of proportion, is unaware of
the *a priori* difference between a twentieth-century exegete and the
Son of Thunder. Likewise he asserts that love of neighbor excludes
all self-love, because he rejects all egoism, even spiritual.[11] But Nygren
does not see that a truly 'natural' self-love does not exist, and that, as
we have shown to the contrary, egoism implies all forms of self-hatred
and is only an apparent love. As for spiritual egoism, it is a contradiction in terms, since where there is spirit, there is no longer any ego.

However, what remains is that I must save my soul, and, according
to Christ if not Anders Nygren, that to gain the whole world does
not compensate for its loss. Lastly, by virtue of his stance on the
Greek *Eros*, which he identifies with gnosis, he constantly opposes
gnosis to agape, attempting to demonstrate that this is the entire thesis of the New Testament. But how explain, then, that St. Paul's most
essential texts on charity[12] are concluded with affirmations of divine
gnosis? Unquestionably there is a gnosis that puffs up with pride,
but through charity we will obtain gnosis of the Divine Pleroma, and
through charity I will know as I am known, that is to say the gnosis
I have of God will be the same gnosis God has of me. The perfection
of Love is eternal Knowledge. And when Nygren supports himself

9   Trans. Philip S. Watson (Philadelphia: Westminster, 1953).
10   Ibid., 152. This love cannot be considered unmotivated, since "we sometimes
find . . . a clause explanatory of the love, introduced by 'because'. . . . 'The Father
Himself loveth you, because ye have loved Me.'"
11   Ibid., 131–32.
12   Eph 3:17–19, 1 Cor 13:12.

with the statement: "The one who does not love does not know God" (1 John 4:8), thus wishing to prove that in this at least St. John does not differ from St. Paul,[13] how can he not see that, by the very same token, the one who loves God can have access to perfect gnosis?[14]

Finally, when the author asks "whether Paul can with certainty be said to use the noun *agape* in the sense of love to God at all,"[15] we simply see intellectual blindness or exegetical scruple: "to them that love God, all things work together unto good" (Rom 8:28), says St. Paul using the verb *agapein*.[16]

As we see, an obsessional fear of Platonism leads to a rather odd blindness. For in reality love clearly leads us much farther than we would like to go. "Rooted and founded in charity," we are to know the "charity of Christ" and enter within the Divine Pleroma. We are constrained to go from created charity to Uncreated Charity, and not only from the love of neighbor to the love of self, not only from the love of self to the love of God, but even to love *in* God, and even to God Himself since God is love. Are we saying that such is the divine gnosis to which love leads us, namely that God is love? Surely. But there is more to say. If charity is the doorway to gnosis, this is because Love in God Himself is the Doorway to Gnosis, or again: this is because God reveals Himself and knows Himself only through His Love. He knows Himself in the Son (Supreme Gnosis) through the Holy Spirit (Supreme *Agape*). And so we must now approach the very essence of love, at the level of its Trinitarian flowering. Only by this can we discover a metaphysics of Charity, a metaphysics distantly reflected in all our previous considerations.

13 Nygren, *Eros and Agape*, 149.
14 St. John in fact writes: "Everyone that loveth, is born of God, and knoweth God. He that loveth not, knoweth not God: for God is charity" (1 John 4:7–8). The Greek text uses the present *ginoskei* (from the same root as *gnosis*) which designates a permanent and definitively acquired knowledge. But to translate "knoweth not" he uses the aorist *egno*, which designates the process of acquiring knowledge. This means that not to love is not to be ready to acquire gnosis. "The one who loves God . . . also shows that he has from God knowledge of the perfected, the authentic gnosis. . . . Those who do not practice charity and actually misunderstand this notion of divine love possess, however much they might claim, nothing of true gnosis." A. Charue, in *La Sainte Bible*, vol. 12 (Paris: Letouzey et Ané, 1951), 545.
15 Nygren, *Eros and Agape*, 124.
16 Also read 1 Cor 2:9, 1 Cor 8:3, and Eph 6:24, where love for God is expressed each time by the word *agapein*.

PART IV

The Metaphysical Structure of Charity in Its Divine Order

INTRODUCTION:
THE TRINITY IS THE TRUE BASIS FOR CHARITY

If everything said up to this point is only a reflection of charity *in divinis*, it follows that the themes we have identified — proximity, relation, person, the revelatory activity of love — should find their completion here.

However, we should point out that charity *in divinis* can be viewed from two perspectives: in its internal dimension — and this is why it can be said that through the door of love we glimpse something of the mystery of divine interiority — and in its external dimension, as creating love. To the structure of cosmic charity we will devote a special part. For we must, if we are to comprehend this love, grasp it first in its supreme root, buried deep in the heart of the Trinitarian mystery.

It is to this mystery, then, that we now turn our attention. This will not involve a complete theological elaboration. As already indicated, we will consider it basically under its aspect of 'subsistent relation'. And here is why.

We have shown that the love of neighbor makes sense only when understood as access to the spiritual degree of proximity; that is, the love of an individual is fulfilled in the love of a relation. At the risk of falling back into the confusion of triumphalist charity, it must be admitted at the same time that this involves the realization of a preexisting relation. Moreover, if to love the neighbor/individual is to love a relation, it follows that this demands identifying the individual with a relation. This is what is required, in the terms of our analysis, so to accomplish the act of charity. Now this requirement does not seem humanly realizable. On the one hand it will be admitted with difficulty that an individual can become a relation. But then how will the other person be transformed into a 'neighbor'? On the other hand it will be admitted with just as much difficulty that a relation, a 'proximity', is identifiable with a person. But then how will we imagine that the neighbor is a person? We touch here on the imperfection of the love of neighbor, that is, on its contradiction. We have rediscovered this contradiction in the love of self and finally in the very love of God where, if it might be so expressed, it is brought to its highest pitch, which is the Cross, the sign of contradiction. We have here described the spiritual transformations to which the Supreme Commandment incites us. In this way we have posited the conditions on which the truth of charity depends in the *human subject*. But to become aware of the demands and effects of charity in man is one thing, to logically establish the charitable structure which nothing specifically human seems able to account for is another. Even supposing that all of these conditions were realized, charity would remain a beautiful dream and finally an illusion if, in the last analysis, its structure was revealed to be 'impossible'. This is why love requires a logical basis for its possibility,[1] without, for all that, this basis ever constituting a determination implying, according to Nygren's interpretation, the negation of *agape* in its essential gratuity. (This we will see when treating of the Holy Spirit, in whom all necessity is grace.) It is in the doctrine of 'subsistent relations' worked out by Scholastic theology that we think we have found this basis, because it is the synthesis of person (subsistence) and relation.

Chapter 12 will lead us directly to the summit of Trinitarian theology while providing the intellectual elements needed for a speculative knowledge of the mystery. In chapter 13 we will make an initial approach towards the Person of the Holy Spirit, according to the traditional perspective. Next, after having proposed, in chapter 14, a new speculative understanding of the Trinitarian mystery, we will make a second approach towards the Person of the Holy Spirit, Who is the key to eternal Love (Chapter 15). Then, having arrived at this summit, we will present, in a fifth and last chapter (Chapter 16), a synthesis of the whole metaphysics of the *Mysterium caritatis*.

---

1 This basis, as we will see, should also be the ontological basis of charity in its *reality*.

I 2

The Theological Doctrine
of the Trinity

THIS DOCTRINE DOES NOT AIM FOR AN INTER-
pretation of the mystery of the Holy Trinity. It simply endeavors to
supply the least inadequate conceptual formulation of this mystery, or
again, to express what we are capable of conceiving about the Mystery
of the Holy Trinity. This corresponds then to the highest and ultimate possibility of conception, beyond which there is only apophatic
intellection, the knowledge which surpasses all understanding. The
theologically certain doctrine of subsistent relations is entrusted with
expressing the real distinction of Persons and their common identity
with the Divine Essence.

I. THE NOTION OF HYPOSTASIS[1]

1. Among the Greeks

The expression 'subsistent relation'[2] is composed of two terms: relation and subsistence (from the Latin *subsistentia*). We should explain
both, then, to better see the importance of what might be called 'the
speculative crown of the Christian West'. We will begin with the
term subsistence.

In Scholastic terminology, a subsistence (*subsistentia*) is a person
or a hypostasis: three nearly synonymous terms. They all designate
the really existing subject, yet with some differences. Hypostasis designates the subject with respect to the accidents which it receives within
itself; subsistence designates a subject's manner of being, namely that
the subject subsists, that is, exists *in and by itself*, "exercises on its
own behalf the act of existing"; the person brings together all these
designations while adding one spiritual in nature. Except for these

---

1 Cf. *La personne et le christianisme ancien*, ed. B. Meunier (Paris: Cerf, 2006).
2 'Subsistence' designates the fact of subsisting in *oneself*, and not a simple
continuance in being, or something that might assure this continuance.

nuances these three terms can, however, be considered equivalent. But this was not always so. This terminology is the result of a long history, and only after centuries of disputes and misunderstandings did the two, Greek and Latin, traditions achieve a relative unification of vocabulary first developed separately. A relative unification, we say, for, as remote as a word might be from its original meaning, the latter is never totally lost. This is the case with *hypostasis*, a word of Greek origin, which, although recognized as the equivalent of *person* in Latin, seems to have retained a slightly different meaning. So we must, then, briefly retrace this evolution while studying each of these traditions separately. We begin with the Greek tradition.

At the time of Christianity's appearance, Greek philosophy already had in place for a long time a precise vocabulary, which could not be utilized as such however in the doctrinal elaboration of dogma without subjecting sacred theology to profane philosophy. When it was a question of designating the divine nature or essence (or substance), let us say Divine Reality, the Greeks used the dedicated term *ousia*. But a problem was posed: by what term should one designate the 'Three'? Recourse was had to *prosopon*, which means countenance, face, aspect. About 205, Hippolytus of Rome spoke of the *prosopa* of the Father and the Son.[3] Now, the term had the disadvantage of not sufficiently marking out the reality of the distinct Persons against Sabellius, for whom the 'Three' were just aspects, modes. This is why *hupostasis* gradually came to the fore, the first reference to which can be read in Origen in 225.[4] At the Synod of Alexandria, in 362, the Church ratified this choice. Its chairman, St. Athanasius, confessed "three hypostases of a single ousia," three Persons of a single essence. But from where does this term come?

There is an occurrence of *hypostasis* in Aristotle, but not in the philosophical sense, which only appeared about the third century with Plotinus, for whom it has the meaning of 'true reality', as distinct from what is only an appearance. But its use in this sense is more ancient outside of philosophy. The first reference to it is in the Epistle to the Hebrews, where the Son is called "the imprint of the hypostasis of

3 *Contra Noetum* 7, 14; PG 10:813–24. Attribution to Hippolytus is widely disputed.

4 *Commentary on St. John* II, 75; *Sources chrétiennes* (Paris: Cerf, 1966), 259.

His Father" (Heb 1:3).[5] This term signifies, then, not the person but the *substance*, that is a 'reality in its own right'. Now this sense will never disappear altogether. And we can understand the debates and hesitations of many Greek Fathers: *hypostasis* should not designate the Persons in their distinctiveness, since it is said of their common reality, of their single divine nature, which the Council of Nicaea in 325 had itself canonized by declaring that the Son was not "of a hypostasis or substance (*ousia*) different from the Father." Thanks to the efforts of St. Gregory Nazianzus, the equivalence of *hypostasis* and *prosopon*, in its distinction from *ousia*, came to be better and better recognized and eventually hallowed by the Church's Magisterium.

2. *Among the Latins*

The Latins did not experience the debates of the Greeks, having been endowed from the start with an adequate terminology. Tertullian was the first to designate each of the Three as *personae* of one sole *substantia*.[6] *Persona*, at first a 'theater mask', then by metonymy a 'personage', had come to signify with Cicero a lawyer's role-playing in a trial. *Persona*, without a philosophical past, did not involve theology in any controversy and brought precision and clarity to its language. This was not the case with *substantia*, a source of difficulties for the East.

How to translate *ousia*, the substantivized present participle of *einai*, 'being'? In classical Latin the verb *esse* has no present participle. Cicero had invented the neologism *essentia* out of the infinitive *esse* (being) and the substantivizing suffix *-ntia*. We read in Seneca: "I desire, if possible, to say the word *essentia* to you and obtain a favorable hearing.... I have Cicero as authority for the use of this word, and I regard him as a powerful authority.... For what can we do, my dear Lucilius? How otherwise can we find a word for that which the Greeks call *ousia*, something that is indispensable, something that is the natural substratum (*substantia*) of everything?"[7] This is an interesting text because in it we find the two Latin translations

5   Also Heb 11:1; the only occurrences of hypostasis = being.
6   *Adversus Praxean* 7, 2–3 and ff. (first occurrence of *trinitas*).
7   Seneca, *Moral Letters to Lucilius*, Bk. VI, 58,6, trans. R. M. Gummere (New York: G. P. Putnam's, 1925), vol. 1, 391. Quintilian attributes the invention of *essentia* to Plautus (II,14,2).

of *ousia* — *essentia* and *substantia* — brought together. Of these two translations the first, *essentia*, was hardly used. Four centuries after Seneca it is still a rare word. But how was *substantia* derived? The majority of specialists agree in seeing it as a transfer from the Greek *hypostasis* (*sub-stantia* = *hypo-stasis*). The Latin Fathers quite naturally inherited the vocabulary of the Latin philosophers, and so for them it is absolutely certain that substance is to be understood by *hypostasis*. Applied to God, the term can therefore only designate the Divine Essence as a whole.

Such is the basic cause for the considerable difficulties that arise between Greeks and Latins when anyone happens to compare their Trinitarian formulations. To assert that in the Trinity there are three hypostases, is, for the Latin ear, to assert that there are three substances, that is to say three divine realities and therefore three Gods. This is tritheism. The unique divine essence is divided, God from God is separated, or then one falls into Arianism, making of Christ a god with a nature other than God. St. Jerome is the most illustrious witness to this long discord. Unable to accept the expression 'three hypostases', he appealed to Pope Damasus: "If you think fit enact a decree; and then I shall not hesitate to speak of three hypostases. Order a new creed to supersede the Nicene; and then, whether we are Arians or orthodox, one confession will do for us all. . . . Whosoever in the name of religion declares that there are in the Godhead three elements, three hypostases, that is, or essences, is striving really to predicate three natures of God."[8] Faced with such resistance, we can readily see how difficult was the work of pacification.

This work we owe first of all to St. Athanasius, but also and above all to those who are called the Cappadocian Fathers (St. Basil, St. Gregory of Nyssa, and St. Gregory of Nazianzus). "We must have done with this ridiculous quarrel raised among brothers, as if our religion consisted in words and not in realities."[9] These words, pronounced at the first Council of Constantinople, bore their fruit. The equivalence

8 *Letter to Pope Damasus* XV, n. 3, 4; PL 22:356–57, in *Nicene and Post-Nicene Fathers of the Christian Church, Second Series*, vol. 6, trans. Fremantle, Lewis, and Martley (New York: The Christian Literature Company, 1893), 19.

9 St. Gregory of Nazianzus, *Orationes* XLII, n. 16, in PG 36:476–77; cited in Vacant-Mangenot, *DTC* 7.1:384.

of *person* and *hypostasis* was recognized by all and actually consecrated in being used by several later Councils. In particular, at the occasion of the second Council of Constantinople (553), the Papacy was led to explicitly specify *personam sive subsistentiam, quam graeci hypostasin dicunt,* "person, that is subsistence, which the Greeks call hypostasis."[10]

However, once this equivalence was recognized, an ambiguity of vocabulary still remained: surely the word *hypostasis* could be transferred as such from Greek to Latin, but unquestionably it would become impossible to continue translating it as *substance* (*substantia*). It was then that the necessity for a neologism appeared, translating hypostasis into the new sense, that of 'person', conferred on it by its theological usage. This is the point of the term *subsistentia*, subsistence. We have seen this term make its appearance in the just-cited conciliar text. And most likely it was in prior use. But the important thing to understand is that, receiving papal backing, its employment was beyond all dispute. That is what occurred, and the term was ratified by the whole later history of theology. *Subsistence* and *person* are synonyms because the person is truly subsistent. It is perhaps regrettable, we think, that the term subsistence has subsequently lost the concrete sense of person (which is that of the Councils) to designate more abstractly a person's manner of being. Be that as it may, according to the definition of St. Thomas, to subsist is said of what exists in itself and not in something else.[11] To speak of subsistent relations is then to speak of relations that subsist in themselves and not in something else. One could then just as well speak of hypostatic relations, that is relations not only proper to an hypostasis but which also characterize a hypostasis in itself. Such is the Infinite Mystery of the Divine Person who is not a person in the manner of human persons. In truth, the term person can be applied here only in an analogical manner.[12]

---

10 Ibid., col. 390. The terminological and philosophical elucidation of these notions in the sixth century was the work of Boethius: *Treatise against Eutyches and Nestorius*, 3; see *Boethius: The Theological Tractates*, trans. H. F. Stewart, E. K. Rand, and S. J. Tester (Cambridge, MA: Harvard University Press, 1918).
11 *Summa Theologiae* I, q. 29, a. 2.
12 *Summa Theologiae* I, q. 29, a. 3. This does not mean that there is truly no Person in God. To the contrary, St. Thomas clearly specifies in the same article that, by reason of the perfection which it implies, the notion of person is suitable for God *'maxime'*, 'to the utmost'.

II. THE NOTION OF SUBSISTENT RELATION

We have just seen the basic notion of person or hypostasis elaborated before our very eyes. Especially in the sixth century it would assume an anthropological meaning, when theology endeavored to define the function of the Hypostasis of the Word with respect to its human nature. But, at origin, this notion is purely theological.

The question posed now is what these persons, these subsistences are. By utilizing this term Christian tradition wanted to indicate the real distinction of the Father from the Son and the Holy Spirit: "As the Father is not the Son, and the Son is not the Father, and the Holy Spirit . . . is neither the Father nor the Son, certainly they are three. . . . Yet, when the question is asked, What three? human language labors altogether under great poverty of speech. The answer, however, is given, three 'persons', not that it might be [completely] spoken, but that it might not be left [wholly] unspoken."[13]

But how then do we avoid speaking of three Gods, since faith obliges us to believe that the three are God? How can they be identical (to God), being all the while distinct from Him? Theology replies to this question by the notion of 'subsistent relations'. The Divine Persons are subsistent Relations.

We will first formulate the solution, after which we will briefly attempt its proof.

1. The Divine Persons are Subsistent Relations

To say that the Persons are Subsistent Relations means that what makes the Father the Father is not a particular quality which the Father should possess (let us say an essence that would characterize Him as father) but simply the relation of paternity. This is not an essence that would characterize a subject, for unless we deny that the Father is God it must be said that the sole essence of the Father is necessarily the Divine Essence, which is also the essence of the Son. To distinguish the Father from the Son, all that remains then is the relation of paternity. It must therefore be said that the Father is identical to the relation of paternity. The Father is nothing but the

---

13 St. Augustine, *De Trinitate*, Bk. V, ch. 9 and Bk. VII, ch. 4; *On the Trinity*, trans. A. W. Haddan (Buffalo: The Christian Literature Company, 1887), 92.

relation of paternity. In the human order Peter is the father of Paul, but he is not only that: he is a man, an American, a baker, bald, etc.; in short he is a subject who, as person, is distinguished by all of these attributes. The Father Himself is nothing but the Father, He is totally Father; He is not a subject who might possess paternity (and therefore be distinguished by it). He is this very Paternity itself and not other than it. Now paternity is a relation (of generation in the active sense of the term). The Father *is* nothing but the eternal begetting of the Son, who *is* Himself nothing but the eternally Begotten, that is: the relation of filiation or sonship (of generation in the passive sense of the term). In this sense the Father is radically distinguished from the Son and vice-versa: filiation is opposed (modern logicians would say 'bijectively') to paternity. This relation, being incommunicable, can therefore constitute a person, since the principal characteristic of the notion of person, in Trinitarian theology, is incommunicability. The upshot of this thesis is that only relation, as identified with the Person, can *distinguish* the Divine Essence without *dividing* It into pieces: the Father is the Divine Essence inasmuch as It begets the Son, the Son is the Divine Essence inasmuch as It is begotten by the Father, the Holy Spirit is the Divine Essence inasmuch as It is animated by the Father in the Son and by the Son in the Father.

Granted, they will say. But this solution is quite formal. How can we identify a relation with a person? The theologian will reply that in fact it is rather the person who is identified with a relation *in divinis*. The Divine Person is conceived of not as something in God but as a Relation, since relation perfectly accounts for the incommunicability of the person, which has only been acknowledged to signify this incommunicability. Without a doubt, anyone objecting to this will retort: but is a relation ultimately something real? It is an abstraction. A relation does not exist alone in 'mid-air'. How then could this constitute the person, something quite real in itself? On the other hand, what have we gained by defining the person as a relation? We must, we are told, view the notion of person in God only in an analogical manner, it must be completely transposed. Is not the same true for the notion of relation? What is the advantage of such a transaction? Does it render the Trinitarian mystery more intelligible? Finally, do we have the right to posit relation in God? Even if it loses all human meaning, we understand that the term 'person' can be used when transposed into God since it indicates a perfection. But relation? God is the Absolute. Does He not exclude all relation?

We will try to answer these questions.

2. A Philosophical Analysis of Relation

"Several doctors have taught," St. Thomas says, "that relations are not realities, but only ideas. But this is plainly seen to be false by the following consideration alone: in themselves things are in a natural coordination with each other."[14] In a general way a relation is the rapport of one reality with another. This rapport, this coordination can be of three kinds: it is a rapport of reason if beings are only coordinated with each other in our mind (if we say for example: the tri-color flag is a symbol of France); it is a mixed rapport — at once real and of reason — if one of the terms depends, *in its own reality*, on the other. For example, the rapport between sensory knowledge and its object: the object is independent of the knowledge we have of it, but knowledge is not independent of the object that gives it form.[15] Lastly, it is a real rapport when the two terms, in their very reality, depend upon each other, in other words when the relation is based on the reality of the terms — as in the relation of father to son and, in general, in all natural realities which are ordered to each other. Moreover, if these realities are all naturally ordered to each other, this is because they belong to the same order of reality. One will better grasp what this means if mixed and real relations are compared with each other. In the case of the mixed relation — knowledge and its object, for example — we clearly see that the two terms do not belong to the same order of reality: one

---

14 *Summa Theologiae* I, q. 3, a. 7. In this difficult account we will give the fewest possible references so as not to annoy the reader. Our analysis is quite faithful to Thomist doctrine, but the mode of expression is our own. The essential references are: Saint Thomas, *Summa Theologiae* I, q. 28 and q. 29, with the commentaries of H. F. Dondaine, *La Trinité*, vol. 1 (Paris: Cerf, 1946), 170–88 and 232–37, which represent the clearest of those we have read on this question; H. D. Gardeil, *Initiation à la Philosophie de saint Thomas d'Aquin*, vol. 4 (Paris: Cerf, 1966), 103–5; Aristotle, *Categories*, ch. 7; *DTC*, article 'Relations subsistantes' (very comprehensive but difficult).

15 Jules Vuillemin, in *De la logique a la théologie* (Paris: Flammarion, 1967), 147–63, denies the possibility of mixed relations. In order to answer his objections, which are important, we would surely have to pass beyond the framework of logic and consider the doctrine of the degrees of reality.

term is of a corporeal nature, the other of a spiritual nature. It is the same in the case of the relation of creature to Creator: the Creator being of another order than the creature, He cannot really be the *correlative* of a creature; in His reality He is even totally independent. But the creature itself, in its own reality, is dependent on the Creator. There is, in this case, a real relation of the created to the Creator, and only a virtual one between the Creator and the creature. It follows that real relations define a real opposition between the two terms: one is truly the correlative of the other and vice-versa; the slave is the correlative of the master and the master is the correlative of the slave. Because of this relation they are really opposed — but not necessarily from other points of view. To summarize, there is a real relation when terms of the *same nature oppose each other correlatively* according to a rapport *based on their very reality*.

A real relation is therefore one that has a real foundation: Peter is really Paul's father to the extent that he actually begets his son. Or again James resembles Andrew — these are the two terms of the relation — because they possess an identical facial configuration; the face is the real basis for the resemblance. But a question arises. Does a real relation differ from its basis? One is tempted to reply yes and no to this question at the same time. No, relation is not distinct from its basis: to be father is nothing apart from the action that makes of the father a generator; to resemble someone else is nothing apart from the fact of having a similar face. And yet at the same time this reply is clearly insufficient: it is not the face of James, as such, that integrally accounts for the relation of resemblance, it is the face as such that corresponds to another one. If this face did not exist, the resemblance would not have any objective basis, and therefore this basis only exists 'in' James. But, insofar as only the face of James is considered, there is no relation. It is the same for the relation of paternity. If Peter does not beget, he will never be a father, and the act of begetting which exists 'in' Peter is indeed the objective basis for the relation. But this basis, viewed in itself, is not the relation: there is relation only if the basis is viewed *insofar as it relates to a son. The relation therefore exists otherwise than through the existence of its basis.* How does it exist? Since this involves real relations, that is relations which do not exist in our mind alone, we must conclude then that a relation exists between the two terms sustaining it. Let us say, if one likes, that the relation has a double existence: considered in its basis, it exists in a subject — this is what Scholastic philosophy calls its *esse in* (its *being-in*), but then it is not rightly a relation; considered in its relational essence, it exists under the form of a rapport of one thing *to another*, it exists for something else — this is what Scholasticism calls its *esse ad* (its *being-for*).

To affirm the ontological autonomy of entity relations is obviously somewhat surprising to say the least and poses a metaphysical problem. We are in fact accustomed to considering only two kinds of beings: individuals and their determinations. What exists is Peter, a cat, a tree, a molecule: these are individuals, or again, as Scholasticism says, substances, which is to say beings capable of existing in themselves and by themselves. But determinations also exist, they characterize Peter: for example, Peter is big, intelligent, has brown hair, is Italian, etc. These determinations also exist, but not by themselves, at least according to our common experience: they exist in Peter and by him. The color brown, which does not exist in itself but in another (in Peter, in a cat, or in a tree), is called an accident of the substance Peter (or of the substance cat or tree).[16] Now we must make room for a third kind of being: relation. Beside substantial being and accidental being there is relational being, which is neither 'in itself' nor 'in another', but 'for another'.

Let us digress for a moment. Such a kind of being will certainly seem less unbelievable if we connect it to what we have said about semantic or intelligible reality. The intelligible is pre-eminently able to be participated in, open, relational. It is this that ties all beings and degrees of reality together among themselves. How can we deny that a being is also an organization, and therefore a sum total of elements ordered among themselves in a structure of relationships — a system of embracings, Ruyer calls it; that it is dependent, in its very reality, on all of the relationships which unite it to other beings and define a world? What is a world if not a system of relationships; what is a world if not order (*cosmos* = order in Greek); what is order if not the sum total of relationships that unite, distinguish, and subject things

16 Accident because this quality 'happens' (*accidere* in Latin) to Peter.

to each other? Now, as will be seen later, a cosmological — and meta-cosmic — function of relation can be attributed to the Eternal Word. He who is pre-eminently the Divine Intellect sustains all relationships in being: He is the Universal Relation, and therefore the order of the world. Such is the metaphysical solution we propose in order to account for the ontological nature of relation. End of digression.

We say that relational being constitutes a third kind of being. But perhaps it would be better to say that the relational being is of itself indifferent to substantial being or accidental being. To be an accident excludes that it is a question of substance, and vice-versa. But to be a relation excludes neither 'accidental' subsistence nor 'substantial' subsistence, because in itself the essence of relation has nothing to say in this respect. When we say that Peter is the father of Paul, this relation is obviously, through its basis, an accident of the substance Peter. It possesses an accidental existence. But, *in itself* (not in its basis), it only refers Peter back to his son. Insofar as it is an accident (its *esse in*), it is not properly a relation, and insofar as it is a relation (its *esse ad*), it is not an accident, it says nothing about the subject, it does not tell us what it is in itself; it only situates this subject *with respect to* another subject, this is its only function: it coordinates each of the terms with each other. Peter is only father relative to his son Paul, and Paul is son only relative to his father Peter. A relation's *basis* clearly says something about the subject, and is moreover an accident of the subject. But, in itself, relation consists only in being completely related to another. This is what is called the 'ecstatic' character of relation.

A very important consequence arises from this 'ecstatic' character of relation: this is that its essence is, by itself, indifferent to its condition of existence. Or again, since the essence expresses what there is of the intelligible in the relation considered, let us say that the intelligibility of the relation is independent of its mode of existence. To clarify once more: the essence of an accident is not independent of its mode of existence. To speak of a color, of a face's form, of any quality whatsoever is necessarily to declare something intelligible and, at the same time, to understand that this intelligible does not exist by itself but in an individual, a substance (at least in the individual world). Likewise, to speak of a substance, of Peter or a cat, is at the same time to understand that the being spoken about exists in itself. But to speak of a relation is to speak of a reality which, by itself (its *esse ad*, its essence), indicates nothing as to its mode of existence. It could, *a priori*, exist just as well in another as in itself. In analyzing its essence, its significance, we find no indication as to its mode of existence, whereas in analyzing the essence of other determinations of a subject, or the essence of a subject, we find indications of its mode of existence. This independence of the intelligibility of a relation with respect to its mode of existence proves that, in the world of individual creatures, relation is what is closest to intelligible reality.[17]

Let us deduce then the consequences of this independent character of relation: on the one hand, since it is by itself indifferent to its mode of existence, we can admit without contradiction that relation can have either an accidental or a substantial being — if it is substantial, it is a *subsistent relation*; on the other hand, and still by virtue of this independence, whatever its mode of existence the intelligibility of a relation remains the same. Therefore, even transposed to the supreme degree *in divinis*, the relation, which will be necessarily then subsistent (since in God there is no accident and since all which is in God is God) — the subsistent relation, we say, will therefore continue to signify the relative opposition (and therefore the distinction) of terms of the same nature according to a real basis.

3. Subsistent Relations in God

We have already implicitly replied to the questions posed by our objector, but it will be useful to clarify the answers. Does one have the right to speak of relation in God, he asked?

But this question presupposes another one: are there relations in God? To this theology can make only a single response: there are relations in God because Revelation has taught us this. The New Testament speaks in fact of a Father, a Son, and a Holy Spirit who proceeds from them. Now to be Father is to maintain a relation of paternity, to be Son is to maintain a relation of filiation. This is the scriptural

---

17 Conclusions of a major importance in metaphysics. They prove that Thomism breaks away from strict Aristotelianism, for which relation is the most deficient of beings, while for Plato and Plotinus it is the *other* dimension of reality: being is also otherness; cf. our *Penser l'analogie* (Geneva: Ad Solem, 2000).

datum. It does not even involve an interpretation, but a formulation of what has been revealed. Surely one can strive to understand it, to the extent possible, but prior to the understanding of faith there is the formulation of this faith itself. In elaborating the Trinitarian dogma, the Church did not seek to render it transparent to reason. It took its departure from a fact: God has revealed himself as Father, Son, and Spirit. How can reason formulate for itself this revealed fact in such a way that it is not purely and simply a contradiction? Here we have quite precisely the proper object of the doctrine of Subsistent Relations. *Why* does God 'exist' in three distinct Persons? This is a mystery only made known by Revelation, a mystery we might try to understand through analogies like those of the Word or Love. *How* does God exist in three distinct Persons? In other words, what does it mean to speak of "a single God in three Persons"? This is what we are dealing with here, and we think the doctrine of subsistent relations responds to this in a satisfying manner.

Revelation obliges us therefore to posit Relations in God, since it affirms explicitly that in God the Second Person proceeds as Son and the Third Person proceeds as Holy Spirit. But a procession founds a relation. Now are these Relations—which are like the static aspect of a processive dynamic—accidental? To this question metaphysical reasoning replies no, and this by reason of the simplicity of the Divine Being. God has said of Himself: "I am who am," which implies that God is all that He is totally, that in Him there is no accident, and therefore that all attributes connected to the Divine Subject are the Divine Subject Himself. God is his own Essence (that is to say, properly speaking, God has no essence). Hence, if relations are attributed to God—and this is what Revelation does in saying that God is Father, that He is Son, and that He is Spirit—in attributing to him the Relations of paternity, filiation and spiration, it must be necessarily affirmed that these Relations are the Divine Being Itself, the Divine Substance: these are then subsistent relations, in other words, relations that enjoy a substantial existence.

Is this logically possible? Yes. We have seen that, of itself, a relation could be either accidental or substantial. In positing relations in God, Revelation makes known that this possibility, which seemed just now purely theoretical, is actually realized.

What remains to be asked is whether these relations are real. Three conditions, as we have seen, are required for there to be a real relation: a real basis is necessary; the terms of the relation must be of the same nature, ordained to each other in the same reality; finally, the terms must be correlatively opposed to each other, and therefore really distinct as a function of the same relation. These three conditions are realized in the case of divine or subsistent relations.

The real basis for this relation is the procession of the Son's generation or the Spirit's spiration. Scripture itself teaches this. That the terms of the relation of procession are ordained to each other in the same Reality is equally certain, since these are *ab intra* processions: God the Father begets the Son within his own Divine Essence. But are the terms of the relation still correlatively opposed to each other, are they still really distinct since they are identified with the Divine Essence?

True, someone might conceive of this identification in the manner of qualities attributed to God. God, it will be said, is good and just at the same time. And, since in God there is no accident, not only must it be said that God is just and good, but also that He is Justice and Goodness, that He is total Justice and total Goodness. Now justice and goodness are distinguished from each other and, for us, can even enter into contradiction. We are however attributing them to God, and rightfully so. Could it not happen in the same way for subsistent relations? Are relations *in divinis* distinguished among themselves in the manner by which Justice and Goodness are distinguished in God?

Let us take a closer look. When we attribute Justice and Goodness to God, we are not, properly speaking, designating a quality of the subject but God himself, for in God all is God. Justice and goodness are, however, notions which by themselves signify a quality of the subject. For them to be transposed into God, it follows that these notions, which by themselves imply an accidental being, have to be entirely transformed, and understood in a purely analogical sense, in such a way that they lose, along with their accidental being, their meaning as particular determinations. Divine Goodness is infinite, Divine Justice is infinite, and one is no longer opposed to the other: for us, they are still distinguished, but in themselves, in the Divine

Reality, they are not,[18] whereas when relations are transposed *in divinis*, although they become then the Divine Essence itself, they continue to signify what they did in creatures; they keep their formal reason, their essence, which is composed of distinction, opposition, ecstasy. Being identical to the Divine Essence, they become subsistent, they exist in themselves and no longer in something else in the manner of an accident.

But being subsistent, by virtue of the privilege of the relation, whose essence is of itself indifferent to its mode of existing, they retain their essence; therefore they do not cease being relations. They possess their subsistence through their identity to the one, same, and only Reality, the Divine Essence, but they continue to be distinguished from and opposed and related to an 'other'. Therefore they introduce a real, irreducible, and incommunicable distinction into God (paternity is not filiation), and yet they do not divide the absolute Substance, they do not 'cut it to pieces'.

4. The Trinitarian Hypostases are Subsistent Relations

The notion of person or hypostasis, as we have seen, designates the subject in its plenary reality, as a real center, let us say, distinct from every other center. Therefore two conditions define the person here, that of reality and that of incommunicability. Now these two conditions are found fully realized by the subsistent relations. As relations, they account for the incommunicability of the Person; as subsistent, they account for its reality: "Such is rightly the Divine Person: it is the *divine subsistent Relation*, and considered precisely as a distinct *Subsistence*. In other words, it is the originating Relation inasmuch as it enjoys in God prerogatives of the substance and of the absolute, all while exercising its intra-divine incommunicability."[19]

---

18 They are not distinguished for us, in our reason, yes. But this is not however a distinction of pure reason, for it has an objective basis: this is a virtual distinction, or again one of analytical reason. For example, in the human being, the reasonable animal, animality and rationality are not really distinguished since they do not form two distinct beings, man being one being. And yet reason is objectively established by distinguishing them, reason has reason to distinguish them (the distinction of *reasoning* reason) since rationality and animality constitute distinct virtualities of the human being (a virtual distinction).

19 Dondaine, *La Trinité*, 245.

Besides, we do not see how it would be possible to formulate the mystery differently. If the Divine Person is conceived of in the manner of human persons, as a subject distinct from its attributes, and for example by the relations which it maintains, then the Father will be posited as different, by His very Essence, both from the Son and from the Divine Essence. In other words, if in saying Person we are positing something of the absolute in God, we deny the dogma of the Holy Trinity. As a consequence, he who says Person in God necessarily says something essentially relational. The Divine Person is constituted entirely by relation and includes no absolute element. The Father is not at first a subject who then begets, but he is God the Father, which is to say God inasmuch as He begets the Son.

Thus the Father, inasmuch as he is Father, is absolutely nothing outside of the relation of begetting; the Father begets the Son essentially and eternally. And the Son, as such, is nothing outside of being begotten, and he is essentially and eternally begotten. "Personal properties," says St. Thomas, "are not to be understood as added to the divine hypostases, as a form is added to a pre-existing subject: but they carry with them their own 'supposita', inasmuch as they are themselves subsisting persons; thus paternity is the Father Himself. . . . By paternity the Father is not only Father, but is a person, and is 'someone', or a hypostasis."[20] And again: "The several persons are the several subsisting relations [*relationes subsistentes*] really distinct from each other. . . . Therefore the subsisting paternity is the person of the Father; and the subsisting filiation is the person of the Son. [*Paternitas igitur subsistens est persona Patris, et filiatio subsistens est persona Filii.*]"[21]

5. Identity and Distinction of the Absolute and the Relative in God

Inasmuch as the relations are subsistent we have seen that they are identified with the essence, and it is by this that they can account for the supreme reality of the Persons. However the relations are only identical to the essence from the viewpoint of their *esse in*, and not of their *esse ad*.

20 *Summa Theologiae* I, q. 40, a. 3.
21 *Summa Theologiae* I, q. 30, a. 2.

This remark means that what is said of the essence cannot be said of the subsistent relations, and what is said of the subsistent relations cannot be said of the essence. In other words, the relations are not essential attributes like goodness, justice, and omnipotence. For example, it is false to say that the Trinitarian mystery obliges us to believe that one equals three or that three equals one. For 'one' is said of the essence and 'three' is said of the Persons formed by the divine subsistent relations. Surely the relations are the One Essence as to their *esse in*, but inasmuch as they are viewed in themselves, as divine relations, according to their *esse ad*, they signify a real distinction and opposition at the very core of Unity.

Therefore there is in God at once identity and distinction between the Absolute and the Relative: consubstantial identity, since the substance of the relations is not other than the divine substance, that is to say real identity, because, in the infinite reality of the divine substance, the relative is substantially (or essentially) nothing but the absolute Substance. But there is a distinction of analytical reason, or a virtual distinction, and this distinction is not for nothing since, to the contrary, "it is truly founded in reality."[22] Such a distinction exists in fact "when the various concepts which the mind forms of one same object are, in truth, formally different and find, in the very virtualities of the object, a solid point of support for their diversity."[23] As a result this distinction has, in God, an objective basis. And this basis is essentially the real distinction existing among the divine relations themselves. In other words, since the relations are distinguished by really opposing each other — paternity cannot be filiation — it is impossible for them to be totally identified with the Divine Essence *in all respects*. There is one respect in which they are distinguished, and this is with respect to their mutual opposition.

This distinction of the essence and the subsistent relations (or divine persons) is of such an importance that its misreading is basically the key to all Trinitarian heresies, to that of Sabellius[24] in particular. This heresy consists in asserting that there is basically no real distinction among

22   *DTC* 13-2:2147.
23   Ibid.
24   Sabellius lived in the third century. We possess none of his texts, but his doctrine was introduced as an anti-Arianism and was quite widespread.

the three Persons, who in reality are therefore only three modes[25] of one same divine substance: there is only one Person. The Sabellians, it seems, even came to assert that each of these modes excluded the other, and therefore that God, at first Father, had next suffered upon the Cross as Son, and had then poured Himself out upon Christians as the Holy Spirit. "God, the Sabellians said, a simple and indivisible monad, is a unique person."[26] As we see, the error of the modalists comes from purely and simply identifying Person with Essence.

To the contrary, traditional theology "reminds us that, in God, paternity and filiation indicate substantial modes which, all the while opposing each other, are to be distinguished from Substance."[27] This is even what Orthodox theology will reproach Latin theology for, which falls, it says,[28] into the Sabellian heresy. But this does not involve ephemeral modes in the manner of the Sabellians; "these modes of the divine nature"[29] are *personal* modes, irreducibly distinct from each other however identical substantially.

It cannot be said then that Christian theology, a creature of a 'massive' monotheism, fiercely denies all relativity in God, since, to the contrary, it expressly posits such a relativity *in divinis*. But it can no longer be accused of brutally identifying this 'supreme' Relativity with the Absolute, since to the contrary it carefully distinguishes what can be said about the One Essence from what can be said about the relative Trinity of Persons. This time, surely, an unreal distinction is involved, but how could it be otherwise under pain of cutting God in two? And unreal distinction does not mean 'illusory distinction',

25 In the present day this heresy is also called modalism.

26 St. Epiphanius, *Haereses*, in PG 41:1052. The Sabellian heresy is a 'Christian' heresy. It denies the divinity neither of the Son nor of the Holy Spirit nor of a certain Trinity. It was basically 'acceptable' for a Christian, and moreover was widely accepted. So much the more remarkable is the condemnation it incurred. For the Sabellians there was a trinity only in the *ad extra* divine operations, in the created world. But there was no real Relativity at the core of the Absolute. Such is, for us, the gravest reproach that can be brought against the Sabellians. It makes of pure Being a monolithic bloc which leaves the world outside Itself and which is therefore opposed to it. This theism will have its 'pay-back' in atheism. Whereas we know of no 'trinitarian' atheism.

27 *DTC* 13-2:2147.

28 P. Evdokimov, *L'orthodoxie* (Neuchâtel: Delachaux & Niestlé, 1965), 135.

29 Th. de Régnon, *Études de théologie positive sur la Sainte-Trinité*, vol. 1 (Paris: Retaux, 1898), 433.

but a distinction based on the nature of the *Res divina*. Thus, in God, the godhead as such is not paternity as such but is objectively and formally distinct from it. The relative Trinity principially 'determines' the Essence in an 'immaculate' manner, so to speak, and reveals it insofar as that is possible.

6. Subsistent Relations in Tradition

Far from being the innovation of a late Scholasticism, the distinction between unity in essence and trinity in the relations is a major theme of the whole Christian tradition, and is summed up in this classic axiom of St. Anselm: "In God all is one wherever the opposition of relation does not intervene." St. Basil writes: "The one who speaks of the Son thinks of the Father, for this expression, inasmuch as *relative*, indicates the Father at the same time." Now these relations and personal properties resulting from them are "signs by which the individual existence of Persons is formed."[30] St. Gregory Nazianzus affirms: "Father is not a name that expresses the Essence or activity, it is a name that indicates the *relation* which the Father possesses with respect to the Son or the Son with respect to the Father."[31] St. Augustine clarifies: "In created and changeable things, that which is not said according to substance must, by necessary alternative, be said according to accident.... And yet what is said about God is not always about substance, which does not mean that this is said about an accident, for in God there is no accident. It is said in relation to something (*dicitur enim ad aliquid*), as the Father in relation to the Son.... Although to be the Father and to be the Son are different, yet their substance is not different; because they are so called, not according to substance, but according to relation [*non secundum substantiam dicuntur sed secundum relativum*]."[32] And St. John Damascene sums up this doctrine in the following manner: "All the aforesaid [absolute] names are to be taken as applying in common, in the same manner ... to the whole Godhead ... but the names 'Father', 'Son' and 'Spirit', 'Uncaused' and 'Caused', 'Unbegotten' and 'Begotten', and 'Proceeding' are to be taken as applying in a different way,

---

30   *Letters*, 38, 7; PG 32:337.
31   *Orations*, 29 (Third Theological Oration); PG 36:96A.
32   *On the Trinity*, Bk. 5, ch. 5, n. 6.

because they declare not the essence, but the mutual relationship and manner of existence [of the Persons]."[33]

7. Conclusion. The Mysticism of Subsistent Relations

"Henceforth, so to grasp the *Res divina*, we should make use of two divine 'categories': substance and relation. It is this irreducible split, short of the beatific vision, that enables our thought to humbly lay hold of the mystery of the Three who are One, without giving way beneath a contradiction."[34]

Unquestionably this Scholastic construction is particularly abstract, difficult and foreign to the inscrutable divine simplicity. What good is all this, someone will say? But it is the honor of the human spirit to aspire to the loftiest of understandings. Actually, through so high — the summit of theology — and, ultimately, so luminous a doctrine, we see the intelligence being purified and rendered a little less unworthy of its divine Object. We will show — and this is basically the entire theme of our book — how this is the key to true charity. But already we can see that it represents a support for an intelligibility whose fruitfulness is rightly inexhaustible. It certainly does not enable us to *comprehend* the Trinitarian Mystery, since It is that which embraces all things, but in a certain manner it speculatively enables us to be established within this Mystery Itself, in the bosom of the Trinity of Hypostases.

There is still more. This is that the doctrine of Subsistent Relations is also the key to our deification. To enter into the Kingdom, says

---

33   *On the Orthodox Faith*, Bk. I, ch. 10, trans. F. H. Chase (New York: Fathers of the Church, 1958); PG 94:837. To be complete, we should add the magisterial texts on the Trinity of Persons. We will only cite this passage from the eleventh Council of Toledo (675): "In the relative names of persons, however, the Father refers to the Son, the Son to the Father, and the Holy Spirit to both, in that while relatively three persons are asserted, we yet believe they are one nature or substance.... For, as He is Father, not to Himself, but to the Son; and as He is Son not to Himself but to the Father, similarly also the Holy Spirit refers in a relative sense not to Himself, but to the Father and to the Son, in that He is proclaimed the Spirit of the Father and the Son. Likewise when we say 'God', no relationship is expressed, as the Father to the Son, or the Son to the Father, or the Holy Ghost to the Father and the Son, but God applies especially to Himself" (*Sources of Catholic Dogma*, trans. R. J. Deferrari [St. Louis MO & London: B. Herder Book Co., 1957], 278–9).

34   Dondaine, *La Trinité*, 176.

Christ, is not to say: Lord, Lord, but is to do the will of the Father. Now what is the will of the Father? It is to beget the Son. And even more: the Father is nothing but the begetting of the Son. The will of the Father is the Father himself Who, in an eternal ecstasy, gives the Divine Essence to the Son. And if the Father were something other than this ecstasy, as truly as God exists, never would we be able to do his Will.

13

The Procession of the Holy Spirit

THE SON PROCEEDS FROM THE FATHER, AND this procession is a procession by filiation. The Holy Spirit equally proceeds from the Father. This is what Scripture teaches, employing this term to define the relation of origin of the Holy Spirit from the Father (*Spiritum veritatis qui a Patre procedit*), as St. John relates (15:26). But nowhere does the Gospel specify or make precise the mode of procession. There is a mystery to the Third Hypostasis.

I. PROCESSIONS AND RELATIONS
1. From the Father through the Son

Just considering the divine processions, and therefore viewing the Trinity in relation to its internal dynamics, we will say that the Father is the Divine Essence inasmuch as It eternally and essentially begets the Son, and likewise for the Son and the Holy Spirit; the Son is the absolute Essence inasmuch as It is eternally and essentially begotten in Him, so that although the Son is not the Divine Essence according to paternity, He is the Divine Essence inasmuch as It is eternally and essentially begotten, that is to say according to filiation. And the Holy Spirit is the Divine Essence inasmuch as It is eternally and essentially 'spirated'[1] by the Father and the Son. Why must we say by the Father and the Son? Here is how St. Thomas explains it, considering things from the viewpoint of the processions. It is said that the Son proceeds from the Father by the mode of the intellect and the Holy Spirit by the mode of will, the essence of which is love. Since intellect does not presuppose will but the will presupposes intellect, so Love presupposes the Word. We know "the Son proceeds by the way of

---

1 The terms 'spirated', 'spiration' are formed from *spirare* — to blow, to breathe — in order to indicate the production of a *spiritus*, and at first have no other meaning.

the intellect as Word, and the Holy Ghost by way of the will as Love. Now Love must proceed from the Word. For we do not love anything unless we apprehend it by a mental conception."[2] But basically the dynamic viewpoint of the processions, which explains why the Holy Spirit proceeds from the Father through the Son as from a common principle, is for St. Thomas only another way of expressing the more static or 'logical' level of the subsistent relations. For the dynamic viewpoint is based upon a mode of analogy—as when humans 'get to know' prior to loving someone—while the viewpoint of subsistent relations expresses the Trinitarian mystery in its 'pure logic'.

2. Passive Spiration

There are in God, we say, two processions. Now each procession implies two extremes: a principle of procession and a term proceeding, or again, an active term and a passive term. Four relations result from this, since each term defines a relation: from the Father to the Son, an active relation of begetting, called paternity; from the Son to the Father, a passive relation of being begotten, called filiation; from the Father and from the Son (or through the Son) to the Holy Spirit, an active relation from proceeding to proceeded, called active spiration; from the Holy Spirit to the Father and to the Son (or through the Son), a passive relation from proceeded to proceeding, called procession (by St. Thomas) or passive spiration (by later theologians). Now active spiration does not set the Father in opposition to the Son—quite the contrary, since it is their common act of love. And two consequences flow from this: 1.—not forming an opposition, this relation does not form a person either, which can therefore only be formed by passive spiration; 2.—the Father and the Son are united (indistinguishable) in the procession of the Holy Spirit.

To say that the active relation of spiration does not form a person—although a real relation, it is not a subsistent relation—this is to say that there is not *one* person who is purely spirating, and nothing other than spirating, like the Father who is not other than paternity. In fact, if active spiration designates the act of love, how could one conceive of there being in God one person and only one

2 *Summa Theologiae* I, q. 36, a. 2.

who is pure loving? Paternity (the relation revealed by the Scriptures) can only be the property of a single person, for it is contradictory to claim that the Son would also possess it. But loving (active spiration) is the act of the entire Divine Essence, in the Father who loves the Son in giving to Him the Divine Essence by his eternal begetting, as well as in the Son who loves the Father in restoring to Him the Divine Essence through his eternal filiation, that is to say through 'knowledge' of the Father as eternal source of the ecstasy of the Godhead. Hence, what alone is opposed to the Father and the Son, in the spirative procession, is not the Divine Essence inasmuch as It loves, but the Divine Essence inasmuch as It is loved. This is passive spiration. The Divine Essence loved by the Father in the Son, by begetting, and by the Son in the Father, by filiation, is the incommunicable Person of the Holy Spirit. And so we can see quite clearly that the Holy Spirit is understood to be the love-knot of the Father and the Son, since He is the Love loved by the Father in the Son and by the Son in the Father.[3]

For St. Thomas, then, there is indeed only one principle of the Holy Spirit, one sole spirating principle, but this is the Son as well as the Father (even though the Son retains this property from the Father):

> because as regards being the principle of the Holy Spirit, the Father and the Son are not opposed to each other, but only as regards the fact that one is the Father, and the other is the Son.... The Holy Spirit is distinguished from the Son, inasmuch as the origin of one is distinguished from the origin of the other; but the difference itself of origin comes from the fact that the Son is only from the Father, whereas the Holy Spirit is from the Father and the Son; for otherwise the processions would not be distinguished from each other.[4]

For St. John the Evangelist,

---

3 This point will be developed in ch. 15.
4 *Summa Theologiae* I, q. 36, a. 2, ad 1 and ad 7.

the Father and the Son are in everything one, wherever there is no distinction between them of opposite relation. Hence since there is no relative opposition between them as the principle of the Holy Spirit it follows that the Father and the Son are one principle of the Holy Spirit.[5]

3. The Non-contradiction of the Greeks and Latins

Without pretending to reconcile the Orthodox and Catholic perspectives, even though both may be perfectly legitimate, we will just say this: the Scholastic perspective does not exclude, at least formally, certain affirmations of Orthodox theology. "The Father spirates the Holy Spirit through the Son," says St. Thomas.[6] It is therefore possible to say that the Holy Spirit proceeds at once from the Father and the Son, and the Holy Spirit proceeds from the Father through the Son. St. Thomas says in effect that in every action it is necessary to consider both the agent which does the action, and the 'virtue' by which it acts. Thus the flame warms: it is the agent, but heat is the virtue. Now the virtue (or the power of fecundity) by which the Father spirates the Holy Spirit is the same as that virtue by which the Son effects the same spiration. In this sense, the Holy Spirit proceeds immediately from the Father and the Son, for this fecundity is the fecundity of the Divine Essence itself. But from the viewpoint of agents, the Holy Spirit proceeds immediately from the Father and only mediately from the Son, for the Son receives this fecundity or spirative virtue from the Father.[7] This distinction of agent and virtue is extremely important. Contrary to what is too often said, Thomism does not deny the monarchy of the Father. At the end of article 3, which we are freely paraphrasing here, St. Thomas utilizes the comparison of the Father to a King. If one considers, he says, the procession of the Holy Spirit relative to the order of the Persons who produce it, then it must be affirmed that the Holy Spirit proceeds from the Father through the Son, a proposition which is not convertible.

---

5 *Summa Theologiae* I, q. 36, a. 4.
6 *Summa Theologiae* I, q. 36, a. 3.
7 Ibid.

II. THE MYSTERY OF THE HOLY SPIRIT

1. The Apophatic Meaning of the Filioque

Thomist 'filioquism' is basically an act of speculative humility and not the affirmation of a rigid dogmatism. The Scholastic perspective is extremely attentive to what one can say or cannot say, or even to what is unsayable. Thus one can consider its essential effort to be an effort at formulation — we will not say of language, for to lead everything back to language is a modern viewpoint, altogether fictitious, if not arbitrary, in which thought is illusorily separated from its expression. The concepts themselves already constitute a language with respect to the super-conceptual Truth, because they are a formulation of what is in itself formless. Written or spoken language is nothing but the passage from a mental to a sensible formulation, but *this passage is obviously only possible because what is thought and spoken is beyond thought and speech*, and this is also why this passage is perilous and cannot be effected finally without 'information loss'. Thus, when we affirm that the Father and the Son are the one principle of the Holy Spirit, we can add that this principle is or is not the Father alone, without it being possible to decide between the two alternatives. "*Non necesse est alterum eorum dare*," St. Thomas says. For what we in this way call 'principle' does not belong in a *fixed* manner to a subject, but in a vague (Latin: *confuse*) and indistinct (Latin: *indistincte*) manner to the first two Divine Persons.[8] There is therefore a mystery in the procession of the Holy Spirit, which is manifest in the impossibility of our choosing between the Father — the sole principle — and the Father and the Son together. There is distinction according to the ordinal viewpoint, and indistinction according to the viewpoint of the Almighty. Inasmuch as the Scholastic viewpoint considers the Trinity in its 'sheer rationality', and therefore as in some way revealing of the Logos, by contrast it necessarily accentuates what, in the Trinity, escapes this viewpoint, and which then appears as especially revealing of the Holy Spirit. In a certain manner the Holy Spirit *is* the mystery *of* the Trinity, inasmuch as it more especially constitutes its 'Mystery'

---

8 *Summa Theologiae* I, q. 36, a. 3, ad 4, 5, 6; this is why we speak of an apophatic meaning: every expression that declares its impotence to name the Inexpressible is apophatic.

aspect. 'Filioquism', which does not distinguish between Father and Son in the procession of the Third Person, expresses apophatically that the intellectual eye's 'separating power' becomes impotent here.

2. *Every Procession Depends on the Holy Spirit*

We can now grasp the difference between the viewpoint of the relations, considered in chapter 12, and that of the processions, considered in chapter 13. In a general way we will say that the doctrine of relations 'sums up' the Trinitarian mystery from the viewpoint of the Word, while the doctrine of the processions 'sums it up' from the viewpoint of the Holy Spirit. Multiple considerations justify this affirmation.

1. We will initially recall that relations and processions are distinguished as static and dynamic, respectively, a distinction parallel in a certain manner to that of the Word-Knowledge and the *Pneuma*-Breath of Love. With the relations this involves 'knowing' the 'logical' structure of the Trinity. With the processions this involves 'entering into' the 'ecstatic' process of emanation of the Son and the Holy Spirit from the Father. Procession is in fact the emanation of one thing from another: the first, the point of departure, is called the principle; the second, the point of arrival, is called the term. Now procession is essentially an action which can end in a term exterior to the principle (transitive procession) or in a term interior or immanent to the principle (immanent procession). In God this evidently has to do with immanent processions, and the idea of immanent activity seems excellently suited to the Holy Spirit. Everything that is procession in some way then arises from the Holy Spirit. So to speak of the procession of the Son is to implicitly declare that the Holy Spirit, as we will see, is no 'stranger' to this procession, not as its principle, but as its 'condition of possibility'.

2. We know that for the Son this involves a procession of intelligence; let us not forget, however, that this qualification is analogical: the human concept remaining immanent to the thought that forms it, this operation is transposed into God, so as to know something of the mystery of the procession of the Son, who also remains immanent to his act of begetting. The Son is thus analogically considered to be the Concept, the mental Word (*Logos*), the term immanent to the Thought of the Father. Now, is it not the *relation* of the concept to the thought

that is illuminating in this analogy? But as for the *operation* or *activity* (conception), it differs greatly in man and in God, for the mental conception in man is not a begetting. Indeed, this mysterious operation (conception) constituting the dynamic of the procession arises from the *Pneuma*. The procession of the will moreover confirms these views. Here, in fact, the analogy seems less illuminating, for the will does not produce a volition in the same way that thought produces a concept; however it is much more revelatory, according to the very analogy of the will, for the idea of procession. In other words, the procession of intelligence is *almost* reduced to a pure relation, is quasi-intelligible then and arises from the *Logos*, while the procession of will is almost reduced to a pure procession, is quasi-unintelligible then and arises from the *Pneuma*; this is why it can be simply called procession.

3. Lastly, we will say that if to speak is to express the intelligible, then we can speak of the Trinity only from the viewpoint of the Word and therefore from the viewpoint of relations. To speak of the processions, in return, is to declare that there is a further side to theological discourse. This is then to bring oneself into the sphere of the Spirit and, thanks to It, to mystically gain access to that further side of theological discourse where we really enter into the Trinity and participate, inasmuch as it is given to a creature, in the generative procession of the Son. This remark takes us out of the purely Trinitarian sphere, since it touches on human participation. But at the same time it supplies a key to the profound identity of procession and the missions, that is, to speak the language of the Greeks, to the theology of the economy: God in Himself and God in the work of salvation. And this key is the Holy Spirit. What is called 'mission' is known as the *sending* by the Father of the Son and the *Pneuma* into the world, either visibly — incarnation, dove, tongue of fire, etc. — or invisibly — in the sanctified soul for example. Now the theologians say: "mission is attributed to time, and yet it does not essentially differ from the eternal procession."[9] "Better said," writes Chardon (died 1651), "the eternal and temporal procession is only one and the same production."[10] This is to say that if the Holy Spirit 'presides' over every procession, He also 'presides' over every mission, which is accomplished, as the prototypical example of

9   Dondaine, *La Trinité*, vol. 2 (Paris: Cerf, 1962), 426 and 437.
10   *La Croix de Jésus*, Third Conversation, ch. 5; éd. F. Florand, 414.

the Annunciation shows, through His operation, and that He realizes their unity in His unique Person.

3. The Holy Spirit 'Summarizes' the Trinity

Thus the Holy Spirit summarizes the whole Trinitarian dynamic. He concentrates within Himself the hypostatic unfolding of the Divine Essence. His procession, whose nature is not revealed to us, is as if the preeminent procession. He does not even have a proper name since, as St. Thomas remarks,[11] the name Spirit is appropriate for the three Persons, and does not express a relation as "Father" or "Son" does. But if this is so, is it not precisely because the Holy Spirit is not a term, but the term, and therefore because He cannot have any particular designation (*proprium nomen*)? And why is He the term if not because in Him is achieved the Trinitarian opening-out of the Essence? He is the divine mystery's 'final word'.[12] He is as if the super-formal 'form' of the Divine Persons, and this is why Rublev's famous icon[13] represents the Three under three identical forms, each that of the Holy Spirit.

He is as if the pre-eminent Hypostasis. "The Son," says St. Augustine, "is therefore the Son of the Father alone, but the Holy Spirit is the Spirit of the Father and the Son and our own."[14] We understand then how the Person or Hypostasis, inasmuch as it is of a spiritual essence, is in some fashion identified with the Holy Spirit. In the Holy Spirit the One Essence 'rediscovers' its unity. He returns It to Itself, and therefore one can equally consider that the identity of forms in Rublev's icon *expresses* the identity of the Essence. But these two interpretations in no way exclude each other, since it is by means of the 'form' of the Holy Spirit that this identity is expressible. And so, if the Person of the Holy Spirit has no *proprium nomen*, this is because He is the preeminent Person.

---

11 *Summa Theologiae* I, q. 36, a. 1. This remark is common among the Fathers.

12 For the Greeks the Son is the Word [French *Parole* = spoken word] of God (*Logos*), and the Holy Spirit is the Word [French *Mot* = a simple word] of the Son (*Rhema*): cf. M. H. Lavocat, *L'Esprit de Vérité et d'Amour* (Paris: Librairie Saint-Dominique, 1968), 79.

13 Rublev's icon synthesizes Trinitarian theology: cf. P. Evdokimov, *The Art of the Icon*, trans. S. Bigham (Redondo Beach, CA: Oakwood Publications, 1990), 243–57.

14 *On the Trinity*, V, 14.

4. The Holy Spirit, the Key to the Circumincession

We also see that, in a certain manner, the Trinity is wholly in each Divine Person. We know, with revealed and theological certainty, that the Father is in the Son and the Son is in the Father, and likewise for the Holy Spirit,[15] since there is nothing which the Father possesses that the Son does not have, without the Son, after all, being the Father, since He is the Son and possesses absolute perfection, in all points consubstantial with the Father's perfection but only inasmuch as He is eternally begotten by the Father. Therefore it is not daring to say that the Trinity is completely present in each hypostasis. This is why a 'representation' of the Trinity has to express this presence of the hypostases in each other, by allowing a permutation of Trinitarian identifications with regard to their pictorial display. In the icon of Rublev, for example, each personage of the icon can be regarded in its turn as Father, Son, or Holy Spirit, according to a certain point of view. It is no longer then a question of the identity of the pneumatic form manifesting, *ad intra*, the identity of the Essence, but it is the gestures and attitudes which take on a different sense according to the identification of the personages. Yet They are Three and no One is the Other. And even more, it is precisely because They are Three and no One is the Other that the Trinity is entirely in each of Them.[16] This possibility of exchange conveys the theological idea of circumincession. There is a 'circulation' of the Divine Essence, which is exchanged among the three hypostases as if Each were *advancing into the Other*[17] in order to give It to Itself. The circumincession of the Three Persons constitutes Divine Life. And because Divine Life is strictly identical to

15 *Summa Theologiae* I, q. 42, a. 5, and John 14:10.

16 According to the constant affirmations of theology, "the Trinity does not produce number." Mathematically it is therefore necessary to represent it not by an addition $(1 + 1 + 1)$, but by a 'multiplication' $(1 \times 1 \times 1 = 1)$.

17 The term "circumincession," from *incedere*, which means to be advancing into, translates the Greek *perichoresis*. It seems to have been St. John of Damascus who first applied this term to Trinitarian life. The Scholastics of the fifteenth century translated it by circuminsession (from *circuminsidere* = to in-dwell), which does not convey the idea of an internal dynamic of *reciprocal ecstasies*. Cf. Labauche, *Leçons de Théologie dogmatique*, vol. 1 (Paris: Bloud & Gay, 1923), 157; and above all Théodore de Régnon, *Études de théologie positive sur la Sainte Trinité*, 4 vols. (Paris, Retaux, 1892–1898), Étude VI, ch. IV, a. 2.

the Divine Essence, the circumincession is eternal and infinite. Being eternal and infinite, it is not completed in the Spirit as in a final term, but it sets out again from the Holy Spirit who sends it back to the Father and the Son. Thus infinite movement is, *in divinis*, the same thing as infinite immobility.

14

The Trinitarian Functions of the Hypostases

INTRODUCTION: A NEW VIEWPOINT

The new viewpoint we propose is as follows: the Trinitarian mystery, equally 'present' in each Divine Person by virtue of the circumincession, 'expresses' in each however a particular aspect of its own structure.

What is the Trinitarian mystery, as seen by its definition, if not a structure with three elements: a single God (element 1) in three (element 2) distinct Persons (element 3)? The first element consists in the Divine Essence or Godhead; the second consists in the Person or Hypostasis, and the third in a distinction, that is to say the subsistent Relation. None of these elements can be isolated from the others: the Godhead, being infinite, cannot be opposed to anything, and therefore includes both Relativity and Personality within itself, since no perfection is lacking to it; as for Relation, it subsists only through its identity with the Divine Essence, although it also gives an idea of the Person as being incommunicable; finally the Person is identified with the Divine Essence, for only the supreme Godhead possesses both supreme Ipseity and undivided Unity, provided that the Person is only formed through relation. Now it can be thought that, in the Person of the Father, the Trinitarian mystery expresses more particularly the 'Godhead' aspect; in the Person of the Son, the 'relation' aspect; and in the Person of the Holy Spirit, the 'hypostasis' aspect. Is not the Father the origin of the Trinity, and does not the Gospel often use the word *God* to indicate the only Father? Is not the Son the primary image of the Father, and is not the image defined here as an ontological relation? And finally, is not the essence of every Person, as we have seen, of the spiritual order?

However, this new perspective will only be fully revealed if we first attempt to fathom its basis in Scripture and dogma.

I. THE FUNCTION OF THE WORD
AS PROTOTYPICAL RELATION
ACCORDING TO SCRIPTURE

1. The Word, the Relation of the Created to the Uncreated

St. Paul, as we know, defines Jesus Christ as "mediator between God and men" (1 Tim 2:5). Christ himself, in affirming that he is the vine and we are the branches (John 15:1–5), presents himself as the 'ontological relation' in whom all beings and all degrees of Creation subsist because joined to him, and in him communicate with the Principle of being. But this is also what St. John's prologue states by saying: *"omnia per ipsum facta sunt"* and *"in ipso vita erat,"* "all things have been made through him" and "in him was life." Notice how these two prepositions *through* and *in* are found again in St. Paul: *"In* him all things were created . . . all things were created *through* him and for him" (Col 1:16), and express the idea of subsistent (*in*) relation (*through*). 'Through' does not directly point to the Creator as such, or to the origin of Creation, but to the creative act, or even the one *by whose agency* Creation has occurred, the One who binds creation to the Creator because he binds Cause to effect. Moreover, the sense of 'through' is specified in the course of the verse: "and without him was not anything made that was made," which expresses, in negative form, the same idea as at the beginning of the verse. The Greek preposition *koris* (= without) means 'separated from', 'apart from', and indicates an absence of relation — which, for the created, would be equivalent to an absence of being.

2. The Word, the Relation of God to God

It is not only considerations of the cosmological order that invite us to attribute a function of prototypical relation to the Son. Besides establishing his title 'Son of God', upon which all other considerations depend, the same text from St. John provides an even more important and decisive testimony for this function.

St. John states in fact: "And the Word was with God." The Latin *apud*, like the English *with*, poorly conveys the Greek *pros* formed with the accusative (*pros ton theon*), a remarkable preposition, since we would normally expect *para* and the dative. Now this preposition means 'turned toward', 'in the presence of', and *'in relation with'* simultaneously. The theological importance of these meanings is clear. On the other hand, notice how the word *God* is preceded here by an article: *the* God; while in the next verse: "and the Word was God," *God* is written without an article. The majority of similar usages of New Testament Greek show that *God* (without an article) designates the Divine Nature, and *the God* designates God the Father.[1] And so, in his prologue, St. John affirms both the identity of the Word with the Divine Essence and its *relational* distinction from the Father. This idea of relation seems all the more certain since, in all cases where New Testament Greek uses *pros* (and the accusative) before the words *the God* or *the Father*, the context indicates a particular sense of relationship of the Son with the Father[2]; while wherever the Gospel uses the preposition *para* to signify 'with God', it seems that this idea of relation to the Father is absent. The most characteristic example is to be found in John: "Father, glorify Thou me in Thy own presence with the glory which I had with Thee" (John 17:5). Although St. John uses *para*, I do not think that the glory which belongs to the Son by virtue of his relation to the Father is involved here, but that glory which comes to him because of his identity with the Divine Essence, an identity which makes him equal to the Father. With respect to the Divine Essence, the Father and the Son are *para*, 'one beside the other'; but, with respect to the Father, the Son is *pros ton theon*, "in a relation of proximity to God the Father." The Johannine verse might then be translated, with gloss, as follows: "The Word was the One nigh to God the Father, the *relation-of-proximity* with the Father."

Therefore, in the bosom of the Trinity, we can appropriate the function of prototypical relation to the Word, so that everything of the order of subsistent relation in the Trinity refers, in a certain way, to the Son, the first relation of the Divine Essence with itself. Correlatively, everything of the hypostatic order refers to the Holy Spirit, just as everything concerning the Godhead refers to the Father.[3] This

---

1   Cf., among others, J. Lebreton, *Histoire du dogme de la Trinité*, vol. 1 (Paris: Beauchesne, 1927), 499; and M. E. Boismard, *Le Prologue de saint Jean* (Paris: Cerf, 1953), 19.
2   Cf. John 1:1, 2; 1 John 1:2 and 2:1.
3   The theory of Trinitarian functions likewise enables us to understand that

function of prototypical relation, such as we have briefly attempted to describe it, is an important acquisition for our research. Other considerations will illustrate it in the course of this study, but right now what it means is that the Son is the metaphysical basis for the relation of proximity.

II. RETROSPECTIVE: HOW THE TRINITARIAN MYSTERY FOUNDS CHARITY

1. Logical Basis and Real Basis

A remark needs to be interjected here. From considering subsistent relations as the general basis for charity, we have passed to a consideration of the Word as the particular basis for the relation of proximity. What is the meaning of this shift? How do we justify proceeding in this way? Clearly, the answer to this question depends on the answer to another question: how does the doctrine of subsistent relations found charity? Actually, up until now we have spoken of a basis for the *possibility* of love. But here we need to examine how this basis is also a basis for the *reality* of love, or even *how* the doctrine of relations really founds love. A comparison will give us a better understanding of the differences between these two questions. We can say that by itself, Being founds the possibility of contingent being, since without Being itself there is no caused being. But we might also ask ourselves: how is such a basis established? And the answer: by its immanence at the heart of contingent being. It is the same in the present instance. Clearly, a structuring of charity is not completely impossible, since theology also presents such a structure as forming the Trinitarian mystery. And this is in a way the *logical basis* of charity. However, this basis needs to be *ontological* as well; it needs to found the reality of charity, for charity is not just a logical possibility. It is also the spiritual activity enjoined by the supreme commandment. Obviously such a distinction is also valid for the Word in its function as prototypical relation. Thus we deem it preferable to examine these two kinds of questions at the same time, so as not to interrupt the flow of our

---

Latin theology, by considering the Trinity according to the pure rationality of these relations, sees it from the viewpoint of the Son, while Greek theology, by considering it according to the hypostases, sees it from the viewpoint of the Holy Spirit.

explanation and to make it possible to compare them with each other; and this will enable us to delve deeper into their respective meanings.

2. *The Trinity is the Real Basis for all Love*

As for the logical founding of charity by the Trinitarian mystery, let us recall the following: 1. — the analysis of charity, in its human order, obliges us to define the charitable structure as a person who is a relation and a relation that is a person; 2. — since this structure is contradictory for human reason, and with charity becoming simply unintelligible on this account, we are compelled to find out how such a structure is possible; 3. — but we find that this structure is the one that constitutes the Trinity as expressed in the doctrine of subsistent relations.

Now we come to the ontological character of the basis itself. As a consequence of the doctrine of subsistent relations, the whole Trinity is Love. And this is the most important feature. The Godhead, or Divine Essence, is basically ecstatic with respect to itself. This *in divinis* love is called *essential Love*, so as to distinguish it from *personal Love*, the Holy Spirit.

Since there is no true charity outside of the Trinity, we must then conclude that, as surprising as it might be for modern man, natural charity is an effective, ontological participation in Trinitarian Charity itself. Every act of love, even the least, whether one wishes it or not, whether one knows it or not, does not exist outside of its ontological participation in essential Love. Such is the way in which Trinitarian Reality actually founds the reality of human charity. We consider an act of love a trifle, and yet with it we are in the presence of the loftiest of all mysteries. Unquestionably we are barely aware of it; it is not easy to *really* become aware of it. Everything we have said about it is nothing but a — hopefully rigorous — chain of reasoning that conveys a sufficient intellectual certainty, but that is unable to give a real awareness of the Holy Trinity, however invisibly and necessarily present.

3. *Every Love Participates in Trinitarian Love*

To conclude, let us again clarify two points. As for the participation of the human in the divine, which *defines every mode of ontological founding*, we must not imagine that essential Love is parceled out or shared. For in its Essence, this Love is perfectly indivisible and therefore completely present — in its Infinity — in every act of love that participates in it. There is limitation only on behalf of the participating subject, not on behalf of the Participated. Only God can give himself, because only God can be other than himself. Indeed, it is then the Trinity as such, in its unfathomable Infinity, which constitutes the reality of every act of love.

On the other hand, this participation occurs, whatever the human subject's degree of faith and even in the case of an atheist, because such participation involves an ontological basis and is therefore dependent on the nature of things. However, contrary to the ontological basis of created existence, which is inseparable from this existence and which permanently sustains the creature in being, the Trinity does not dwell in the being properly speaking, but in the act of love as such. In this sense, every act of love is a participation in the Trinitarian ecstasy. The being of the act participates, not the being of the acting subject. But how is this possible? Far from being an exception, this is to the contrary very frequently the case, and the vast majority of people have the power to accomplish acts that far surpass the abilities of acting beings. Only among the saints are acting and being of equal dignity. Thus no one can say "Jesus" if not by the Holy Spirit who speaks through his mouth. But who is there among us whose being is the actual temple of the Holy Spirit? Every act of love is therefore, by nature, supernatural. However, as we have pointed out already, God is thus present in an 'objective' way in every act of love. What, then, does faith and, even more, holiness add to such a presence? It adds spiritual awareness of this presence — or, in other words, knowledge of the true nature of charity. But is this an appreciable change? It is a radical change, for cognitive awareness is not just anything; it is not a simple accident of the human being; quite the contrary, it is a human being's specific essence. Through the spiritual awareness of faith the Holy Trinity is not only present in the act of love, but also in the acting *person*, or at the very least it can become so, little by little, in proportion to our spiritual progress. We now see the great value of the distinction made previously between participation by acting and participation by being. When the being is a conscious being, participation by *acting* can be transformed into participation by the acting *being* only through an awakening of consciousness. Surely this does not depend on an awareness of the Trinity as the basis for the act of love, since the Trinity is there through what the theologians call the *presence of immensity*. But it does depend on the awareness that this presence may become a personal and, hence, a sanctifying presence.

III. THE WORD AS BASIS FOR THE RELATION OF PROXIMITY

1. The Word as Logical Basis

With respect to the Trinity (under its aspect of subsistent relations) as the general basis for charity, we could say that the Word represents the specific instance of this basis, or even that the Word represents, within the general basis of charity, the basis for the relation of proximity, integral to being a neighbor, just as the Holy Spirit is both the particular basis of the person and the revelatory function of love, a dual function of the divine *Pneuma* that somehow 'frames' the function of the Word: you will love (revelatory love, the Holy Spirit) the neighbor (relation of proximity, the Word) as yourself (person, the Holy Spirit). Thus, *in divinis*, the Holy Spirit leads to the Son as to the Spirit's own heart; but likewise, on earth, human charity is another way for the Spirit to effect the same revelation.

We come now to the functioning of the Word. To love the neighbor, as we have said, is to discover that a person is a relation of proximity. To be possible, such a discovery requires a logical basis, which is truly provided by the idea of subsistent relations, insofar as the Divine Person is identical to a *Relation*. As we have seen, we can with good reason appropriate for the Word a prototypical function of relation — and conversely, as we will see later, the Holy Spirit shows us how a relation can be a *Person*. Therefore we need to connect the specific basis of the person, seen as a relation of proximity, with the Word, the basis that makes it possible for others to be transformed into the neighbor. In other words, the discovery of the neighbor is the discovery of the Word. Without doubt this discovery is the work of the Holy Spirit, of the act of love, but what is revealed somehow 'preexists' — just as the Word hypostatically "precedes" the Holy Spirit — and constitutes its meaning and its purpose. The act of love is effected with a view to revealing the immutable relation of proximity that is, in truth, no longer altogether of the order of love, but of the order of what love accomplishes: knowledge. Already we see — and we will see it better later — that love is the doorway of gnosis, that love leads to knowledge, that the Holy Spirit leads to the Word; but also, in the alchemy of the spiritual man, love is the pneumatization (Holy Spirit) of the intellect (*Logos*).[4]

2. The Hypostasis of the Word is the Real Basis for the Relation of Proximity

Now we need to examine not just the logical basis, but also the ontological basis of 'proximity' for this function of the Word. Here the most interesting considerations will become apparent, and it is from this that we will harvest the fruit of previous analyses.

We will start with this idea: because of the presence of immensity, the Word is not truly the basis for the relation of proximity. The reason for this is that the presence of immensity is that of the Divine Essence, which excludes of itself the distinction of hypostases, unless we attribute it to the Father in his role as the prototypical Godhead. But, even then, it could not be distinctively allocated to the Son. Additionally, we should point out that in considering the relation of proximity, we have left behind the order of 'natural' charity (however supernatural in its unknown essence), so as to pass to the subjective order of fraternal charity, that which is not only the love of other people, but also a search for the 'neighbor'. Spiritual awareness is therefore implied. In other words, we will no longer consider charity 'objectively' but 'subjectively', as a properly *Christian* act. And therefore it will no longer involve the atheist, who never has access as such to this properly religious dimension and for whom there is no neighbor.

This is why the relation of proximity requires the personal presence of the Word, the prototypical relation of proximity. But even more, since an essentially *Christian* dimension is involved here, it calls for the presence of the Christic Word and, we say, necessitates the Incarnation/Redemption; for how, once the presence of immensity is set aside, could the Word be present, in person, to the act of

---

4 All of the themes of this study are closely linked: they are only different reverberations, on different planes, of a unique theme: the Holy Spirit, the hypostatic Love of the Father and the Son.

Christian love if not by becoming personally incarnate and by remaining, through his grace, as the specific basis for the religious way that he has founded? It is a *fact* that Christ Jesus, the human incarnation of the second Hypostasis, is the founder of Christianity. It is a fact, which is to say that no *a priori* deduction could have accounted for it; one can only start from it, as from an irreducible datum. This fact is, however, not unintelligible. Quite the contrary.

How appropriate, then, that it is the second Hypostasis who becomes incarnate. The Incarnation is essentially a work of mediation: Jesus is *mediator Dei et hominum*, "mediator between God and man," according to St. Paul's definition (1 Tim 2:5). Now the function of mediator is obviously connected to the function of prototypical relation, the Christic Word being the *medium quo*, the means by which the relation between God and man can be reestablished, because he is the *medium quo* eternally, the means by which the Divine Essence enters into relation with itself. It is through the Christic Word, the Mediator by essence, that people enter into a relation of proximity with each other; it is through Him too that they enter into a relation of proximity with God. It is in Jesus Christ that we love God, but it is also in Him that man becomes God's neighbor; it is through the humanity of the Son that God can love all men. This is not to subject the incarnation of the second Hypostasis to a reasoned necessity, but simply to 'read' the mystery itself as an intelligible sign. The presence of the Christic Word as an ontological basis for the relation of proximity is therefore essentially dependent on the Incarnation, and is impossible without it. It is an effect of the Incarnation. No one can say "my neighbor," if not through Christ. Hence the love of one's neighbor is no longer a participation in the Word by (supernatural) 'nature', but a participation by grace, since the Incarnation is wholly of the order of grace and not of the order of nature. Grace, however, does not destroy nature; it fulfills it.

3. The Love of Neighbor is Quasi-sacramental

Our analysis thus leads to a very clear understanding of how charity can truly be a spiritual way. Having arrived at these summits, let us cast a glance backward and survey the road traversed. To love one's neighbor is to enter, quite truly, into the Christic Word, is to be quite truly established in the relation of proximity, is to participate quite truly — to let oneself be traversed by — the hypostatic Relation. Such a love has also something of the quasi-sacramental about it, and this is surely the reason why such a love seems, in the eyes of so many Christians today, to take the place of all religion. However, if we accept this, we not only destroy love but even render it impossible. For its quasi-sacramentality is dependent, as we have said, on the Incarnation and, hence, on the *continuance of the Incarnation* in the sacraments communicated by the Church. To be able to encounter Christ in our brothers, where (with respect to our spiritual awareness) he is only 'in potency', we need *first* to meet him in the sacraments where he is 'in act'. Only under the effect of the *act*-ual sacramental presence will the charitable presence be actualized. Precisely because it is a spiritual way, entry into the relation of proximity claims for itself, under pain of being totally impossible, the grace of the actual presence of the Christic Word in the sacraments and, most especially, in the Eucharist. Every spiritual way becomes increasingly aware of the *actualness* of a Reality that was, to begin with, only faith and hope. But it is strictly impossible for such a dawning of awareness to occur unless this very reality is bestowed *in act*, under one form or another, on the conscious being, for nothing can be brought from potency to act if not by a being in act.

4. The Neighbor is Christ because Christ is the Neighbor

We will conclude by showing what light these principles shed upon several Gospel passages. It seems that these texts will thus receive a clear and precise sense, and interpretations based on the deadly confusions of 'triumphalist' charity will be better avoided.

If we again consider the parable of the Good Samaritan, a conclusion (which happens to confirm our speculative analysis) will become quite obvious. In it the two previously advanced interpretations are combined in a most profound way, which is none other than the traditional interpretation enriched with all the just-deduced theological significance. Christ is indeed the 'neighbor' — since the Good Samaritan designates Christ in particular, or since he represents others — because there is no neighbor outside of the Christic Word, who is the Relation of proximity, and because others are the neighbor only by participation in the Christic Relation of proximity. The other elements of the parable are now recognized and the need for their presence becomes apparent: the Good Samaritan, who comes from 'elsewhere' than Jewish territory, is the incarnation of the Christic Word who comes down from Heaven; by the grace of the Incarnation the *participated* presence of the hypostatic neighbor is made possible. The wine and oil which heal the traveler's wounds are, as we have just seen, the sacraments needed, being *in act*, to actualize the spiritual awareness of the Divine Proximity.

We should also look at those texts where Christ declares that he is the true subject of charitable acts: "Who welcomes you welcomes me, and who welcomes me welcomes the one who sent me" (Matt 10:40). "Whoever welcomes a little child such as this [or a man become a child] for my name's sake, it is I whom he welcomes" (Matt 17:5). "Amen, I say to you, in the measure that you did it to one of these, the least of my brothers, you did it for me" (Matt 25:40). We might, with respect to these texts, be content with a vague understanding that emotionally identifies others with Christ. We might also — and this is the whole deviation of modernist charity — superimpose upon the texts the categories of Marxist sociology and transform the "least" into the "proletariat." Lastly, we might — and this is more properly the subversion of triumphalist charity — identify God with others, making of others the only God of a new religion. These last two interpretations obviously negate all spiritual charity and, hence, all the 'objective' charity that is its visible manifestation; they do not correspond then to any possibility. The first kind of charity is all that remains. But, such as it is, this charity offers too little speculative consistency not to fall sooner or later into the heresies and apostasies of Modernism. Unquestionably, the affirmations of Christ find a direct echo in the Christian soul; the heart is nobly stirred and rejoices that Christ's words confer such a dimension on an act of fraternal love, be it only the gift of a glass of water. Before so dazzling an identification, the intellect believes that it must fall silent in order to let our inmost soul speak. But at the same time — and this only seems paradoxical by lack of reflection — such a simple emotional understanding does not grasp the *metaphysical reason* for these declarations; rather it sees only hyperbole, a divine exaggeration whose entire value resides in the

powerful impetus it gives to the duties of charity. Emotional charity
confidently accepts, for itself, the most dizzying ellipses, and this is
one of them; but this charity can also go mentally hand-in-hand with
a prosaic and anti-mystical rationalism. To the contrary, we need to
give Christ's declarations their entire metaphysical dimension: "It is
to Me that you have done it": not to the Father or the Holy Spirit,
but to the second Hypostasis, for, by virtue of the hypostatic union
of the divine and human natures in the unique Hypostasis of the Son,
there is only one Self in Christ Jesus. And it could not be otherwise,
precisely because to love the neighbor is to enter into the relation of
proximity, because this relation of proximity is the Divine Word, and
because outside of Him such a relation could not exist. Through his
Word, then, Christ himself comes to confirm our analysis. Unless we
attribute only a symbolic and moral value to these words, we clearly
need to admit their eminent theological import. Must we then fall
into the perversions of triumphalist charity — it also attributes a doctrinal value to these words — which draws from them the basis for a
religion of the neighbor, which it would be best to call *the religion of
others*, since it puts others in the place of God? No. What is not yet
understood is that the aim of the act of love is not 'others' as such,
but others as neighbor. Now what are others as neighbor? Quite precisely it is others insofar as they are, in a sense under the heading of
occasional cause, the means for entering into the relation of proximity.
They are not the aim of the act of love, nor am I its true source. The
last cause and the first is the Divine Neighbor himself, that hypostatic
Proximity which, so as to unfold its effects in the relative order, utilizes both others and myself as created supports for uncreated Proximity. And, since we have spoken of the quasi-sacramentality of the
'neighbor', let us say that others are as if the matter of proximity, while
the Word is its eternal form.[5]

We can state with great accuracy that such is the Christic basis of
charity. However, having arrived at this basis, we run the risk of no
longer understanding the 'inverse' relationship that joins charity to its

5   As is known, form and matter are analogically distinguished in the sacraments;
thus, in the sacrament of Penance, its matter is the external acts of the penitent, the
avowal of faults, while its form is the absolution. In Baptism the matter is the water
of ablution and the form is the baptismal words.

basis. At the core of the pure necessity of the Logos, the prototypical relation, we need to discover the mysterious movement of love and its gratuity; after discovering the basis of charity, we should also discover the charity of its basis. This reversal is effected in the person of the Holy Spirit. We have said that the Holy Spirit is the last word of the Trinity, its perfection and fulfillment. But this fulfillment is endless; this last word is coeternal with the first. Within it is effected the 'conversion' of the Divine Essence that is returned to the Father through the Son, for the Trinity is superabundant life. And our account, wedded to the movement of the Trinitarian circumincession, must now show how the Holy Spirit is eternal Love's point of departure.

15

The Hypostatic and Maternal Functions of the Holy Spirit

THE FOLLOWING CONSIDERATIONS ARE EVEN more unusual than those just set out. In truth, the person of the Holy Spirit has never finished yielding up to us all of His secrets. But surely the time has come to deepen the theology of the divine *Pneuma*, and to enrich ourselves not only from the tradition of the Ancients, but also from the remarks of more recent theologians; not only from the Latin tradition, but also from the treasures of Greek theology.

I. THE SCRIPTURAL BASIS FOR THE HYPOSTATIC FUNCTION

1. The Hypostatic Function in Man

In declaring that the Word is the prototype of the subsistent relation we mean this: the Son gives us an understanding of how a person can be a relation. Now declaring, with theology, that the Holy Spirit is the bond of Love of the Father and the Son, we mean this: the Holy Spirit gives us an understanding of how a bond can be a person; and this is why we have said that the Holy Spirit was like the prototype of the Person *in divinis* — or even that He preeminently exercised a hypostatic function. In its revelation of the Holy Spirit, the New Testament seems to suggest this hypostatic function. If we consider all the scriptural data concerning him, and all the elaborations of the Eastern and Western theologians,[1] one statement clearly stands out: the only term certainly attributed to the Third Person by Scripture is 'Holy Spirit'. We should be instructed first, then, by meditating on this term. Now what is spirit? It is that which inspires. The idea of inspiration contains two elements: the idea of an internal principle

---

1   The already-cited book by Lavocat, *L'Ésprit de Vérité et d'Amour*, identifies many of these indications (184).

(the prefix 'in-'), and the idea of a movement, the effect of something that moves from within — a dynamic interiority. Such is the notion of spirit. This is also why this notion is so difficult to grasp, for the spirit is in some way at the heart of all our proceedings; it moves us from within, it is truly more intimate to ourselves than ourselves, it *precedes us in interiority*, it is 'already there'; one can grasp it only through itself; it is the spirit who awakens us to the awareness of spirit, and therefore it cannot truly become an object for religious consciousness, which presupposes it in all its operations. It is preeminently the transcendent person.

Scripture witnesses to this: St. Paul affirms the hypostatic function of the Holy Spirit in its relation with the human soul when he says: "I bend the knee before the Father ... in order that He agree to strengthen in you, by his Spirit, the inner man" (Eph 3:14–16). Christ himself also seems to suggest this function: "The Spirit of Truth which the world cannot receive ... you, you know him, because He dwells with you and because He is in you" (John 14:17). In the same way Christ connects Spirit and interiority: "According to the words of Scripture, from his bosom will flow rivers of living water. Now this he said of the Spirit" (John 7:39). Lastly, we can equally identify the kingdom of God, *which is within us*, with the Holy Spirit. Christ says in fact: "If it is by the Spirit of God that I chase out demons, the kingdom of God has already come to you" (Matt 12:29), a saying which the Greek Fathers relate to this other one: "the kingdom of God does not come in an observable manner, as if one could say: it is here, or: it is there; for the kingdom of God is within you" (Luke 17:20–21).[2] St. Cyril of Alexandria thus writes: "Here [Matthew's text on the demons], I believe, Christ calls 'the kingdom of God' the divine work accomplished in the Holy Spirit, or perhaps the Holy Spirit Himself, which would be in perfect harmony with this saying: the kingdom of God is within you."[3]

---

2 Today *entos umon, intra vos* is often translated by "in the midst of you," Christ designating Himself in this way in the midst of the Pharisees as the kingdom. This sense is not to be excluded. However, in a general manner, *entos* signifies 'within', 'inside'. If the Kingdom cannot be localized (neither *here* nor *there*), this is precisely because it is not in space but comes into the heart's interiority.

3 Cf. St. Cyril of Alexandria, *De Trinitate*, VII, in PG 75:1114.

2. The Hypostatic Function in God

But can we go further and find in Scripture the indication of a hypostatic function *in divinis*? Recall that the very name of Spirit seems to point in this direction — for what is Spirit if not that auto-dynamism we will see as constituting the ultimate note of the person, or else that which, ever interior and invisible, is known from its effects and productions? Now is this not what Christ said in connection with the sin against the Spirit: "for it is by the fruit that the tree is recognized" (Matt 12:33)? But above all there is the text from St. Paul that seems to imply such an interpretation: "We speak the wisdom of God in a mystery, a wisdom which is hidden, which God ordained before the world, unto our glory. . . . But to us God hath revealed [this] by his Spirit. For the Spirit searcheth all things, yea, the deep things of God. For what man knoweth the things of a man, but the spirit of a man that is in him? So the things also that are of God, no man knoweth, but the Spirit of God" (1 Cor 2:7–11). If therefore the spirit is alone in knowing what is within the interior of man — because only the spirit is within the interior of man and even more because it is this very interiority, and since this is equally true of God, inasmuch as the Spirit is the most secret interiority of the Divine Essence — then it seems to us that it would be difficult to avoid seeing in the divine *Pneuma* of St. Paul the prototypical face of the person.

The theological and philosophical examination of the notion of person leads us toward the same truth. Here we rediscover the same connected notions of mystery, secret, interiority, life. Now for the proof of this.

II. THE THEOLOGICAL BASIS FOR THE HYPOSTATIC FUNCTION

1. The Person is Unnameable

Let us then consider the person. We will not enter into the details of a discussion about nature and hypostasis, which would require quite lengthy explanations. We will only say this: the person is always 'behind' what can be said of it. It is the completely unobservable subject that produces and sustains everything in the being that can be attributed to

301

it. As such it is imperceptible, and this is why the name of person fits it better than any other, for in Greek as in Latin it signifies the mask and therefore what is masked, what *sounds through* (*per-son*), as that through which someone speaks. Actually this name is itself a mask; this name does not express the reality so designated, for this reality is inexpressible. In its very utterance the term hints at this reality while openly declining to act as a *proprium nomen*, while openly betraying its inadequacy. The person is nobody. It has no name, yet all names are suitable. Now this is precisely a characteristic of the Holy Spirit. Already we have seen St. Thomas declare that the Holy Spirit has no proper name. St. Gregory of Nazianzus,[4] starting from the same evidence, understands that this implies for the Holy Spirit the possibility of receiving all names. "I am seized with dread," he says, "when I think of the abundance of titles . . . the Spirit of God, the Spirit of Christ, the Mind of Christ . . . the Spirit of adoption. . . . The Creator-Spirit, who by Baptism and by resurrection creates anew . . . who bloweth where and to what extent He listeth . . . who giveth light, or rather is the very Light and Life; who maketh temples; who deifieth. . . . He is another Paraclete in the sense of another God." Whereas St. Symeon the New Theologian sings the apophatism[5] of the Third Person: "Come, true light; come, eternal life; come, hidden mystery; come, treasure without name; come, unutterable thing; come, unknowable person . . . come, invisible one, wholly intangible and impalpable. . . . Thy name, so greatly desired and constantly proclaimed, none is able to say what it is. . . . Come, breath of my own life, consolation of my lowly heart."[6]

2. The Person is Manifested as Will

This secret, mysterious, and unnameable character of the Holy Spirit, which shows how He can be regarded as the pre-eminent Person, is found again in the Scholastic terms that designate the person

4 St. Gregory of Nazianzus, *Orat.* XXXI (*Theologica V*), 29, in PG 36:159BC; cited by Vladimir Lossky, *The Mystical Theology of the Eastern Church* (Crestwood, NY: St. Vladimir's Seminary Press, 1976), 163. At the beginning of paragraph 29, not quoted by Lossky, St. Gregory declares: "All names given by Scripture to the Most High, sovereign Lord of all things, it applies all of them to the Holy Spirit, except for that of Father and Son, because the Divine Persons must not be confused."
 5 Apophatism consists in naming God while showing how He cannot be named.
 6 Cf. Lossky, *Mystical Theology*, 160–61.

and which St. Thomas defines in the *Prima Pars* of the *Summa*:[7] hypo-stasis, sub-stance, sup-positum. But we must weigh up what distinguishes the person from all of the preceding terms.[8] Certainly the person is a hypostasis, a substance, a subsistence, a suppositum. However, to all of these ideas, it adds that of free will. The person is grasped in all of his perfection only when one adds the notion of sovereign and autonomous agent to that of reasonable substance. "Further still, in a more special and perfect way, the particular and the individual [in an absolute sense where God is involved] are found in the rational substances [that is, *in divinis*, substances of an intellectual nature and not in the sense of discursive reason][9] which have dominion over their own actions [*dominum sui actus*]; and which are not only made to act, like others; but which can act of themselves; for actions belong to singulars. Therefore also the individuals of the rational nature have a special name even among other substances; and this name is 'person.'"[10] Thus the person is properly defined only through the dominion or mastery over action. That which is moved by itself: this is the ultimate distinction of the person.

The same idea is found again in Greek theology. If the human person were identical to human nature, then fallen nature could never be saved. It is clearly necessary that the person be, in one way or another, free with respect to his nature in order to lose or save it. The proper sense of the human person resides then in "the fact that we are free from necessity, and not in bondage to any natural power, but have decision in our own power as we please; for virtue is a voluntary thing, subject to no dominion."[11] This is not to say however that we conceive

7   *Summa Theologiae* I, q. 29, a. 1.

8   One of the major conclusions of the joint work edited by Bernard Meunier, *La personne et le christianisme ancien*, is that the Latin *persona*, with no philosophical past, endowed Latin theology with a concept ultimately more efficacious than that of hypostasis for designating what is the spiritual being's mystery of interiority.

9   "It may be said that God has a rational 'nature', if reason be taken to mean, not discursive thought, but in a general sense, an intelligent nature. But God cannot be called an 'individual' in the sense that His individuality comes from matter; but only in the sense which implies incommunicability" (*Summa Theologiae* I, q. 29, a. 3, ad 4).

10   *Summa Theologiae* I, q. 29, a. 1.

11   St. Gregory of Nyssa, *On the Making of Man*, XVI, 11 (trans. H. A. Wilson); PG 44:184. Ch. XVI of *On the Making of Man* (col. 178–88) is devoted to man, the image of God. If Sartrean existentialism were less willfully ignorant, it would have found in theology a doctrine of the transcendence of the person and of his freedom

of the person more as will than as intelligence, but that the person is *revealed* more directly by will than by intelligence. There is in the intelligence something of the super-individual, by essence, which seems to dissolve the point-like quality of the person in the light of knowledge, while the will is, by definition, the affirmation of self and includes an obscure and unintelligible element by which person becomes presence. Thus the person, imperceptible in itself, reveals its presence through its effects. It is that which exerts, moves, acts; that which, as sheer interiority, can only be inferred from exteriority where it consents to radiate. But we see then how these characteristics of the person are appropriate for the Holy Spirit, He who proceeds from the Father by mode of will; He who is Freedom and not necessity like the *Logos*—if one can make this distinction in God—for the Spirit blows where He will; He who is preeminently the Active One, the Doer of all things, who in the beginning 'broods' over the primordial waters of Universal Existence, just as He overshadows the virginal substance of Mary.

3. The Person of the Holy Spirit is an Imageless Image

But the hypostatic function of the Holy Spirit can also be established by a third consideration which is, in truth, only a return to the two previous ones relative to unnameability and will: this has to do with the Holy Spirit as an imageless image. It is chiefly Orthodox theology that has drawn from this formulation its implied consequences. "The Son," says St. John Damascene, "is the image of the Father and the Spirit is the image of the Son."[12] Lossky, who quotes this statement,[13] comments on it in these terms: "It follows that the third hypostasis of the Trinity is the only one not having His image in another person." We could say: the Father is the non-reflecting-reflected, the Son is the reflecting-reflected, and the Holy Spirit is the reflecting-nonreflected.

This perspective, although the rightful property of the East's theological treasury,[14] is not however totally absent from the Latin

---

with respect to human nature even more ample and serene than the simplistic and melodramatic theory Sartre has presented.

12   *On the Orthodox Faith*, I, 13, in PG 94:856.

13   Lossky, *Mystical Theology*, 160.

14   This is an opportunity to say how a certain ecumenism seems dangerous for the Latins as well as for the East. The wealth of Christianity is partly in its variety. The extraordinary spiritual dynamism of Orthodox theology is a precious benefit for

tradition. St. Thomas writes: "the Son is properly called the Image because He proceeds by way of a word [since His procession by mode of intellect implies likeness to its principle], although the Holy Spirit also is like to the Father."[15] Yet if the Son is image as Word, which is to say as person, the Holy Spirit is not image as Holy Spirit but as God, and this is why it can be said here more readily that the third hypostasis is the image of the Father, source of the divinity, and not only that of the Son as the expression of St. John Damascene would have it.[16] Being non-reflected, the Holy Spirit remains, like the image itself, mysterious and 'not manifested'. He is the image or manifestation of what cannot be imaged, of what is eternally unmanifested and unmanifestable *in divinis*. We dare to say: He is the image of the non-image, just as in his procession by mode of will, as eternal Activity, he is the affirmation *of* Non-affirmation. He reveals then — and every revelation supposes a certain immanence — the radical transcendence of the person. He is this very Revelation. He is the revelatory immanence of hypostatic transcendence, as the Father is the transcendence of the immanent Godhead, the rootless root of the Divine Essence, the model-less model which unfolds its infinity as far as the imageless image. And so, just as the immortal person is as if

---

all Christians. But surely the organic unity of the Eastern perspective is incompatible with the organic unity of the Latin perspective, and each one has developed its own virtualities while being *practically* unaware of the other's. Each one also has its own altogether inevitable limits. And it is to be feared that, in wanting to reunite them, we might add the limits of one to the limits of the other, and both will be corrupted: Latin dogmatism will suffocate the mystical spontaneity of the East, and the relative aversion of the East to exterior formulations, its pneumatic 'realism' composed of immediacy and interiority, will accentuate among present-day Westerners a scorn for theology, and will sanction a confusion of the individual soul's movements with the motions of the Holy Spirit. It is good that hatred or scorn cease between Orthodox and Catholics. It is to be hoped that the 'primacy' of the throne of St. Peter be recognized on all sides. But it would be catastrophic for this ecumenism to lead to the destruction of that which forms the irreplaceable specificity of each one.

15 *Summa Theologiae* I, q. 38, a. 2, ad 1; also I, q. 3, a. 2, and *Contra Errores Graecorum*, ch. 10. (Bracketed phrase is author's gloss. — *Trans.*)

16 Actually, for St. John Damascene, the function of image concerns the exterior manifestation of God in the world and not the intra-Trinitarian life; cf. Lossky, *Mystical Theology*, 84–5. But it is not possible to maintain this distinction in an absolute manner, for all that concerns the exterior world must find its sufficient reason in the interior world of the Trinity, and this is why the term 'image' can be adequately transposed from the exterior to the interior for characterizing the subsistent relations.

veiled by the human nature that it receives, and remains invisible, so the Third Hypostasis remains hidden by the image which It reflects. Its reality as image of the Divine Essence is its mask, its *persona*. It reveals while veiling itself, and this is why it is like the prototype of the hypostasis. Finally, utilizing an allied symbolism of the image, we will say that It is the pure mirror, invisible in itself and only made visible by the image it reflects. However, at the same time that the image 'proves' the existence of the mirror, it hides and completely covers it. The mirror is veiled by its own revelation.

Being non-reflected, as we have said, the Holy Spirit expresses the transcendence of the hypostasis. But being a reflector He expresses the blossoming of the Divine Essence. It is then that the hypostatic function becomes hypostatic maternity and we understand that the name of the Holy Spirit is Love and Gift.

III. THE HYPOSTATIC MATERNITY OF THE HOLY SPIRIT

1. Theological Aspects

What better symbol of the Spirit of Love than that of the mirror? Indeed, the mirror is wholly itself in the gift which it makes of the image. Its existence is gift; just as the person of the Holy Spirit is gift and the gift is His Person. But more must be said. Not only is the Holy Spirit gift and love, but He is Gift and Love in such a way that Gift and Love are actually proper names for the Third Hypostasis. "If [Love is] taken personally it is the proper name of the Holy Spirit,"[17] St. Thomas says; and again: "Gift... is the proper name of the Holy Spirit."[18] As we see, everything that is gift and love, the gift being the very act of love, is, in the depths of the Trinity, in direct relation to the Holy Spirit. Now what does the Father do in begetting the Son? He entirely divests Himself of the Divine Essence, as we have said, in order to give it to the Son. And what does the Son do in the relation of filiation? He entirely divests Himself of the Divine Essence in order to return it to the Father. By eternal generation the Divine Essence is *loved* by the Father in the Son; by eternal filiation the Divine Essence

17 *Summa Theologiae* I, q. 37, a. 1.
18 *Summa Theologiae* I, q. 38, a. 2.

is *loved* by the Son in the Father. Thus the Holy Spirit is hypostatic Love and Gift *in which* the Father and the Son are united. We repeat, the Holy Spirit is as if what makes possible the active spiration of the love of the Father and the Son, and this is why theology refers to him as passive spiration. As hypostatic Charity, he makes possible the Love-in-act of the Father for the Son and of the Son for the Father. It is therefore Himself, the Holy Spirit, it is therefore itself, hypostatic Charity, that reveals the Father to the Son and the Son to the Father. He does not beget, but He *delivers* [Fr. *accouche* = birth/delivery] the Son to the Father. Being reflector of the Divine Essence, being the Divine Essence inasmuch as It gives Itself and is loved, He makes it in some way burst forth between the Hypostasis of the Father and that of the Son, and this is why we can truly speak of a hypostatic motherhood.

The expression 'hypostatic motherhood' is borrowed from Father Bulgakov.[19] It belongs to Eastern theology then, and unquestionably runs the risk of seeming strange in the West. And yet this truth, if not the same formulation, is not totally absent from Latin theology. It could be supposed that for St. Thomas, since the Father and the Son are the common principle of the Holy Spirit — which is to say that the Father and the Son are not distinguished in the procession of the Third Hypostasis — it follows that one cannot attribute to the Holy Spirit the function of hypostatic motherhood, namely the function of revealing the Hypostasis of the Father and that of the Son to each other. But St. Thomas writes: "If we consider the spirative power, the Holy Ghost proceeds from the Father and the Son as they are one in the spirative power, which in a certain way signifies the nature with the property.... Nor is there any reason against one property being in two 'supposita' that possess one common nature. But if we consider the 'supposita' of the spiration, then we may say that the *Holy Ghost proceeds from the Father and the Son, [inasmuch as they are] distinct*; for He proceeds from them as the unitive love of both."[20] Consequently it is necessary to say: "because of His kind of procession — the union of love — the Holy Spirit requires a distinction

19 *Chapters on the Trinity*, in Russian; cited by P. Evdokimov in *Woman and the Salvation of the World*, trans. A. P. Gythiel (Crestwood, NY: St. Vladimir's Seminary Press, 1994), 220–21.
20 *Summa Theologiae* I, q. 36, a. 4, ad 1.

between those from whom He proceeds,"[21] for what is indistinct cannot be united. And there are not two loves, one of the Father for the Son and the other of the Son for the Father, but only one, which is the Holy Spirit. John of St. Thomas comments as follows: "by a single act, their common spiration, the Father and the Son are one *in* the Love which proceeds from them."[22] Thus Love is a person and, because Love is a person, it implies a hypostatic distinction in what It unites. It reveals the hypostases to themselves by giving them, by offering them the 'possibility' of being hypostases, since, we repeat, the Father is the hypostatic Father or paternal Hypostasis only inasmuch as He begets the Son, that is only and absolutely inasmuch as He *gives* the Divine Essence to the Son. And the Son is the hypostatic Son or the Hypostasis of filiation only inasmuch as he is begotten by the Father, that is solely and absolutely only inasmuch as he *returns* the Divine Essence to the Father.

Now, as we have said, the Holy Spirit is the image of the Godhead. The Godhead *given* from the Father to the Son and from the Son to the Father is the Holy Spirit. If the Divine Aseity is not closed upon Itself, it is the *Person* of the Holy Spirit who realizes this unifying explosion. This is why the Three are One in a total immanence. As a result, although the Father is the active source and the monarchic origin of the Divine Essence's self-communication, the Holy Spirit, the charitable Hypostasis, is its passive 'condition' through which generation and spiration are co-eternally in act. For surely there is nothing passive (in the privative sense) in God, but it is inasmuch as he is passive spiration that the Holy Spirit is Hypostasis actively and eternally revealing the Father to the Son and the Son to the Father. And we think we have found in St. Thomas the analogy to hypostatic motherhood when he says: "The Holy Spirit is said to be the bond [*nexus*] of the Father and Son, inasmuch as He is Love; since the Father loves Himself and the Son with one Love, and conversely, there is expressed in the Holy Spirit, as Love, the relation of the Father to the Son, and conversely."[23]

---

21 St. Thomas, *Responsio ad magistrum Joannes de Vercellis de 108 articulis*, q. 25.
22 *Cursus theo.* q. XXXVI, disp. XV, a. 4, n. S, 6 and 26.
23 *Summa Theologiae* I, q. 37, a. 1, ad 3.

2. *Its Foundations in Scripture and Tradition*

What remains to be asked is whether or not there exists, in the tradition of Holy Scripture and the Fathers, any basis for a doctrine of the Holy Spirit's hypostatic motherhood. This is what we shall briefly examine now.

First of all notice how this notion of pneumatic motherhood touches on two fundamental themes: that of a maternal and therefore feminine aspect of the Holy Spirit, and that of His revelatory function *in divinis*, for we have understood these two themes previously as closely connected and even altogether inseparable.

The first theme should not surprise us: obviously there is neither masculine nor feminine, properly speaking, in God. However there is certainly found in Him the principle of positive and distinct perfections which represent man and woman on earth. There is absolutely no question then of defining the Person of the Holy Spirit as feminine in contrast to that of the Father as masculine. This is to say that if we seek for the divine prototype of feminine perfections, it will be found, but without sexual polarizations of any kind, in the Trinitarian function of the Holy Spirit, rather than in that of the Father or the Son. The use of an analogous term, such as that of hypostatic motherhood, is found to be justified then at the same time.

In the second verse of Genesis it is said that "the Spirit of God brooded over the surface of the waters." As we know: *Ruah Elohim* is feminine in Hebrew. True, the exegetes refuse to draw any conclusion from this, unless this femininity points to the *Ruah Elohim* not as a person but as a thing. Yet this 'brooding' activity seems to indeed confirm the *Ruah*'s feminine role, obviously on condition that one accept this translation of *m(e)rahepheth*.[24] We think that in any case, and in conformity with Sacred Scripture, which admits of multiple related meanings, it is impossible to exclude this translation, a translation which, besides, perfectly agrees with what Revelation teaches us about the 'Comforter', the One who "covers with His shadow" the pure and virgin water of the Marian substance, so that, not begetting

---

24   This is the case for, among others, Edmund Fleg, *Le livre du commencement* (Paris: Éd. de Minuit, 1959).

(which depends upon the Father exclusively) but effecting the conception of the Son, according to the words of the Creed, "the only Son is conceived of the Holy Spirit."[25]

Next we must recall this saying which the Gospel according to the Hebrews placed on the lips of Jesus: "The Savior Himself says, 'My mother [who is] the Holy Spirit took me just now [in Christ's temptation in the desert] by one of my hairs and carried me off to the great mount Tabor.'"[26] This apocryphal gospel, whose existence we know of from references by Clement of Alexandria and through the quotations of Origen, Eusebius, and above all St. Jerome, poses problems variously resolved. However, two points are to be retained: on the one hand its antiquity, as it certainly dates back to the end of the first century—it is perhaps even the most ancient of the apocryphas[27]—and on the other, as Father Manteau-Bonamy remarks, this affirmation of the maternal aspect of the Holy Spirit in no way astonishes St. Jerome who, to the contrary, "has a great esteem for this non-canonical Gospel."[28] "*The Gospel According to the Hebrews*," says St. Jerome, "was written in the Chaldean and even Syriac [Aramaic] language, but in Hebrew characters, and it is in use to this day among the Nazarenes; some think that it is even from the Apostles, but the majority presume that it is from Matthew."[29] It even seemed so important to St. Jerome that he made a translation of it into Greek and Latin.[30] Here is moreover what is said today about this Gospel: "In the orthodox Judeo-Christian communities circulated a gospel which was, for the faithful of these Churches, simply the *Gospel*, for

25 On this subject, read Rev. Manteau-Bonamy's book *La Vierge Marie et le Saint-Esprit* (Paris: Lethielleux, 1970), one of the best contemporary works on the theology of the Virgin.

26 Cited by Origen, *Commentary on St. John*, 2:12; trans. A. Menzies, in *Ante-Nicene Fathers of the Christian Church*, vol. 9 (New York: Charles Scribner's Sons, 1912), 329.

27 Cf. Jean Daniélou, *Theology of Jewish Christianity* (London: Darton, Longman & Todd, 1964), 22–23.

28 Manteau-Bonamy, *La Vierge Marie*, 29.

29 St. Jerome, *Contra Pelagius* III, 2, PL 23:597; the term 'Nazarene' is applied to a Jewish Christian community of the first century that combined Mosaism and Christianity.

30 *De viris illustribus*, II; PL 23:611. French translation by Delphine Viellard, *Jérôme, Les hommes illustres* (Paris: Migne, 2009), 61. Recent criticism (Pléiade, 455) obviously does not believe in the existence of these translations.

they knew only that one. People foreign to these communities called it the *Gospel According to the Hebrews*, since it was in use among the Christians speaking Hebrew (or, more exactly, Aramaic)."[31]

Lastly, we can quote, along with Father Manteau-Bonamy, a text from one of the first Syriac Fathers, Aphraates (mid-fourth century). His works constitute the most ancient monument of Syriac literature. He was nicknamed the "Sage of Persia."[32] This perfectly orthodox Father—he was one of the first to explicitly and vigorously teach the Divinity of the Holy Spirit and His perfect distinctness from the Father and the Son—declares: "From the law we have heard it said: 'man will abandon his father and mother; and he will attach himself to his spouse, and they will become one single flesh.' In truth this is a great and sublime prophecy. Who are the father and mother then that one abandons when one takes a spouse? The meaning is as follows: the man, inasmuch as he has no woman, loves and honors God his father and the Holy Spirit his mother: and there is no other love in him. But from the time that he has taken a woman, the man abandons father and mother, namely those whom we have just designated."[33]

Finally there is the text of the *Apostles' Creed*[34] which teaches that "Jesus Christ, the only Son [of God], our Lord, was conceived of the Holy Spirit." This creed is known to enjoy the highest authority and includes such precious truths that in the first centuries it was forbidden to write it down and it could only be transmitted orally:[35] *Qui conceptus est de Spiritu Sancto, natus est ex Maria Virgine.* Here again, following the commentaries of Father Manteau-Bonamy, we will say that each of the Creed's affirmations can be considered from seperate

31   *Dictionnaire de la Bible*, Supplement, vol. I, ed. Pirot, Robert, et al. (Paris: Letouzey et Ané, 1926), col. 471.

32   Cf. *Patrologia Syriaca*, vol. 1, ed. R. Graffin et al. (Paris: Firmin-Didot, 1926), XII.

33   This involves a text on virginity; cf. *Demonstratio*, XVIII, 10, *De virginitate et sanctitate. Patrologia Syriaca*, vol. I, col. 839 (we have used the Latin translation of the Syriac text).

34   Although it is not possible to historically prove the *apostolic* origin of this Creed, it is however beyond doubt that it goes back to highest antiquity. A summary of the history of the Creed is found in Dumeige, *La Foi catholique*, 5. A more substantial account is given by Father H. de Lubac in *The Christian Faith: An Essay on the Structure of the Apostles' Creed* (San Francisco CA: Ignatius Press, 1986), 19–53.

35   Cf. H. de Lubac, *The Christian Faith*, 22.

sides. This is in fact because birth from the Virgin Mary is manifested temporally, while the *Conceptus est de Spiritu Sancto* is eternal. This springs from both Scripture and theology at once. From Scripture since St. Paul writes: "Blessed be the God and Father of Our Lord Jesus Christ, who has blessed us with spiritual blessings in heavenly places, in Christ: as he chose us in him *before the foundation of the world*" (Eph 1:3–4). From theology, for, if the Son is conceived of the Holy Spirit, this is so with a view to the Incarnation, however the mission or sending, as we have said, is brought back in the end to the procession. And so, as for himself, the Son is eternally conceived of the Holy Spirit and born of the Virgin Mary. "His physical conception, in Mary, is the revelation, the manifestation of His divine *conception* in the Holy Spirit."[36] If the Father is the eternal Conceiver, the Holy Spirit is the hypostatic Conception. "When the Holy Spirit is sent to the Virgin, in order that she may conceive Christ, it is not He Himself, the Spirit of the Father, who changes, but it is she, remaining Virgin all the while, who becomes pregnant with the Son of God. Thus the Holy Spirit assumes in time the attribute of the divine source of motherhood. . . ."[37] In other words, the Gift that God makes of his Son in Jesus Christ is eternal, and therefore Christ is eternally conceived of the Holy Spirit, but for us He is revealed in the historical and truly human Incarnation *ex Maria Virgine*, who receives from the Holy Spirit, because He possesses it from all eternity, *the relation of divine motherhood*.

---

36 Manteau-Bonamy, *La Vierge Marie*, 25.
37 Ibid., 27.

16

A Metaphysical Synthesis of the 'Mysterium Caritatis'

WE HAVE NOW REACHED THE METAPHYSICAL pole of charity. All of the themes we have set out are to find their fulfillment here. This is what we will try to show, while collecting all the threads of our meditation and weaving them together in a manner as systematic as possible, so as to reveal the irreducibly mysterious dimension of Charity.

Our analysis has finally identified three basic notions that we think will aid us in elaborating a theology of charity. These notions, which have provided us with an exegesis to the parable of the Good Samaritan, are the following: 1. — a dynamic element, the energy of love or charitable power or ecstatic movement; 2. — a static element, the relation of proximity, pre-existing and foundational; 3. — an element at once static and dynamic, the person. And so the divine commandment is composed of these three elements: love (element 1) your neighbor (element 2) as yourself (element 3). The relation of proximity (element 2) is of the supernatural order by 'Christic institution', since there is no relation of proximity outside of Jesus Christ. The person (element 3) belongs at once to the natural and supernatural orders, in which it is supernatural by 'nature' or essence, not by grace (God having created it transcendent to nature). However, as we will see, only grace can actualize this supernature. Lastly, the power of love (element 1) is, in a certain manner, neutral with respect to the nature/supernature distinction, and this is why, in its operations, it can confuse the two orders.

Inasmuch as it operates according to the natural order, or even inasmuch as it is neutral with respect to this distinction, we have related charitable power, the act of love, to the ecstatic Essence of the Trinity. Element 2, relation, we have related to the Word, the prototypical relation. What remains is to relate element 3, the person, to the Holy Spirit, since the Holy Spirit is the pre-eminent hypostasis.

313

Further, making a return to origins, we will also relate Him to element 1, but now in its supernatural operation, which is to say that inasmuch as the act of love is 'revelatory' of the relation of proximity, since the Holy Spirit, by his hypostatic motherhood, exercises, in the bosom of the Trinity, an analogous function. In this way personal love is led back to essential love, to the ecstatic Essence revealing to Itself its own ecstasy.

However, in order to glimpse as much as possible how human charity is in this way ontologically founded *in divinis*, we must show how human charity's demands are fulfilled and its imperfections overcome in divine super-perfection, which implies, as will be recalled at least briefly, the structure and limits of human love under its dual natural and supernatural form. We are therefore led first to envisage the plane of natural human love; secondly, the plane of supernatural human love; thirdly, the plane of divine love; and finally, in fourth place, supernatural love's mode of participation in its divine ground.

I. NATURAL LOVE

From a general point of view, and regardless of the nature/supernature distinction, we can consider three forms of love, expressed by the Greek terms *eros*, *philia*, and *agape*: *eros* or love between man and woman, *philia* or friendship, *agape* or fraternal charity. These are relative distinctions, for no form excludes the other, but neither are they baseless as distinctions. We will examine each one from the viewpoint of the tri-elementary structure with which we started. Unquestionably this examination poses a difficulty, for how can this structure, valid for Christian charity proper and including a supernatural element, still be valid for *eros*, *philia*, or natural charity? What then becomes of the relation of proximity which we have expressly ascribed to the Word Incarnate? Actually we have already answered this question. In *eros*, *philia*, or natural charity the relation is not a relation of proximity. As we will see, a relation of unity is involved in the first case and one of unicity in the second — whereas supernatural charity provides a typical structure for all love. And so we must rediscover this structure in all of love's forms. But, even though it is always possible to speak of person and energy, for these non-sacred forms we should speak of a relation whose type will have to be determined each time.[1]

1. Eros

As for *eros*, we must first point out that it can be seen from the viewpoint of nature[2] or from the viewpoint of structure properly speaking. A necessary distinction, for *eros* is the most natural of all loves, the one where nature plays the greatest role. That is to say, analysis according to structure is less instructive with regard to this than analysis according to nature.

According to nature, *eros* manifests the cosmic masculine/feminine polarity, whose symbolic prototype is the polarity of Heaven and Earth. The energy of *eros*, which leads the sexes towards one another, has its principle in the desire to reunite the human being's two halves. As such, this love is not love of a person but of the masculine or feminine nature as such.

According to structure, that is independently of the sex of the lovers, the energy of love is at first a feeling that possesses only a purely subjective certainty. This certainty is also rightly 'blinding': love is perfectly sure of itself, or rather it is this very certainty; not being shared seems unintelligible to it. But, and here is its contradiction: love, in its pure movement, is a tendency *ad aliud*, a desire for what is not one's self. It burns to prove its truth, for it suffers within itself from an essential lack of objectivity that only recognition by the other can make up for. When this recognition occurs it comes as such a 'novelty' from the start, it seems so miraculous, that it is impossible to see only a result or a product of the erotic impulse here. It is a grace which comes from elsewhere, from beyond *eros*, and which

---

1 As we see, the nature of love depends on the nature of the relation which determines it principially, just as *in divinis* the Holy Spirit, Divine Love, depends principially, in its procession, on the Word, the prototypical relation.

2 By nature we mean here the essence of a being inasmuch as it accounts for the operations of this being. It does not tally with the nature/supernature distinction. Moreover, it goes without saying that all forms of love can be sacralized. This is the case with *eros* in the sacrament of marriage. Yet remember that of all the Christian sacraments, marriage is the only one not exclusively Christian. Also, it goes without saying that in the present account the words *eros* or 'erotic' absolutely do not have the purely physical meaning attributed to them in modern language. They designate the love of every man for every woman and vice versa.

makes all that preceded it illusory. The consequence of this miracle is *the revelation of the person*, my own as well as someone else's; the *ad aliud* (toward something) becomes *ad alterum* (toward someone). Actually, there can be a complete discontinuity with respect to the energy of *eros* only in *starting* from a free and conscious subjectivity, that is from a person. Things cannot simply *respond* to my call. The demand for erotic objectivity can only be satisfied in its recognition by an autonomous center perfectly free to refuse it. The only elsewhere for self is the elsewhere of another self. Thus, in *eros*, erotic energy makes its appearance as the revealer of the person. And this is also true for my own person, for, although subjectivity might forget itself in the first moment of erotic energy and be somehow identified with it when the response that this energy calls forth occurs, the further side of myself out of which it arises puts myself into myself as its own further side. To be precise, this involves a Revelation in the active sense of the term. I learn to discover the person at the outer limit of erotic dynamics. I experience the living reality of the person as the end claimed by *eros* for its fulfillment. This does not then involve a revelation for philosophical awareness which would reflect *a posteriori* upon a lived fact, but a revelation for a loving awareness which forms an integral part of the lived fact itself. Such a revelation does indeed exist for the philosophical awareness when, for example, there is brought to light that *preexisting relationship of intersubjectivity* in which each consciousness discovers itself by discovering mutual awareness.[3] And yet I have no effective awareness of this intersubjective relationship in particular, unless through a philosophical 'retracing'. It might be said then that the person 'reveals' the relationship, but, in this case, a passive revelation is involved. This is to say that, for an attentive philosophical awareness, the person 'reveals' the prior and subjacent existence of the relationship because its situation demands it, just as heat reveals the presence of fire, but not as light actively reveals it by snatching the existence of a thing from the nothingness

---

3   This thesis, which seems right to us, has been strongly established by phenomenology. Husserl, G. Marcel, Sartre, Nédoncelle, and Buber have given good descriptions of it. The pessimistic conclusions drawn by Sartre (with the other being the indispensable mediator between I and myself, and my awareness the other's prisoner) are in conformity with the sentimental *pathos* of that author.

of night—we will find this distinction again *in divinis*. Let us say, for the moment, that the function of active revelation can be the source of an illusion, which would not be the case for passive revelation. This illusion is that of the creation of a person. Love thinks itself (or wishes itself) the creator of a person, like Pygmalion and his statue. This illusion assumes multiple forms, the most current of which is that of a certain romanticism: "Before meeting you I did not exist. In loving you, I have created you." This desire, or illusion, is natural to *eros*, for its recognition by the other implies that it renounces its own self-sufficient certainty, and puts its fate into another's hands. As it cannot do without a limit however—this is its contradiction, as we mentioned—it has a tendency to want to seize upon the other as an effect of its creative power, or even suppose that the loved person has no existence independent of that loving impulse which brings us outside the indistinctness of the human species.

2. Philia

As for *philia*, it might be said that from the viewpoint of nature, it is essentially based on human nature's specific unity in each individual. It expresses a community, and not a complementary duality like *eros*. If, in *eros*, nature sighs after the unity of the human being, in *philia* nature sighs after the unicity of humanity's essence repeated in the multiplicity of individual subjects. By this we see that both *eros* and *philia* belong to the natural order.

From the viewpoint of the tri-elementary structure, we might say that the dominant element here is not energy, as in *eros*, but the person; and this arises from the difference of roles played by nature in *eros* and *philia* respectively. With *eros* nature is as if cut in two, each half seeking the other with a quasi-impersonal impulse. And that is why this impulse finds its end in the revelation of the person. With *philia* the one nature, multiplied in its subjects, tends to *recognize* its unity despite this multiplicity. The energy, which always expresses the 'voice of nature', is not here then that of a nature vitally seeking to reconstitute its unity, since this unity is unbroken, being entire in each person. The energy of friendship can therefore only be expressed through the person, since it is the multiplicity of persons that seems to contradict the unicity of human nature. And here persons find their end and their limit in the relation which unites them. In *philia* the person is the revealer of relation. Also, *philia* is fulfilled in communicated knowledge. And this is how Christ himself defines it: "I call you friends *because all which I have learned from my Father, I have made it known to you*" (John 15:15). Relation, being of a spiritual nature, can only be revealed in knowledge. Is friendship anything else than the awareness of a bond uniting two people? In this it is quite different from *eros* in which the relation is not consciously posited for itself, in which it is not therefore revealed in the active sense of the term. It is true that in the love between man and woman a relationship can also be discovered, but this comes from *philia*'s ability to be concretely mingled with *eros*, since, as we said at the start, the *eros-philia-agape* distinction is relative. This is a real discovery, then, because in a pure (and abstract) kind of *eros* the relation is in fact 'covered over' or 'hidden' by erotic energy, and because it is hard to distinguish between this *eros* and *philia*. Finally, just as the corruption of *eros* is a corruption of the revelatory function which expresses erotic energy with respect to the person, a function perverted by creative power, so with *philia* the revelatory function the person exercises with respect to relation can be perverted by the creative function. For, as with everything, its strength can be its weakness. This is conveyed quite exactly in the expression: "to form bonds". Friendship, perverted in this way, ceases to be honor rendered to our unique and noble human nature, which unites us despite all of our accepted (because secondary) differences. It craves common acts, identical tastes, similar choices, anything to create this unity. It does not tolerate difference, distance, or silence. It banishes that miraculous confidence through which each friend knows that none of the others are lacking in that human dignity about which their friendship is precisely a celebration.

In each of the preceding cases, as anyone can see, relation is determined by the natural principle of the acts of *eros* or *philia*. The relation pre-existent to the *eros* of lovers is in fact based on the pre-existence of the essence of the prototypical Adam in whom man and woman are united at the world's beginning. "The two shall be one flesh": this is a relation of unity. The relation pre-existent to the *philia* of friends is based on the pre-existence of the unique human nature in which friends recognize each other as identical: this is a relation of unicity.

Now what is the natural principle of worldly charity and the resulting relation? It seems that this principle can only be the person. This does not involve then a natural principle comparable to the preceding two, since the person belongs in a certain manner to the supernatural order.

3. Natural Charity

Now we would like to briefly establish just what a person is. To the extent that it is legitimate to distinguish between natural *philia* and *agape* — and we admit this at least in principle — we think that what inspires *agape* is not human nature as such, but the fact that this nature is subjectivized in a consciousness. Basically, natural *agape* is hardly distinguished from what is called altruism. From the outset the other is understood as a person, as another I, not at first as another man or woman. This means that it is understood from the outset as an appeal not to be egotistic. What first incites (and impels) altruistic activity is not that human nature is stricken with misery or injustice, but that this misery and injustice is suffered by a consciousness and that, by this, such suffering eludes me and calls out to me for relief, if not to share in it directly. Altruistic acts will perhaps be performed in the name of human solidarity, but *a posteriori* this justification would not be enough to set such acts in motion if it were not preceded by a graphic representation of suffering's *personal* character. As a result, since we have here a 'natural' principle inspiring *agape*, the relation determined by it tends to abolish the duality of consciousnesses; in other words, it transforms the person into a relation. Now, on the natural plane, this transformation is impossible; such a relation which is also a person does not exist. This is why the energy of *agape* seeks to create it. It is only its revealer, however; and with the further reservation that, on the natural plane, it can only reveal a need and not the relation itself. And yet if we disregard this reservation we see that, structurally speaking, *agape* is as if a synthesis of *eros* and *philia*. In *eros* energy reveals the person. In *philia* the person reveals a relation. *Agape* combines the revelatory function of the energy of *eros* with the revealed object of *philia*: in *agape* energy reveals relation.

Surely, on the natural plane, such a function comes up against a near impossibility. The impulse of profane charity clearly leads to the discovery of a relation which, according to the needs inspired by this impulse, should unite people among themselves. But, as we have said, such a relation at this level does not exist. The intervention of the grace of Christ is needed here. Consequently altruism falls back to the level of *philia* and becomes again a relation based on the unicity of human nature: it is in truth a philanthropy. Thus natural *agape* is a compromise or a mixture of *eros* and *philia* rather than a true synthesis. It might claim to love human nature with a true love, but such an impulse to love can in reality only be addressed to the person and not to nature. This particular situation explains the attractive force of worldly charity, the quasi-erotic emotive power of declarations on its behalf and the pseudo-mysticism of that *religion of humanity* whose consummate type is represented by Auguste Comte.

II. SUPERNATURAL LOVE

1. The Three Degrees of Sacred Love

We are therefore invited, so as to realize the promises of nature, to enter into the order of grace, into the order of true *agape*. We are also going to rediscover, at the very heart of supernatural *agape*, those just-described three forms of love, and first of all *agape* properly speaking, the love of neighbor.

Since we are in the order of grace, here the energy of fraternal love can no longer stem from nature, even that supernatural nature which is the person. It stems from divine grace and corresponds to a divine commandment: "you shall love." However, grace does not abolish nature; it itself appeals to a 'natural reason': "you shall love (your neighbor) as yourself," or even, according to an interpretation proposed by certain Jewish exegetes, *"for he is like you."* Thus the reason put forward by the divine commandment is indeed the very one we have now discovered by philosophical analysis: the person. In the same way we can repeat what we said above concerning the energy of *agape* in its function of revealing the relation of proximity, but with this difference: this time, the need that resides in the charitable power can be fulfilled because it is taken in charge and assumed by the Word Incarnate, the prototypical relation, provided that the charitable power discover, at the same time as its desire, its impotence to realize this by itself. Charity's impetus makes us discover that to the extent that the other is my neighbor, he is a person open to my approach. Access to the person of the other, unattainable by natural charity, is attained by sacred *agape*, thanks precisely to the relation of proximity. The person ceases being altruism's impenetrable subjectivity. Opened and transpierced by the relation of proximity, the person enters into the circumincession of Christian love.

But since *agape* is a synthesis of *eros* and *philia*, it should be possible to find *eros* and *philia* again, integrated into the rightful forms of spiritual *agape*.[4] We can see then in charitable *philia* the type of the love of self and in charitable *eros* the type of the love of God. And so we obtain those three dimensions of charity we established at the beginning of this metaphysics of love, and rediscovered in the cross of St. Paul.

That *philia* provides an adequate type for love of self is immediately apparent if we consider *eros* to be set aside at the outset, except in the case of narcissism, which is its perversion. But the analogy of *philia* to *agape* is more profound and more rigorous than with *eros*. True love of self, we have said, implies an interiorization of the relation of proximity: loving oneself as the neighbor. Now we have just seen that in *philia*, the person reveals the relation. Here, in charitable *philia*, it is the same: the person accedes to the relation of proximity with himself through the grace of Christ that lives in him. This analogy according to structure is coupled with an analogy according to nature. What in fact inspires *philia* is human nature. Now if Christ, inasmuch as He is God, makes access to the relation of proximity possible, he who is the prototypical hypostatic relation, inasmuch as he is now *true man*, the New Adam, he restores in each one of us the truth of human nature.

As for charitable *eros*, it is clearly an adequate type of the love of God. And this already from the viewpoint of structure. But is there need to insist on it and show that the only perfectly transcendent 'beyond' that calls forth the power of love can only be found in

4   There exists a sacralization proper to *eros* and *philia* that we only mention as a reminder. The sacralization of *eros* is marriage; the relation of unity, in conformity with Love in general, is assumed there by Christ in his function as the New Adam, for in Him, St. Paul says, there is no longer either man or woman (Gal 3:28), which the Icon of the *Deisis* represents. The hallowing of *philia* is fraternal charity, especially for consecrated religious; the relation of unicity is equally assumed here by Christ in his function as head of the Mystical Body.

the revelation of the supreme Person who mercifully condescends to respond to the thirst for absolute certainty which inspires the creature? From the viewpoint of nature it is at once sacred literature and mystical literature which proves it. What could we add to the *Song of Songs* or to St. John of the Cross? The creature, smitten with the Uncreated, traverses the night of the world to seek out its Beloved:

> O guiding night!
> O night more lovely than the dawn!
> O night that has united
> The Lover with His beloved,
> Transforming the beloved into her Lover.[5]

Is this all? No: since supernatural *agape* is truly a synthesis, all forms of love are found again in each one of its forms. We will see this later for fraternal charity. This can be shown immediately though for charitable *philia*: in love of self, or access to interior proximity, not only can one define a properly charitable dimension of charity toward oneself, but one can do so even for *eros*, to the extent that the relationships between the *psyche* and the *I* are analogically identified with the relationships between the feminine and masculine: within ourselves as well it is necessary to restore the primordial Adam by the *metanoia* of the *I* which turns away from the fascinating psyche and towards the spiritual sun. And likewise, with charitable *eros*, we are introduced to divine friendship because we recognize between God and ourselves, by grace of adoption, a *community of divine nature*: "we are made participants of the divine nature" (2 Peter 1:4), at the same time that God reveals himself as the only and unique Neighbor.

2. The Radical Imperfection of Created Love

Such, it seems, are the essential forms of human love, both natural and supernatural, systematically aligned with each other and in accord with the fundamental principles of our metaphysics. If we now attempt to characterize these forms globally from the viewpoint of

---

5 *The Dark Night of the Soul*, stanza 5, in *The Collected Works of St. John of the Cross*, trans. Kavanaugh and Rodriguez (Washington, DC: ICS Publications, 1973), 296.

their inevitable limitations, inherent to the very nature of the created, we must turn to fraternal charity, since it constitutes what a mathematician would call the base 'differential'. This limitation, this imperfection is easily identified. It necessarily betrays itself and is manifested at the very point at which charity can be corrupted. Now it seems to us that this corruption can be described as the illusory transformation of the revelatory function into the creative function.

Charitable power, which is basically a desire to abolish the ontological separativity of human persons, is by itself impotent to realize this desire. It can only attain it by renouncing and abandoning its own power. Impotent for, as we have said repeatedly, the satisfaction of this desire requires a person to be a relation and a relation a person, which is impossible in nature, since only in God is the Person constituted by the Relation. On earth, even if one admits that consciousness might entertain an intersubjective relation, it must be said that this relation is concerned with consciousness, not the person. It is a cognitive basis for becoming conscious of self, not an ontological basis: the person is a being. Besides, even though an intersubjective relation 'opens' the consciousness, it 'shuts out' the person, if it can be so expressed, by accentuating to the eyes of consciousness itself the impenetrability of the person. In these conditions it is understood that the charitable power experiences the need to be illusorily endowed with a creative capacity: "The encounter which makes a neighbor out of the other *requires a creation*," writes Marcel Légaut.[6]

Such is basically the key to the corruption of charity, which we have uncovered in all degrees and under all forms of human love. With *eros* the revelatory function of the power or energy of love arrogates to itself the very creation of the person. With *philia* the person imagines engendering a relation on its own. This close tie between revelation and creation should not surprise us. Metaphysically, and from the viewpoint of God, creation is a revelation. Conversely, for man the temptation to make of revelation a creation is great: now, how are we to deny that the loving impetus that obliges us to become aware of someone else in *eros*, *philia*, or *agape*, according to the order of

6 Cited in *Catéchistes d'aujour'hui* (Paris: Maison de la bonne Presse, Nov. 1972), 21; a statement betraying a naturalist and therefore deviated mysticism.

nature or of grace, obliges us to become aware of the other, and that it is then the revealer of the other as person, or as relation, or as their impossible synthesis? How could the creature not cling henceforth to its own power to love, since it is through this that it enters into love, and since it is, in any case, to the creature that the command to love is given? It is the creature that should pledge its own existence and prove to God that it is not altogether unworthy of heaven. This spiritual work requires the whole creature, it needs the convergence of all of the soul's powers, it is addressed to the very depths of being and asks it to ponder quite precisely with every fiber of its being; in short, it demands that it commit itself to and be at risk in its own, simple affirmation, and yet it has to finally renounce itself and vanish. For that person, who no longer has any other certainty than that of his own will and love, since it is this that God himself asks of him, is asked at the same time to abandon all of his own certainty.

Now we can better understand why, before arriving here, we had to bring together and systematize all forms of love in order to lead all of them to one and the same truth. It was a lengthy and sometimes dry process, but it was necessary, prior to the ultimate ascent to the last metaphysical summit, to know truly if all roads were indeed leading to this destination, to this humanly insurmountable rift. Yes, we can say, all ways have been explored, and we have seen them connected, joined, and unified in supernatural charity; we have seen them progressively homogenized and interiorized, the stitches and their interweavings tightened into this unique and vibrant cord of pure charity, drawing behind them the immense weft of human loves. Let us state then the law of charity one last time: the act of charity reveals the neighbor, but between the charitable power's act and the ontological proximity to which it gives us access there is a rift, an essential, unbridgeable discontinuity. The miracle is that, through charity, other people and myself become neighbors. It is here that the destiny of charity is played out. The power by which it is charged can be illusorily thought capable of filling up the emptiness which separates the will to love from ontological proximity, and can therefore believe itself the creator of the neighbor. Now, in doing this it transforms itself into 'triumphalist' charity and perverts its own nature, since it then denies what forms its sufficient reason and its foundation.

3. *Created Love is Freely Dependent on its Foundation*

Now we shall consider the 'founding' function of this foundation, that is: we shall consider the *relation of proximity in its rapport with charitable power*, which we have not done until now. And here we shall discover an important truth, one that Nygren has not seen. In assigning to charity a determining and founding reason, one surely destroys the gratuity of love, and thus one would decide in favor of Nygren if this determination (ontological proximity) could necessarily engender charity. But it does not engender it: it founds it. This is what defines the direction of charitable movement — that towards which it tends — but it does not produce it, no more than the movement of love itself attains to the foundation. Thus we hold that on the plane of human love there is a gap between the elements of the charitable structure, which is the very mark of its inherent imperfection. Pure charity is, at this level, in some manner imperceptible: it is not in the charitable movement, which is not yet charity; nor is it, strictly speaking, in ontological proximity, which is other than love, since it must be connected to the *Logos*. Therefore it is truly a miracle, it is the miraculous bond that unites the elements of the charitable structure among themselves. It is not we ourselves but St. Paul who calls it 'bond', the bond of perfection (*vinculum perfectionis*). By this he situates charity very precisely with respect to perfection. There is not, moreover, space enough to ask what perfection is involved here, as do certain exegetes,[7] since in reality this involves everything that is capable of receiving its completion, that is to say, everything which, even though imperfect in its present reality, longs for perfection — a need intrinsic to its very nature. Charity is precisely this 'passage', this invisible and unobservable *Pascha*, this dynamic interlinking. It is, if one likes, the passage from potency to act, the mysterious completion of all things, or rather the very movement by which all things are led to their completion, not perfection accomplished but the link to perfection. A mystery and a miracle irreducible on the human plane. Every lover knows indeed that

---

7 Prat (in *Theology of Paul*, vol. 2) discusses the different interpretations of the Pauline definition at length. "The principal point is to know to what charity serves as a bond" (335). Either charity serves as link to the other virtues, or else it unites Christians. But this formula should be interpreted in a much more universal manner.

by *eros* he or she is carried toward the other in a relation of unity that is pre-existent to both of them and is their perfection. But this relation is also understood to remain inaccessible and never realized in its earthly modality. The founding relation is thus present and absent at the same time. And it is the same for *philia* and *agape*. Besides, would there be charitable movement if the relations of unity, unicity, or proximity were realized here and now? Surely not, since there can only be movement where there is imperfection. At least this is so here below. We can see then, in a general way, that charity, in the full sweep of its movement, is what ties earth to Heaven, imperfection to the Supreme Perfection; it is the ultimate act of Universal Existence, breathed in like an ocean by the Divine Breath of Love towards Heaven.

III. LOVE 'IN DIVINIS'

1. In God, Three Loves that are only One

We are led back then to the Divine *Pneuma* in which we recognize the divine prototype of charity. It is then necessary for us to broach the difficult question of the Holy Spirit, personal Love in the Trinity.

If we return to what we said in connection with the procession of the Holy Spirit,[8] we find ourselves undeniably in the presence of three Loves: the essential Love or ecstasy of the whole Divine Essence, the Love of the active spiration of the Father and the Son spirating the Holy Spirit, finally the Holy Spirit himself, personal Love.[9] But quite clearly there is only one single Love, seen by us in several different ways. This is what we will show first.

Essential Love, we say, is the ecstasy of the whole Divine Essence; it is therefore the Divine Essence viewed in its act of love. Notional Love is situated, not at the level of the Absolute, but at that of the relations; it is this same Divine Essence as the spirative force of the Father and the Son in their mutual ecstasy. The spirative force, the

---

8 Cf. 275ff.

9 Cf. *Summa Theologiae* I, q. 37, a. 1. St. Thomas calls active spiration 'notional love' because love is viewed here as the 'notion' (knowledge) that we can have of the procession of the Holy Spirit (procession by way of love). There are, in the Trinity, five notions: innascibility, paternity, filiation, active spiration, and passive spiration; four real relations: paternity, filiation, and the two spirations; three subsistent relations: paternity, filiation, and passive spiration; two processions: of knowledge and love.

virtus spirativa as we have already mentioned,[10] is not in its very nature the property of the Father or the Son but of the Essence[11] — it is *fecundity*, the fecundity of the Divine Essence itself. Therefore, viewed in itself, the act of spiration is nothing but Essential Love. The Father and the Son possess it only by being agents of the spiration. In other words, since God is Love, and since there is only one Father and one Son, it is indeed Love as the Father who loves God in the Son and as the Son who loves God in the Father. Or specifically, this God who is loved by the Love of the Father in the Son and vice-versa — what is he if not Love Itself, but this time hypostatic Love, which is to say God as 'Loved'?

2. The Holy Spirit proceeds from the Common Love of the Father and the Son as the unique Weight of Love impelling them from within to Love One Another

How can we glimpse this mysterious procession of love which is also a weight of love? St. Thomas writes: "when anyone loves an object, a certain impression results, so to speak, of the thing loved in the affection of the lover; by reason of which the object loved is said to be in the lover."[12] This beautiful doctrine, merely a seed in St. Augustine ("my love is my weight"), is developed at length by St. Thomas in the *Contra Gentiles*. But how is the beloved (who is such only because I love him or her) actually in me? Obviously not by him- or herself, but by an

10   *Summa Theologiae* I, q. 36, a. 3.

11   Is there an insurmountable difference between Greeks and Latins in connection with the Holy Spirit? Can we not compare St. Thomas distinguishing between spirative virtue and spirating agents (*Summa Theologiae* I, q. 36, a. 3, ad 1 and 2) and St. Gregory Palamas declaring: "When you hear it said that the Holy Spirit proceeds from two, because He essentially springs from the Father through the Son, you must understand [this] teaching in this sense: what is poured out are the essential powers and energies of God, but not the divine hypostasis of the Spirit" (cited by John Meyendorff, *Introduction à l'étude de Gregoire Palamas* [Paris: Université de Paris/Seuil, 1959], 314)? For St. Thomas, active spiration, or spirative virtue (the uncreated energy which is poured out, according to the Palamite) cannot constitute the hypostasis of the Holy Spirit either; we have seen what St. Thomas declares in this respect: "Although there are four relations in God, one of them, spiration, is not separated from the person of the Father and of the Son, but belongs to both; thus, although it is a relation, it is not called a property, because it does not belong to only one subject; nor is it a personal relation — i.e., constituting a hypostasis [*neque relatio personalis, id est constituens personam*]" (I, q. 30, a. 2, ad 1).

12   *Summa Theologiae* I, q. 37, a. 1.

attraction, a 'weight' that draws me, makes me fall towards him or her. It has become in me a power that impels me from within towards itself. This is what I call 'my love'. This involves then a kind of reaction of the lover to his love for the beloved. Love is first a movement casting me towards the other, but once the other is discovered as 'loved' there is as if an inversion that occurs: I discover that it is the beloved-other who moves me from within towards him- or herself. This is what St. Thomas calls 'impression'. "Because the beloved in the will," he says, "exists as inclining, and somehow inwardly impelling the lover toward the very thing beloved, and an impulse of a living thing from within belongs to a spirit, this is suitable: that God proceeding by way of love be called His 'spirit', as it were a kind of existing spiration."[13]

Now, given the infinite perfection of the Divine Essence which is such that everything within It is infinitely perfect, it follows that this Spirit, impelling from within, necessarily possesses hypostatic perfection. Here we see as clearly as possible how the person of the Holy Spirit is constituted by passive spiration.[14] Indeed, this Person clearly proceeds from active spiration, since it is by active spiration that there is a 'beloved'. But this active spiration, this love of the Father for the Divine Essence presented in the Son, and of the Son for the Divine Essence originated in the Father, in some way 'induces' in the unique deity of the Father and the Son a 'weight of love' drawing them towards each other, and which is in opposition to the Two who spirate it (who breathe it forth) only from the viewpoint of passive spiration, that is to say only as *That which is spirated*. It is self-evident that in God, the two faces of Love are co-eternal. We previously stated that by the act of love I discover a beloved, and that, next, with the movement reversing itself, I breathe forth a breath of love which moves me from within toward the beloved.

13 *Contra Gentiles*, IV, 19 [10], trans. C. J. O'Neil (New York: Doubleday, 1967), 119.

14 Strictly speaking, we could be accused of mixing together the viewpoints of the relations and the processions here. There are two processions, of knowledge and of love. Each procession, considered in its 'result', requires two relations which are nothing but those between the principle and term of procession. As we stated, the viewpoint of the relations corresponds to the Trinity seen from the Word, while that of the processions is ascribed to the Holy Spirit. Here is precisely the difficulty: the names of the relations of the Holy Spirit are in fact the names of procession. Cf. *Summa Theologiae* I, q. 28, a. 4, resp.

But obviously, in God we can only distinguish these two 'moments' in a quite provisional manner. This means that active spiration, or the common act of love of the Father and the Son, as such, is spiration only inasmuch as it is a reaction, a breathing-forth of love 'provoked' by the weight of love, the fiery Heart that urges the Father and the Son towards one another. As for origin, the Spirit proceeds from the Father through the Son as 'effect' of the charitable fecundity of the Divine Essence which is given to the Son by the Father: God loves Himself in the common spiration of Father and Son; but this love is 'incited' by the Holy Spirit, hypostatic Love, the Presence of God within Himself, the charitable Center of gravity which 'impels' God to love Himself. We repeat: Essential Love, through which the Father and the Son love each other, only becomes *spiration* by reason of the weight of love which the Father and the Son both spirate. "The same act of appetite is at once a *loving*, that is to say an affectionate inclination toward the object, and a *spirating*, that is to say a vital reaction to the attractive influence of the object. Under the attraction of the good the will grows heavy with the weight of love, 'breathes forth' this interior breath in loving this good."[15] But this *spirating* is, quite precisely, only to be qualified as such thanks to the *Spirated* (the Spirit) who proceeds from it, in the same way, says St. Thomas, that the action of flowering is qualified by the flowers producing this activity.[16]

Surely this weight of love that is hypostatic Charity is at once in the Father and the Son as that which draws them towards one another, as that which 'invites' them to actively spirate the same love. But there are not two weights of Love, for there is only a single spiration. This weight of Love is the unique Divine Essence imparted to itself, it is the sole Godhead inasmuch as it is loved, inasmuch as it exercises upon itself and within itself a charitable attraction; it is the unique Heart of God which from its most unfathomable depth calls itself to come towards itself. And by this — the Holy Spirit's presence at the single Heart of Father and Son — it is verified that he is indeed the key to the circumincession.[17]

15   Dondaine, *La Trinité*, 403.

16   *Summa Theologiae* I, q. 37, a. 2.

17   As we see, we are quite far from the sterility that Thomist doctrine, in the words of the Orthodox, would impose on the Holy Spirit. How would the Holy Spirit be sterile if he is, by very virtue of the spirative fecundity, hypostatic Fecundity?

3. Hypostatic Love Alone Reveals Essential Love

Two themes seem to emerge from this description: that of a hypostatic function and, as a consequence of the preceding, that of hypostatic maternity or a self-revelatory function. We think, in fact, that all the notes just attributed to the Holy Spirit, as impelling the Father and the Son from within to spirate Love, as a mysterious weight of love, remain as such in the innermost Divine Essence, being even its own Heart impressed within itself. All of these notes are exceedingly apt for a definition of the Person. As for hypostatic maternity, the self-revelatory function, it seems implicit to Thomistic analysis at every turn — without, we think, forcing the texts. One remark is imperative, though. As we mentioned, two modes of revelation need to be distinguished: an active mode (for example, God reveals his true Name to Moses) and a passive mode (for example, movement reveals life). The first mode should not be transposed *in divinis*, because God knows himself instantaneously. The second, suitably transposed, can retain a certain analogical significance. Here below this mode rests upon the relation of cause to effect: the effect is the sign of the cause. *In divinis* there is no effect in any proper sense; however St. Thomas, as has been seen, is not averse to comparing the Holy Spirit to an effect, to a flower sprung from a tree.[18] Surely there is a great difference between being caused and proceeding: to be caused is to hold one's being from the cause to which the effect can always be reduced; to proceed indicates only an origin. And so there can be causal processions and non-causal and immanent processions which indicate nothing but a simple relation of origin between the proceeding term and the principle.[19] In this type of procession the proceeding term is irreducible to its principle: the Son could not be reduced to the Father, the Hypostases are co-eternally distinct from each other. In

---

18 *Summa Theologiae* I, q. 37, a. 2.

19 In his fine book *The Comforter* (trans. B. Jakim [Grand Rapids, MI/Cambridge, UK: Eerdmans, 2004], 124–29), Father Bulgakov critiques the notion of causal procession, stating that it was never noticed that one would be introducing in this way the notion of causality into God. We sometimes wonder if Orthodox theologians, even the greatest, have read St. Thomas directly. The *Summa Theologiae* declares, in the first article of the first question of the treatise on the Trinity (I, q. 27, a. 1): "Procession, therefore, is not to be understood from what it is in bodies, either according to local movement or *by way of a cause proceeding forth to its exterior effect.*"

this sense one can say that the Person of the Holy Spirit 'testifies' to the fecundity of spirative virtue, just as the Son 'testifies' to the Father.

However, that about which the Holy Spirit first gives testimony, that for which he is the revealing Hypostasis, is the relation that unites the Son to the Father and the Father to the Son. This is what we would now like to stress. The Holy Spirit, as we have seen, requires or implies the distinction of those whom he unites, or of those from whom he proceeds as their unity. In other words, if the Father and the Son are 'essentially' One, by essence and not 'hypostatically', they are also a single principle inasmuch as they spirate the Holy Spirit, their common Love. It is therefore with respect to the Holy Spirit and in his spiration that they are One. They are both face-to-face, they are one in a Third. Now the unity in which they are one is not identified with themselves hypostatically, in such a way that they would be confused in it, but it is itself posited as a distinct Hypostasis, the Holy Spirit, in whom they are united. We see then, insofar as this is possible, that they clearly need to be hypostatically distinct in themselves if they are *only* united in a third hypostasis. Since there is a third, who is their unity, they clearly need to be two considered apart from this third. Such is basically the hypostatic Maternity of the Holy Spirit which *reveals* by his own hypostasis, by his hypostatic reality, the Son to the Father and the Father to the Son; he is as if Unity made Hypostasis.

We have said along with theological Tradition: only the Essence is one; the Hypostases are three. And yet, in the very order of the hypostases, we dare to say that there is as if a hypostatic 'translation' of the unity of the Essence — the divine *Pneuma*. And this is why we also declare that he is the pre-eminent Hypostasis, since he is in some manner the divine Unity made Hypostasis. Hypostatic Love reveals active spiration through its very being as Hypostasis, just as, according to a remote analogy, the dot on a white page reveals, by its very being and without exercising any action, all the dimensions and relations of the page, which are then determined and become exterior to each other with respect to it. Thus the Holy Spirit does not 'reveal' the charitable energy of the ecstatic Essence, the Love-Essence directly, but more precisely the relation of active spiration, that is, the charitable dimension of the begetting relation. If God is Love, it is in the tri-hypostatic blossoming that we see it. But this Trinitarian blossoming itself would be reduced to the abstraction of a system of logical relations if the Hypostasis of the Holy Spirit, constituted by one of these relations, did not come to reveal, since it is Love, that this ecstasy of relation, its *esse ad*, is by essence charitable. It is in the Person of the Holy Spirit that God 'betrays' His inmost essence which is revealed to Himself as hypostatic Love. The begetting of the Son discloses an act of love which would not be apparent if a Person-Love were not proceeding from it.

4. Only 'in the Unity' of the Holy Spirit is the Divine Essence able to enter into Relation with Itself

One objection might come from our initial characterization of the maternity of the Holy Spirit as the revealing of the Son to the Father, then, secondly, as the revealing of active spiration. But there is no uncertainty here: "active spiration, while it is opposed to passive spiration, is not opposed to, and hence not really distinct from either paternity or filiation."[20] Recall that active spiration is not in fact a subsistent relation, that it does not constitute a Person (there are not four Persons in God). Hence it is quite obvious that it cannot be really distinct from the relations of paternity and filiation. However, it does not amount to them either, purely and simply, at least as to its notion. But what is the result? The result is that, as we have said, it forms the unique charitable dimension which is at the heart of the procession of intelligence. Now, once again, this dimension would be in some manner 'invisible' if it were not manifested by the term which proceeds from it, hypostatic Love. It is in this then that active spiration can be truly called Spiration. Outside of this it cannot be distinguished from the relations of filiation and paternity. In qualifying as 'charitable' the relation of filiation (and at the same stroke that of paternity, for it is in the Son that the Father is Father), the charitable Hypostasis is indeed therefore the revelation of the love of the Father for the Son and of the Son for the Father. It is in this love that the Father begets the Son as his Word. It can also be said, according to a remote analogy, that the maternal Hypostasis who delivers to the Father the Son whom the Father has begotten is, in some manner, the

20 Garrigou-Lagrange, *Reality: A Synthesis of Thomistic Thought* (St. Louis & London: Herder, 1950), 145.

One who 'offers' the Father the 'possibility' of begetting. Not that it actively urges the Father to beget, but it is as if the 'matrix' in which the Father pronounces His Word.

Actually, inasmuch as the Father begets His Son, God puts Himself, to all intents and purposes, at a distance from Himself. This distancing is only possible because it is effected (eternally and intemporally) in a 'divine space' which unites profoundly and 'below the surface' those distinguished in this way in the procession of knowledge. Repeating a formula of Meister Eckhart, we will say that in the Holy Spirit the Father and the Son are *fused*, but through him they are not *confused*. Allowing Unity to beget itself so as in this to rediscover its Unity: this is the role of the divine *Pneuma*. How could the Father entirely divest Himself of the Divine Essence in order to give it to the Son without ceasing to be God, or the Son entirely divest Himself of the Divine Essence in order to give it to the Father without ceasing to be God, if at the very instant of this divesting, an eternal instant, the Divine Essence were not given back to the Father and the Son in the 'Unity of the Holy Spirit'? In begetting the Son, if the Father remains perfectly within Himself, this is 'thanks' to the Holy Spirit, and likewise for the Son. He is the *immanence* of the divine processions. He is, in truth, the matrix in which God begets Himself, and therefore through which God remains within Himself. Surely some will say that there is thus as if two unities in God: the Unity of the Essence and the Unity of the Holy Spirit. In a certain manner, yes, in the sense that the Holy Spirit is as if the image of the Essence, the Godhead's 'non-manifested manifestation'.[21] And that is necessary, if the Divine Essence is not to be posited as a fourth hypostasis beside the other three. In reality, this *function of unity* is not assumed by the Divine Essence (the Godhead), which assumes no function, not even that of unifying the three Persons, for the Godhead is not 'possible' in any manner and no one can say anything about it, unless by apophasis. The only unity that might be conceived of in a distinct manner from the terms which it unites, and hence about which we can speak, is that of the Holy Spirit.

---

21   This equally enables us to account for the nearly 'impersonal' character of the Third Person, who comes into the world, in Person surely, but as a power, an 'energy', rather than as a 'being'. This is because He is the image of the Godhead.

5. Identity and Otherness in God

Such is the mystery of Supreme Charity, of the divine *Pneuma*, the eternal *vinculum perfectionis* of the Trinitarian Mystery. The Greek theologians in general refuse to follow St. Augustine in calling the Holy Spirit Love. Instead, they like to call him the perfecting quality. Now it seems that once the metaphysical meaning of the Pauline definition of charity as the link of perfection is recognized, there is no longer anything opposed to bringing about a synthesis of both perspectives, as much in the divine order as in the human. In the divine order let us cite the text of St. Gregory Nazianzus: "What Godhead can there be if It is not perfect? And how can that be perfect which lacks something of perfection? And surely there is something lacking if it has not the Holy, and how would it have this if it were without the Spirit?"[22] In the order of creation here then is a text from Basil of Caesarea: "In the creation think you first, I pray you, of the original [principial] cause of all things that are made, the Father; of the creative [demiurgic] cause, the Son; of the perfecting cause, the Spirit."[23]

In the same way, if one remembers what we have said about the Son as prototypical Relation and about the Holy Spirit as prototypical Hypostasis, it seems to us that the difference of 'position' of the *Pneuma* in Eastern and Latin theologies is minimized. The East takes the process of Trinitarian development to be rectilineal: from the Father to the Holy Spirit through the Son, so that the Son is link and the Spirit term. For the Latins, the bond of Father and Son is the Spirit who is 'in the midst'.[24] Both perspectives are true. The 'new viewpoint' we are proposing will enable us to see why. We will say with the Greeks that the true Trinitarian bond is indeed the Word, as we have shown. But this bond *unites while distinguishing*, whereas the Holy Spirit, end-point and prototypical Hypostasis, *distinguishes while uniting*. Or

---

22   St. Gregory Nazianzus, *Discourse 31* (Theological Oration V), IV; trans. Browne and Swallow, *Nicene and Post-Nicene Fathers of the Christian Church, Second Series*, vol. 7 (New York: The Christian Literature Company, 1894), 319.

23   St. Basil of Caesarea, *On the Holy Spirit*, ch. XVI, 38; trans. Jackson, *Nicene and Post-Nicene Fathers of the Christian Church, Second Series*, vol. 8 (New York: The Christian Literature Company, 1895), 23.

24   These patterns are represented in this way:

$$\text{Father} \rightarrow \text{Son} \rightarrow \text{Spirit} \qquad \begin{matrix} \text{Father} \rightarrow \text{Son} \\ \nwarrow \text{Spirit} \nearrow \end{matrix}$$

again, as already mentioned, in the Word we understand how a person is a relation and in the Holy Spirit how a relation is a person. In the Son, the Father and the Spirit eternally 'access' the relation of proximity. God is God's neighbor: it is through the Son as intermediary between Father and Spirit that the Father 'produces' the Spirit, and it is through him that the Spirit draws near the Father. He unites the Father to the *Pneuma* while inseparably distinguishing them according to the subsistent relation. Or again, if the Father is the Model, the Son is the Image, and the Spirit is the Mirror in which the Image is reflected. And it is in reflecting this Image (that of the Father), and therefore through its intermediary, that the Spirit is united to the Father. The Word, *Logos* or Reason or Relation or Eternal Rapport, is the supreme Symbol through which the Godhead enters into communication with Itself.

The unity of the Holy Spirit is different: it is not in any manner a negative unity, which unites because it does not divide (a relation opposes without dividing the substance), but a positive unity, that is a unity which expresses in and through itself *what the terms it unites have in common*. The first unity is a unity of structure, the second is a unity of contents; and this is why this unity implies the distinction of what it unites, since it is-what-there-is-in-common-for-two-opposed-terms. What is eternally affirmed in the divine *Pneuma* is the unity of the Essence of the Father and the Son, under the mode of a Hypostasis. In some manner this is the interior unity of the divine Persons, whereas the Word expresses their 'exterior' unity, that is the unity of their mutual relations. The Son is 'in the midst' of the Father and the Holy Spirit because he is 'between' the Father and the Holy Spirit. But the Holy Spirit is 'in the midst' of the Father and the Son because he is what is innermost to each of them, their unique Heart.

God is Love, says St. John, declaring in this way the ecstatic nature of the Divine Essence. This eternal ecstasy, which is also eternal enstasy, this *esse ad aliud* which is also *esse ad se*, is resolved in the person of the Son and that of the Holy Spirit; the Mystery of an identity and an otherness inseparably conjoined. The Son is otherness in identity, the Spirit is identity in otherness. The Son is Relation, the Spirit is Person, the identity which subsists in the bosom of otherness, and which therefore renders it 'possible' and reveals it as otherness in the bosom of identity.

6. The Assumption of all
Human Loves into Divine Love

If therefore we turn now to the three elements of the charitable structure that we have identified, we will understand how divine Charity achieves their perfection: irreducibly separated upon the human
plane, we see them in some manner reduced to unity on the divine
plane. Charitable power, we have said, is active spiration, the *virtus
spirativa*. But this active spiration is itself nothing but the relation of
proximity of the Father and the Son, or rather, as we have pointed
out, it is rightly its charitable dimension. Yet it is not this that reveals
the relation of proximity, but the person of the Holy Spirit who,
however, proceeds from it. And so the very thing that is a human
imperfection is divine super-perfection. Let us consider *agape*. On
earth, as in Heaven, the relation of proximity is primary with respect
to charitable power (active spiration), for *in divinis*, active spiration
is as if the reaction of the Father to the attraction of the Good shown
forth in the Son; one loves what one first knows. But — now the
inverse analogy — charitable power is 'first' with respect to the relation of proximity, if one considers that the *virtus spirativa*, communicated to the Son by the Father, is in reality the ecstatic energy of
the Divine Essence itself. It is by virtue of this essential Ecstasy that
the Son, which is to say the relation of proximity, proceeds. On the
other hand let us consider *eros*. On earth, as in Heaven, the impetus to love is first with respect to the person; but contrariwise, *in
divinis*, this impetus to love is capable of producing the person — the
Holy Spirit proceeds by active spiration — and in return, also contrary to human *eros*, the person of the Holy Spirit is the revealer of
active spiration. Finally let us consider *philia*. Here again we find
these two aspects of a direct and an inverse analogy. Actually, as in
human *philia*, the 'reason' for divine ecstasy is the Love of God for
Himself,[25] and it is therefore the unique Essence that is loved in the
Son by the Father and by the Father in the Son. But — a wonderful
mystery — this unique nature, even inasmuch as it is loved, 'becomes'
a Person, that of the Holy Spirit, thus realizing that unity between

---

25   This love is moreover theologically characterized as love of friendship.

nature and hypostasis sighed after by human *philia*. As we see, direct and inverse analogy are differently articulated according to whether *eros*, *agape*, or *philia* is involved. For *agape* the analogy essentially concerns relation, for *eros* it basically concerns the charitable impetus. For *philia* it involves the person. God is at once True Neighbor, all-powerful Love, and the unique Friend.

IV. THE HOLY SPIRIT AS BASIS FOR CHARITY

We are in this way led to clarify the mode of participation of human charity in the grace of the Holy Spirit. We will be brief after our just-completed long and extraordinary voyage to the core of divine Charity. One might wish to consider such a participation for all aspects of *agape*, yet for our purposes it will be enough to simply deal with fraternal charity. Besides, as promised,[26] the moment has come to show that *eros* and *philia* are to be rediscovered in *agape*. This will become clear in the following consideration: "you will love" is related to *eros*, "your neighbor" properly speaking to *agape*, and lastly "as yourself" to *philia*. By this the perfect agreement of the charitable structure with each of its forms is shown once more, and at the same time the coherence of our analysis.

1. How Charitable Eros is united with the Holy Spirit, its Foundation

First, let us consider the erotic dimension of *agape*. The divine *Pneuma* cannot be the basis for charitable power in its very act, which necessarily remains human. But he transforms and supernaturalizes it while associating himself with its operation from within. By this he renders this operation capable of attaining its supernatural end, the discovery of the Christic Word as the only Neighbor. Being what is most charitable at the heart of the charitable impetus, he thus enables man to obey Christ's commandment.

However, for the operation of divine love to be associated with the operation of human love, human love needs to conversely 'enter' into the Breath of eternal Love, that is, to allow the Breath of Love to

26   Cf. ch. 10, "The Love of Neighbor."

imbue it, for it is only thus that the Spirit can allow the participation of its own operation through a human operation. This requires that charitable power renounce itself, or let us say: that the human subject cease identifying with its power to love, that it cease recognizing itself in it and delighting in it. Only then is it possible to love one's neighbor, for it is only then that the Holy Spirit can accomplish its function as Revelation of the Christic Word in the relation of proximity. Just as Jesus descends into Mary through the operation of the Holy Spirit, so, through His operation, Jesus 'assumes' the relation of proximity. For the work of the Holy Spirit, in all things, is to lead us to Christ and reveal Him: "No one can say that Jesus is Lord but in the Holy Spirit," says St. Paul.[27] In the same way, when the loving heart discovers the Christic Word in the relation of proximity, it is the Spirit who makes him known to it. It is the Spirit then who gives us the understanding that charitable power could not be creative of the neighbor; it is he alone who enables us to escape from the trap of triumphalist charity, and it is precisely in this that the true spiritual operation of charity resides.

In this founding of the charitable operation by the *Pneuma*, we grasp a specific feature which differentiates this mode from the Christic mode of the founding of a relation. As we have shown, the Word as Person founds relation, which is to say that he himself is that relation and it does not exist outside of him. Things transpire differently here. The *Pneuma*, even if present in person, which we would hesitate to affirm, exerts in all cases this presence under the form of an association with the charitable operation, not in substituting himself for it. Let us say even more: this association is so close that it is impossible to distinguish then between the divine and the human operation, just as in so many of St. Paul's passages we do not know if he is speaking of the Spirit of God or of man. The only criterion for distinguishing eludes discourse, for it is of the interior and lived order: it is our inner renunciation that will make our participation in the divine Energy of love increase. But even then we cannot know if the Holy Spirit has substituted his mode of operation for ours or if our human mode has not rather been supernaturalized and divinized.

27   1 Cor 12:3.

2. How the Charitable Person is united to the Holy Spirit who is the Foundation of our Person

We find ourselves in the presence of the same mystery once more if we consider the *philia* aspect of *agape*. Here, however, we will not hesitate to say that it is the Holy Spirit in person, in his hypostatic function, who comes to found the third term of the charitable structure. The "as yourself" expresses, as already mentioned, the 'natural' reason that Christ ascribes to the second commandment of supernatural charity. Remember, philosophical analysis has identified the person as the principle of natural charity. We rediscover then the same affirmation on all sides. For we must not let ourselves be misled: when we speak of 'person' we understand the fact of person, not the other's person or mine. And Christ did not say anything else: the "as yourself" means in fact: "for he is as you are," that is: *for he is a person*. What I love in myself is the person. And, since the other is also a person, this is what I should love in him. Perhaps it will be better understood now why we should speak of 'person' as such, without specifying what might be involved (myself or others), just as we should speak of the relation of proximity rather than the neighbor.

We are quite aware of how disconcerting such expressions can be, but we wanted to delve into the metaphysical structure of charity. We thus had to go beyond the psychological plane of the reciprocity of personal relationships and meditate upon pure concepts, so as to determine their full significance and logic. If the person, therefore, is the inspiring principle of charitable energy, how can the Holy Spirit be so in his turn, which is required in the supernatural order? To this we must reply that it could not be otherwise, and that, far from raising a question, the personal presence of the Spirit alone makes the accomplishment of the divine Commandment possible. Indeed, how do we love ourselves, love our own person, outside of the Holy Spirit? Either this love is possessive love of self (but then it cannot serve as model for the love of others since it makes this impossible) or it is access to the true *I*, as we attempted to show in our anthropology, that is to say to true interiority, which as a matter of fact does not exist outside of the Holy Spirit. Here, not only does the subject renounce ownership of his charitable operation, but he even renounces himself. And just as the first renunciation allows him to enter into the movement of the vivifying Spirit, of the One who comes to vivify the relation of proximity, who comes to make it alive and manifest it, so the second renunciation makes us delve into the interiority of the Spirit who comes to pneumatize our intellect, that is, who makes me understand that the interiority of the other could not be exterior to the interiority of my own person. There is only one interiority: that of the Holy Spirit. In Him we are fused without being confused. For in me, as in others, this clearly has to do with what is most interior in others as in myself. We repeat: with the Word, the prototypical relation, we understand how the person is a relation, a neighbor; with the divine *Pneuma* we understand how a relation, the common love of the other's person and my own, is *one* Person. Yes, the interiority of my being is incommunicable and irreducible, and yet I can only have access to it in the unique interiority of God, the Holy Spirit. In this presence of the divine Spirit at the heart of our heart, as pure charity, through whom we are drawn and spirated toward Heaven from within ourselves, it is truly God who calls out to Himself and who Himself comes and unites us to Himself, from the depth of our nothingness, like a rediscovered face of His Identity.

Such is the mystery of Christian charity. Such is its inexhaustible Beauty which triumphalist charity intends to desecrate. Such is the entirety of the second commandment, and how it is alike to the first. Here below Christian charity is truly a sacrosanct mystery which imitates, as much as this is possible, the circumincession of the Eternal Trinity, and even more which brings us into its very depths. Yes, we are called to *triumphant* Charity, if it is true that tri-umph, from the Greek *tris-ambos*, designates a dance in three measures: for there are three dancing, in the circumincession of Life Eternal, the dance of Supreme Love.

PART V

The Metaphysical Structure of Charity in Its Cosmic Order: Charity and Creation

GOD IS LOVE, SAYS ST. JOHN. THE VERY SUPER-abundance of Divine Love implies creation. *Bonum diffusivum sui esse* [The good is diffusive of itself]: these few words say everything.

This actually means that creation is at once necessary and gratuitous, that it is at once in God and outside of God. It is necessary because the Divine Essence with its superabundant Love possesses, by nature, creative power. The world is thus God's 'neighbor'.[1] But it is gratuitous because this necessity is that of Grace itself. On the other hand, Creation is outside of God because God is not Creation. But Creation is in God because outside of God there is nothing, and because his Love envelops and includes everything. Charity is the insurmountable distance separating Creator from creature, as well as the irresistible movement which leads the creature back to the Creator. We say insurmountable distance — this is not only the existentiating act that projects the possibilities of creation into the nothingness by *giving them* being, which is the perfect act of love,

---

1 We know how strongly theology affirms that creation is gratuitous and God could just as well not have created. However, unless we conceive of this gratuity only in a negative manner and as a consequence place contingency in God Himself, which is an impossibility, it must be clearly understood that true gratuity does not exclude the perfection of necessity. To deny the *bonum diffusivum sui* in an absolute manner, except in the case of a providentially opportune formulation, is to deny the very possibility of creation. Surely the *bonum diffusivum sui* is also a formulation and can give way to pantheism, and yet it is the Holy Spirit himself who fills all of creation and vivifies it. "*In quantum bonus est, sumus,* in as much as God is good, we are," says St. Augustine (*On Christian Doctrine* I, 32). To say that God was able to not create indicates nothing but the creature's total dependence on the Creator. "Goodness is described as self-diffusive," says St. Thomas, "in the sense that an end is said to move" (*Summa Theologiae* I, q. 5, a. 4).

but also an effect of divine mercy tempering in this way the intensity of its radiance.

Divine Love is then the very fabric of Universal Existence. The play of its intersectings is indefinite and inexhaustible, and anything we might say about it is unable to account for it.

We will attempt first to clarify the general conditions for a theology of creation in its relation to the Creator (Chapter 17). We will then encounter the Virgin Mary, the creature who has been immaculately conceived: we will identify the metaphysical and cosmological significance of this (Chapter 18). Finally, at the cosmic level, we will seek out the traces of the Trinity and their angelic ramifications (Chapter 19).

17

Remarks on a Theology of Creation

WHO SAYS CREATION *IPSO FACTO* DISTINGUISHES between a created and a Creator? This duality, irreducible on its own plane, has been the object of numerous critiques. Unquestionably, it safeguards divine transcendence, but by making God a correlative of the creature. At least this is what certain philosophers think—who, for this reason, prefer the Eastern doctrine of manifestation. How are we to imagine that God is Absolute Being, outside of which there is nothing, and that creation is outside of God? Is not pantheism the solution to creationist dualism, as the example of Spinoza proves? The theology of creation is, in fact, quite remote from the caricature under which it is sometimes presented; as we will see, it explicitly presents God as non-correlative to the creature. As for the continuity/discontinuity between created and Uncreated, which India has expressed under the concept of *maya*, it seems that Christianity expresses this under the concept of cosmic charity. This is basically what we want to show. In the same manner, the most standard theology has resolved some problems often reputed to be insoluble, such as that of the temporal beginning of the created: "And what was there before?" Such are some of the questions to be dealt with now, although the present chapter, despite its somewhat ambitious title, cannot take the place of a systematic account of the theology of creation.

I. CREATION AND BEGINNING

1. Knowledge of the Relative is Relative

God has created the world through love. One could just as well say that God has created the world in Love. Love is therefore the key of creation. But to better understand what intellection is opened to us by this key, we must first pose the conditions for an understanding having creation as object. When the mind contemplates the mystery of the Trinity, the 'object' of contemplation being unconditioned, absolute, and eternal, the knowledge we have of it is equally unconditioned, absolute, and eternal; it is limited by nothing other than our intellectual capacity. But within itself it is limitless. If our mind is capable — and it actually is — of gaining a certain idea of the Absolute, this, by definition, proves that only the Absolute is worthy of our intelligence, that this alone defines it in its essence. The idea of the Absolute is the most simple, most clear, and most certain of all ideas. The Absolute is neither before nor after our recognition of it. Being strictly intemporal, it eludes 'before' and 'after' alike. It cannot be the object of a reflection; it would always be one step ahead of this reflection. It is not a thing and, as a matter of fact, neither is it an object. It does not transpire in the same way for creation. Creation is always already there; it precedes every knowledge that takes it for an object. This insurmountable previousness means that there is something of the completely inexplicable about it. The Absolute is not inexplicable. It is the superintelligible peace of the intellect; in a certain manner It clearly outstrips the intellect, but as a very good host who anticipates our least desires while satisfying them. It fulfills the intellect. Nothing can be said about it, but it is every word. On the contrary, the world is radically inexplicable, radically, that is to say in its root. The inexplicability of the world is the mystery of cosmic charity; or again, it is by integrating inexplicability with the world itself, by making its fabric and substance out of it, that it is alone possible to adequately describe an awareness of the world. This substance of unintelligibility that is the world, what India calls *maya*, appears then as a mystery of love, as cosmic charity. Charity is the *locus*, receptacle, matrix in which God can establish the creation. One could just as well say that God, wishing to create, sees that there is nothing outside of Himself. It is then at first necessary that there be a space outside of Him in which to place creation. He then casts His Divine Charity before Himself and by this He creates the exteriority wherein He will be able to project creatures. But because this exteriority is charity, it is love of God and leads everything back to Him, being nothing but the mode according to which God comes toward Himself out of His own Beyond. Charity alone can account for the unimaginable otherness that is creation with respect to the Creator.

2. The True Beginning is Intemporal

We have said that creation (or the world) always precedes any knowledge which takes it for object, and that this previousness expresses the condition of all created knowledge. This is to say that the idea of beginning is inseparable from the idea of the world. If the world is an exterior, it is also a before, an anterior. This is why it is said: "In the beginning God created." But by this we also see that this beginning is intemporal. It is the source of time, the origin of time, but it is not itself in time, for otherwise it would not be a beginning.[1] To ask, as the human mind is invincibly led to do, *when* this beginning took place is to pose a meaningless question. Time implies or requires a beginning, but the beginning does not imply time. The beginning is contemporary to all times, it is the permanent origin of the temporal flow; it is not a moment of time. We have just shown that knowledge of the world is always framed by the world, but it would perhaps be better to say that the world is the frame itself; the idea of the world is the idea of a frame for knowledge. This framing which defines the unsurpassable limit of our knowledge of nature, and which we do not see any more than we see the edge of our ocular vision, but which is 'always there', is temporal as well as spatial. It is beginning and end, as well as beyond and within. We do not say that it is before and after, for these are not limits and without limits there is no longer any world. The world is necessarily finite. Any affirmation to the contrary is strictly meaningless, since the ideas of world and finiteness are basically identical. But this finiteness is "analytically inexhaustible";[2] like the edge of my vision or my horizon, it is unattainable in itself. It is for itself its own exhaustion, it is a perpetual passing to the limit. Its finiteness is indefinite, its limitation is everywhere. By this we see that this limitation is ontological. The world-frame does not define an *a priori* condition of knowledge in the Kantian manner, which separates being and knowledge, thinking in this way to escape from the illusion of a knowledge ignorant of itself, but in reality reinforcing it. This

---

1 This is why, in our translation of Genesis 1–3 (*La Poème de la Création*, Ad Solem, 2002), we have translated the beginning of the text as "In the Origin."

2 Cf. René Guénon, *The Metaphysical Principles of Infinitesimal Calculus* (Hillsdale, NY: Sophia Perennis, 2001).

has to do with an ontological condition integral to the very substance of the world, and this is why the beginning, which defines a modality of this ontological finiteness, is an ontological beginning and not the beginning of a temporal series. It is an absolute beginning and not a relative one. Before this beginning there is nothing, not even God. Hence it must be said that the world has always existed, always temporally, in the sense that there never was a time when the world had not been. And perhaps this is what the notion of the eternity of the world meant in antiquity. For "even supposing that the world always was, it would not be equal to God in eternity."[3]

3. To enter into Sacred History we must depart from Time

The cosmogonic *Fiat Lux* is therefore actually intemporal. There never was a *time* when God had not created. Nor is creation an event which would happen on behalf of God, who is perfectly immutable, or on behalf of the creature, "since there is neither territory nor material support nor duration for something to occur before before the world itself already is."[4] For the act of creation is instantaneous, as St. Thomas repeats in several places. There is no successive relationship between the First Cause and its effect; the former produces the latter immediately. To adequately think about creation, it is therefore necessary to raise oneself above temporal succession, and, inasmuch as such an effort is impossible for the human mind, it must be said to the contrary that it cannot do otherwise, that it is led to it necessarily by the very notion of beginning. It is impossible for us to imagine a time without beginning, because time is only one of the conditions of cosmic existence and therefore it is always conceived of within a framework. It cannot be thought about as merely flowing. Rather it only flows between a before without beforehand and an after without afterwards, between a beginning and an end. But, on the other hand, it is not possible for us to think of a temporal beginning of time — no more than of a temporal end.[5] Consequently the idea of the beginning

---

3 *Summa Theologiae* I, q. 46, a. 2.

4 P. Sertillanges, in his contribution to *Initiation théologique*, vol. 2, bk. 2 (Paris: Cerf, 1952), 215.

5 What we have said about the beginning is in fact equally true for the end. The end of time is necessarily outside of time, since it marks precisely the 'moment' when time finishes. According to René Guénon's formula, which we have already

(identical to that of the end) saves human speculation from bondage to the temporal condition. The beginning is the 'instant' when there is at once a passing from eternity into time and a passing from time into eternity. And this is why sacred history begins at the Beginning: in order to delve into the reading of this history, it is in a certain manner necessary to depart from time. To know Revelation, in the world, is already to escape from the world, since this revelation obliges me to pass through knowledge of the world's beginning. What remains, however, is that the relative before and after have a meaning inside the beginning/end framework, but a symbolic one. Or rather their very being is a symbol, which is their whole reality. "God is prior to the world by priority of duration," St. Thomas says, "but the word 'prior' signifies priority not of time, but of eternity."[6] Now, if the word 'prior' can be laden with such a dignity that it designates the primacy of eternity, then the word "beginning" also designates, transposed *in divinis*, the Principle itself within which the world was created, and not the *priority* of eternity with respect to time; this is because the temporal 'prior' really represents, in time itself, the primacy of eternity over time. And here we have the true basis for Tradition.

II. THE TRANSCENDENCE AND IMMANENCE OF GOD

1. Creation is a Relationship

Up until now we have spoken of the world and creation inseparably. We must now distinguish them. In the active sense, creation designates the act by which God makes something from nothing, and this is how St. Thomas understands it. As for the world, it is the universality of created beings. This distinction is necessary if we are to identify the essence of the creative act and bring to light the paradox which characterizes it. But what we have just said about the 'beginning', which was meant to assist our speculative gaze in ridding itself of its temporal conditioning,

---

recalled and which is basic to all of these questions, "the indefinite is analytically inexhaustible." But the indefinite is only one aspect of the finite, which by definition is synthetically exhaustible, or again which is exhausted by the very finiteness of its manifestation. Space is limited because it is not time, or life, or thought.

6 *Summa Theologiae* I, q. 46, a. 1.

will surely facilitate the reception of this paradox. The paradox is as follows: the creative act, reduced to itself, is a relationship. Inasmuch as this act comes forth from God so as to end up with the creature, we should be spontaneously led to conceive of this relationship as proceeding from Creator to creature. Indeed an act supposes an agent, an action, and something acted upon, that is to say an object upon which the action is exerted. Creation being an action, we understand it as the intermediary which goes from creative Agent to created object.

Now this general idea of action is inadequate here, for there is not any object upon which the creative action might be exerted; the creative act is in fact an existentiating act, it is the source of the being of the object itself since creation is *ex nihilo*. This act therefore excludes every change, succession, or passage from an uncreated before to a created after. The world does not arise as the result of something produced. There is no 'being made' in the creative act prior to being made. All that may be said is that it is created, which is to say that this act defines the 'creaturely state'. Thus, to declare that the creative act created its object is to affirm that this act constitutes the whole being of the object, is to recognize that it is in truth simply an ontological relationship. For once every idea of movement is eliminated from this act as incompatible with divine immutability as well as with the 'nihilian' origin of creation, only a relationship remains: "Now when movement is removed from action and passion, only relation remains.... Hence creation in the creature is only a certain relation to the Creator as to the principle of its being."[7] But what relationship is involved here? We have said an ontological relationship, that is to say a relationship of being. Now what is the reality of this relationship? This relationship is real inasmuch as it is relationship to created being, since it is through this that created being exists. In other words: created being is real, and consequently the relationship causing it to be is equally real; if not it would cease to be. In its depths, it is this very being. But as much cannot be said if we consider the relationship of God to the creature. For God being Above-Being, according to the expression of Father Sertillanges,[8] He does not enter into a real relationship with anything other than Himself, and thus there can be no real relationship of God

7   *Summa Theologiae* I, q. 45, a. 3.
8   *Saint Thomas d'Aquin*, vol. 1 (Paris: Alcan, 1912), 305.

to the created, but only a relationship of reason, that is according to the viewpoint of human knowledge — without which it would not in any way be possible to speak about creation. Creatures are really tied to God because their reality depends upon this relationship, but God is not really tied to creatures, because His reality is totally independent. Our intellects spontaneously posit a relationship of God to creatures, whereas in reality there is only a relationship of creatures to God. And it must even be said along with St. Thomas that the relationship of Creator to creature has its real basis in the relationship of the creature to the Creator.[9] If we try to translate into metaphysical terms this doctrine of the real relationship of created to Uncreated and the rational relationship (or *secundum rationem tantum*) of Uncreated to created, one can say that in order to understand how God has produced creation — relationship according to reason — it is in reality necessary for the creature to *actually* rise again from its relative being to its eternal Source, to a real relationship. Here, no more than elsewhere in theology, knowledge cannot be separated from being. The whole movement of neo-theology, which sees in Thomism only an alienation in conceptual objectivity, conducive to making us forget our existence, in reality only bears witness to its own profound misunderstanding.[10]

2. God is Immanent to Creation

Insofar then as creation is something in the creature, it is a relationship. "Creation is not a change, but the very dependency of the created act of being upon the principle from which it is produced. And thus, creation is a kind of relation."[11] But insofar as this relationship is an act, namely the creative act, this act pertains to the Divine Essence and is only one with It. "Creation signified actively means the divine

---

9 *Summa Theologiae* I, q. 13, a. 7. "Creatures are really related to God Himself; whereas in God there is no real relation to creatures, but a relation only in idea [*secundum rationem tantum*], inasmuch as creatures are referred to Him." Meister Eckhart, affirming that "when all creatures say 'God' — then God [inasmuch as Creator] comes to be," has drawn out all the consequences of the Thomistic doctrine of dual relationship.

10 We are grateful to Father Chenu for having on the contrary emphasized the 'existential' dimension of Thomist doctrine in his short book on St. Thomas Aquinas (*Saint Thomas d'Aquin et la théologie* [Paris: Seuil, 1959]).

11 *Contra Gentiles* II, 18 [2], trans. Anderson, 55. Cf. likewise *C. G.* II, chs. 11–19.

action, which is God's essence."[12] Now, since divine causality is inseparable from its Essence, it follows that this causality is really immanent
and that God Himself, by His Essence, is totally immanent to the
being of the creature, so that it is unnecessary to say that created
being is separated from creative Being by the act of creation, since,
to the contrary, it is in this very act that the eternal Essence is wholly
present in the depths of the creature, but this is by the ontological
relationship of dependence of the created with respect to the Uncreated. Not from God's vantage point are we outside of God, but from
the world's.[13] This conclusion derived from the theological doctrine of
the both rational and real relationship between created and Uncreated
should never be lost from sight:

> since God is very being by His own essence, created
> being must be His proper effect; as to ignite is the proper
> effect of fire. Now God causes this effect in things not
> only when they first begin to be, but as long as they are
> preserved in being.... Therefore as long as a thing has
> being, God must be present to it, according to its mode
> of being. But being is innermost in each thing and most
> fundamentally inherent in all things since it is formal in
> respect of everything found in a thing.... Hence it must
> be that God is in all things, and innermostly.... [God]
> acts immediately in all things. Hence nothing is distant
> from Him, as if it could be without God in itself.[14]

And this immanence of God to creatures is extended down to the
demons themselves, inasmuch as they exist.[15]

---

12 *Summa Theologiae* I, q. 45, a. 3, ad 1.

13 "God sees Himself in Himself, because He sees Himself through His essence;
and He sees other things not in themselves, but in Himself; inasmuch as His essence
contains the archetype [*similitudinem*] of things other than Himself" (*Summa Theologiae* I, q. 14, a. 5).

14 *Summa Theologiae* I, q. 8, a. 1.

15 *Summa Theologiae* I, q. 8, a. 1, ad 4. By this we see how inexact it is to see
in Thomist creationism a thoroughgoing conception of divine transcendence. Truly,
for St. Thomas (cf. all of question 8 in the *prima pars*), divine transcendence implies
its immanence.

18

Metaphysics of the Immaculate Conception

THE FOREGOING CONSIDERATIONS CONSTI-
tute a first approach to the mystery of creation. As brief as they might
be, they have perhaps already resolved certain difficulties that are tied
more to the misreading of a theological perspective than to the very
nature of this perspective. The following considerations will lead us
into a greater depth of the mystery. Faithful to our method, we will
continue to rely on Thomist doctrine, while placing it however in a
light in which it is rarely viewed, because this light confers on the
conclusions of this master an unsuspected import, an import that
could be truly characterized as esoteric or 'gnostic'. Not only the most
standard theology, but also the most official dogmatic definitions of
the Catholic Church reveal by this light their highest significance and
rejoin the supreme metaphysical truth. Until now we have seen creation in its dependence with respect to the Creator; next we will see
the Uncreated in its ontological immanence within the created. But
now we have another immanence, that of the created in the Uncreated,
of the relative in the Absolute.

I. INFINITE POSSIBILITY AND
IMMACULATE CONCEPTION

1. Creatures have, in God, an Uncreated Being

Now we turn to an understanding of how God's immanence to creatures is made possible by another immanence, that of creatures in
God, and this expresses a still greater mystery of charity, if possible,
than that of the creative act which gives to things their being. It is
the mystery of the Divine Essence which allows itself, *in divinis*, to
participate by the Ideas of things. "By divine knowledge and will

351

things are more truly [*magis*] in God than God in things"[1] — *magis* meaning in a more eminent manner. God in fact sees or knows everything which is other than Himself only in Himself; through Himself "God sees other beings not in themselves, but in Himself."[2] And the knowledge that God has of things in Himself, joined to His will, is the cause of things.[3]

But what are things in God? Things are said to be in God as Ideas that God determines by the knowledge which He has of His Infinity. These are possibilities of existence or creation whose 'place' is the Divine Word, the knowledge of the Father. Now these possibilities of creation are nothing but the Divine Essence Itself insofar as It consents to be imitated and shared by the various beings.[4] We could say: at the very core of the Absolute, God allows Himself to be devoured by the innumerable multiplicity of beings, so great is the mystery of charity. God then makes things pass into created existence, guided by their models or exemplars within Himself. Not that He is compelled in some manner, for in God the Ideas or Archetypes are nothing but Himself; "in God these Ideas do not differ from the infinite Essence, they are this very Essence."[5] And so, although the possibilities have, in the world, a created existence, in God they have an uncreated existence; but, obviously, this uncreated being does not pertain to their nature as creatures:

> If form only, and not matter, belonged to natural things, then in all respects natural things would exist more truly in the divine mind, by the ideas of them, than in themselves. For which reason, in fact, Plato held that the 'separate' man was the true man; and that man as he exists in matter, is man only by participation. But since matter enters into the essence of natural things, we must say that those things have their absolute being [*esse simpliciter*]

1 *Summa Theologiae* I, q. 8, a. 3.
2 *Summa Theologiae* I, q. 14, a. 5.
3 *Summa Theologiae* I, q. 14, a. 8. The most important work about knowledge in God is the French translation (with commentary) of St. Thomas's *On Truth or Knowledge in God* by S. T. Bonino (Paris: Cerf, 1996).
4 *Summa Theologiae* I, q. 15, a. 2.
5 *Summa Theologiae* I, q. 18, a. 4.

more truly in the Divine Understanding than in themselves, for they have in the Divine Understanding an
uncreated being, while in themselves they have only a created being; nevertheless their relative being [*esse hoc*], the
particular nature of man or horse as such, is more truly to
be found in their own nature than in the Divine Understanding, because material being belongs to the truth of
man and because man does not have this material being
in the Divine Understanding.[6]

Do we then have to imagine all of these possibilities, existing in God
with an uncreated existence, as an infinity within the Infinite? Do we
have to understand that there is an infinity of possibilities in God, with
God bestowing a created existence upon those of His choosing? This
would be a crude interpretation. It is God Himself who, according to
the expression of Father Sertillanges, is an 'infinity of possibility',[7] or
again, who is Universal Possibility or All-Possibility. And so Father
Sertillanges declares: "the possibility which is in God is God Himself,
such as He knows Himself and such as He is . . . and it is our existence
in God that establishes our possibility and not the opposite."[8]

2. The Three Interpretations of the Immaculate Conception

1. Infinite Possibility, which is God Himself inasmuch as He knows
Himself as archetype of every possible thing, may be defined, we think,
as the Conception God has of Himself; God conceives of Himself,
and the fruit of this Conception is the infinity of possibilities. And
precisely because these possibilities are absolutely infinite, it might
be said that the Divine Conception is immaculate, since it excludes
every determination, every limitation, which would constitute a stain,
a 'mark' (like that of an umbilical cord) indicating the origin of a
thing, its dependence, its closure upon itself. For each possibility is
God Himself inasmuch as He is infinitely conceiving of Himself as a
model shared by every possible being, and therefore each possibility

6 Ibid.
7 Cited by J. Chevalier, *Histoire de la Pensée*, vol. 2 (Paris: Flammarion, 1956),
777. We have discussed this doctrine in *Problèmes de gnose*, 167–211.
8 Cited by J. Chevalier, 777.

is without origin or closure, but infinitely open to the illimitability of the Divine Essence.

Such is the most general metaphysical significance of the Immaculate Conception understood as infinite Possibility.

Is this doctrine in harmony with the dogma of the Immaculate Conception's Marian character? Three considerations seem to favor this approach. To begin with, what does this privilege mean for Mary if not that she is a creature preserved, from her conception, from Original Sin? And here is precisely the first interpretation of the dogma. Now what is a creature preserved from Original Sin if not the creature in all of its purity, that is to say in perfect conformity with its archetype *in divinis*? Thus Mary's immaculate conception refers directly to the immaculate conception that God has of Mary. But, on the other hand, and this is the second consideration, Mary herself has told us at Lourdes not: "my conception is immaculate," but: "I am the Immaculate Conception" — literally: *Que soy era Immaculada Counceptiou* — an indisputable statement which, in our eyes, constitutes the major theological event of modern times. Therefore Mary is not one immaculate conception among others, but the Immaculate Conception itself. In the third place it must be admitted, since Mary is a creature, that she is a creature apart: all creatures have in God an uncreated being, but Mary's uncreated archetype is the Divine Essence inasmuch as it also conceives all archetypes. Mary is then the human face of *in divinis* Possibility in which she, according to her own words, participates mysteriously.[9]

2. If this doctrine is now applied to the Christian theology of the Divine Mystery, a second interpretation is immediately identified, which, as a matter of fact, is only another formulation of the preceding one; this one concerns the Divine Essence, the Godhead, in relation to its Trinitarian unfolding. Is not the Trinitarian unfolding in fact the Conception according to which the Divine Essence 'reveals' Itself to Itself? Thus the Immaculate Conception could be understood as the 'interior matrix' of the Divine Essence, the unfathomable depths of the Godhead, the shoreless Ocean of absolute Substance,

---

9 The most profound reality of the Marian being is not, in this sense, of a feminine nature, but beyond the masculine/feminine distinction. It seems that this is why St. Bernadette always designated the apparition by the neuter pronoun: *aquero* (that).

the more-than-luminous Darkness of the superessential thearchy, in which the Trinitarian relationships are eternally deployed. This is in fact a perfectly immaculate conception, since the real distinction of each Hypostasis in no way *determines* or limits the Godhead, which remains one, unique, and infinite in each of them.

The Marian dimension of this second interpretation seems to be illustrated for us in that 'celestial icon', the apparition at Pontmain. The children actually first saw the Blessed Virgin at the center of a triangle formed by three stars, after which the Virgin faded away and was merged with the immaculate blue enclosed within the triangle, immaculate because devoid of all stellar light, while the three stars continued to twinkle — as if Mary were being identified with the depth of the trinitary Essence itself.

3. A third equally supreme theological interpretation of the Immaculate Conception is clearly warranted, but this time at the properly hypostatic level of the Trinitarian deployment. It will be enough to recall that, in Catholic tradition, the Word is designated as the Concept, fruit of the begetting of the Son by the Father through the mode of knowledge. If the Father is Conceiver and the Son Concept, the Holy Spirit will therefore be considered as the Conception itself, that is to say the 'unitary space' through which and in which the Divine Essence, as Father, can beget itself, as Son. And here we rediscover the hypostatic maternity of the Holy Spirit, which we have already emphasized at length. This interpretation is so much the more consistent since the Word is traditionally viewed as the 'place of divine possibilities', the entirety or summation of all possible Concepts, and since we have appropriately started by considering the divine possibilities in order to define the metaphysical notion of the immaculate Conception. So then to the Word — hypostatic Synthesis of the archetypes, hypostatic and infinite Concept which the Godhead, as Father Conceiver, forms of Itself — responds, by virtue of Its eternal possibility, the Holy Spirit as hypostatic and immaculate Conception.

From the Marian point of view, it is clear that here the Mother of Christ, as Immaculate Conception, is related to the Holy Spirit, as hypostatic Maternity. This relationship, which makes of Mary a 'manifestation' of the Holy Spirit — and not an incarnation, which is excluded — was developed in particular, as we have seen, by Father Manteau-Bonamy. But it must be added that the amazing working-out of the theology of the Immaculate, a teaching given by Father Maximilian Kolbe not only in his writings but even in his life, is now the better known.[10] It follows that if Mary is indeed the Mother of God, because Mother of Christ who is God, she is also the Mother of God in a transposed sense, inasmuch as the Holy Spirit, her divine prototype, exercises His 'maternal' function within the bosom of the Divine Trinity.

We have come to understand in this way the Immaculate Conception or infinite Possibility, first in Mary, as the privilege proper to her election by virtue of being Mother of the Savior, next in the Divine Essence as the root of its Trinitarian fecundity, and lastly in the Holy Spirit as maternal Hypostasis of the Word's engendering. And so we see how the figure of Mary casts light even on the highest mysteries of theology. But is it not the (pre-Conciliar) liturgy itself which invites us to such a metaphysical ascension? Does not the liturgy itself identify, in a certain respect, the Virgin with Divine Wisdom? For example this reading from the Mass of the Nativity of the Virgin: "The Lord possessed me in the beginning of his ways, before anything had been made, at the beginning.... When he was preparing the Heavens, I was there; when he hollowed out the abysses and fixed their law... I was there. I was with him, ordaining everything."[11]

II. PRIME MATTER AND
IMMACULATE CONCEPTION

Marian theology, however, is not to be entirely reduced to the dogma of the Immaculate Conception; it includes another pole, that of Christ's virginal Conception. Although the first mystery looks toward the Divine Essence in itself, the second rather concerns God inasmuch

10 This doctrine was given to us by the Abbé André Gircourt, who was inspired with it on December 8, 1942, without any exterior contact. [Cf. Abbé Henri Stéphane (pseudonym of Abbé André Gircourt), *Introduction à l'ésotérisme chrétien*, vol. 1 (Paris: Dervy-Livres, 1979), 89–91. — *Trans.*] By a miraculous convergence, three Catholic theologians, without the least collaboration, ended up with an identical conclusion. And some claim that theology is not a rigorous science!

11 Proverbs 8:22–35; Mass of September 8 in the traditional liturgical calendar.

as He is given to the world. And just as the first mystery has served as a model for understanding how creatures have in God an uncreated being, and are therefore archetypically identified with God Himself, so the second mystery will enable us to understand how creatures, viewed in their created being, are distinct and separate from Him, so that there is as if an inverse analogy between the two mysteries.

1. The Infinite Charity of the Divine Essence or Principial Imitability

We have said that *in divinis* the Absolute Essence lets itself be 'devoured' by the non-quantitative multiplicity of archetypes. It lets itself be shared or, again, imitated by the infinity of creatures, so that we should speak of it as infinitely imitable. The doctrine of the *principial imitability* of the Divine Essence founds Thomist exemplarism.

> Since the exemplars of all beings are in the Divine Intellect, it is necessary that there is, in Its Intellect, a multiplicity of Ideas, but as so many conceptions.... God actually knows His Essence perfectly and, consequently, He knows It according to all of the modes by which It is knowable. Now It can know Itself not only according to what It is in Itself, but also as it is able to be *participated* in by creatures according to their mode of likeness to the Divine Essence. Each creature then possesses its own intelligible form, according to which it participates in a likeness to the Divine Essence through such or such a mode. So then, inasmuch as God knows His essence as *imitable* by such a creature, He knows It as exemplar [or archetype] and as the idea of this creature.[12]

The central intuition of Thomism is rightly to be seen in this doctrine of the participability of the Divine Essence.

We can envisage in God then, in the very terms of St. Thomas, two 'aspects' of the Divine Essence: the Godhead in Itself, in its absoluteness, and the Godhead inasmuch as it is imitable or participable by all

---

12 *Summa Theologiae* I, q. 15, a. 2.

creatures, which, in this principial Imitability, are so many modes of knowledge of the infinite Essence through Itself. Imitability *in divinis* is basically nothing but the Immaculate Conception and is identified therefore with the infinite Charity of the Essence.

2. Materia Prima

However, if we keep to the just-given description, the creature as such would disappear, since the archetype is God Himself; this is why St. Thomas can say, as seen at the beginning of this chapter, that creatures have their (uncreated) being more truly in God than in themselves. But, he adds, it is in the nature of the creature to be not only form, but also matter. If it were only form, it would be identical to the archetype and, ultimately, to God, since form is the projection of the archetype within a matter. What is this matter then which *differentiates* the created from the Uncreated, and which, for this reason, we will characterize as a cosmic differential?

Without dwelling on an extremely subtle question (we are thinking of the difficulties which St. Augustine tells us he encountered in understanding this notion in Book 12 of the *Confessions*), we will recall only this: considering the Paros marble statue of Apollo, we can distinguish the form (Apollo), the intelligible structure, and the matter (marble) which is given form by this structure. But this matter is itself of marble, that is to say already composed of an intelligible form (Paros marble) giving form to a matter, stone. But stone, since it is distinguished from other materials, is itself given form, and therefore includes the combination of a form and a matter, and so forth for all creatures. If we pursue this division towards the bottom, we end up with a *prime matter* which is no longer given form by anything, and which is therefore neither graspable nor intelligible; towards the top we end up with a form of forms which is the *Logos* Itself. This first matter is obviously non-corporeal — it is the same with psychic and even angelic matter for St. Bonaventure. It is the universal substratum from which all things are made, it is that which receives within itself all created forms, but has no form itself and remains always virgin with respect to all its determinations. It seems, though, that the mystery of *materia prima* is somewhat illuminated when viewed as cosmic charity. Does not St. Paul say that "charity upholds everything"?

Now, is not *materia prima* also the universal upholder, that which untiringly gives itself to all the forms it receives, that which is the cosmic receptacle, the very receptivity of the created? Genesis presents *materia prima* under the symbol of water because, St. Thomas says, "it is apt, like water, to be given form by all of the forms."[13] But also cosmic charity because through it God created the world; that is to say, through it, through this unconceivable otherness which defines it, God projects the pure forms into this other-than-Himself. It is the very substance of cosmic love, since it testifies, through its mysterious nature, that God consents to what is other than Himself.

But is it not this that calls for a comparison with the virginal conception of Christ in Mary? To the cosmic kenosis of God consenting to project the possibilities just this side of Pure Being, which is *materia prima*, corresponds the kenosis of the Divine Word consenting to be clothed with human form in the bosom of the Virgin Mary. This is a much more profound analogy, since the uncreated Word is precisely the Form of forms, the hypostatic Synthesis of all possible creatures, so that one can quite really affirm that in Mary the whole of creation is made flesh. Still it is necessary to understand, moreover, that the work accomplished in Mary is more astounding than that accomplished at the creation of the world, since within her it is the whole of creation, through the grace of Christ, that is renewed in its principial splendor. Finally, just as in the Beginning the Holy Spirit brooded over the Primordial Waters of Universal Existence so that the creatures might be produced, so *Maria* (in Latin *maria* = the waters) is overshadowed, covered by the shadow of the Paraclete so that the Word may be conceived in her. And so the symbolic equivalences of *Maria, Mater, Materia,* and matrix become apparent, for only a virgin creature can be Mother of the Uncreated, only perfect emptiness can contain total Fullness.

3. Materia Prima is the Inverted Reflection of Principial Imitability

We come now to the last aspect of this doctrine, and here again it is the Marian mystery which serves us as guide.

---

13 *Summa Theologiae* I, q. 66, a. 1.

Since the virginal Conception of Christ in Mary implies the Immaculate Conception of the receptacle, we are likewise invited to connect *materia prima* with Divine Imitability. And by this a sure-to-be-raised difficulty is resolved. Is there not actually a risk of making the *materia prima* a principle of creation juxtaposed with the divine principle, thereby negating creation *ex nihilo*? But Marian symbolism in particular teaches us that these two notions are inseparable and as if two faces of the same reality. Just as the virginal Conception implies the Immaculate Conception, so *materia* implies Imitability, the distant reflection of which it is and in which it finds its model and divine prototype. This is because God consents, in the bosom of His own Essence, to let Himself be shared and imitated according to an infinity of possibilities, because here below something-other-than-Himself can exist, that existential otherness which is only another name for *materia prima*.

Yet, from the One to the other, the analogy is inverse and it might even be said doubly so, if the two poles of the Marian mystery are equally taken into consideration.

On the one hand, in fact, the *Imitability/materia prima* relation defines the axis of creation, while the Immaculate Conception/virginal Conception relation defines the axis of Redemption; and the work of Redemption is in a certain manner the inverse of the work of creation, since it leads back to God that which was separated from Him under the effect of sin. On the other hand, there is an inverse analogy between *Materia prima* and its Divine Prototype, since it founds the possibility of an other-than-God by its unintelligibility and indetermination, while principial Imitability founds the possibility of Divine Intelligibles by its superdetermination. In other words, the superabundant fullness of divine possibilities is necessarily reflected in the poverty of *materia prima*. And perhaps St Thomas had such an inverse analogy in mind when he declared: "Although matter as regards its potentiality recedes from likeness to God [who is in act], yet, inasmuch as this potentiality is its *being*, it retains within itself a certain likeness to the Divine Being."[14]

14 *Summa Theologiae* I, q. 14, a. 11, ad 3.

III. THE COSMIC VIRGIN AND THE HOLY SPIRIT

1. The Spiritual Significance of Prime Matter

The mystery of creation is indeed a mystery of Charity, since the Most Holy Virgin, who is created charity, sums up in herself all aspects of this mystery. The Church, Tradition, the Fathers, and the Liturgy have designated Mary in multiple ways. Throughout these designations we find ever and again the presence of the universal protoplasmic, always virgin 'substance', the cosmic differential between created and Uncreated, distance and proximity, separation and union. Let us recall a few of these figures: Jacob's Ladder, which unites Heaven and Earth and which *supports* the ascending and descending angels, is the Most Holy Virgin Mary, whom the Middle Ages called 'ladder of Paradise'; the Burning Bush, "which burned without being consumed," says the Bible, and which *supports* the Manifestation of God — that is, the Word — is, according to the third antiphon of the Vespers of the Circumcision, the Most Holy Virgin Mary; the Ark of the Covenant, made from acacia wood (symbolizing purity and innocence), summary of the World, which *bears* the Tablets of the Law, that is to say the 'lettered' incarnation of the Divine Word, is the Most Holy Virgin Mary, queen of Creation and receptacle of the Divine Immanence. But the Most Holy Virgin Mary is also the closed Garden of the Earthly Paradise, the sealed Fountain, the City of Jerusalem, Holy Mount Zion, the Temple where the Presence of God reposes, Noah's Ark, the golden Urn containing the true Manna, the guarded Table *bearing* the living Shewbread.

However, the analogy that we have emphasized between Mary and the *materia prima*, which has already yielded so many teachings, once more enlightens us about one of the least-noticed aspects of the protoplasmic substratum, and this, it might be said, is its spiritual function and meaning.

What is *materia*, insofar as it is seen as a type of the Virgin, if not, in some manner, the creature in its pure state, the creature totally reduced to itself, the creature in its virginity, the merely created, short of which there is only nothingness? This is, in the most literal sense of the term, the *creatum ex nihilo*, the further side of nothingness. We have called it a cosmic differential, that is to say the indeterminate and ungraspable boundary between created and Uncreated; but also boundary between existence and non-existence: it is non-nonexistence, the quasi-absolute miracle that distinguishes the *creatum* from the *nihil*; it is the *ex*. As pure submission to the creative Will, it constrains it in some way to pour forth its illuminating flux that gives birth to the *logoi* of all creatures. It is ontologically wedded to the Holy Spirit in its creative effusions, it is inseparable from them. It gives him its passivity so that he may manifest his activity there, which is to reveal the cosmic words.

We have here a first positive meaning of *materia*. We can go yet further if we consider the relation by which Mary is united to the Holy Spirit. It is said, as we shall see in the following chapter, that God created the world *in* the Holy Spirit. It might also be admitted that He created *in the materia*. But these two 'receptacles' do not have the same function and, in one sense, there is no common measure between them. First, because one of these receptacles is created, since it is even the creation as receptacle, whereas the Second is uncreated. But also because the first receptacle separates, whereas the Second unifies. The first receptacle separates, this is to say fragments or segments. This is *materia prima* as principle of individuation, for Aristotle and St. Thomas, because it makes creatures other than God and then because it unthinkably isolates them from their ontological Source. But also, and by way of consequence, it isolates them from each other, since they can only be united in their common nature which is the uncreated Word.

Thus each creature is limited by its own receptivity, each creature is separated from all others from the instant that it is 'received', that is to say from the instant that God consents to what is other than Himself and therefore to what is welcomed within itself. This 'within itself' is moreover not a true ipseity, which is only found in God. It is only its reflection, the reflected modality, for the Ipseity cannot be reverberated to the confines of creation. It manifests itself then as an obscure point-state which, although no creature is 'in itself', it is not in any others either. This is a negative ipseity, and this is the cause of the individuating or separating power of *materia prima*. All created things thus appear as isolated from one another by their deep-rootedness in an obscure point, which defines their otherness with respect to God and the rest of creation, their 'being outside of God'.

But, by a wondrous logic, this is also what effects a saving reversal. And this reversal is actually effected in Mary, according to the order of grace, in such a manner that she is indeed Co-Redemptrix for the entire world. For this 'being outside of God' is also the 'from what' by which creatures may go toward God in giving themselves to Him. The virginal creature, Mary in each one of us, is the root-point from which we are able to grow up to the heavens. And this is why the Liturgy sings: "*Ave Regina caelorum, Ave Domina angelorum, Salve Radix, Salve Porta*: Hail Queen of Heaven, Hail Lady of the Angels, Hail Root, Hail Door." And how is this reversal effected in Mary if not by her *fiat* to the message of the archangel Gabriel? And what is the *fiat* if not the act of passivity, the liberty of obedience, the response of *materia prima* to the recreative act? Thus the true meaning of the *materia* becomes apparent, the meaning it possessed before Original Sin and which expresses its pure nature: the *materia* is not a principle independent of God, but, as passivity's receptiveness, it is the response of the created to the creative act; it is the *ontological yes* which the creature silently utters by the very existence of its being, an instantaneous and immediate response, the *adsum* [unto me] of the creature to the creative Will, the creature's presence and submission: "Behold the handmaid of the Lord, be it done unto me according to Thy word." The *fiat* of the creature is the returning echo of the *Fiat Lux* of Creation.

So once again we discover a truth for which we had already felt the need in anthropology: it is impossible, we say, to define the nature of man without taking into account his spiritual finality. What is true for man is also true for all creation. There is no pure cosmology, but the truth of creation only appears in the recreative work of the redemption. However, this cosmic salvation, through which the created reveals its true nature, is only accomplished through the ministry of the human creature, and first through the ministry of Mary, the perfect creature.

2. Cosmic Alchemy

The work of the *materia* is therefore made explicit in the figure of Mary. Thanks to the perfect receptivity of her perfect passivity, the *Virgin/Materia* in some manner constrains the Creative Spirit to pour forth its existentiating flux into the cosmic indefiniteness of the primordial Waters so that the 'word-forms' of all creatures are given birth there, just as Mary's perfect humility offers its nothingness to the paracletic overshadowing in order that the Word might take flesh there.

Clearly then, here as well as there, matter can only receive form through the operation of the Holy Spirit. The form, whose sacred prototype is the Christ-Word, requires, for its manifestation, the Marian charity of the *materia* in its pure receptivity, but also the hypostatic Charity of the Holy Spirit in its pure Effusion. At the seam of the matter/form composite there is the love of the Divine *Pneuma*.

With the help of these three elements, form, matter, and *Pneuma*, cosmic alchemy is realized. We have seen how, at the lowest point of creation, virginal matter constitutes a divine 'hither-side' out of which the other-than-God can make a return to the Principle. But this return also and necessarily passes through the mediation of form, for it is as if the 'cosmic memory' of metacosmic archetypes, since the created words are images of the Uncreated Word, the unique Mediator and hypostatic Relation. Just as the Word has descended into Man in order that man ascend into God, so the Divine Archetypes have descended into the created so that the created might ascend back to the Divine Word. Finally, hypostatic Love establishes the cosmic circumincession, which "moves the sun and the stars." This is the will-to-form which is inwardly open to the universality of created beings and aspires to fall toward the Principle. And so we rediscover the already-mentioned alchemical symbolism of the *solve et coagula*. The Holy Spirit realizes his intelligible coagulations — the creatures — by uniting them to some matter, next dissolving them in the circumincession of cosmic Love and then in the circumincession of Divine Love, where they realize their uncreated prototype. The Holy Spirit is the true Alchemist, the Word of Wisdom is the true Philosopher's Stone, and the Virgin is the true Athanor. The cosmological *solve et coagula* is likewise mentioned by St. Maximus the Confessor: "The essence of all things . . . has always been in motion and moves in the manner of expansion [*diastolé*] and contraction [*systolé*]. For it moves from the most general genus, through the less general genera, to the species, through which and in which it finds itself divided, and it presses on down to the most specific kinds of being, where its expansion comes against a limit, which circumscribes its being on the 'downward' side; then once again, it moves from the most specific kinds of being through more and more general categories, until it is included in the most generic genus of all, and there its contraction meets its end, limiting its being on the 'upward' side."[15] Notice how the interpretation here of the *diastolé/systolé* movement is the reverse of the one which we have given for *solve et coagula*. But in reality these two interpretations are complementary. What is contraction with respect to the creature is expansion by irradiation from the viewpoint of God, the Irradiant Source, and vice-versa. There can be no absolute viewpoint here. We can represent the Principle as a point, the transcendent center of the cosmic sphere, as well as by an infinite sphere that surrounds the cosmic point from all sides.

15 *Ambigua*, PG 91:1345B–C, quoted from Hans Urs von Balthasar, *Cosmic Liturgy* (San Francisco: Ignatius Press, 2003), 158. The texts of St Maximus the Confessor and their commentaries in the "Syntheses of the Cosmos" chapter of *Cosmic Liturgy* should be read.

19

Trinity and Creation

IN EXPLAINING THE METAPHYSICS OF THE
Immaculate Conception we have striven to situate ourselves first at
the root of the Trinitarian mystery, in the depthless Abyss of the
Godhead, and then at the level of its hypostatic deployment. But
the tree of the Trinity casts its shade over all creation, even to the
uttermost reaches of the world. Therefore it is fitting to identify its
traces, and to appropriate them to each Hypostasis.

I. APPROPRIATION OF PRODUCTIVE CAUSES

The three Persons of the Trinity have only one will, one action, one
operation. But a particular aspect of the creative act, and therefore
of created being, can be more especially appropriate to a specific
Person. This is the unanimous teaching of Catholic theology. St.
Athanasius summarizes this doctrine in the following formula: "The
Father has created everything through the Son in the Holy Spirit,
for wherever the Word is there is the Spirit, and what the Father
produces receives its existence through the Word in the Holy Spirit."[1]
In fact the Word contains the exemplary causes of all things, and
so it is that the Father creates the world *through him*: "All things
were created by the Logos who is as it were a divine nexus, the
threshold from which flow the creative outpourings, the particular
logoi of creatures, and the center towards which in their turn all
created beings tend, as to their final end."[2] And, in the same vein,
St. Thomas declares: "To the Father is appropriated power which is
chiefly shown in creation, and therefore it is attributed to Him to
be the Creator. To the Son is appropriated wisdom, through which
the intellectual agent acts; and therefore it is said: *through whom all
things were made*. And to the Holy Spirit is appropriated goodness,

---

1 *Epistola III ad Serapionem*, 5, in PG 26:632B–C.
2 Lossky, *Mystical Theology*, 99.

to which belong both government, which brings things to their proper end, and the giving of life — for life consists in a certain interior movement; and the first mover is the end, and goodness."[3] But St. Basil of Caesarea already had declared: "In the creation bethink thee first . . . of the original [principial] cause of all things that are made, the Father; of the creative [demiurgic] cause, the Son; of the perfecting cause, the Spirit. . . . For the first principle of existing things is One, creating through the Son and perfecting through the Spirit."[4] In this way the perfecting role of the Holy Spirit is clarified. As to the relationship between charity and perfection, we see that the Holy Spirit, He who is Love itself and within whom God has created, actualizes the perfection of all things, since through Him all things are led to their ultimate fulfillment, which is God. God cannot create *in* anything else but the Holy Spirit, since the Holy Spirit is hypostatic charity. The Father gives being; in other words, being is a gift. Now Gift is one of the proper names of the Holy Spirit. And so, for creatures, being is conferred on them in the Holy Spirit; it is the Holy Spirit who conveys being from the Principle to creatures. But, through the fire of His charity, it is also He who restores all things to their Principle. Equilibrating the centrifugal effects of creative power exerted toward the periphery of the Cosmic Wheel (*Rota Mundi*), He is the universal magnet that holds together the totality of created beings with the attractive power of love, a power that 'spirates' the circumference towards its uncreated Center. If mankind lives, if plants grow, if stars revolve in the sky, it is because they are moved by the Holy Spirit. He alone prevents them from falling into nothingness. Thus, for creatures, Creation is a formidable act since, in its creative explosion, it distances them from the Principle. But it is likewise and simultaneously a permanent return from exteriority toward the interiority of the One, since the Holy Spirit gathers up this cosmic scattering by encompassing everything within the arms of his eternal Love.

3   *Summa Theologiae* I, q. 45, a. 6.
4   St. Basil of Caesarea, *On the Holy Spirit*, 16.38, in *Nicene and Post-Nicene Fathers of the Christian Church, Second Series*, vol. 8 (New York: The Christian Literature Company, 1895), 23.

II. APPROPRIATION OF EFFECTS

1. The Triple Reflection of the Uncreated in the Created

From the appropriation of productive causes, we turn now to the appropriation of their effects in creatures, through which we discover the *vestigia* or traces of the Holy Trinity. But, in this respect, a distinction has to be made between man and other beings. Thus, if man exhibits a true image of the Trinity, other beings show only traces; in man there are both vestiges and the image, in other beings only vestiges: an image in his spiritual being because man possesses being (with reference to the Father), intellect (with reference to the Son), and will or love (with reference to the Holy Spirit) — in other words exhibits an image of the Trinity in his active and conscious being:

> But in all creatures there is found the trace of the Trinity, inasmuch as in every creature are found some things which are necessarily reduced to the divine Persons as to their cause. For every creature subsists in its own *being*, and has a *form*, whereby it is determined to a species, and has *relation* to something else. Therefore as it is a created substance, it represents the cause and principle; and so in that manner it shows the Person of the Father, Who is the principle from no principle. According as it has a form and species, it represents the Word as the form of the thing made by art is from the conception of the craftsman. According as it has relation of order, it represents the Holy Spirit, inasmuch as he is love, because the order of the effect to something else is from the will of the Creator. And therefore St. Augustine says (*De Trinitate* vi) that the trace [*vestigium*] of the Trinity is found in every creature, according as *it is one individual*, and according as *it is formed by a species*, and according as *it has a certain relation of order* ... and also (*QQ.* 83, q. 18): *that which exists; whereby it is distinguished; whereby it agrees.* For a thing exists by its substance, is distinct by

its form, and agrees by its order. Other similar expressions may be easily reduced to the above.[5]

2. The Holy Spirit Vibrates the Architectures of the Logos

This caption conveys what we would like to say about the Holy Spirit. And so from one perspective we see that, in creation, the Divine Word and the divine *Pneuma* are opposed to one another, since one distinguishes and the other unites. This view is, however, much too superficial. These appropriations by no means exclude but rather imply each other. Nothing can be systematic here, for each one may be found again in the other two. The hierarchical ordering of beings with respect to each other, and of all creation with respect to the Creator, is appropriated to the Holy Spirit; but, basically, it lies in the nature of things, in the quiddities, essences, or forms of things that are appropriated to the Word, the place of the Intelligibles. The respective functions of the Word and the Holy Spirit's 'traces' therefore need to be made specific here.

When we studied charity *in divinis*, we saw in the *Logos* the prototype of the subsistent relation, and so we need to realize that creatures are analogically connected among themselves and to the Principle by their *logoi*, by their 'intelligible forms', since it is in the *Logos* that they have their exemplary causality. Therefore insofar as they bear a trace of the *Logos*, insofar as the *Logos* is manifested in them, they are ontologically related. But this hierarchical ordering, depending as it does on the essence of the *Logos*, would be a pure state of being as well as a pure ontological situation, and, as such, would not manifest itself if not somehow dynamized by the Holy Spirit who supports and expresses this ordering throughout all creation. It is the Holy Spirit who is the revealer of this cosmic and metacosmic congruence. A being is not only a state of existence; it is also a will. As a pure state of existence, as a pure intelligible structure one being is clearly

---

5 *Summa Theologiae* I, q. 45, a. 7. The separative power of matter and the unifying power of form, that is to say the distinguishing and determining function of the Word, must not be confused. We speak of an individuation by matter and an individuation by form, but these are not the same individuation: matter separates and fragments, form qualifies. Through matter a being is not other beings, through form it is itself.

ordinated to all other beings, but, we could say, simply by interior relationships, as each point on the circumference is connected to all others through its relationship with the center, whose projection it is (following the radius). On the other hand the Holy Spirit is 'circular'. Through his presence he creates the circumference of the worlds, where each point is exchanged for all of the others; he makes of this circumference a vibration emanating from the supreme Center and, through these spiritual vibrations, brings back to the Center that desire for eternity which animates everything from the angel to the dust of the road: "The whole creation has been groaning in travail," says St. Paul (Rom 8:22). These groanings and sufferings are the work of the Holy Spirit. And, in this, he is indeed cosmic charity; he is cosmic charity in this universal interconnectedness and exchange, where each thing gives itself to the others and all give themselves together, through the priesthood of man, to God in order to fulfill their nature.

3. Order and Ordination

Matters could also be expressed in this way: through the Word created being receives a form — or essence or *logos*. This form *determines* the existence of the created being. But this is a dual determination: it simultaneously defines both the nature of a created being and its hierarchical situation in the cosmic order. To determine the nature of a thing, its quiddity, what it is, is also to determine everything that it is not and, hence, is also to assign a thing its rank among all creatures, for its nature is not the only nature (the possibility called 'nature' is not exhausted by itself alone). Nor is it completely separate from all of the other possible natures either; otherwise it would be as if nonexistent for the rest of creation and vice versa. Because it is what it is (cardinal determination), a creature is also an element of universal order (ordinal determination). Thus a musical note, *because it is itself*, that is, such or such a specific note, defines its own place within the octave. By its very nature a creature is a nexus of relationships implying the entire universe. And this is why it is right to appropriate this function of ontological relationship to the *Logos*. Without doubt this doctrine of a dual — cardinal and ordinal — determination asks that we see the creature as a harmonious totality, as a cosmic hierarchy in which each thing has its *raison d'être* and occupies a position suitable to its nature. Surely, it also has as a consequence the doctrine of universal correspondence, the doctrine that corporeal, animic, and angelic creation, which define for man the three basic degrees of cosmic reality, are like so many reverberations of the Unique *Logos*. Thus, the doctrine of universal correspondence is just another way of expressing the unity of creation in the multiplicity of its aspects and, hence, the very notion of cosmic hierarchy. But it is clear that these notions are actually inseparable from the notion of creation, and that, in the Bible, the goodness and beauty of the universe do not represent poetic themes but metaphysical axioms. Here, briefly summarized, is what St. Thomas calls the Word's "work of distinction."

However, a created being does not possess its nature in act *ab initio*. It realizes it by a relative passage from potency to act. In this sense it provides the end for which it was created, an end that cannot be attained for it by any other creature. But the realization of this end is tied to the ordinating work of the Holy Spirit. It is he, the *vinculum perfectionis*, the "bond of perfection," who actualizes and perfects creatures while ordinating them to their end. Now such is the condition of every creature: that it can fulfill its proper end, and therefore realize its own nature, only by giving itself to another creature. Only through otherness does it discover its own identity. And likewise all creatures realize themselves by giving themselves to creation, while all creation does so by giving itself to God. For the end of everything is truly endless, infinite; otherwise, for a creature to realize its end would simply mean its destruction and annihilation. By this we see that the two meanings of 'end'—annihilation and perfection—are two aspects of one and the same realization: "If the grain of wheat does not die, it will not bear fruit." The end as death is the means to the end as fulfillment. Thus the roots of the tree give themselves to the sap-bearing trunk, finding their fulfillment therein; the trunk does the same for the branches, and the branches for the leaves, flowers, and fruits. The fruit has its end solely in the continuity of the species, but the species is not an end in itself—it manifests an aspect of Divine Beauty, and, through it, incarnates an archetype of the Eternal Truth that instructs us. Then, *through the ministry of the contemplative spirit*, the species itself becomes conscious, for consciousness, that cosmic chimney which burns on its hearth the tree of creation and bears it in its flames up to heaven, "is a '*raison-d'être*' for the states in question."[6]

Clearly, Love ordinates everything to everything else. If the Word is order, the Holy Spirit is ordination, the One who animates and reveals the universal intersection of cardinal and ordinal determinations. In this way we glimpse the metaphysics of charity in all of its unity. According to the order of fraternal charity, the Holy Spirit is animator and revealer of ontological proximity, which should be related to the Word; according to the order of Divine Charity, we see Him through His function of hypostatic maternity, revealer of the *Logos*; now we see him as animator and revealer of the 'word' of creatures in his function as cosmic charity — the work of creation requires the concurrence of the "two hands of God,"[7] the Word and the Holy Spirit. If a palpable reality can symbolize an intelligible reality, it is by virtue of an ontological correspondence, the work of the Divine Word. But it is the work of the Third Person to *set* palpable and intelligible realities in correspondence, to *bring* the symbolizing toward the symbolized (i.e., the symbol itself in its ordinating function of relating the one to the other). Creation thus proceeds like a musical score: the staff and notes have been composed by the *Logos*, but it is the Holy Spirit who sings it.

III. THE CHOIR OF ANGELS AND THE COSMIC HYMN

1. The Uncreated Spirit and Created Spirits

Finally, to be complete, we must come to the consideration of angels, for, as we have observed at the beginning of this work,[8] there can be no cosmology that does not take into account angelic existence.

It is fitting, after all, that we treat of them at the very moment when the Holy Spirit comes into view as the one who makes the

6 R. Guénon, *The Multiple States of Being* (Ghent, NY: Sophia Perennis, 2001), 42.

7 Cf. St. Irenaeus, *Contra Haereses* IV, Praefatio, in PG 7:975B.

8 Ch. 7, section 2, 4. On angels, consult Father Serge Bonino's dossier-book, *Les Anges et les Démons* (Les Plans sur Bex: Parole et Silence, 2007). Tiziana Suarez-Mani has shown the great philosophical importance of medieval angelology: *Les Anges et la Philosophie* (Paris: Vrin, 2000).

cosmic Harp of the *Logos* sing. For the angels have their place in the universal concert, to the very extent whereby the choir which they form is itself, in some manner, only the created reverberation of the uncreated Angel who is the divine *Pneuma*. There is in fact an altogether direct relationship between the angels and the Holy Spirit, so that it is possible to consider the former as a created prolongation of the latter. We will focus briefly this relationship inasmuch as it concerns the nature as well as the function of the angels.

As to their nature, angels are known to be purely spiritual creatures, whereas the human spirit is united to a sensible body. These creatures are therefore clothed with the spiritual form for which the Holy Spirit is the divine prototype, so that the angels are so many images or reflections of the Third Hypostasis.

As to their function, on the other hand, since the word *angel* signifies messenger, bearer of news (ev-angel means good-news, good 'angeling'), repre*sen*tative, spokesman [*porte-parole* (Fr.) = word-bearer], lieutenant [*lieu-tenant* (Fr.) = place-taker or -holder] of God. Now, as we have seen, in the bosom of the Trinity the Holy Spirit is Gift, Outpouring, Energy, Procession, while to the Word can be related the more static function of Relation: to speak of hypostatic relations is to envisage the Trinity from the viewpoint of the *Logos*, to speak of Trinitarian processions is to envisage It from the viewpoint of the Spirit. Likewise we have seen how this function of the Spirit's supreme Dynamism is linked to its function of hypostatic maternity, inasmuch as this Hypostasis is 'revelatory' of the Word *in divinis*.

In the same way, *ad extra*, the Spirit is in its cosmic missions an animating outpouring spread through all creation and through the revelation of the Word of God in Tradition, Holy Scriptures, and the Church's teaching. But notice how these two missions of animating outpouring and prophetic revelation are only one in reality, once we observe that creation is another Book of divine revelation, a veritable 'cosmic prophecy', while the Holy Book, the Word of the Lord is another world, that of the divine recreation, a veritable 'prophetic cosmos'. This junction of Word and World is explicitly realized moreover in the sacrificial liturgy of the Mass, wherein creation, completely summarized in the Eucharistic bread, is transubstantiated into the Body of the Eternal Word. And this shows that a third function of the Spirit must be added to the preceding two, the liturgical function which, in the new liturgy, before the consecration, underscores the invocation to the Holy Spirit (epiclesis). Animating function, revelatory function, liturgical function — these are precisely the three essential functions of angelic creatures.

2. *Governing Angels*

As for the first function, perhaps the least recognized today, we will say this: the existence of angels as governors and animators of the sensible world is not only a datum of faith, but also a requirement for every cosmological philosophy. God knows how much the Scholastic (but first Platonico-Aristotelian) notion of the *angelus rector*, the angel-governor of the celestial spheres, has been ridiculed. And yet a scientist as eminent as Kepler makes constant use of them. Now, recalling what we have said in our outline of cosmology, it will be understood that, for corporeal beings as much as for their causal interactions, the existence of angels is required. The unity of a corporeal being cannot be material and must be related to a superior principle of spiritual nature. And it is the same, for example, for the movement of a celestial body. How many people know that one of the direct consequences of the theory of relativity is that, since there is no absolute space able to serve as immobile referent, the simple idea of trajectory or the displacement of a star *makes strictly no sense in itself*? But do we need to conclude that this displacement has no reality and that the world is a phantasmagoria? This subjectivist idealism is untenable. What then? It is realism itself which obliges us to posit a transpatial 'cosmic consciousness' that makes up the unity and therefore the reality of this movement; otherwise it is quite simply inconceivable. In the same way the simple growth of a tree is inexplicable in purely determinist terms: it is in effect an incarnation, across a dispersive space/time multiplicity, of a specific and unifying theme which, consequently, comes necessarily from beyond the corporeal world. And this is why St. Thomas has reason to say with Origen that the world has need of angels who "preside over animals at their birth, and over the growth of shrubbery, plants, and other things."[9]

---

9 *Summa Theologiae* I, q. 110, a. 1.

Finally, at the human level, we encounter the guardian angel whom God has appointed to assist us. But here this is no longer a matter of realizing the corporeal and psychic unity of a being and its acts. It is also a matter now of realizing its spiritual unity. From this viewpoint the guardian angel is like the perfect form of each essence — or, still more profoundly, it is the created model of our uncreated archetype *in divinis*. That is to say, in it is expressed the Will of God at our side. Each uncreated archetype, by virtue of the divine Imitability, is as if the unique face which God turns toward such or such a unique creature. The guardian angel is the created mirror of the unique Face of God for me, which it is responsible for reflecting down to me so that I may be illuminated by it. And this is why Christ affirms: "See that you despise not one of these little ones [men who have attained to perfect charity] for I say to you, that their Angels in heaven contemplate always the face of my Father who is in heaven" (Matt 18:10). Or again, and according to another symbolism, the guardian angel is like the ray which, traversing the entire cosmos, unites the archetype to the person: it is thus the bearer of the celestial message which God addresses to our being. It keeps our immortal essence pure and restores it to us when the moment has come.

3. Revelatory Angels

Of the prophetic or revealing function of angels we will say only a few things, since it is attested to throughout the whole of Scripture. We will simply remark, along with Cardinal Daniélou, that the Gospel is much more (ev-)angelic than one ordinarily thinks, for the fundamental mysteries of Jesus Christ are directly revealed there by the angels. In other words, contrary to the heretical theses of modern exegetes who, with Bultmann, see in the Gospels the mythological constructions of the primitive Christian community expressing the kerygma according to its culture, the evangelists affirm that neither the Incarnation nor the Resurrection nor the Ascension is a human interpretation (*even inspired!*) of the facts, whose witnesses they themselves or others were. But these mysteries are 'explanations' coming directly from angels. For it is all too evident that they themselves understood nothing and would have indeed been incapable of formulating such mysteries. As a result, then, *the source of our theology is essentially angelic.*

4. Serving Angels

Finally, we will conclude with the liturgical function. It is the Epistle to the Hebrews[10] that calls the angels 'liturgical *pneuma*', that is to say, serving or 'ministering spirits'. And it is the Second Epistle of Peter[11] that calls them 'Glories'. Glory is, as we know, the radiant presence of God in Himself and in creation. The angels are themselves glories because they are, each in its rank, so many pure mirrors in which are collected the myriad rays of the Divine Sun and who reflect them back to the supreme Source, so that through them creation as a whole becomes a sparkling of lights, all of which celebrate the unique Light of the Word. But the celebration of this cosmic liturgy, in which the Word becomes light and the Light word, is only possible on condition of the perfect submission of the reflecting mirror, on condition that it sacrifice itself to become nothing but a crystalline transparency. Otherwise the mirror becomes dark and reflects its shadow over the whole of creation: such are Satan and his legions. The angel is 'glory' only if it is 'servant'.

This perfect effacement of the created is what is realized on earth in sacramental mode and pre-eminently in the transubstantiation of the 'bread of angels'. This is what, in all worlds, the Virgin Mary, Queen of Angels, realizes, because she is the most pure mirror that God has ever formed in which to have His glory rest. Here, then, Heaven and Earth are invited to celebrate the splendor of the Father; here the cosmic immensity of men and things, embraced in the infinite circle of the Holy Spirit, is assembled around the mystical Lamb; here the celestial armies are surrounding the crowned Virgin; here is the eternal *Trisagion* that ascends to the super-essential Thearchy.

10 Heb 1:14.
11 2 Pet 2:10.

PART VI

The Spiritual Life of Charity

INTRODUCTION:
"CHARITY IS THE DOOR TO GNOSIS"

WE BEGAN WITH THE QUESTION: HOW CAN charity be, in Christianity, the preeminent spiritual way? We can now suggest an answer, with which the metaphysics of the *Mysterium caritatis* will be complete. The most universal formulation which can be given to this answer is the following: the Holy Spirit is the revealer of the Word from whom He is inseparable, and such is the Essence of every spiritual way. To us this seems equivalent to saying that charity is the door to gnosis, that is, to divine knowledge which consists of eternal life, since charity should in fact be related to the Holy Spirit and gnosis to the *Logos*, and since we gain access to the *Logos* through the Holy Spirit.

For such a formulation to be admissible over the many objections raised, we will start from God in order to go towards man while passing through Christ. In the first place, therefore, we will touch on the relationships of love and gnosis *in divinis* (Chapter 20). Next we will see how love and gnosis are crucified and reconciled at the same time on Good Friday (Chapter 21). After that we will study their relationship to the spiritual way, with the help of some major expressions of Christian spirituality (Chapter 22). Lastly, we will conclude with a brief study of what is also the end of the spiritual way: the deification of man in Jesus Christ (Chapter 23).

20

Love and Gnosis 'In Divinis'

OBVIOUSLY WE WILL NOT REITERATE EVERY-
thing we have explained on divine charity, but will try to grasp as
precisely as possible the way of love in its metaphysical principle—in
other words, show that in God also, in God first of all, love is the door
to gnosis. We suppose as taken for granted then everything we have
previously established, but we will explain it in a new way, and draw
from it a perhaps not-yet-perceived consequence. However, because
this involves the principle of the spiritual way, we first need to deal
with what serves as basis for the way of triumphalist charity, a basis
that justifies all of its follies.

I. GOD IS LOVE, BUT ALL LOVE IS NOT GOD
1. The Nature of Spiritual Statements

Before broaching the question at hand, we have to refute one last time
the false assertions of triumphalist charity. This charity, which we have
challenged everywhere, finally takes refuge, as in an impregnable fortress,
behind the words of St. John: "God is Love" (1 John 4:8). And since
God is Love, every love is a road towards God. This inference from the
Johannine proposition serves as justification for the theses of modernist religion. Now this inference rests upon the heretical confusion
between the order of ontological statements and that of spiritual ones,
the former being concerned with the Cause and the latter with effects.

What is a spiritual way? A spiritual way is a path that leads from
illusion to Reality, and by which what is not goes toward What is.
Actually the word 'way' designates the route and the journey at the
same time. It binds together and, by the same token, separates. Therefore it requires us to renounce what falsely gives itself as reality — this
is what illusion is — in order to unite us to That which alone is real,
but at present seems illusory. Recall here the famous saying: "we must
burn what we have adored, and adore what we have burned." Spirituality in this sense belongs to the order of becoming, but not under

this order's temporal form alone, for, as Origen has said, we should also attend the "School of the Souls." If a spirituality or a way exists, this is because we have not arrived wherever we should be. And if we have not arrived there, this is because, in a certain manner, we are in ignorance about our true state. Conversely, this ignorance implies a false knowing and therefore a false certainty: we live as if our present situation were the only reality and the definitive term of our existence. If we were truly aware of not having arrived, we would have already departed. This is why every spiritual way consists in a conversion or even a reversal, which means two things: first, 'to turn away from', and second, 'to turn towards'. Now how do we turn away from something if this something is truly real? Could it be that the spiritual way begins in a lie? Are the injunctions of our spiritual teacher, Jesus of Nazareth, the Son of God, mere idle chatter? "If someone comes to me and hates not his father, his mother, his wife, his brothers and sisters, and even his own life, he cannot be my disciple."[1] Must we then set St. John at variance with Christ, He who never said that God was love? It is clear to see that, if every love is God, there is no longer any spiritual way. A spiritual statement therefore needs to teach two things: to turn oneself away from what is not, and to turn oneself toward What is. We could just as well say that the Cross is the preeminent spiritual statement, because every spirituality is crucifying, and, hence, every spiritual statement should be explicitly or implicitly built on a crucial model, or be related to it, that is to say, be comprised of two propositions, one stating what is not and the other What is. It cannot not denounce an illusion from which we must detach ourselves. Being realization, it is a call to Reality, it is a voice, the voice of Reality, crying out in the desert of cosmic unreality.

2. The Nature of Ontological Statements

As for the ontological statement, that is to say a statement about Being, it is necessarily made by mode of analogy. With no reality of the created world providing the human mind with an adequate concept of Uncreated Being, it is only possible to speak about Being by transposing to the level of Pure Being those of our concepts that are

1 Luke 14:26.

open to such a transposition by virtue of a certain analogy with it. This does not mean that we have no 'idea' or intuition of Being. Quite the contrary: an ontological transposition is only possible through an ontological intuition that defines this transposition's higher term and its meaning. But notice that this involves an ontological statement and not the intuition that is its source, which in itself cannot to be formulated, precisely because formulations are situated completely outside of the necessarily supra-formal degree of Pure Being. This statement, ontological in its object, can therefore only be analogical in its mode. And yet analogical transposition equally requires, beside ontological intuition, a symbolic intuition defining the lower term of the transposition, that is, an intuition that perceives in created realities what they reflect of Creative Being. For analogical transposition, if it is not founded *in re*, upon the nature of things, could not serve as an adequate support for an ontological statement. It follows that every ontological statement, inasmuch as it is expressed, implies a certain indistinction between created and Uncreated unless its analogical nature is explicitly declared. When in Exodus God says, "I am who I am," He explicitly denounces, by this very formulation, the inevitable analogical use of the word *being*, if we might dare express ourselves in this way, while unveiling the discontinuity between every being and Pure Being: there is no being if it is not *the* Being. This is the supreme ontological statement and therefore the metaphysical key to all other ontological statements.

But when St. John declares that God is Love, this statement, which is clearly ontological since it has to do with Pure Being, rests upon an analogy (that of created love with the divine nature) but an unavowed analogy. The analogical transposition is therefore implicit in this instance. It is much more legitimate to be 'ignorant of' the analogical transposition's mediation, since created love is a very real reflection of Uncreated Love and even alike to this Love. In the order of being every love is Love. And this is true for an objective truth, but not for a subjective one, according to which it should be enough to love — no matter whom or what — in order to enter into God. From the subjective viewpoint of spiritual realization, we are able to enter into Divine Love only by renouncing human love, or again, by renouncing what there is of the human in our love. "By this we recognize that we love the children of God, when we love God" (1 John 5:2), says St. John some lines after saying *Deus Caritas est*. The ontological statement designates the Cause while declaring its effect, but inasmuch as the Cause is present with the effect and ultimately inasmuch as it is entirely reabsorbed by it. Again we could say: the ontological statement is posited, *a priori*, from the viewpoint of God who sees all things *within* Himself. This is why we can say, along with St. John, *Deus Caritas est*. But to see from God's viewpoint is the privilege of objective intelligence. This is not the viewpoint of spiritual doctrine, which might be called subjective intelligence because it is an understanding of our subjectivity. From this viewpoint the effect must go back toward its Cause, that is, become aware of being only an effect and therefore renounce taking itself for Cause. The heretical confusion between these two orders destroys both. An ontological statement is treated as an existential fact: God is love; therefore everything that exists as love is God and causes us to realize God, so that those who hold such a view no longer see why man should make an effort to rejoin God, since, by modernist definition, all that he is *is* already God. This is truly a sin against the Spirit. Only ontological statements have the right and the duty to be absolute, that is to ignore the inevitably contingent mode of their formulations — whereas spiritual statements cannot ignore the relative, since their aim is to save what is relative by teaching it to become aware of its relativity. The "*Sum qui Sum*" of the ontological order corresponds, in the spiritual order, to the "You are the one who is not" of Christ to St. Catherine of Siena.

3. Infinite Love loves only the Infinite

Simple logic, for all that, is enough to reduce to nil the modernist interpretation. God is Love, they say, and consequently Love is God. And in the same way, "To sum up, Absolute Being is revealed to be composed of Love."[2] Such propositions make no sense and only make the underlying woolly philosophy more obvious. When we say: God is Absolute Being, we are defining the name 'God' in a way that is equivalent to saying God or Absolute Being. But how might

---

2 A definition given by a congress of theologians. Cf. *Le Monde*, September 26, 1969.

we define it? By a definition that is at once positive — Being — and negative — absolute. Being is affirmed by mode of analogy; *absolute* indicates the inadequacy of all analogy, since it signifies what is not relative and is bound to nothing. Hence, to say that God is the Absolute Being is to say that He is transcendent with respect to everything that can be stated and known about Him distinctively (*Sum qui Sum*), and therefore that He is the supreme, irreducible, and strictly non-predicable Subject.[3] This also means that everything attributed to God is unconnected to Him, or again that every relation of attribution is 'absolved' in Him. With respect to this real Subject, there are only apparent subjects. "HE WHO IS [the Absolute Being] is the principal of all names applied to God; for it completely encompasses Being like the infinite ocean and is without determinations of substance." This statement by St. John of Damascus is commented on in this way by St. Thomas: "All other names determine some mode of substance, whereas the name HE WHO IS determines no mode of being, but is indeterminate to every determination, and this is why it denominates the 'infinite ocean of substance.'"[4] Whenever it is affirmed that Love is God or Love is Absolute Being, the intent is to define the Essence of the Absolute Being through one of its modes. Not only do they limit God, but they even destroy Love, the essential attribute; for it is God who 'absolutizes' Love, it is in God that Love exists in perfection, and not Love that absolutizes God.

To say that God is Love is thus to say that in God Love is infinite. Now Love can only be infinite if applied to an infinite object. This infinite object can only be God. It follows that, in saying God is Love, we are saying that God loves Himself with an infinite Love. When this Love is poured out upon creatures, it is still God who is loving Himself through them, since, if He loves them, this is in order to render them similar to Himself. Also, the fire of this deifying Love is capable of burning up all the lies and illusions of human love. And this is why we must "hate our brothers" in order to come to God, for, inasmuch as we have not come to Him, we cannot love in truth. "By this we recognize that we love the children of God, when we love God and keep

3   That which can never become an attribute (predicate).
4   *Summa Theologiae* I, q. 13, a. 11.

his commandments" (1 John 5:2). Divine Love has something of the implacable about it, going as far as the crucifixion of one's humanity. "The one who does not love anything human loves all men."[5]

II. MORE THAN LUMINOUS DARKNESS

1. Love and Darkness

"God is Love," says St. John; but he also says at the beginning of the same epistle: "And this is the declaration which we have heard from Him [Christ] and declare unto you: that God is Light" (1 John 1:5). These two theological definitions are inseparable, even though it is the former that enjoys a great success among the modernists for whom it serves as justification. However, to take things literally, we must give primacy to the latter, which in St. John's testimony comes from Christ himself. In universal symbolism Light designates Knowledge or Truth. Likewise Light, Truth, Truthfulness, and Eternal Life are closely linked for St. John.[6] "The one who does the Truth, comes to the Light" (John 3:21). This Light is the Word; "He is the true Light" (John 1:9). To know this Light is to escape from sin and death. "We know that whosoever is born of God does not sin, but the generation of God preserves him and the wicked one does not touch him. We know that we are of God and the whole world lies in the power of the evil one [*mundus totus in maligno positus est*]. And we know that the Son of God is come. And that He has given us understanding [*sensus*, spiritual intelligence] that we may know God, the Truthful One, and that we may be in the Truthful One, his Son. This is the true God and life eternal" (1 John 5:18–21).

God is love. This, as we have said, means that God loves Himself with an infinite love. Inasmuch as God loves, Love is an essential attribute of Him. Inasmuch as it is he himself who is loved, Love is the Holy Spirit's proper name. "In God the term 'love' can be taken in two senses: essentially and personally. If taken personally, it is the proper name of the Holy Spirit."[7] But it is the whole Divine Essence

5 St. Maximus the Confessor, *Texts on Love*, III, 37.
6 Cf. Jules Lebreton, *Histoire du Dogme de la Trinité*, vol. 1 (Paris: Beauchesne, 1910), 516–20.
7 *Summa Theologiae* I, q. 37, a. 1.

that, through Love, blossoms in the three hypostases. At the very least, Love is given to us as the key to the blossoming of the Divine Essence, and it casts a glimmer upon the super-intelligible mystery of the Trinity. Here we glimpse the supreme sense of the formula: Charity is the door to Gnosis; and we will add that the theological formulation is in this case indistinguishable from its Object: God is Light, God is pure Knowledge, or again, God is totally revealed to Himself. This self-revelation of the Divine Essence is 'borne' by essential Love. It is in the Gift that God makes of Himself to Himself that He knows Himself as pure Knowledge. The more-than-luminous darkness mentioned by St. Dionysius the Areopagite is the Love (Darkness) that is as if the 'support' or 'substance' of Trinitarian Gnosis. Let us take the image of physical light. It is pure light through and through, and this translucency is inseparable from its luminosity. If light were 'itself', in the manner of a reality which, in order to be itself, should belong to itself like the human ego, it would be impenetrable and would obscure by its opaqueness. If it 'was' not at all, there would only be night. It is necessary then, in order for light to be, that it be in itself an *esse ad aliud*, that its ipseity be formed by its own otherness, or again that it be, in its very 'interiority', 'exteriority', that is to say a pure gift, pure love, pure *mysterium caritatis*. Each corpuscle of light—to be precise, any part whatsoever of luminous 'substance' *is* indiscriminately a corpuscle, in other words there is no 'intercorpuscular space'—each corpuscle of light is, we say, a tiny bit of obscurity divested of itself, a black diamond offering its own substance to the flame that instantaneously devours it. Light is made of consumed obscurity. And so it is for the Divine Essence. The Divine Essence is pure Gnosis and, inseparably, pure Love. Its *esse ipsum* is mysteriously an *esse ad aliud*; Love is the substance of Its Knowledge. Its Knowledge is the Truth of Its Love. Supreme Gnosis is the radiant Light from the core of supreme Charity. In the divine Night of His essential Love God reveals Himself to be an Ocean of Light. "Light shines in the darkness," says St. John, "and the darkness has not comprehended it." It is the same *in divinis*. The eternal Darkness in which the Light shines is Love, the matrix of Gnosis. But conversely, this Darkness does not 'contain' the Light, because it is the Light that contains It. Finally, we shall mention the ontology of the Burning

Bush. God is revealed there in His Aseity. The support of this revelation is a bush that burns without being consumed. Transposed into God: the eternally burning bush is Divine Love, the support of His Self-Revelation.[8]

2. The Burning Bush

What we have tried to express so clumsily about the Divine Essence is equally true for the Persons or Hypostases. We will just recall what we have said of the hypostatic maternity of the Holy Spirit, who is Person-Love, in whom the Father reveals Himself through the Son, the hypostatic Gnosis. If we observe again that the liturgy and the Fathers have seen in the Burning Bush a symbol of the Virgin, and in the ontological declaration a symbol of the Word, it will be understood, as much as this is possible, that the *Theotokos*, the Virgin as Mother of God, is mysteriously identified under a certain aspect with Essential Love and under another with Personal Love, that is with the Holy Spirit. This is how Christian iconography, as exemplified by Nicholas Froment, interprets the Burning Bush.[9] The Virgin appears there as the very flame of the bush, presenting to Moses the Incarnate Word who holds in his hand *a mirror wherein is reflected the Virgin and Child*, a mirror in which it is possible to see a symbol of the Holy Spirit. This aspect of hypostatic maternity is also expressed in the West by what is called "the maternal role of the Holy Spirit."[10] "The Holy Spirit is for man a Mother who nourishes him at the breast of My divine Charity." These words of God to St. Catherine of Siena sum up the whole doctrine that we have just suggested.

"Superessential and more than divine and more than good Trinity, You who preside over divine Christian wisdom, lead us not only

8 What we say of the Light that contains the Darkness can also be understood of the Knowledge that contains Ignorance. From this viewpoint the *Mysterium caritatis* is supreme Ignorance which, like the burning bush not consuming itself, is the eternal extinction of itself; that is to say not ignorance of something, but a sheer and absolute ignorance, totally immanent to pure Knowledge.

9 *The Burning Bush*, 1476, oil on canvas by Nicholas Froment, Cathedral of Aix-en-Provence. Art historians view Froment with a certain disdain. True, his painting is no longer altogether sacred in its form. But the meaning and symbolism of his canvases evince a sure theological science and mystical development.

10 Cf. Lemonnyer, *Le rôle maternel du Saint-Esprit* (Paris: Librairie de l'Arc, 1920).

beyond all light, but even beyond unknowing up to the highest summit of the mystical Scriptures, there where the simple, absolute and incorruptible mysteries of theology reveal themselves in the more-than-luminous Darkness of Silence: in Silence one understands in fact the secrets of this Darkness, about which it is saying too little to assert that it blazes with the most dazzling light in the bosom of blackest obscurity, and that, all while itself remaining perfectly intangible and perfectly invisible, it fills with splendors more beautiful than beauty those intellects that know how to shut their eyes."[11]

11   Cf. Dionysius the Areopagite, *The Mystical Theology* 1, 997A–997B.

21

Love and Gnosis in the Crucified Mediator

CHRIST'S DEATH ON THE CROSS SEEMS, IN MODern eyes, to prove the folly of love. Does St. Paul not speak of the "folly of the Cross"? And do we not also see here the justification for all excesses into which triumphalist charity leads Christians? Why should God, who can do all things, have to sacrifice his Son to save us—when a single word from Him would suffice—unless by a kind of excess of love? Nor is it truly understood, from this triumphalist perspective, that this Love is realized in sacrifice. How can so good a God be angry at man for his sin? Should He not pardon everything? How can he let his Son be an occasion for hatred and murder? Jesus was, after all, innocent and his Crucifixion an assassination; his sacrifice, the proof of his love, a work of hatred. What satisfaction did divine justice derive from this expiation on the Cross? Viewing the Crucifixion in this way, from the side of justice in its implacable rigor, we surely understand that reparation *can* be made, but we no longer understand how this reparation is the work of Divine Love. And yet it is, since it is God Himself who gives Himself in sacrifice. On the other hand, viewing the Crucifixion from the side of mercy—once its motive becomes clear and justified in itself as gratuitous love—we fail to see why this mercy should achieve its purposes under the form of a bloody crucifixion, the cruelty of which seems especially incompatible with an all-merciful God.

Here as elsewhere triumphalist charity manifests its heretical incomprehension of pure charity, which inevitably leads to a rejection of the Crucifixion and its sacrificial reality, and then, as a consequence, to a negation of original sin, redemption, and finally the Incarnation itself, for God became incarnate with a view to death on the Cross and not to pleasing men. Every step of His earthly life led to the gibbet. There, upon the Cross, is the heart and center of his Incarnation; it is the sword of this cross that rends the veil of creation, opening the door to eternal life that is *gnosis* of the Divine Essence.

391

This sacrifice—the prototypical sacrifice—of the crucified Mediator realizes the union of love and gnosis, or again, of charity and truth, under the form of mercy and justice. Not only does it realize this union, but even makes it possible because it *is* this same union. To say that love is the doorway to gnosis is to say that the Word, the eternal gnosis of the Father, died upon the Cross of his love so that man, through love of the Cross, might have access to eternal gnosis. Christ's charity is not some indefinite and unformed love-impulse, but is mortally espoused to the rigor of the Cross. Because Christ's love is true Love, it is the Love of Truth. The Cross is the cross of both Love and Gnosis. Divine Gnosis is crucified by Love, and human Love is crucified by Gnosis in the person of the God-Man, he who is made of Love and Gnosis, *"plenum gratiae et veritatis,"* "full of grace and truth" (John 1:14). And so, just as charitable power does not produce the relation of proximity but gives access to it, so the Divine Will's love for man does not produce the Cross, but leads to it as to that which alone can bestow on him the seal of truth, because the Cross is the symbol of the ontological relation itself.

We need to be reminded, then, of the Crucifixion's 'gnostic' dimension, which shows how the idea of justice refers to that of truth and expresses it in the created order.

I. ORIGINAL JUSTICE IS TRUTH
1. Justice is a Hierarchy

Modern man spontaneously thinks of sin in a subjective way and has completely lost sight of its objective side. This error undermines his entire spiritual and moral life, and all his ways of thinking about original sin and redemption. But, in reality, justice is defined as order and original sin as disorder. This doctrine is objective because it lies within the nature of things. Original justice is order, and order is hierarchical harmony reflecting and actualizing unity in multiplicity. Justice is, in fact, the quality of what is just. Justness marks the relationship between things, for what is just is to have one thing in a relationship with something else in conformity with their respective natures, and thus in conformity with the right that they have to actualize these natures. A just relationship makes it possible for a reality to be what it is. This possibility is not actually realized *ipso facto* in the world of created things, and this for two reasons: first, no reality is in its own being identical to its nature, but to the contrary it finds itself subject to becoming; second, the world being complete, the actualization of a particular nature will clash with the actualizations of all other natures. If the first reason establishes the right for a created being to be what it should be by nature, the second establishes the idea of hierarchy. Viewed in itself, a right is always absolute and therefore excludes all others. But it is impossible to translate this absoluteness into equality and to say that since all rights are absolute they are all equal, for equality destroys rights. This right is in fact the right of a nature to be what it is. Now equality is realized only on the purely quantitative plane of numerical unities ($1 = 1$); thus, under its sway, everything tends to a numerical juxtaposition, which is only possible through the destruction of all of the qualitative differences that specifically make up these natures, so that, with equality, a right is the right to nothing.[1] Hence, to preserve this right (its absoluteness being unable to express itself through an egalitarian juxtaposition), there remains only a hierarchical superpositioning, one in which this right, renouncing its absoluteness, consents to its own relativity; in other words: a superpositioning where one right may have more of a right to something than another. But for this renunciation to be not just resignation and compromise, it has to be based on something other than constraint.

Conversely, for there to be a hierarchical subordination, a principle of hierarchization regulating the subordination of natures by their degree of proximity to the Principle is needed. These two requirements are satisfied in a single and unique operation: the submission of the creature to the Creator, of the relative to the Absolute. All rights are established by the creature renouncing its absoluteness in the face of the rights of the Absolute; and it is even through this obedience alone that these rights are established. By this act of submission all natures have access to a formal and qualitative equality, not horizontally among themselves, but vertically with respect to God. Adverting

---

1   The democratic ideal, whether one likes it or not, is necessarily condemned to reduce human relationships to mathematical ones. This curse is already expressed in the *more geometrico* style of Rousseau's *Social Contract*, which has corrupted all of Western political thought; or which, if you prefer, is its original sin.

to this absolute Criterion, each is seen — simultaneously — in its own truth, which defines its hierarchical rank. Justice consists, then, in the subjection of lower to higher, because this subjection is in conformity with ontological truth. But, being a subjection, it is an act of the will; for if, by definition, the intellect is subject to the true, it is nonetheless powerless to bring itself into subjection, which is an operation proper to the will. The intellect does not obey; it is in itself obedience. But the will obeys, in the active sense of this verb, because it can always refuse to be subject to the truth perceived by the intellect. Therefore, if the will obeys, which it cannot do merely by being aware of the nature of things, it must be an effect of Divine Grace. Hierarchical harmony, which gives definition to justice, is indeed based on the nature of things, but for it to be actualized by the will the power of grace is required. Thus justice is the effect of truth, but also the effect of supernatural grace.

2. Justice is the Truth of Nature realized by Grace

Adam was created in a state of original justice. In him

> reason was subject to God, the lower powers to reason, and
> the body to the soul: and the first subjection was the cause
> of both the second and the third; since while reason was
> subject to God, the lower powers remained subject to rea-
> son. . . . Now it is clear that such a subjection of the body
> to the soul and of the lower powers to reason, was not
> from nature; otherwise it would have remained after sin. . . .
> Hence it is clear that also the primitive subjection by virtue
> of which reason was subject to God, was not a merely nat-
> ural gift, but a supernatural endowment of grace.[2]

This state of original justice, which is defined by hierarchical harmony, was therefore an effect of grace, but in its turn also had the effect of allowing each nature to realize itself in keeping with its degree of hierarchical perfection, and in this sense this effect is also a grace. Original sin consists in the destruction of this hierarchical harmony,

2 *Summa Theologiae* I, q. 95, a. 1.

through the revolt of reason against God. Instead of being subject to Divine Law, the reasonable soul has turned back upon itself (this is an *anti-metanoia*) and desired its own lower powers, an act of revolt that had instantaneous repercussions all along the hierarchical axis. The natures forming this axis were not destroyed in themselves, *but they could no longer actualize themselves according to their truth*: they are the stones of a toppled building scattered on the ground. By Adam's sin "original justice was taken away, whereby not only were the lower powers of the soul held together under the control of reason, without any disorder whatsoever, but the whole body was held together in subjection to the soul, without any defect."[3] Human nature is wounded, not destroyed.

But neither does the healing of nature (the reconstruction of the building) suppress fallen nature so as to replace it with grace; what it does do is restore the order of original justice. Thus, insofar as justice is truth, this restorative work is the work of truth. And truth, says St. Thomas, is either the conformity of the intellect to things or the conformity of things to the intellect; in architecture, for example, a material building is true if it conforms to the rules of art: "Therefore God's justice, which establishes things in the order conformable to the rule of his wisdom, which is the law of his justice, is suitably called truth."[4]

We must now ask ourselves why this work of truth has to be accomplished in a sacrificial mode, and, after this, we will see how only God could offer it.

II. THE NATURE OF SACRIFICE

1. The Destruction of the Old Man

No extrinsic reason can justify the redemptive sacrifice, because this sacrifice is its own justification (*justitiam facere*). But to ask why Our Lord would need to sacrifice himself in so bloody and cruel a way is to ask why Adam's sin had such consequences.[5] Was not God able

---

3 *Summa Theologiae* I-II, q. 85, a. 5.

4 *Summa Theologiae* I, q. 21, a. 2.

5 All of those questions about the crucified Mediator — so exciting to the Modernists — are not new, and reflect no present-day need. The Socinians, in particular, denied the redemptive sacrifice, and saw in Christ's death on the Cross only a

to prevent a single revolt from involving the destruction of the entire human order? No indeed! God could not do it, for that would be equivalent to asking whether truth can be error, or a circle a square. The natural order is not true just because it is willed by God, but also, and at the same time, it is willed by God because it is true. No one is held responsible for understanding this *metaphysical proof*, but neither does anyone have the right, for all that, to poison theological understanding with their own contradictions. The truth of the natural order requires submission of the reason to God, of the lower soul to reason and of the body to the soul. *It is not within anyone's power, not even God's, to destroy this order while maintaining the integrity and perfection of natural realities which this order is charged with assuring* — for hierarchical harmony and the perfecting of natures are inseparable; the world is not composed of independent and autonomous natural elements, but, to the contrary, each of its elements is able to actualize itself only in its relation to the whole.[6] Through sin a new human order was set up, which is actually a disorder; a new human structure — the work of the devil — was established, which is in truth a 'destructuring'. Therefore this human order needs to be destroyed in its turn, so that the Divine Order may be rediscovered; this 'new man', which St. Paul calls by its true name, the 'old man', must die so that the new man might be born. The fallen Adam has to be sacrificed, so that the primordial Adam can sacrifice himself to God once more.

2. The Cross of Sacrifice

What is sacrifice? To sacrifice is to immolate, to renounce, to set apart; it is also to render sacred (*sacrum facere*). Immolation and oblation, two dimensions — one negative and the other positive — in a single act: the horizontal branch of the cross immolates, the vertical branch offers up to God. Why immolate? To immolate is to grind (*molo*, "to chew"), to break bad connections, to destroy a structure. Fallen man is constructed poorly, his reason is subject to his soul and his soul

---

beautiful example of virtue given to mankind. Socinian and modernist Christologies are basically identical.

6 Nature in itself is not destroyed but altered in its effects by sin; no longer is it able to realize the perfection of its being. Hierarchical harmony and the perfection of natures are inseparable, but not identical. In this lies the whole *mysterium creationis*.

to his body. This hierarchical subversion has to be abolished; these chains of subjection have to be broken. What is united by sin needs to be separated, and this is a true death, because each 'part' of man illusorily believes that its life and its joy are to be found in subjection to a lower one. Reason has to die, and this is the 'crowning with thorns'; the will has to die, and this is the 'carrying of the cross'; the body has to die, and this is 'crucifixion' itself.[7] And in just this way is justice accomplished. The instant that immolation becomes oblation, what has been sacrificed is rendered sacred: God takes possession of whatever renounces self-possession.

III. THE GNOSIS OF GOOD FRIDAY

1. Christ's Humanity is Open to all Men

Only God, as we mentioned, could have accomplished this sacrifice of Truth, and this from two points of view: as to the redemptive effects and the communication of redemptive grace on the one hand, and as to the sacrificial mode itself, to the sacrifice of the Cross on the other. And this is what we will turn to now.

What is immolated and offered in this way is God himself made man. The Word Incarnate not having any human personality, any human ego, since the Divine Hypostasis itself is the subject of human nature,[8] we can say that Christ's human nature is not that of such or such an individual, but that it is total human nature, an integral humanity that all human persons can, in principle, have a share in, and in which, as a consequence, they have all been ransomed. Thus we see how the unicity of the Redeemer, the New Adam, reestablishes in some manner the unicity of the Old Adam through whom sin came to mankind. This is, in fact, quite necessary, since we have all sinned in Adam, and since it is human nature as such that has been wounded through him. Now Adam, being a creature, possesses a human personality, which means that, for him, nature is enclosed in a subject. Hence, not being human nature as such, it was most necessary that he be the only one to possess human nature, which

7 The third, fourth, and fifth of the Sorrowful Mysteries.

8 This is what theology calls the 'Hypostatic Union', the union of divine and human nature in the hypostasis of the Word.

was as if completely gathered together in him. This is a quantitative unicity that corresponds to the qualitative unicity of the Redeemer's human nature.[9]

Only God, hypostatically united with a human nature devoid of an individual human ego, can realize what theology calls 'vicarious satisfaction', a giving of satisfaction in our place, because in this nature, being open to all men, all are ontologically delegated, all are present. Surely this does not suffice to 'explain' the Redemption, which is excluded *a priori*, but it does suffice to demonstrate both the possibility of the Redemption and the indestructible coherence of Catholic dogma.

2. The only Gnosis of Sin is the Death of Christ

But only when we look deeply into the sacrificial mode itself, the sacrifice of the Cross, do we see the truly gnostic dimension of Good Friday. Original justice has been destroyed and must be reestablished, a reestablishment that can only be brought about by the destruction of injustice, and this is why the work of justification (doing justice) necessarily includes an immolation. Does mankind need to be completely immolated then? If yes, who but God alone can immolate it? If immolation is the work of God alone, it is indistinguishable from a punishment that befalls a guilty being, a being that can do nothing but submit to it: this is no longer an immolation; it is a chastisement. The fault having come through a man, it is fitting that it should be redressed by a man. Hence only a God-Man can offer the sacrifice of his humanity to his divinity. But let us once more approach this mystery, which involves leaving behind the world of sin and rediscovering the doorway to heaven. Not by killing the sinner along with the sin will justice be reestablished, not in completely

9 Remember that the 'scientific' denials of monogenism have strictly no value. However, the same people who refuse to admit to a first man do not hesitate to admit to a unique nucleus of energy. It is unworthy of their 'reason' that we are all children of one and the same human father, but not that we arise, through mutation, out of a lump of matter. Actually, human nature is not, strictly speaking, wholly contained in Adam, since it also exists in Eve. Genetics has established that present-day humans all have the same ancestor ("On a retrouvé Adam! Une enquête génétique sur les premiers hommes aboutit à une tribu d'Afrique," *Science et Vie*, no. 967 [Montrouge, France: Mondadori Magazines, 1998]).

sacrificing sinful mankind will hierarchical harmony be restored, for then there would no longer be anything to hierarchize. The first and indispensable condition for quitting the circle of sin is to become aware of the truth of sin. Sin could not be lived in its whole truth by the sinner. In fact sin, we dare say, does not exist in a 'pure state'. At its root it is not a positive entity; otherwise it would be a good, albeit a defective one, an absence, a disequilibrium. It created, as we said, a new order. Doubtless this new order is, in reality, a disorder, but this disorder is not self-apparent, precisely because there is no longer access to the criterion of the original hierarchy, which alone could reveal it to be a disorder. Also, this disorder is inevitably lived as an order. The circle of sin is not the circle of happiness, and here created realities betray their limitations; but then these realities always conceal, with their positivity, the negativity of sin. Besides, this is why Catholic theology has always maintained that the goodness of nature was not destroyed by sin, but only wounded. To abandon this truth would mean the total collapse of Christianity: "The principle of the logicians, that contraries do not meet in the same thing, suffers an exception. Good can be without evil, but evil could not be without good. What is evil actually if not the corruption of the good?"[10] By this we see that, in a certain manner, Adam could not have known the truth of his sin. Moreover it is not by chance that the dogma of original sin was not 'elaborated' by the Old Testament, but by St. Paul.[11] This is because we actually needed to wait for Christ's Passion to understand what happened on the last day of the earthly Paradise. We needed to wait for the Incarnation of that One who is Truth, infinite Wisdom, Sun of Justice, Hypostatic Hierarchy, the Divine Word, for the injustice of sin to be fully and totally revealed. And this is why

---

10 St. Augustine, *Enchiridion*, XIV; cf. *Summa Theologiae* I-II, q. 55, a. 2.

11 Rom 5:12: "Therefore as sin came into the world through one man and death through sin, and so death spread to all men [*in omnes homines mors pertransit*], all having sinned in this man [*in quo omnes peccaverunt*]." Our translation runs contrary to the interpretation of modern exegetes who think that *in quo* means "because" and not "in whom" (according to the Greek *eph'o*). But we agree with Saints Ambrose, Augustine, and Thomas. Contrary to what many exegetes assert, the traditional construction is perfectly defensible grammatically: cf. Stanislas Lyonnet, S. J., "Le péché originel et l'exégèse de Rm V, 12–14," Appendix II in Father Joseph Huby, *Saint Paul, Epître aux Romains* (Paris: Beauchesnes, 1957), 521–57.

the state of ransomed man is superior to the state of primordial man. For although original justice, an effect of supernatural grace, resided in a natural hierarchy, in the state of Christic justice it is the Hypostatic Hierarchy that takes the place of the vanished natural hierarchy; it is the ontological Relation itself that becomes, through the transformation of the crucified body into the Mystical Body, the bond of grace uniting man both to himself and to other men through their union with God. By this is also resolved the apparent contradiction of the God-Man, he who assumes human nature except for sin and yet must *know* sin. But how can he know sin without being defiled by it? Indeed, only the reverse is possible. To know the truth of sin, it is inevitably necessary to escape from sin: not for Christ to be a sinner and share in the Fall, but for him to be made sin (2 Cor 5:21), and from the bottom of this nothingness (Phil 2:7), reached only by the Beyond of all things, to 'take away' the sin of the world. To know sin is therefore to bring it to its completion, to realize it in all of its negativity, to lead it to its objective end which is death. From the beginning of time this cup waited to be drunk and had to be drunk to the dregs. All men have drenched their lips, but none have drunk to the last drop. The Passion of Jesus Christ is the truth of sin.

3. Discrimination by the Unifying Cross of Gnosis

Such is the sacrificial union of love and gnosis in the crucified Mediator. And so the sacrifice of the Cross actualizes a metaphysical discrimination between darkness and light. The truth of the Cross fatally tears the illusion out of fallen nature, and yet it is necessary to accept being nailed there: love for men has led Jesus Christ to the gnosis of the excruciating cross, so that the love of God might lead men to the cross of unifying gnosis. Love is the carrying of the cross; gnosis is the crucifixion. But it is even more necessary to say that true gnosis *is* the cross; Christ, in dying on the cross, has shown what true knowledge is and that the doorway to it is charity.

In Jesus crucified the highest mystery of metaphysical knowledge has been accomplished. In him "love and truth have met, justice and peace have been given the kiss of reconciliation" (Psalm 84:11).

22

Love and Gnosis in the
Pneumatized Intellect

INTRODUCTION: HISTORICAL REMARKS

UNTIL NOW WE HAVE SPOKEN OF GNOSIS WITH-
out defining what meaning should be given to this term. We will
now say a few words about this. "Since the early Church, the word
'gnosis' designated an understanding of the faith that jettisons faith
and is substituted for it."[1] This definition has no other interest than
to show what a rather typical modern theologian thinks of gnosis;
but this is obviously inexact in its historical content as well as its
doctrinal content.[2]

The word *gnosis*, transliterated from the Greek *gnōsis*, means
knowledge. If it is helpful to use it, this is because ordinary knowledge is not involved here, but sacred knowledge: a knowledge sacred
not only in its object, which is the Divine Essence, but also in its
'mode', which is a participation in God's self-knowledge. This term,
however, is also used to characterize an early Christian heresy that
was, in truth, an angelism, which it would be best to label 'gnosticism'. This gnosticism is defined by two essential traits: first, the
rejection of creation and the Incarnation, and, second, the pretence
of reducing Truth and its Revelation to mental diagrams,[3] while losing sight of its irreducibly superintelligible dimension. The attitude
of many exegetes and theologians, which consists in applying the
term 'gnosis' to something that is its counterfeit, proves how much
they have been contaminated by those very things they mean to combat. The heresy of gnosticism has at least succeeded in convincing
its adversaries that there is only a single gnosis, its own. Hence, for
Christianity, gnosis is stricken with suspicion: it has become the

---

1   P. Manaranche, *Je crois en Jésus-Christ aujourd'hui* (Paris: Seuil, 1968), 38.
2   We have discussed this topic in *Problèmes de gnose*.
3   In this respect Hegel's philosophism is a gnosticism.

chief sin of the intellect. The consequences of such a rejection will be terrible. As all mystical knowledge of God is rejected, theology is reduced to a purely rational knowledge. This knowledge being human and natural in its mode, even if divine in its object, what happens is that we see in it only a profane exercise indistinguishable from philosophic speculation and ultimately useless for salvation. This is the Lutheran reaction.

Finally, even this useless knowledge will be seen as dangerous and alienating: only the 'existential' Christianity matters. This is Bultmann's heresy, which makes the existential the criterion for both hermeneutics and theology, for both the interpretation of Scripture and the working-out of doctrine. *Praxis* becomes the criterion for *theoria*, and so *theoria* becomes no more than a doctrine of good *praxis*, an *orthopraxis* according to the expression of certain modernists.[4] All of this basically rests on a negation of true *theoria*, which is now conceived of as only a philosophic mode, a mental construction, whereas what it really is is contemplative knowledge. But human existence is too heavy to be held in the webbing of a mental construct; it always rips right through. This is why, in the name of the existential, discredit and even anathema have been cast upon sacred theology. Forgotten is that other knowledge which is not ratiocination but realization, a knowing which is also a being by the grace of the *Logos*, namely that gnosis actualized in us by the Holy Spirit which is the inner basis for sacred theology.[5] This inner basis having disappeared, speculative theology, ceasing to be seen as the mental objectivization of mystical theology, as the expression of contemplation, is no longer anything but the rational husk of a fruit, a fruit decreed to be nonexistent because some no longer know how to taste of it.

But, to the contrary, speculative (or scholastic) theology, far from being opposed to mystical theology (or gnosis), gives access to it because, satisfying the human reason's need for causality, it settles and pacifies the human thought-world, and because, by its very imperfection, it calls for its own surpassing, inviting reason to be subject to spiritual understanding.

4 Cf. what we have said about the natural virtues and the alienating theory of *praxis*.

5 Revelation is its outer basis.

I. LOVE AND GNOSIS IN ST. PAUL

1. Gnosis in the Gospel

The above definition reflecting the ordinary idea of gnosis is, as we have stated, both doctrinally and historically false. Recall — and this is essential — that gnosis (both the word and what it designates) has an extremely precise Scriptural basis. The term 'gnosis' (*gnōsis*) is first found in the Gospel designating an intimate and deifying knowledge of revealed truths. "Woe to you doctors of the law, for you have taken away the key of gnosis. You yourselves have not entered in, and those that were entering in, you have hindered" (Luke 11:52). A comparison of this text with the corresponding one in Matthew is illuminating. St. Matthew does not speak of "the key of gnosis," but of a shutting of "the kingdom of heaven" (Matt 23:13). These two expressions are thus equivalent, revealing that true gnosis is the kingdom of God.[6]

2. From False Gnosis to True Gnosis

Only with St. Paul does the term assume its full meaning.[7] Actually, although the term *gnôsis* in classical Greek means abstract and discursive knowledge, St. Paul uses it to designate sacred knowledge, or true knowledge as opposed to profane knowledge. In other words, only sacred knowledge merits its name; profane or even theoretical knowledge of divine things is not true knowledge. True gnosis eludes all other gnosis. True knowledge is not known as knowledge; a knowledge without mode, it is a knowing by unknowing: "We know that we all have gnosis [but] gnosis [the known, modal gnosis] puffs up, while charity edifies. And if any man think that he knows anything, he still does not know as he ought to know" (1 Cor 8:1–2).[8]

With St. Paul we see a doctrine being formulated with the following features: a distinction between so-called gnosis and true gnosis;

6 Unquestionably there are grounds for distinguishing the kingdom of heaven from the kingdom of God.

7 In the New Testament we find the words *gnosis* and *epignosis*, the second term meaning perfect knowledge. *Gnosis* occurs 29 times (24 times in St. Paul); *epignosis* occurs 20 times (15 times in St. Paul). These are the numbers given in the *Concordance du Nouveau Testament* (Paris: Cerf & Desclée De Brouwer, 1970).

8 We are imitating the Greek as exactly as possible.

within true gnosis, a distinction between simple faith, which is already a true gnosis, and gnosis itself, which is perfect faith; finally, pure gnosis is, in its essence, the work of love by which we open ourselves to God's knowledge of us.

St. Paul's insistence on distinguishing a true from a false gnosis by opposing them to each other is sufficient to show that, for him, there is indeed a mystical knowledge which enables us to participate in supernatural Life: "O Timothy, keep that which is committed to thy trust, avoiding the profane novelties of words and oppositions of a gnosis falsely so called; which some promising, have erred concerning the faith" (1 Tim 6:20–21). However, true gnosis cannot be given to all, and must not be a scandal for those with a weak conscience (1 Cor 8:7). Besides, St. Paul himself always observed this rule: "And I, brethren, could not speak to you as unto spiritual men [pneumatics], but as unto carnal. As unto little ones in Christ, I gave you milk to drink, not meat" (1 Cor 3:1–2). This is because there is as if a dual faith, or rather several stages proceeding from an obscure faith to a luminous one, *ex fide in fidem* (Rom 1:17),[9] the first seeming to be nearly exterior (*ex fide* = outside of faith) to the other (*in fidem* = immersed in faith). The gnosis of the first faith is therefore called on to disappear, or rather to be integrated and actualized in the immutable gnosis of perfect faith: "Gnosis [the modal gnosis to be distinguished from charity] shall be destroyed. For our gnosis is partial [*ex parte* = from a particular point of view].... But, when that which is perfect is come, that which is *ex parte* shall be done away" (1 Cor 13:8–10).

3. Supreme Gnosis, a Work of Love

What is this pure gnosis then? How can we attain it and what is its essence? "For God, who commanded the light to shine out of darkness, hath shined in our hearts, to give the light of the gnosis of the glory of God, in the face of Christ Jesus" (2 Cor 4:6). But here this gnosis, which is a hyper-knowledge, an epi-gnosis, is at first a gift of God: "that the God of our Lord Jesus Christ, the Father of glory, may give unto you the spirit of wisdom and of revelation, in the deep knowledge [*epignosis*] of him" (Eph 1:17). "To one indeed,

---

9 The Pauline formula *ex fide in fidem* has given rise to many commentaries.

by the Spirit, is given the *logos* of wisdom; and to another, the *logos* of gnosis, according to the same Spirit" (1 Cor 12:8). It is by this gift that the unity of faith and gnosis is realized, and it is by this unity that we, surpassing the state of Adamic nature, attain to the ideal of the *perfect man*, the one whom nothing else can measure unless it is that which surpasses every measure, the *pleroma* of Christ:

> He that descended is the same also that ascended above all the heavens, that he might fill all things [with his gifts]. And he gave some to be apostles, and some prophets, and still others evangelists, pastors and doctors; for the perfecting of the saints, for the work of the ministry, for the edifying of the body of Christ; until we all meet into the unity of faith and of the deep knowledge of the Son of God, unto a perfect man, unto the measure of the age of the pleroma of Christ; that henceforth we be no more children, tossed to and fro and carried about with every wind of doctrine, by the wickedness of men, by cunning craftiness by which they lie in wait to deceive. (Eph 4:10–14)

But this gift of supreme gnosis, which alone establishes us in immutable doctrine, must be merited and attained to by the renunciation of every particular and determinate knowledge: to say it positively, by pure love. In beginning, we recalled: "If any man think that he knoweth anything, he hath not yet known as he ought to know" (1 Cor 8:2). And this is how St. Paul teaches unknowing with a view to divine gnosis: "We pull down fortifications, destroy counsels . . . and every height that exalteth itself against the gnosis of God; and bring into captivity every understanding unto the obedience of Christ" (2 Cor 10:5). For this gnosis is of such great value that nothing compares with it, and everything should be renounced for its sake: "I count all things to be but loss for the supreme gnosis of Jesus Christ, my Lord" (Phil 3:8). A passage through unknowing is truly necessary — and this passage is even, somehow, eternal — because in deep knowledge, in supreme gnosis, it is not really I who know God, but God who knows Himself in me when my understanding is completely divested of itself. Now, since I need to renounce all of myself, what is that power which can even renounce the highest speculative knowledge if not the charitable power? This is why, after having said: "If any man think that he knoweth anything, he hath not yet known as he ought to know,"[10] St. Paul adds: "But if any man love God, the same is known by him" (1 Cor 8:3). Here we understand that the knowing of gnosis is also a being, and that the bond of the union of knowing and being is charity, the doorway to true gnosis: "Charity will never pass away." It is this, then, that leads us from speculative gnosis to ontological and eternal gnosis: "We see now through a glass in a dark manner [*in aenigmate*]; but then face to face. Now I know in part [*ex parte*]; but then I shall know even as I am known" (1 Cor 13:12).[11]

II. LOVE AND GNOSIS IN
ST. CLEMENT OF ALEXANDRIA

1. Gnosis in the Church and Scriptures

The history of the early Church exhibits a remarkable continuity as to the doctrine of gnosis. St. Irenaeus' chief work, *Against the Heresies*, far from being directed against gnosis, has the following title in the original Greek: "Exposition and Refutation of Pseudognosis [*pseudonumos gnosis*]," its aim being to establish the Christian doctrine of true gnosis (*gnosis alethes*) according to apostolic tradition. But it is with St. Clement of Alexandria that Christianity discovers its first doctor of Christian gnosis.

The 'gnostic edifice' spoken about by St. Clement[12] is nothing but the full blossoming of faith. Without doubt, two unequally perfect degrees can be distinguished in Paul's epistles, just as two receptacles of unequal capacity can be equally full. But these two states are interconnected by a divine accord: faith and gnosis mutually strengthen each other. Faith, being an anticipation, precedes gnosis and is its foundation.[13] But, in reality, more than any human course faith is

10 Three times have we repeated this formula. And we only want to restate this: it contains the whole of gnosis, and nothing else can be said in any tongue. Let whoever understands, understand!

11 This section was written before we read Dom Jacques Dupont's book *Gnosis, La Connaissance religieuse dans les Épîtres de saint Paul* (Paris: Gabalda, 1949).

12 *Strom.* V, ch. 4; PG 9:45.

13 *Strom.* II, ch. 4; PG 8:948.

the very voice of God conveyed to our soul, it is an eye given to us by God for knowing him, even though we might not see Him.[14] Hence, through faith, the two basic coordinates of gnosis are found to be defined: Scripture on the one hand and Catholic Tradition on the other. There is nothing here to remind us of the poisonous fruits of a self-intoxicated intellect which proudly supposes it has access, by its own strength, to the mysteries of divinity.[15] Knowledge is certainly involved here, and not will or action. But such a knowledge — and this is the very depths of holy gnosis — has its source in Scripture and Catholic Tradition. An understanding of Scripture is even the rightful property of the gnostic: the name of gnostic is only merited by one who, "having grown old in the Scriptures, and maintaining apostolic and ecclesiastic orthodoxy in doctrines, lives most correctly in accordance with the Gospel."[16] As for Catholic Tradition, the Church constitutes — and not just for St. Clement — the only rule of faith and the only means of salvation because it is a creation of the Holy Spirit and the incarnation of His will.[17] But it must even be said that this Church, *recognized by the immutability of its tradition just as the sects are recognized by their innovation,* is gnosis itself: men of good will agree that perfect gnosis "is in the truth alone and in the ancient Church."[18]

2. *Gnosis, the Perfection of Love*

Although the tree of gnosis is rooted by faith in Scripture and Catholic Tradition, its growth is the working of Christ in the soul. First, because the gnostic tradition goes back to Christ;[19] next, because Gnosis is

14   *Strom.* VI, ch. 17; PG 9:384.

15   Recall Origen, that pure gnostic, who was martyred at more than seventy years of age by the Emperor Decius. "Without doubt, it did not seem appropriate to execute this illustrious man, but an iron collar was forced upon him, and he was set on the rack in such a way that his feet were stretched up to the fourth foramen for entire days at a time. He was threatened with torture by fire. And yet all this violence was for nought" (Hans von Campenhausen, *Les Pères Grecs* [Paris: Ed. de l'Orante, 1963], 78). But what were they asking of him? To deny his gnosis? That would be of no interest to the Emperor. They were asking that he deny his faith in the Holy Catholic Church and its sacraments.

16   *Strom.* VII, ch. 16; PG 9:544.

17   *Paed.*, Bk. I, ch. 1; PG 8:281, 300.

18   *Strom.* VII, ch. 15; PG 9:528.

19   *Strom.* VI, ch. 7; PG 9:277. "The Lord has taught us gnosis through His presence and the prophets."

Christ himself, he who is "our spiritual garden into whom we are transplanted."[20] Now, what corresponds to Christ's work in us is charity.
Here, with St. Clement's help, we can see how charity is the doorway
to gnosis, or, again, how the Christian only enters into gnosis through
the doorway of charity. Gnosis is, in fact, that perfect knowledge
wherein the knowing subject is wholly united to the known Object,
because, knowing as he is known, the knowledge which he has of God
and the knowledge which God has of him are one and the same knowledge. Being absolutely unknowable by any one other than himself, it
is clearly necessary that God cause the creature to participate — in the
Holy Spirit — in the knowledge which He has of Himself through
His Word. "When a created intellect sees God through his Essence,
it is the very Essence of God which becomes the intelligible form for
the intellect," says St. Thomas.[21] Thus, according to Christ's prayer,
we become one as the Father and the Son are One. Now, 'before' oneness, there is a unification which is the work of love. And charity, says
St. Clement, endows us with the character of the One, renders us
'monadic'; charity prepares, perfects, and completes us in unity. To be
Christian, to believe in Christ, is to become monadic.[22] But why, at
this level, do we still need to distinguish between love and gnosis? In
reality, it is impossible to separate them, since *the substance of gnosis is
love and the essence of love is gnosis*. But it has to be understood that
only the gnostic dimension of charity can disinterestedly realize the
complete and absolute dimensions of pure love. Gnosis is centered on
the Truth, and Truth alone is what it is. In the last analysis, only "the
Truth delivers" us — instantaneously — from all the bonds of relativity
by its Aseity. Gnosis is the immutable and invisible vertical axis which
the dance of love envelops like a flame. Does not saying that charity
is the doorway to gnosis attribute to gnosis, then, a superiority over
charity? Recent commentators are not sparing in their reproaches of St.
Clement of Alexandria, insofar as they feel at ease with heaping scorn
upon gnosis, and insofar as they feel self-assured as to the superiority

20 *Strom.* VI, ch. 1; PG 9:209. "Our gnosis, and our spiritual garden, is the
Savior himself; into whom we are planted, being transferred and transplanted, from
our old life, into the good land."
21 *Summa Theologiae* I, q. 12, a. 5.
22 *Strom.* IV, ch. 25.

of love over knowledge. There is much Phariseeism and false humility in this attitude. His gnosis, it is said, "oscillates dangerously between complete rationalism and false mysticism."[23] We repeat: love and gnosis are truly indissociable. However, if the term 'gnosis' is preferable to 'love' for designating the supreme monadic state, this is just because love, in its essence, is a desire for ontological knowledge, and therefore because *realized* love is gnosis, or even because gnosis is the truth of love. This is why St. Clement can write: "Could we, then, suppose any one proposing to the gnostic whether he would choose the gnosis of God or everlasting salvation; and if these, which are entirely identical, were separable, he would without the least hesitation choose the gnosis of God, deeming that transcendent property of faith, which from love ascends to perfect gnosis, desirable, for its own sake."[24]

III. LOVE AND GNOSIS IN EVAGRIUS OF PONTUS

We will conclude these few remarks on Christian gnosis by mentioning the doctrine of Evagrius of Pontus[25] as explained in his *Treatise*

---

23   On this question cf. T. Camelot, *Foi et gnose chez Clement d'Alexandrie* (Paris: Vrin, 1944).

24   *Strom.* IV, ch. 22; PG 8:1348. We have drawn inspiration from A. Mehat's translation in *Études sur les Stromates* (Paris: Seuil, 1966), 455. To complete the gnostic doctrine of St. Clement, we should add that, although gnosis is rooted in Scripture and Catholic Tradition and it is Christ's work in us by means of charity, it is no less nourished by the sacraments, especially the Eucharist: "To receive the Divine Logos as food and drink is to have gnosis of the Divine Essence [*brosis kai posis tou theiou logou e gnosis esti tes theias ousias*]." Cf. *Strom.* V, ch. 11; PG 9:101, 105. Also notice how the stages (the 'dwellings') of the soul's ascension towards God correspond to ontological stages, to the very hierarchy of created beings, to the angelic hierarchies in particular. Cf. *Strom.* VII, ch. 2; PG 8:413–6. This feature is the basic difference between a mysticism of gnosis and 'affective' mysticism. In the latter, the stages of the soul are rather hard to define and must be described quite subjectively; hence the possiblity of writing psychological treatises on the "great religious figures" (whereas the spiritual is by essence of a super-psychological nature). The former, to the contrary, exhibits an objective and serene character, which in no way excludes mystery, the indescribable, and tears. But for the gnostic, the most painful vicissitudes have a kind of impersonality, objectivity; are something matter of fact. He is condemned to serenity, which becomes a veritable crucifixion. At least this is what can be grasped and said from the 'outside'. As for the inner reality of the gnostic and lover . . . that is a secret between the soul and God.

25   Here we base ourselves on the work of Father Hausherr, *Les Leçons d'un contemplatif* (Paris: Beauchesne, 1960), a translation of and commentary on St. Evagrius's

on Prayer. Evagrius was the first to articulate the formula that we have taken as this chapter's theme: "Charity is the doorway to gnosis."[26] With him, what seems a metaphysical dissertation comes to life and becomes prayer. Certain aspects of gnosis, sometimes only implicit in St. Clement, become explicit in him, especially the clear distinction between ratiocination (or mental discourse) and gnosis, an important distinction above all for a modern Western thinker who cannot conceive of any knowledge other than the scientific.

1. The Identity of Prayer and Gnosis in the Intellect

We will begin at the top. Evagrius identifies three states:[27] the state of pure (or naked) intellect, the state of pure prayer and the state of pure gnosis (or the gnosis of the Holy Trinity) — "the state of intellection is the peak of the intellect radiant with the light of the Holy Trinity at the time of prayer." If we then ask ourselves what the loftiest activity of the intellect is, we would have to answer: 'prayer'; and it is by prayer alone that gnosis is obtained: "Prayer is an ascent of the intellect towards God."[28] This gnosis has, then, nothing to do with a rational knowledge: "The gnosis of Christ has no need of a dialectical soul, but of a soul with clear vision."[29] "As for rationality, despise it, because it is useless to us along our way. For Our Lord has said: 'Come, O blessed of my Father, and inherit the kingdom prepared for you from the foundation of the world; for I was hungry and you gave me food, I was thirsty and you gave me drink, I was a stranger and you welcomed me' (Matt 25:34–5). See how he nowhere mentions rationality."[30] And

---

Treatise on Prayer. John Meyendorff (*St Gregory Palamas and Orthodox Spirituality*, trans. A. Fiske [Crestwood, NY: St. Vladimir's Seminary Press, 1974]) asserts (23) that Evagrius does not allude to Jesus in his treatise. This is excessive and ultimately tendentious, like reproaching someone for not speaking about the air he breathes whenever he speaks. Evagrius truly loved Jesus Christ more than anything and above all. His life testifies to it. That he does not write the Name of the one whom he loved more than himself (although he speaks at length about Christ): is this not detailed proof of the veneration in which he held this sacrosanct Name?

26 Evagrius, *Letter to Anatolios*; PG 40:1221C.

27 *Treatise on Prayer* (in Hausherr, *Les Leçons d'un contemplatif*), 53.

28 Ibid., 53.

29 Ibid., 85. We are translating *dioratikos* as 'clear vision'. Hausherr transliterates it as 'dioratic', which means both vision and discernment in Greek.

30 Ibid., 86.

so it is not profane and exterior knowledge that befits the dignity of our intellect, but rather "prayer is the activity which befits the dignity of our intellect, in other words, is its best and most adequate use."[31] In fact, among all the realities subject to becoming, the intellect alone is capable of the gnosis of the Holy Trinity. Now, all of creation has been made with a view to this gnosis. And prayer is the act through which the intellect realizes its deiform nature; this is what God wants of it and what he has destined it to.[32] For perpetual and continual prayer "knocks at the door of gnosis so as to awaken the master of the house, the giver of spiritual bread to those who ask for it,"[33] since the Scriptural basis for perpetual prayer, says St. Evagrius, is the parable of the unjust judge:[34] "Thus God will do justice to those who cry to Him day and night, and promptly. Be therefore of good courage and valiantly persevere in holy prayer."[35] All prayer is therefore a gnosis, and every gnosis is a prayer, at whatever degree it is situated, because it is the intellect that prays in knowledge and knows in prayer, or even because knowledge is the prayer of the intellect. Father Hausherr writes in his commentary: "Represent the ascent of prayer on the one hand and gnosis on the other as two lines, parallel if you like, but being reunited in the infinity of God: the two slopes of the 'spiritual mountain', or better yet the two uprights of 'Jacob's ladder' whose summit reaches heaven and upon which the Lord leaned."[36] "At each step of the ascent there is prayer and there is gnosis, both of equal value. We can therefore characterize someone's spiritual level equally by either his state of prayer or his state of contemplation."[37]

2. *The Steps of the Gnostic Ladder*

But what are the steps of this spiritual ladder made up of prayer and gnosis? These degrees of prayer, which are also degrees of gnosis or contemplation, states of the intellect progressively stripped of all

---

31   Ibid., 117.

32   Ibid., 115. "Prayer causes the activity proper to it to be exercised by the intellect."

33   Ibid., 122.

34   Luke 13:4–5.

35   Hausherr, *Les Leçons d'un contemplatif*, 122.

36   Evagrius of Pontus, *Centuries* IV, 43.

37   Hausherr, *Les Leçons d'un contemplatif*, 121.

forms, are founded upon the Scriptural and world-wide doctrine of the anthropological tripartition (body, soul, and spirit), which corresponds to the cosmological tripartition. To these three a fourth degree must be added, which, as a matter of fact, is not a degree at all but the 'place of God'. If there are four steps, there are also three transitions, three passages, three renunciations or privations. "May the virtues of the body [somatic] serve you as a basis for obtaining the virtues of the soul [psychic]; the virtues of the soul for obtaining the spiritual [pneumatic] virtues, and the spiritual virtues for obtaining immaterial and essential gnosis."[38] Three things, we could say, bind the intellect, which in its pure state is itself perfectly free of every imprint, to objects and forms: the desires of the body, the passions of the soul, and the thoughts of the reason. Desires, passions, and thoughts do not work independently of each other, but mutually avail themselves of each other's support; passion reinforces desire and thought reinforces passion, which itself binds thought to desired objects. We need, then, to combat desires and passions with virtue; this is the object of *praxis*, which leads the intellect to a state of impassibility (*apatheia*), while *theoria* gives access to pure thoughts and the reasons of things. "We approach the virtues with a view to the 'reasons' of created things, and the latter with a view to the Lord who has made them; as for Him, He is accustomed to appearing in the state of prayer."[39] Actually, it is impossible to separate *praxis* from *theoria*, or, in other words, *praxis* (the 'energies of the commandments'[40]) is insufficient for attaining impassibility; there also must be 'corresponding contemplations', contemplations that deal with 'reasons for beings in becoming' ('physical' beings: *physis* = in becoming), the essences or principles of creatures. Evagrius calls this degree of contemplation natural or lower or secondary contemplation,[41] while only primary contemplation merits the name of theology. And so we have the ternary mentioned by Evagrius in his Prologue: *praxis*, natural contemplation, and theology.

But this basic outline should be enriched and made more flexible: "Among the gnoses, some are immaterial, others are known in

38 Ibid., 166.
39 Ibid., 75.
40 Ibid., 77.
41 Ibid., 76.

material objects, while gnosis of the Holy Trinity surpasses all."[42] In this respect it should be pointed out that the immaterial gnoses include both a gnosis of the Holy Trinity, which is truly the primary contemplation, the state of perfect prayer, the place of God, and also a gnosis of the intelligibles, which has to do with celestial beings, and which is again a part of secondary or natural contemplation, even though by possessing this alone we would become equal to the angels. Material gnosis consists, moreover, in seeing not creatures themselves but their principles, their reasons (*logoi*), or, according to Father Hausherr's commentary, "the reflection of divine attributes whose effects, mirrors, and symbols they are."[43] This is why it is said that material gnoses are known *in* objects: what there is of gnosis in an object is its symbolism, the divine attribute which is reflected in it and which it incarnates. The object as symbol is thus an objective gnosis which becomes visible to the intellect of the human subject, and it is to this material gnosis that *praxis* leads: "Intellect, having entered into the service of God's commandments — *praxis* — evolves in thought the object of this world."[44]

From bottom to top, then, we can distinguish the following levels: *praxis*, which introduces us to material gnosis, since, freeing the thought-of-objects from a passional attachment to objects, it gives the intellect the ability to see, across the thoughts or concepts themselves, the reasons of objects, their symbolic transparency, the ability to see them as 'simple expressions'; next, material gnosis leads to immaterial or spiritual gnosis, by which the intellect is nourished with the intelligible natures themselves, with pure spiritual realities, as with its proper diet, for its native land is there. And this is why such a spiritual contemplation can still be called 'natural': not only because it deals with the intelligibles, the heaven of the created cosmos, but also because it suits the nature of the intellect, so that, in attaining spiritual gnosis, the intellect does not become perplexed: "for it meets with a kindred and beloved contemplation."[45] And so "to perceive the contemplation of natures is within the intellect's power, but to

42 Ibid., 94.
43 Ibid., 95.
44 Ibid., 93.
45 Ibid., 116.

contemplate the Holy Trinity does not belong to it, for that is an eminent gift of grace."[46] Besides, the spiritual contemplation of the intelligibles implies a certain (non-quantitative) multiplicity[47] which is like a 'final garment'. *Praxis*, material gnosis, natural immaterial gnosis, and Trinitarian gnosis: "The intellect cannot see the place of God in itself, unless it become superior to all thoughts of objects; and it will not become superior to them unless stripped of the passions which, through thoughts, bind the intellect to sense objects. Now, it abandons the passions through the virtues [impassibility], simple thoughts through spiritual contemplation, and this, in its turn, is abandoned with the appearing of that light which, at the time of prayer, impresses [within it] the place of God."[48]

3. Under the Activity of the Holy Spirit the Gnostic gains access to the Logos

We have seen the top of the spiritual ladder; its various steps have been outlined. What remains to be seen is how it is possible to gain access to it, and by what power we might raise ourselves from step to step. It has to be understood, then, that these steps (being the degrees of gnosis) should refer to the Word, the Logos, while the power to ascend spiritually — which is charity — should refer to the Holy Spirit and his angels who ascend and descend upon this ladder; and so, once more, the principle of the inseparability of the *Logos* and the *Pneuma* (and their reflections within man as intellect and love) will be borne out, a principle which constitutes the basic theme of our entire study.

Evagrius describes the function of the Holy Spirit in this way: "The Holy Spirit, out of compassion for our weakness, comes to us even when we are impure. And if only he finds our intellect praying to him, he enters it and puts to flight the whole array of thoughts and reasonings that beset it, and urges it on to love [or to works] of spiritual prayer."[49] Love is therefore the effect of Holy Spirit's operation within us. Sometimes it is said that Evagrius has not developed a true Trinitarian doctrine and does not really distinguish between

46 Ibid., 82.
47 Ibid., 80.
48 Ibid., 80–81.
49 Ibid., 88.

the work of the Son and that of the Holy Spirit. However, what matters here as elsewhere is not so much finding easily identifiable doctrinal formulations as recognizing the very realities which these formulas express. But his entire *On Prayer* speaks of the Holy Spirit, since it is a treatise on spirituality. The Holy Spirit may not always be named as author of spiritual books, but this is because He somehow hides behind His workings. As we have shown at length, the Holy Spirit is the unnameable Name, the Hidden One, the preeminently Mysterious One, whereas the Word is seen in broad daylight. The Word is the crucial center upon which the mystic should concentrate, the indisputable Mediator visible from East to West, an axis raised above cosmic horizontality. "Originally," Evagrius states in *The Centuries*, "the intellect had the revelation of the Spirit for a teacher, but it turned away and became a student of the senses. It will again have its original teacher once it is perfected in Christ."[50]

4. *Charity is Oil for the Intellectual Lamp*

It is not possible to cite here all of the chapters where Evagrius speaks of the relationship between charity and gnosis. Basically, we should make a distinction between two aspects of charity: charity as ascesis, as an operative key for spiritual alchemy, and charity an a 'state of love' or that supreme love which can no longer be separated (or distinguished) from gnosis, because it is also a fruit of gnosis. Charity is the doorway to gnosis, but when the soul has arrived at supreme contemplation — knowledge of the Trinity — it does not abandon love. Quite the contrary: gnosis itself radiates then with the infinite radiance of Love. Having attained to Christ, the eternal Gnosis of the Father, through charity, we participate in his outpouring of Love — the Holy Spirit.

The operative function of charity basically consists in the alchemical separation of the psychic from the spiritual. This fundamental theme, which we have approached from so many viewpoints, is found abundantly illustrated in Evagrius. For want of somehow understanding this operative character, this spiritual technique, we run the risk of seeing here only moral precepts. The distinction of the psychic from the spiritual corresponds, in Evagrian anthropology, to the distinction

50   *Century* III, 55.

of the irascible/concupiscible[51] from the pneumatic. "Prayer is the offspring of meekness and the absence of anger."[52] Father Hausherr comments on this statement of Evagrius by citing another text from the same author: "When the intellect begins to pray without distraction, it is in the irascible part of the soul, then, that an all-out battle is waged day and night."[53] Only charity, with God's help, can conquer this disorder of the soul in us. But what is charity?

> Charity is an excellent habitus of the rational soul through which it is impossible to love anything in the world more than the knowledge of God. . . . Whoever acquires charity scorns eating and wealth and the world's glory, and, along with this, even denies the body for the love of the knowledge of God. . . . If, as it is written, our God is charity, then love of this wicked world is the enemy of charity. It is therefore impossible to acquire charity if we do not hate the world, nor to hate the world if we do not divest ourselves of the passions out of which our old man is composed, being corrupted with aberrant desires.[54]

Charity, however, is not ascesis or fasting. "Of more worth is a man of the world, if he is meek, than an angry and passionate monk."[55] "I am," says Evagrius,

> a panegyrist of temperance [of ascesis], and I wish to live with her in all forbearance and charity. For, without the latter, what name can we give to temperance? It is the cinder left after the fire which had kindled the ardor of Charity. Temperance, and it alone, is similar to that foolish virgin excluded from the wedding chamber, because oil was lacking and her lamp extinguished. I call this lamp the intellect made to receive the blessed light, but fallen,

---

51 Terms used in the Platonic tradition.
52 *On Prayer*, ch. 14.
53 *Les leçons d'un contemplatif*, 29.
54 Ibid., 31–33.
55 Ibid., 35.

because of its hardness, from the knowledge of God. For
there where oil [unction] is lacking, anger reigns.[56]

Charity's likeness to the oil of the intellect/lamp, an oil which, in being
consumed, makes the manifestation of the light possible, verifies our
previous use of a symbolism of darkness. This comparison also proves
that a spiritual alchemy (and not just moral precepts) is involved here.

True, the irascible is connected to the concupiscible, and therefore
meekness is connected to temperance: "The reason why I suppress
desires is to cut off the pretexts for anger. For I know that the latter
is always arguing about the subject of pleasures, that it troubles my
intellect and drives out contemplation."[57] And so ascesis and charity
must be seen as two — negative and positive — aspects of the selfsame
praxis.[58] Ascesis leads to 'impassibility', which is as if the substance
of fraternal charity. "Perfect *apatheia* [impassibility or purity]," says
Evagrius, "is accompanied by humility, compunction, tears, a vast love
of God and an immeasurable zeal for works."[59] Charity is thus "the
daughter of *apatheia*."[60]

5. Charity Pneumatizes and Unifies the Intellect

If charity alone renders the intellect capable of supreme contemplation, this is because it is a recollection; it gathers, reunites, and leads
back to the One, whereas the irascible tendency is dispersive. "Anger
dissipates contemplation, but forbearance gathers it."[61]

Charity 'gathers' contemplation because it eliminates dispersion. To
eliminate dispersion is to divest us of our passions. Once the passions
are cast off, we obtain 'nakedness of the intellect'. And the naked intellect is the 'spiritual' or pneumatic intellect.[62] The proper function of
charity is therefore — through the alchemical work of denuding — to

---

56 Ibid., 42.
57 Ibid., 43.
58 *Praxis* designates spiritual labor: "*Praxis* is a spiritual method which purifies
the passionate part of the soul" (ibid., 15). Derived from it is the adjective *practicos*,
designating that which relates to *praxis*.
59 Ibid., 78.
60 Ibid., 16.
61 Ibid., 35.
62 Ibid., 45.

pneumatize the intellect, to render the intellect spiritual, to introduce the intellect into the spiration of the Holy Spirit. And here we find bound together inseparably every theme of our study. Now "the spiritual intellect is the seer of the Holy Trinity."[63] With contemplation of the Trinity being the supreme gnosis or supreme prayer, we can grasp, as far as possible, why charity is the doorway to gnosis. However, as previously stated, this gnosis by no means excludes love, since it is a disclosure of supreme charity, so that the gnostic state or the habitus of gnosis is also the habitus of love.[64] "The first and principal commandment (through the practice of which we obtain contemplation) is charity, thanks to which the intellect sees primal charity, that is to say God. For by our charity we see God's charity towards us, as it is said in the Psalm: He teaches his ways to the meek."[65]

But what act accomplishes the work of charity and leads to the awakening of the intellect? It is prayer: "The state of prayer is an impassible habitus which, by a supreme love, ravishes the philosophic [*philosophale* in French] and pneumatic intellect to intellectual heights."[66] In this state — the concrete union of love and knowledge — supreme contemplation does not extinguish prayer, but instills in it a peerless "zeal, fervor, and loving impetuosity."[67] And this love of God is, as Evagrius again declares, "the perfect and spiritual holiness by which prayer passes into act in spirit and in truth." By it the monk, the one who is one (*monos*), "separated from all and united to all,"[68] separated from and stripped of all scatteredness by the charity uniting him to all beings — the monk, we say, realizes the unity of virtue and gnosis, just as the crucified Mediator has realized the unity of mercy and justice: "the *gnosticos* and the *practicos* have met and in the midst of the two stands the Lord."[69]

---

63 Ibid., 78.

64 From the viewpoint of spiritual realization, we need to distinguish between two modes of awareness of the Divine: *habitus* and *diathesis*. (These terms are borrowed from Aristotle; see ibid., 76.) A *habitus* is a stable and permanent state, *diathesis* an ephemeral contact.

65 Ibid., 34.

66 Ibid., 76. *Philosophale* literally means 'smitten with wisdom'.

67 Ibid., 121.

68 Ibid., 124.

69 Ibid., 161.

Such, briefly expressed, is the Evagrian doctrine of a gnostic ascent through charity. We will not leave St. Evagrius, however, without relating some of his propositions about the supreme state of the intellect, because many of the themes we have encountered are to be found there, and because, in our opinion, these propositions represent the summit of Christian mysticism, formulating its highest doctrine: deification.

6. The Deified Intellect

We might say this: for the deified intellect, to contemplate the Holy Trinity is, in a certain manner, to contemplate itself. Surely the audacity of this formulation might seem excessive. But we have to understand that it is denying neither grace or transcendence.

"When the intellect, after stripping away the old man, puts on grace, then it will also see its own state at the time of prayer, alike to sapphire or the color of the sky; the state which Scripture calls the place of God, and which was seen of God on Mount Sinai."[70] This 'place of God', which is a 'state of the intellect', is the heaven where the vision of the Trinity arises. "The state of the intellect, that is to say the state of pure intellection, is the intellectual summit, alike to the color of the sky, upon which, at the time of prayer, the light of the Holy Trinity is resplendent."[71] We have seen, and Evagrius untiringly repeats, that only the intellect — a perfectly stripped intellect — is able to see the Trinity. But it is even preferable to say that such an intellect is a 'seeing of the Holy Trinity', that *this vision is its very essence*. Becoming what it knows, the intellect through this second contemplation is rendered 'isangelic', equal to the angels. At this stage, man is truly no longer a man: "the world changes and names are abolished."[72] But a total stripping is even beyond every intelligible form, and is thus a question of the informal intellect. "Go, immaterial one, into the immaterial, and you will understand," says Evagrius. This is because God himself is in-formal, '*aneidos*'.[73] "The intellect, having entered into the service of God's commandments — *praxis* — evolves

---

70 Ibid., 34.
71 Ibid., 78.
72 Ibid., 144. This abolishing of names corresponds quite exactly to what Hindu spirituality calls the surpassing of the *nama-rupa*, of name and form.
73 Ibid., 93.

in thought this world's objects; having entered into (inferior) gnosis, it evolves in contemplation; but, having entered into prayer, it penetrates into the formless light which is the place of God."[74] With this entry the intellect becomes God by grace. Thus contemplation of the Trinity coincides with the intellect's vision of its own state: "When the intellect is judged worthy to contemplate the Holy Trinity, then, by grace, it is also called god, having been completed in the likeness of its Creator." This is why "it is of God even as it praises God."[75] Thus the intellect, "in contemplating itself, possesses the spiritual world."[76]

The intellect is then raised to an infinite dignity, a dignity it possesses by very virtue of its intellectual nature. Western theologians will be tempted to see in these assertions a confusion of nature and grace: "The naked intellect," declares Evagrius, "is the one that is consumed in the vision of itself and has merited communing with the contemplation of the Holy Trinity."[77] The intellect that is perfectly itself shines with its own light, and this light is the place of God. However, there is no confusion here between the two orders, for the pure nature of the intellect is a gift of God. There is only a total fusion in an eternal transformation. The intellect, we say, is to be identified with its supernatural nature, its prototype *in divinis*. It could not be otherwise: "just as the light which shows us everything has no need of another light in order to be seen, so God, who has made us to see everything, has no need of a light by which to see him; for he is by essence light."[78] Here we touch on one of the loftiest mysteries of spiritual science. God can only be seen by Himself, and therefore, if the intellect sees God, it can only be God Himself seeing Himself in His own light. The intellect is transformed by this vision into God Himself, and it is also by its own light, then, that it sees God. We should refrain from trying to settle the matter here, either by denying the Evagrian perspective in the name of overly formal distinctions or by imagining some 'out-and-out' identity between creature and Creator: *this is neither a dualist distinction nor a monist identification*. This mystery is more profound than such distinctions, and its profundity is even

74 Ibid., 94.
75 Ibid., 85.
76 Ibid., 155.
77 Ibid., 146.
78 Ibid., 145.

infinite. Let us listen to this wonderful story from Evagrius: "On the subject of this holy light [of prayer], the servant of God Ammonios and myself asked St. John of the Thebaid if it is the nature of the intellect that is luminous and if it is from this that the light comes, or if something illuminates it from without. He answered: No man is capable of deciding this question; but, in any case, without God's grace the intellect could not be illuminated in prayer and delivered from those numerous enemies intent on its loss."[79]

7. Infinite Ignorance

All of these considerations lead us to identify supreme gnosis with 'infinite ignorance'. We think we have sufficiently shown that such was indeed what St. Paul taught. But a Pauline thesis is not all that is involved here. 'Unknowing' is the very substance of epignosis, of deep knowledge. Here we can only touch lightly on the doctrine of supreme ignorance, but let us at least recognize that it is somehow based on the very nature of things. It rightly belongs to no particular author, and may be typified by Christ's word from the Cross: "*Eli, Eli lama sabacthani.*" All knowledge is knowledge of what is. At the same time it is, then, a discrimination between being and nothingness, between what is real and what illusory. Now being is ultimately God and, in this respect, all knowledge is knowledge of God. For man, on the other hand, to know is to have an object in front of oneself. The meaning of an object is inherent to the act of knowing. But these two qualities of knowledge — (1) that to know is to know an object, and (2) that this object is Being which is distinguished from nothingness — disappear at the stage of supreme knowledge. As we have seen in the testimonies of both Evagrius himself and the greatest mystics, the object known by the intellect in a state of privation is the intellect itself. Such an intellect's intellection can no longer be defined by the meaning of an object; on the other hand, the intellect cannot know if it is itself or God that knows, or if it is God or itself that is known, for the simple reason that such a question can no longer be posed then, and, therefore, should not be posed. This unknowing is

---

79 Ibid., 47. "No contemplative reputation has ever surpassed that of the 'Seer' of the Thebaid."

actually identical to that spoken of by St. Dionysius the Areopagite: "the intellect which knows how to shut its eyes . . . knows, then, in its unknowing." And Evagrius declares: "Blessed the intellect which, at the time of prayer, attains infinite ignorance."[80]

Father Hausherr is not of this opinion. In a 'brief treatise',[81] he denies any similarity between Dionysius and Evagrius. Dionysian doctrine is 'ecstatic', whereas Evagrian doctrine is unaware of the term 'ecstasy', except in the sense of folly. "We risk confusing differing doctrines if we omit, in the definition of ecstasy, what is its most essential factor: going out of oneself, not through the unconsciousness of a 'suspension of the senses', but through a kind of projection, under the impetus of love, outside of the laws of the intellect itself" — whereas for Evagrius the intellect does not go out of its own nature to contemplate the Holy Trinity. After all, says Father Hausherr, "to know absolutely is to know nothing at all." It seems that here the Jesuit priest falls victim to his prejudice against Dionysius, which he has exhibited in other writings. To not know absolutely is not that kind of unknowing. Quite the contrary: ordinary ignorance is always only relative — ignorance of such or such a fact, for example. But it is the same with knowledge: all knowledge is knowledge of something; it is relative. Therefore we need to renounce every definite knowledge to attain absolute knowledge, and this is indeed an absolute ignorance. There is, necessarily, a 'moment' of total obscurity. And it is in this darkness that the Divine Essence is 'known'. Is this going out of oneself? Surely — but going outside of my fallen and possessive self, and this going-out is clearly also a reentry into our true self. Let us not use Evagrius to combat Dionysius. This is a lack of spiritual courtesy, an impropriety. These giants have said what they had to say, as was appropriate. And now, this is neither Dionysius nor Evagrius, but the Eternal Word: "If you wish to save your life [find yourself again, reenter into yourself] it is necessary to lose it [ecstasy] for my sake." The most prodigious erudition is blind if it does not know how to stand aside for the sake of spiritual understanding. To understand absolute ignorance, the most learned of men must become ignorant.

80 *On Prayer*, 117.
81 *Hesychasm et Prière*, Orientalia Christiana Analecta 176 (Rome: Pont. Institutum Studiorum, 1966), 38–49.

What remains is that Dionysius did not write a treatise on prayer, and Evagrius did not write a treatise on mystical theology. But they expressed one and the same truth in different styles: the nakedness of the intellect (or infinite ignorance) and the cloud of unknowing both symbolically represent the non-modal way by which the creature can become immanent to divine transcendence. And for us this non-modal way is the highest stage of charity. Returning once more to the image of light, we will say this: a milieu filled with light is in itself darkness, since it is such as soon as the light is withdrawn. *Lux in tenebris lucet et tenebrae eam non comprehenderunt.* The non-understanding of darkness is also supreme ignorance. For darkness to be united with the true Light, it has to renounce its borrowed and relative lights. Insofar as the intellect is not God, its light is not the true Light. It is outside of God and therefore 'ecstatic' with respect to the Divine. And so it has to realize its own non-divine substance, *its ontological ignorance.* The divine Light instantly pervades it through and through and bears it away into its own transcendence, united with it as its most intimate and most invisible secret. The Blessed Virgin knew this secret, she who was the pure darkness where the Light of the world took flesh. We will be beatified by spiritual poverty, for by renouncing all we will possess the All. By being nothing, we will become Being; by definitively dying, we will enter into Life. By being ignorant of every created thing, from the least blade of grass to the highest of the angels, we will gain access to that Knowledge which knows us. Like a newborn with closed eyes, with fragile and silent flesh, the Mother of God will envelop us in the swaddling-clothes of her Love.

23

Deifying Charity

IN THE TERMS OF OUR ANALYSES, IT IS QUITE apparent that the end of charity is deification. Being the bond of perfection, this is what binds us to the Supreme Perfection by bringing us into conformity with it. This is what makes us sons of God, 'other Christs'. Viewed from the side of divine activity it is therefore the work of the Holy Spirit, whose proper operation is to make us deiform. It is this point that we will examine briefly in closing.

I. THE THEOLOGICAL
FOUNDATIONS OF DEIFICATION
1. Wisdom is the Fruit of Charity

What we have said concerning the relationship between charity and gnosis was illustrated with the help of the Greek rather than the Latin tradition, because it seems that the former tradition has provided us with its most vigorous expressions. Yet it would be false to believe that Western theology is ignorant of this relationship. Returning to St. Thomas, the Common Doctor, we actually encounter the clearest affirmation in this respect: "After having treated of hope, we will speak of charity: first, charity itself, and then the corresponding gift of wisdom."[1]

As a gift of the Holy Spirit, wisdom is seen to be distinguished from knowledge, which regards created things more directly: it consists, says St. Thomas, "in judging and setting in order all things according to divine rules. Now man obtains this judgment through the Holy Spirit, according to 1 Corinthians 2:15: 'the spiritual man judges all things,' because, as stated (1 Cor 2:10), 'the spirit searches all things, even the secrets of God.' Wherefore it is evident that wisdom is a gift of the Holy Spirit."[2] The two fundamental acts of the intellect, perception

---

1 *Summa Theologiae* II-II, q. 23.
2 *Summa Theologiae* II-II, q. 45, a. 1.

and judgment, are therefore transformed in such a way by the gift of wisdom that they bear the mark of divine presence. Also, sapiential knowledge implies a certain deiformity. We must, in order to receive this gift, assimilate ourselves in some way to the divine nature. Now this assimilation is the work of charity. There is no denying that in wisdom, as St. Thomas describes it, we rediscover many characteristics of true gnosis, and therefore that charity is the doorway to gnosis: "Wisdom, which is a gift of the Holy Spirit, causes divine things to be judged rightly, or other things according to divine rules, by the effect of a certain connaturality, or by a certain union with the divine, a connaturality which is the work of charity."[3] In fact, "this conformity of nature with divine things is accomplished through charity, which unites us to God according to these words: 'He who is united with God, forms only one spirit with him' (1 Cor 6:17). So then wisdom, as gift, indeed has charity as its cause."[4] And again: "Uncreated wisdom [Christ] unites itself to us by the gift of charity, and consequently reveals to us the mysteries, knowledge of which is nothing else than infused wisdom [the gift of wisdom]. Hence infused wisdom, inasmuch as it is a gift, is not the cause but the effect of charity."[5]

2. By Wisdom we become Children of God

Returning to the terms of our study, we will say that the proper work of charity is to *pneumatize the intellect,* and that the pneumatization of the intellect renders it capable of receiving the gift of wisdom or gnosis. Now the gift of wisdom, inasmuch as it is perfectly actualized by a creature, corresponds to that creature's state of deification. Wisdom, the first gift of the Holy Spirit, contains all of the gifts. In the enumeration of their development, each subsequent gift is like the condition for manifestation, or secondary cause, of the prior gift. Thus wisdom supposes understanding, which supposes counsel, and so on from justice to fear, the seventh and last gift which is nonetheless the 'beginning of wisdom', so that the end rejoins the beginning—since, as we have often mentioned, circular motion is the mark of the Holy Spirit. Thus wisdom, being the originating and

3 *Summa Theologiae* II-II, q. 45, a. 2.
4 Ibid.
5 *Summa Theologiae* II-II, q. 45, a. 6.

terminating synthesis where all the gifts happen to converge, corresponds in the order of grace to deification, which is the originating
and terminating synthesis of all creation in the order of spiritual
alchemy, where all sanctifying transformations happen to converge.
This is what St. Thomas says. Showing that the gift of Wisdom must
be placed in correspondence with the seventh beatitude: "Blessed the
peacemakers for they shall be called the Sons of God," St. Thomas
writes: "Now those are called the children of God insofar as they
participate in the likeness of the only-begotten and natural Son of
God, according to these words: 'Those whom God has foreknown,
they are also predestined to be conformed in the image of his Son'
(Rom 8:29), Who is wisdom begotten. Hence, by participating in
the gift of wisdom, man is raised even to divine sonship."[6] "God's
charity has been poured forth into our hearts by the Holy Spirit who
has been given to us." And this Spirit which we have received is "the
spirit of adoption of sons, whereby we cry: *Abba*, Father."[7]

3. Gnosis of the Essence and Deification

Finally, the divine sonship to which we are called, and which is the
fruit of charity, is likewise for St. Thomas identified with gnosis, that
is to say with knowledge of the Divine Essence, with the vision of
the Essence.

This doctrine proceeds directly from Johannine theology. Christ
in fact says in St. John's Gospel: "Eternal life is to know You, You
the only true God, and the one whom you have sent, Jesus Christ"
(John 17:3). And furthermore: "We know that when He shall appear,
we shall be like Him: *because* we shall see Him as He is" (1 John 3:2).
To see God as He is will therefore be the cause of our likeness to

6 Ibid. The foreknowledge spoken of by St. Paul does not mean that God sets
apart certain beings in advance for deification. This error, that of Luther in his treatise *On the Servile Will*, is not only a gross interpretation, but even a stupid one. It
supposes in fact a coexistence of time and eternity, and passes from one order of
things to the other as if they were comparable. Eternal prescience is not 'before' the
temporal unfolding, or 'after' it. St. Paul's words mean only this: our deification is
a consequence of the knowledge that God has of our being; or again: to be deified,
to become conformed to the image of the Son—*conformes fieri imaginis Filii*—is to
be identified with the knowledge which God has of us from all eternity. The eternal
gnosis that God has of us is our deification.

7 Rom 5:5 and 8:15.

Him. Or again, knowledge of the Divine Essence is the very content of deification. To this gnosis of the Essence Latin theology has given the name of 'intuitive vision'.

The Greeks are known to deny the possibility of such a knowledge, deification for them being effected by participation in the 'Divine Energies' which they carefully distinguish from the absolutely unknowable Essence. There is, they think, among Latins a 'mystical ambition' which they are ready to brand as pantheism. Let us briefly recall, then, the doctrine of St. Thomas.

On the one hand, Scripture teaches that we will know God "as He is."[8] On the other, human nature itself requires such a knowledge. In effect: "As the ultimate beatitude of man consists in the use of his highest function, which is the operation of the intellect, if we suppose that the created intellect could never see the Divine Essence, it would either never attain beatitude, or its beatitude would consist in something else beside God."[9] But no created intelligence can see God by itself. This is why it has need of a 'light of glory' which "perfects the intellect, strengthening it to see God."[10] The effect of this light of glory is to bestow on the intellect the form of God: "When any created intellect sees the essence of God, the essence of God itself becomes the intelligible form of the intellect."[11] Must we then conclude, by reason of the wholly supernatural character of the beatific vision, that man is totally unable to gain access to the divine? Is there a kind of incompatibility between human nature and God? If this were so, the gift of deiformity would be impossible, it would contradict human nature. Now God himself cannot make a circle assume the form of a square. The form of the Divine Essence given to the intellect is indeed the supreme grace, but the intellect is 'capable' of receiving this grace. How? By the 'obediential power', that is the power possessed by human nature to *obey* all the operations that God wishes to realize within it. Thus we are under obligation to obey the supreme orders of God, since we have the ability to do so.[12] In the notion of obediential power, nature and

8   1 John 3:1ff.; Matt 5:8; 1 Cor 13:12; etc.
9   *Summa Theologiae* I, q. 12, a. 1.
10 *Summa Theologiae* I, q. 12, a. 5.
11 Ibid.
12 *Summa Theologiae* III, q. 2, a. 1.

supernature are join together and articulated — an obediential power whose incarnate prototype is the Virgin Mary.

Now, are vision of the Divine Essence and deification the same thing? We have seen what St. John affirms: "Dearly beloved, we are now the sons of God: and it hath not yet appeared what we shall be. We know that when he shall appear, *we shall be like to him because we shall see him as he is*" (1 John 3:2). And St. Thomas, who always returns to this verse in order to support the doctrine of the beatific vision, declares: "the final perfection of the human intellect is by union with God, Who is the first principle of the human soul and of its enlightenment."[13] "For perfect happiness the intellect needs to reach the very Essence of the First Cause. And thus it will have its perfection through union with God, as with that object in which alone human happiness consists."[14]

Is this created or uncreated happiness? It is necessary to say, replies St. Thomas, that it is uncreated in its Object,[15] but, inasmuch as it is human happiness, it is created.[16] Only this creation of deifying happiness in man is a new creation: it is, on God's part, an act more important than the creation of heaven and earth.[17]

As for the term 'deification', St. Thomas himself uses it: "God alone deifies in communicating a partaking of the Divine Nature."[18] This communication begets in man a new, properly divine existence, a divine manner of being real: "grace perfects the essence of the soul [and not just the soul's powers] insofar as the soul participates in divine existence."[19] One theologian summarizes the doctrine of Thomas in this way:

> Grace causes us to participate in divine nature, not such as we might conceive of it. . . . It assimilates us to God, not by reason of understanding or love, of life or of being, of *esse subsistens*, but by reason of the Godhead; it assimilates

13 *Summa Theologiae* I-II, q. 3. a. 7.
14 *Summa Theologiae* I-II, q. 3, a. 8.
15 *Summa Theologiae* I-II, q. 2, a. 8.
16 *Summa Theologiae* I-II, q. 3, a. 1.
17 *Summa Theologiae* I-II, q. 112, a. 1.
18 Ibid.
19 *Summa Theologiae* III, q. 62, a. 2.

us to the divine nature, such as It is in Itself, such as It
subsists in its own mystery, beyond all our limited concepts.... The Divine Nature to which we are assimilated
is that very one by which the Father and the Son are One.
St. Thomas says this explicitly....[20] Thus the grace that
divinizes us assimilates us to the Divine Nature even inasmuch as divine, that is even in that which is known only
by It alone...; grace opens us to Divine Nature, such as It
is within itself in the bosom of the unfathomable Trinity.[21]

And therefore It opens us to the Absoluteness of God at the heart
of the Trinitarian Relations. This is why, since we are 'adopted' by
the one Divine Nature in the Three Hypostases, "Christ is not the
Son of the whole Trinity, as we are."[22] Such is the true breadth of a
doctrine where certain people see only the limits of Latin rationalism.

II. FRATERNAL CHARITY AND DEIFICATION
OR THE MYSTERY OF THE VISITATION
1. Fraternal Charity and Altruism

Charity is the alchemical ferment of our deification; it effects the distinction of the psychic and the spiritual, it leads to gnosis, it realizes
the pneumatization of the intellect. But some might think that there
is only charity for God and not for the neighbor in all this. In reality
the two are inseparable; not that we must choose in this way and, on
principle, perpetually refer the first to the second. This voluntarist
and calculating attitude is opposed to true spirituality. Some consider themselves insured in this way against pharisaism and 'spiritual'
egoism, but they cannot mislead God. Present-day Christianity sometimes seems filled with publicans who vaunt their sins and repeat:
"We are not like those pre-conciliar pharisees."

Actually, fraternal charity is unconnected to any 'ethics', 'altruism',
or 'philanthropy'. This does not exclude that acts of philanthropy

20 *In Joannem* 17, Bk. 5, 2.
21 H. T. Conus, "Divinisation chez S. Thomas," in *Dictionnaire de Spiritualité,*
vol. 3 (Paris: Beauchesne, 1967), col. 1426–32.
22 *Summa Theologiae* III, q. 23, a. 2.

may resemble acts of charity exteriorly. Anyone in whom the least doubt subsists in this respect is incapable of understanding the true nature of charity.

The spiritual function of fraternal charity is to allow others and oneself access to deification by means of our access to the degree of *proximity*.

2. Visitation and Deification[23]

"The Truth must illumine this saying: I must love my neighbor as myself. But who am I? Nothing, a nothing (negative) before God. And I must become 'nothing' (positive)—or virgin—so that the Father begets in me the only-begotten Son; such is perfect Humility. It is the same for my neighbor. I must love this 'nothing' who is, he as well, mysteriously identified with the Virgin in whom is accomplished the operation of the Holy Spirit or the Incarnation of the Word. Here again we find the *Mysterium caritatis* who is God himself. God cannot give anything other than Himself. . . .

"On the human plane it is therefore an impossibility and an absurdity to love one's neighbor as oneself. Charity is a mystery, not an altruism. It is therefore impossible that a human individual possess the charity involved here with respect to another human individual, the altruist illusion is on the same level as the egocentric illusion. . . .

"When the human individuality vanishes—the Mystery of Humility—to the point of realizing the perfect virginity of Mary, only then is such a transfigured individuality '*my neighbor*' and am I '*his neighbor*', both having realized the 'divine proximity' that is the *mysterium caritatis*. But then it is no longer individual x who gives alms to an individual y: it is God who gives God to God.

"'What you do to the least of my own, it is to Me that you do it' (Matt 25:40.). The 'least' of my own does not mean the 'sub-proletariat' or the most miserable of men; it means the one who has realized perfect humility, as mentioned above: 'For the Kingdom of Heaven is for the little ones and those who resemble them'. . . .

"We will conclude these few remarks with the 'historical model' of the *mysterium caritatis* as realized with respect to the neighbor—the

23 The texts in quotes are by the Abbé Henri Stephane, *Introduction à l'ésotérisme chrétien* (Paris: Dervy, 1979), 223–24.

mystery of the Visitation of Mary to her cousin Elizabeth — and this account will serve to illustrate everything we have just said.

"The Mystery of the Annunciation was just accomplished in Mary, and the *Mysterium caritatis* required that this be communicated to the 'neighbor', represented here by Elizabeth. 'In haste,' says the Gospel, 'Mary went away to the hill country. . . . Now at the time that Elizabeth had heard Mary's salutation, the child leaped in her womb, and she was filled with the Holy Spirit.' The essential contents of the *Mysterium caritatis* cannot be better described: Mary, bearer of the Incarnate Word, greeted Elizabeth who was filled with the Holy Spirit. Such is the 'Gift of God' to Elizabeth through Mary. In return, Elizabeth, filled with the Holy Spirit, bears witness to Mary: 'Blessed are you among all women, and blessed is the fruit of your womb'. . . .

"This Gospel episode 'incarnates', on the human plane, the *mysterium caritatis* with respect to the neighbor: ultimately this involves, in imitation of Mary, the Virgin soul and bearer of the Word making the infant John the Baptist, that is to say the Precursor who recognized Christ, leap in the womb of the other, and, in the course of this 'recognition', the soul of the neighbor is filled with the Holy Spirit."

3. Fraternal Charity and Deification of the World

With the text from which we have just given some excerpts, we see what the spiritual essence of fraternal charity is through its historical prototype, the Visitation. One can equally consider, as a consequence of what has just been said, that this mystery realizes, on the plane of the relative, an image of the Holy Trinity. Sacred iconography suggests this analogy. One depiction of the Visitation[24] shows St. Elizabeth welcoming Mary. They stand embracing each other. St. Elizabeth gazes at Mary, who gazes in front of, or rather within, herself. On the other hand, St. Elizabeth has placed her right hand on the womb of the Virgin. This image is decidedly similar to those medieval representations of the Trinity in which the Father and the Son stand embracing each other, while a dove unites the breath of their mouths. But here it is the Word who is invisibly present. Mary can then be regarded as an image of the Father, and St. Elizabeth as an image of

24 A pre-romanesque fresco of the small church of Ris in Puy de Dome (first pillar to the left).

the Holy Spirit, a manifestation of whom St. John the Baptist will be. By gaining access to ontological proximity, Elizabeth is enabled to 'realize' the Word. Note well, however: this Word is not begotten by an act of the charitable power. As we have repeated all through our study, that is an idea arising from triumphalist charity. The Word is already there, in Mary. It is she who takes the initiative and greets St. Elizabeth first. It is by her that St. Elizabeth is filled with the Holy Spirit. On this subject St. Bernadine of Siena is not afraid to say: "From the time that the Virgin Mother conceived the Divine Word in her womb she obtained a kind of jurisdiction, so to say, over all the temporal manifestations of the Holy Spirit; so that no creature can obtain any grace from God that is not dispensed by this tender and compassionate Mother."[25]

If the Annunciation descends vertically from Heaven to Earth, the Visitation radiates horizontally across the cosmic environment. It indeed corresponds to the second commandment, which is like to the first, that is to say, is its image. The Visitation is like a second Annunciation. Through it the creature is rendered prophetic. What was interior becomes exterior, so that exteriority might be brought back to interiority. The second commandment, which is the radiance of the first, also finds its end here because its function is to bring back. Fraternal charity is the mode under which the cosmos realizes its deification.

III. DEIFICATION AND SPIRATION OF LOVE

1. Deifying Spiration

The pneumatization of the intellect, charity's *magnum opus*, gives us access to *spiritual maternity*. We—we too—must become in some manner the Mother of God: spiritual virginity with a view to spiritual maternity. The state of spiritual maternity should be connected with the hypostatic Maternity of the Holy Spirit. This function, under its uncreated aspect as under its created aspect, can only be pneumatic.

We are deified because we are 'sons of God'. But, as a complementary mystery, by becoming sons of God we also become the mother of God. Jesus has said, extending his hand above his disciples, "Here

25 Cited by St. Alphonsus Liguori, *Glories of Mary* (Rockford, IL: TAN Books, 1977), 345.

are my mother and my brothers. Whoever does the will of my heavenly Father, that one is my brother, and my sister, and my mother" (Matt 12:49–50). Now the Father's will is to beget the Son. To do the will of the Father is therefore to beget the Son in oneself. The Holy Spirit, through passive spiration, is, as we have said, the One who 'reveals' the Son to the Father. Similarly, in the creature, the work of the Holy Spirit is to permit the conception of the Son. The creature, filled with the Holy Spirit, is 'transformed' by Him into a 'Mother of God', and 'reveals' to the Father its own 'filial' reality through its creaturehood.[26]

It is then that the creature 'enters' into the passive spiration, and, through it, into the circumincession, as testified to by St. John of the Cross. What was a dogmatic formulation becomes a spiritual reality. This interiorization of the dogma and doctrine of subsistent relations shows to what level theology can be raised, and reduces to naught the pretentious objections of modernist theologians.

This is what St. John of the Cross says:

> By His divine breath-like spiration, the Holy Spirit elevates the soul sublimely and informs her and makes her capable of breathing in God the same spiration of love that the Father breathes in the Son and the Son in the Father, which is the Holy Spirit Himself, Who in the Father and the Son breathes out to her in this transformation.... And this kind of spiration of the Holy Spirit in the soul, by which God transforms her into Himself, is so sublime, delicate, and deep a delight that a mortal tongue finds it indescribable, nor can the human intellect as such, in any way grasp it. Even that which comes to pass in the communication given in this temporal transformation is unspeakable, for the soul united and transformed in God breathes out in God to God the very divine spiration which God — she being transformed in Him — breathes out in Himself to her.[27]

26 This doctrine is the basis of Meister Eckhart's thought on deification. Moreover, we know how much the teaching of the Meister influenced St. John of the Cross.
27 *Spiritual Canticle*, 39, Commentary, in *Collected Works*, 558.

2. *Identity and Distinction in Deification*

This entry of the creature into the Trinitarian circumincession is effected precisely by the spiration of love. This means that in God the creature will not cease to give itself eternally to the Creator, and this is why charity will not pass away, for it is the eternal passage from the relative to the Absolute. This is what is sometimes called the Supreme Identity. But need we fear seeing in this, as do certain neo-Thomists, the heresy of an 'entitative' union with God?[28] Surely there is the quite frequently committed error which we have already termed 'out-and-out identification'. But the truth is far indeed from these gross simplifications, of which the East as well as the West has been guilty.[29] To the contrary, only by integrally realizing its creaturely nature can a relative being become a partaker of the Divine Nature.[30] The natural and profane man believes in the autonomous and independent reality of his being. In this he takes himself for God and attributes to himself a perfection that belongs only to Absolute Being. He lies about his nature as a created being. What then is the truth of this nature? It is that created being is a being received, a being given. To the precise extent that a being becomes ontologically aware of the gift of being, he allows the Divine Being to flow into himself. To the precise extent that the creature abases itself and gives itself to the Creator, it ceases being an obstacle to this flow of Being; and not only is it no longer an obstacle, but it even desires and wants nothing else but Him, and becomes itself this flowing. At last it is a pure creature, at last it is the unimaginable further side of God, where God can pour out the irresistible effusion of his Infinity. It wants nothing more than what the Divine Essence wants. It can no longer want anything

---

28   Cf. J. Maritain, *The Degrees of Knowledge*, trans. G. B. Phelan (Notre Dame, IN: University of Notre Dame Press, 1995), 400.

29   "Even when there is eviction of duality (between God and man)
>   O Lord, I am Yours,
>   You are not mine.
>   The waves belong to the ocean,
>   the ocean never belongs to the waves."

Shankara, *Vishnusadpadi*, cited in Paul Martin-Dubost, *Çankara et le Vedanta* (Paris: Seuil, 1973), 97.

30   This doctrine is explained more amply in *The Sense of the Supernatural*, trans. G. J. Champoux (Edinburgh: T & T Clark, 1998), 127–40.

but the Divine Essence itself. And since the Essence has willed this creature, it finally consents to offer itself as receptacle for this eternal will, because it has finally understood that in this creature that it is, it is the uncreated Essence itself that has willed itself.

Yes, there is a truth higher than the one claiming to deny the irreducible duality of Creator and creature on their own plane; a truth deeper than the one claiming to aspire to a union such that creation is at last entirely reabsorbed into a solidly homogeneous Absolute. This is the truth of the Supreme Godhead which, being beyond duality as well as unity, contains them and conceives of them within Itself in an immaculate manner, so that within It alone the relative and the created are what they ought to be. Charity is the substance of this mystery which is beyond language and which the intellect, however, perceives in a flash; charity is the substance of this mystery at all levels of its reality, from the helping hand which a brother holds out to his brother, and by which the duality of beings is finally justified, to the spiration of love that breathes eternally between the Father and the Son, and by which the relativity of the Trinitarian Hypostases blossoms and is unified at the very core of the Absolute.

INDICES

Index of Names

Meaning of abbreviations accompanying certain names of religious:

A. A.: Augustinian Assumptionists
O. F. M.: Order of Friars Minor (Franciscans)
O. P.: Order of Preachers (Dominicans)
O. S. B.: Order of Saint Benedict (Benedictines)
S. J.: Society of Jesus (Jesuits)

A

Abelard, 206
Abram, 184
Adam, 62, 102, 115–56, 139, 141, 144–48, 160–61, 172, 192, 229, 318, 394–99; New, 321, 397; Old, 397; primordial, 147, 322, 396
Alexander of Aphrodisias, 181
Allmen, J. J. von, 183
Alphonsus Liguori (saint), 433
Ambrose (saint), 203, 399
Amiel, Henri-Frédéric, 72
Ammonios, 421
Andrade e Silva, J. L., 23, 79
Anselm (saint), 271
Apollinaris of Laodicea (saint), 195–96
Apollo, 178, 358
Apuleius, 101, 110
Aristotle, 2, 72, 77, 91, 173–74, 178–84, 189–90, 194, 211–12, 254, 260, 362, 418
Athanasius (saint), 254, 256, 367
Augustine (saint), 107–10, 125–26, 157, 203–5, 258, 271, 282, 327, 334, 341, 358, 369, 399
Averroes, 181
Avicenna, 181

B

Bacon, Roger, 181
Bartmann, Mgr Bernard, 154, 157, 169
Basil of Caesarea (saint), 238, 256, 271, 334, 368
Benedict XVI, vii, 1
Bergson, Henri, 72
Bernadette (saint), 354
Bernard of Clairvaux (saint), 205, 217–18, 233
Bildad the Shuhite, 189
Boethius, 127, 257
Bohr, Niels, 79
Boltzmann, Ludwig, 30
Bonaventure (saint), 358
Bonino, Serge, O. P., 352, 373
Bonnet, Serge, O. P., 45
Bonsirven, Joseph, S. J., 187
Bossuet, Jacques-Bénigne, 74
Bréhier, Émile, 105
Brillouin, Léon, 30
Broglie, Louis de, 79–80
Brun, Jean, 104
Buber, Martin, 316
Bulgakov, Sergius, 307, 330
Burckhardt, Titus, 144

C

Calmet, Augustin, O. S. B., 109
Camelot, Thomas, O. P., 409

Index of Subjects

A

absolute, 9, 11, 13, 18, 20, 26, 42–45, 58, 60, 63, 68, 93, 113, 123, 134, 146, 158, 243, 248, 260, 267–71, 275, 283, 326, 343–44, 346, 351–52, 354, 357, 384–85, 388–89, 393, 408, 430, 435–36

accident, 224, 253, 262–67, 271, 290

agape, 249–50, 252, 314, 318–23, 326, 336–37, 339

agony of Christ, 46

alchemy, 94, 144, 150, 161–62, 176, 201, 242, 248, 292, 363–64, 415, 417, 427

anima, 115–17, 132, 148, 151, 155–56, 165, 171, 180, 184, 186, 203–7

animus, 116, 119–20, 124–25, 132, 151, 158, 171, 184, 186, 204–6, 208

Annunciation, 282, 432–33

anthropology, 37, 49–50, 71–72, 77, 104, 114, 137, 153–55, 159, 163, 167, 169–71, 182, 188, 190–1, 194–96, 198–201, 203, 205–7, 231, 235, 339, 363, 415

Ascension, 78, 196–97, 376

athanor, 364

B

beatitude, 156–57, 220, 427–28

Bible, 105, 107, 117, 147, 172, 183, 190, 209, 361, 372

buddhi, 125

C

Calvary, 148

Cartesianism, 59

charity, fraternal, 217, 227, 292, 314, 321–23, 337, 417, 430–33; infinite, 357–58; revolutionary, 17; triumphalist, 214, 227, 232, 251, 294–96, 324, 338, 340, 381, 391, 433; triumphant, 340

Cherubim, 231

circumincession, 241, 283–85, 297, 321, 329, 340, 364, 434–35

civilization, industrial, 63, 69

conditions of existence, 96

Constantinople, council of, 170, 196, 256–57

contemplation, 126, 172, 207, 225, 344, 402, 411–15, 417–20

corpus, 115–17, 133, 148, 151, 156, 165, 171, 180, 203, 206; *Christi*, 143; *natum*, 160

cosmology, 2, 77–78, 103–4, 107, 111–13, 363, 375

Creation, 35–36, 45–47, 56, 92, 105–6, 112–15, 134–35, 139, 143, 178, 182, 188, 190, 193, 196, 200, 221–22, 225, 227, 242, 286, 323, 334, 341–52, 359–64, 367–68, 370–74, 377, 391, 401, 411, 427, 429, 436

Creed, Apostles', 101, 311; Nicene, 256

cross, 10–12, 15, 53, 107, 112, 192, 217, 219, 236–45, 247–48, 252, 270, 321, 382, 391–92, 395–98, 400, 421

culture, 36–37, 43, 49–52, 54–57, 60, 84, 103, 109, 120, 124–25, 153–54, 163, 200, 213, 376

D

darkness, 43, 47, 98, 106, 108, 140, 144, 167, 183, 400, 404, 417; more-than-luminous, 355, 386–89, 422–23

295; natural, 320, 339; *nous* and, 158; pure, 267; rapport of, 260; relationship of, 349; seminal, 107; sufficient, 306, 324

relation, subsistent, 9, 233, 251–53, 257–58, 264–67, 269, 271–72, 276, 285, 287–89, 291, 299, 305, 326, 332, 335, 370, 434

religion, 1, 28, 36–37, 39–40, 42, 43–44, 47, 50, 72, 112, 129, 139, 149, 256, 294–96; Catholic, 42; (of) humanity, 320; Jewish, 101; modernist, 381; Platonic, 110; primordial, 139

Resurrection, 78, 96, 160, 183, 185, 201–2, 302, 376

Revelation, 1, 18, 26–27, 35–36, 39–41, 49, 55, 77–78, 110, 153, 155, 157, 159, 183, 197–98, 214, 229, 233, 247, 264–65, 291, 299, 305–6, 309, 312, 316–17, 322–23, 330, 332, 338, 347, 374, 387–88, 401–2, 404, 415

Rosary, 47, 150, 239

Rota Mundi, 368

ruah, 183–86, 188; *Elohim*, 309

S

sacrament, 5, 129, 143, 149, 229, 238–39, 294–96, 315, 407, 409

sacrifice, 3, 11–12, 17, 20, 47, 132, 142, 150, 165, 192, 213, 236, 238, 377, 391–92, 395–98, 400

Samaritan (the Good), 225, 228–29, 234, 294–95, 313

Satan, 1, 68, 107, 242–43, 377

semantic, 88–90, 92–98, 100, 104, 113, 160, 262

sin, original, 41, 62, 102, 115, 142, 144, 148, 159, 229, 236, 246, 354, 363, 391–94, 399

solve et coagula, 241, 364–65

spiracle, 188–93

spiraculum, 187–89

spiration, 192–93, 265–66, 275–78, 307–8, 326–29, 331–32, 336, 418, 433–36

spiritus, 115, 129–30, 132, 151, 171, 185–87, 203, 205–8, 243, 275

structuralism, 43, 60, 62

subsistentia, 253, 257

substantia, 255–57

subtle, 82–83, 98, 101, 104, 106, 108–9, 115, 119, 131, 144, 148, 205, 207; body, 147, 201; energies, 103; world, 83, 93–94, 98, 101, 105, 144, 193, 199

supernaturalism, 72

supposit(s), 268, 303, 307

symbol, 36, 51, 53–54, 57–58, 60, 94, 114, 116, 120, 142–45, 147, 151, 157, 174–75, 193, 222, 226, 247, 260, 306, 335, 347, 359, 373, 388, 392, 413

T

Talmud, 230–31

theoria, 402, 412

theosis (*see* deification), 238

Thrones, 113

transcendence, 19, 44, 46, 96, 114, 131, 133–34, 137, 182, 204, 241–42, 303, 305–6, 343, 347, 350, 419, 423

trans-spatial, 81–82, 88, 97, 100, 113

tree of the knowledge of good and evil, 146

trichotomism, 154, 169, 175, 177, 195, 198, 203, 209

Trinity, 9, 251, 253, 256, 258, 268, 270–72, 275, 279–83, 285, 287–91, 297, 304–7, 313–14, 326, 328, 330, 340, 342, 344, 356, 367, 369, 374, 387–88, 410–11, 413–15, 418–20, 422, 430, 432

U

union, hypostatic, 195, 296, 397

V

Vedanta, 104, 107, 120, 184, 193, 201, 435

vestigia, 369

virginity, 311, 361, 433; Marian, 41, 147, 431

virtues, 5–6, 10–11, 16, 40, 43, 55, 129, 151, 325, 412, 414; natural, 19, 27, 36, 42, 44, 46–47, 49, 54, 61, 63–66, 69–70, 402; theological, 5, 35

vision, beatific, 176, 272, 428–29

vision of the Divine Essence, 157, 427, 429

Visitation, 430–33

W

waters, 141, 309; above/upper, 105, 242; animic, 36, 140; below/lower, 105, 242; existential, 246; Maria, 359; mental, 124; primordial, 36, 304, 359, 364; psychic, 140–41; toxic, 54

will, 6–13, 39–41, 62, 65–66, 84, 94, 103, 121, 130–35, 137, 147, 151, 158, 163, 165–66, 171, 210, 240, 243, 275–76, 281, 302, 304, 324, 328–29, 362, 364, 367, 369–70, 394, 397, 407; creative, 361–62; Divine, 46, 56, 62, 351–52, 392; eternal, 436; (of the) Father, 273, 434; free, 303; (of) God, 41, 105, 165, 376, 407; good, 198, 407; procession, 281, 305; servile, 427

Word, 6, 36, 39–41, 45, 107, 112–13, 195, 238–40, 247–48, 258, 265, 275–76, 280–82, 286–88, 291, 293, 296, 299, 305, 313, 328, 332–35, 338, 340, 355, 359, 361, 364, 367, 369–74, 377, 379, 386, 388, 392, 397, 408, 414–15, 431–33; Christic, 292–95, 337–38; Divine, 7, 11, 296, 352, 359, 361, 364, 370, 373, 399, 433; Eternal, 36, 52, 196, 263, 374, 422; (of) God, 6, 39, 46, 161; Incarnate, 47, 161, 196, 314, 315, 320, 388, 397, 432; made-flesh, 247; revealed, 41; uncreated, 359, 362, 364

Scriptural Index

OLD TESTAMENT